The CIA on Campus

The CIA on Campus

Essays on Academic Freedom and the National Security State

Edited by PHILIP ZWERLING

McFarland & Company, Inc., Publishers
Jefferson, North Carolina, and London

Library of Congress Cataloguing-in-Publication Data

The CIA on campus : essays on academic freedom and the national
security state / edited by Philip Zwerling.
        p.   cm.
    Includes bibliographical references and index.

    ISBN 978-0-7864-6346-6
    softcover : 50# alkaline paper ∞

    1. Academic freedom — United States.   2. United States.
Central Intelligence Agency.   3. Espionage — United States.
4. National security — United States.   I. Zwerling, Philip.
LC72.2.C53   2011
371.1'04 — dc23   2011026227

British Library cataloguing data are available

Cover image © 2011 Shutterstock

Manufactured in the United States of America

McFarland & Company, Inc., Publishers
   Box 611, Jefferson, North Carolina 28640
      www.mcfarlandpub.com

To the memory of
Benjamin Ernest Linder,
graduated from the University of Washington, 1983,
murdered by the CIA, 1987

Acknowledgments

I thank all of my contributors for their hard work and offer special thanks to Jose Skinner for editing the editor and to Susan Zwerling for her unwavering support.

Contents

Acknowledgments   ix

Preface: The Search for Truth   1

1. Template for Terror
   PHILIP ZWERLING   7

2. Uninvited Guests: A Short History of the CIA on Campus
   DAVID PRICE   33

3. South of the Border: The CIA in Latin America
   DAVID CARLSON   61

4. The Spooks in the Stacks: Academic Libraries and the National
   Security State Since 9/11
   DEIRDRE MCDONALD   88

5. Deception Detection and Torture: The American Psychological
   Association Serves the Intelligence Services
   STEPHEN SOLDZ   113

6. CHAOS on Campus: I Spied for the CIA
   VERNE LYON   147

7. Never Too Young: The U.S. Intelligence Community's
   Summer Spy Camp for Kids
   ROBERTO GONZÁLEZ   168

8. Nine Steps to a Spy-Free Campus
   PHILIP ZWERLING   191

9. Which Side Are You On? Intelligence Agencies on Campus
   and the Class Struggle
   DAVID ANSHEN   216

                        About the Contributors   241
                              Index   243

Preface: The Search for Truth

Philip Zwerling

I enthusiastically threw the first 20 years of my working life into the parish ministry. I preached, prayed, counseled, visited the sick and jailed, clothed the homeless, fed the hungry, and tried to speak truth to power. Always I found time to write.

I returned to school to learn to write better and, against my will, fell in love with teaching. Contrary to all my memories of rote learning, authoritarian or absent-minded professors, apathetic and bored students, the forced accumulation of miscellaneous bits of undifferentiated knowledge that had no bearing in the real world, I discovered a real place called academia; a place where the truth mattered and professors learned from and with the students they taught. As a new immigrant in the hallowed groves of the academy it seemed I had entered an intellectual Garden of Eden. Here I got paid (not enough, mind you, but paid, nonetheless) to think, read, learn, research, write, and teach full time. I had enlisted in a search for truth and knowledge.

In the midst of a competitive, consumerist, commercialized and commodified society, these little islands of thought and contemplation, some 4,000 universities and colleges scattered among our 50 states and territories, stand as oases, or liberated zones, where knowledge trumps power, and intellectual inquiry supersedes financial gain.

You could say I was just a little idealistic. But so were most of my colleagues and even more of my students. How could we not be? The old brick buildings on campus, swathed in ivy, fronted with ionic columns, and etched with Latin mottos inspire a higher calling. The school colors carried high each year at commencement bespeak a tradition of intellectual progress through the ages. And the institutional mottos all claim a universal purpose. Harvard, one of my alma maters and the country's oldest institution of higher learning, chose its motto first and kept it simple: *Veritas*, Latin for "Truth."

1

Brandeis, another school I attended, and one of our country's youngest universities, chose *Emet*, Hebrew for "Truth." I earned my Ph.D. at the University of California Santa Barbara. Its beautiful seal is a shining open book with the Latin motto *Fiat Lux*, "Let There Be Light."

Today I teach at the University of Texas Pan American, one of fifteen campuses in the University of Texas system. The UT system has a motto, also in Latin: *Disciplina Presidium Civitatis*, "The Cultivated Mind Is the Guardian Genius of Democracy." These are big words and bigger ideas. They indicate that the work of the institution matters and that work links the pursuit of knowledge with the greater social good.

The goal of creating and enlarging knowledge in a search for truth depends upon openness, sharing information and data, and collaboration across disciplines and departments. A campus is a privileged space where people contest, argue, disagree, verbally spar, share new discoveries and create a synergy where my truth and your truth might lead to a new Truth.

We don't keep secrets on campus. It's our job to share what we know. If I design a new technique for teaching playwriting (my speciality) I publish it in a journal, present it in a paper at a conference, or share it in a seminar with colleagues. I don't classify my discovery, or stamp it "Top Secret" so that revealing it becomes a crime. I don't burn my notes or refuse to discuss my findings with peers. Secrecy is the enemy of truth, and we don't have secrets on campus. Public records will tell you how many students attend, how many commute and how many live on campus, where they come from and their ethnicity, who the faculty are, where they earned their degrees, what they've published, and even what they are paid.

The Central Intelligence Agency and the 15 other agencies that make up the so-called U.S. Intelligence Community (Air Force Intelligence, Surveillance, and Reconnaissance Agency, Army Intelligence, Defense Intelligence Agency, Marine Corps Intelligence Activity, National Geospatial-Intelligence Agency, National Reconnaissance Office, National Security Agency, Office of Naval Intelligence, [Department of Energy] Office of Intelligence and Counterintelligence, [Department of Homeland Security] Office of Intelligence and Analysis, Coast Guard Investigative Service, Federal Bureau of Investigation, Drug Enforcement Agency, [Department of Sate] Bureau of Intelligence and Research, and [Department of Treasury] Office of Terrorism and Financial Intelligence) are by definition secret. They will not tell you how many employees they have, what their budget is and how it is allocated, who their employees are or where they come from. They will not publish all of their research or share their discoveries with everyone. The shredder, the burn bag, the bug, the "top secret" classification, the covert operation and the sealed lips are among their standard operating procedures.

The idea of the university in the West is based on the model of Plato's Academy, which met in a sanctuary dedicated to Athena, the goddess of Wisdom, located outside the walls of Athens. Here, among the olive groves (thus the phrase "the groves of academia"), Plato taught whoever came to learn, using the diaologic method of his mentor, Socrates, in which teachers and students discovered knowledge together through inquiry, questioning, and open debate. Significantly this school was outside the city, in a religious sanctuary where politicians, bureaucrats, and the military were unwelcome unless they attended as students. Modern ideas of academic freedom and tenure as necessary protections to those dedicated to critical inquiry trace back to this ancient place.

The sanctuary that is the university has always been vulnerable. Today, as in the past, the Central Intelligence Agency seeks to penetrate the academy to access the best brains in the country, skew research, recruit students, burnish its image, and spy on faculty. As former CIA Personnel Director F. W. M. Janney wrote: "It is absolutely essential that the Agency have available to it the greatest single source of expertise: the American academic community."[1]

CIA projects on campus involve recruitment (they need to generate 10,000 applicants each year) and "curriculum modification" (to teach courses their way), and have drawn faculty and students into dangerous mind control experiments, election fraud and the training of police torturers and military death squads. Such projects always involve secrecy and the subversion of an independent faculty. They have been so successful that, in 1988, CIA spokesperson Sharon Foster announced: "The CIA has enough professors under Agency contract to staff a large university."[2]

On the evening of January 17, 1961, following decades of service to his country as Army officer, president of Columbia University and two-term president of the United States, Dwight David Eisenhower appeared on the three national television networks to offer his valedictory from the office he would relinquish in three days. After famously warning his country men and women of the rise of the military-industrial complex he turned to his fears for the future of the country's universities:

> The free university, historically the fountainhead of free ideas and scientific discovery, has experienced a revolution in the conduct of research. Partly because of the huge costs involved, a government contract becomes virtually a substitute for intellectual curiosity. For every old blackboard there are now hundreds of new electronic computers. The prospect of domination of the nation's scholars by Federal employment, project allocations, and the power of money is ever present — and is gravely to be regarded.[3]

Eisenhower's farewell originally named this mortal threat to American democracy as the "military-industrial-academic complex" though he deleted that phrase from the final draft of the speech.[4] America ignored Eisenhower's warning and government and corporate sponsors now buy and sell research on campuses, influence degree plans and faculty hiring. This book is a response to the new CIA penetration of U.S. universities through programs like the Intelligence Community/Centers for Academic Excellence and the Intelligence Analysis Campus. The CIA, obscuring its hand through the Office of the Director of National Intelligence, quietly pours tens of millions of dollars into college campuses just as Eisenhower warned. The authors of this book are professors who fear that their campuses are becoming spy schools.

One of my committee responsibilities at UTPA is to serve on the Admissions Committee for our MFA Program in Creative Writing. As you can imagine we require a student application form as well as a portfolio of his or her creative work. On the form the applicant enters personal information (i.e., name, address), educational history, contact information for those offering references, and attaches academic transcripts. Recently I accessed online the application form for a program at the University of Texas El Paso, one of the other campuses in the University of Texas system. The program is called the UTEP Intelligence Community Center of Academic Excellence, sponsored by the University College and the Office of the Director of National Intelligence. You can find the full six-page application at the UTEP Intelligence Community Center of Academic Excellence IC CAE Scholars Application. The initial five pages request the same kind of material as our own MFA application. The difference comes on page six when applicants are asked to study an image and to

> answer the following questions in a concise 1-page essay.... (1) What is the image below? (2) What details of the image tell you about the activity taking place? (3) How was the image taken. When was the image taken? Explain how you arrive at your conclusions? (4) What is the context of the image? What do you believe is going on in the areas beyond the image's range? Explain how you arrive at your conclusions.[5]

The image is on the following page.

I don't know what it is. Is this a satellite photo of a Somali port, an Amazonian marina, or a terrorist training camp? These are questions for secret agents, not college students. But it graphically demonstrates what a spy school looks like: training future secret agents, not scholars. Though no university has yet chosen *Dolus malus*, "Deceit," for its motto, the threat to American democracy posed by the covert intelligence services' subversion and penetration of U.S. higher education may yet surpass the danger posed by the terrorists they seek to defeat.

Ironically, engraved in stone in the CIA headquarters building in Langley, Virginia, is the New Testament verse "And ye shall know the Truth and the

The photograph from the University of Texas El Paso scholars program application.

Truth shall make you free" (John 8:32). We only hope that this book can yet make the university free ... free of the CIA, secrecy and deception and dedicated once again to *Veritas*.

NOTES

1. Quoted in Ami Chen Mills, *CIA Off Campus: Building the Movement Against Recruitment and Research* (Boston: South End, 1991), 29.

2. Ibid., 37.

3. Quoted in Henry Giroux, *The University in Chains: Confronting the Military-Industrial-Academic Complex* (Boulder, CO: Paradigm, 2007), 15.

4. Ibid., 14.

5. https://academics.utep.edu/Portals/1729/pdf/IC_CAE_Scholars_Application.pdf, accessed August 10, 2010.

WORKS CITED

Giroux, Henry. *The University in Chains: Confronting the Military-Industrial-Academic Complex.* Boulder, CO: Paradigm, 2007.

Mills, Ami Chen. *CIA Off Campus: Building the Movement Against Recruitment and Research.* Boston: South End, 1991.

UTEP Intelligence Community Center of Academic Excellence IC CAE Scholars Application, https://academics.utep.edu/Portals/1729/pdf/IC_CAE_Scholars_Application.pdf.

1

Template for Terror

PHILIP ZWERLING

Murder in Paradise

I first ran into the CIA in one of the most beautiful places on earth. I had rarely traveled outside North America before 1980 when I ventured south to observe the Literacy Crusade in Nicaragua. Then, in the summer of 1982, on little more than a whim, I made a spontaneous decision to step beyond a fairly ordered life in Los Angeles to visit Grenada just a year before the U.S. invasion. At that time I was mispronouncing the name of this small island off the coast of South America, north of Trinidad and south of Barbados, as Grenada, with short "a" sound and a Spanish inflection.

The trip just happened. A member of my church had a daughter working on the local newspaper there and thought she would show my wife and me around if we visited. It seemed an attractive offer, combining a visit to one of the most beautiful and least visited islands in the Caribbean with a chance to observe a self-styled revolutionary government attempting to reverse centuries of underdevelopment, simultaneously rankling the U.S. government with ties to Cuba and the Soviet Union.

When the never encountered daughter withdrew the invitation because of a holiday she had planned on the nearby island of Carriacou we decided to go anyway though we knew no one there and had no contacts, letters of introduction, or even a vague sense of what we would find.

Lacking direct flights, we flew a circuitous route from New York since Grenada's old airport could not accommodate large passenger planes and the new airport at Point Salines was under construction. We switched to a small plane in Barbados that sat no more than 24 and, flying out, looked back to see our baggage lying in a heap on the tarmac below. This meant three days without a hair dryer, contact lens solution, or a change of underwear.

I can't remember, 30 years later, if we rented a car or hopped in a shuttle for the 45 minute drive up and down mountain roads traversing the island to the capital of St. George's. Not only too small to accommodate modern jet aircraft, Pearl's airport only operated in daylight. We landed as night fell.

We played tourist for two weeks. Our little hotel sat on Grand Anse Beach, often rated the most beautiful beach in the world. The poet Kate Braverman caught the tropical images of Grenada I saw in her "Transformations in Green":

> On Grand Anse Beach
> I am encircled by women
> in cobalt and crimson print gingham
> waving hand sewn dresses like flags
> and the world dissolves
> behind blue stripes and red dots
> shimmering like a flock of plumed
> and sun-struck iridescent jungle birds....
>
> In Grenada, the main street
> is vine-swallowed. Women pass,
> boxes of Coca Cola bottles
> balanced on their heads
> and one can resist by sheer grace.....
>
> In a shantytown, windowless shacks
> and shattered boards, women sew,
> beige and brown piglets at their feet
> in shadows of a dynasty of green volcanoes....[1]

We strolled the powdered white sand for miles, stopped in at tiny shacks to eat freshly grilled fish, and observed whole families of Grenadians bathing at the water's edge after work. Occasionally a large cruise ship berthed off shore and an array of small boats quickly set up a bar and a steel drum band for tourists who drank and danced for a few hours. We dined on turtle soup at a restaurant on the Carenage along St. George's picturesque bay. We visited a fishing cooperative, one of 28 economic cooperatives set up by the revolutionary New Jewel Movement and Maurice Bishop, its Prime Minister. I have snapshots of a young woman, a member of one cooperative, proudly selling fish at the side of the road. We drove inland to visit a nutmeg farm, its product giving Grenada its nickname, "Spice Island," exporter of one-third the world's nutmeg.

One day we took our rental car and drove to a compound high on a hill housing the office of the prime minister. We had no appointment. Back in the States we had seen numerous newscasts of President Reagan and State Department officials labeling Bishop, who had taken control in a 1979 coup, a client of Havana and Moscow and a threat to U.S. security.[2] Bishop and the New Jewel Movement overthrew the corrupt and brutal regime of Eric Gairy, a UFO enthusiast and U.S. client. We were surprised to find the building's drive guarded by a single young soldier, looking all of 12 years old, dwarfed by the rifle he struggled to carry. He looked into our car, asked me to open the trunk for a quick peek, and then waved us forward. Inside, we sat for an hour or so with a government official whose name I no longer remember who gave us an informal briefing on the revolutionary government and its development projects, including a literacy crusade, new schools, teacher training, health initiatives, free milk for children, and putting more women in government, even while it left private businesses undisturbed.[3] I asked about the new airport under construction at Point Salines which the minister saw as a great boon to tourism development.

The airport had been first proposed by the British in 1954. They had succeeded the French as colonialists who had earlier wiped out the original Carib inhabitants. There had been airport feasibility studies in 1969, 1976, and 1979. Construction had begun just prior to the revolution and only then had become the focal point of U.S. evidence of a Soviet threat. Excavation work was being done by the Layne Dredging Company of Florida as communications gear was installed by Plessy, a British multinational, while the Cubans ran the earth moving machines.[4]

The presence of the Cubans drove the Americans into a frenzy. Nestor Sanchez, formerly a CIA agent and then Deputy Assistant Secretary of State, accused the Russians of planning to use the airport, presumably when completed, for a nuclear attack on the United States[5] and President Reagan charged that Grenada (a mere 21 miles long and 10 miles wide, a little bigger than Martha's Vineyard, with a population of but 110,000) threatened U.S. security,[6] saying on U.S. television: "Grenada doesn't even have an air force. Who is it [the airport] intended for?... The rapid buildup of Grenada's military potential is unrelated to any conceivable threat.... The Soviet-Cuban militarization of Grenada ... can only be seen as a power projection into the region."[7]

Often cited as proof of its nefarious intent was the fact that the main airport runway under construction was to be 9,000 feet long, a length unnecessary for tourist planes, the president told Americans, but just right for Soviet bombers. The American Security Council Foundation produced a movie, *Attack on the Americas*, quoting U.S. State Department officials to the effect that the new airport would be much larger than necessary to serve tourists and asserting: "With its strategic location, the airfield could serve as a staging area and refueling stop for Cuban troops on the way to Africa or South America, and another Soviet base in the Western hemisphere capable of servicing Soviet Bombers, including the new Supersonic Backfire."[8]

Meanwhile the Heritage Foundation, which had supported Reagan's election, opined: "Ever since 1898 America's worldwide reach has rested on a quiescent Caribbean and a supportive South America. The Caribbean, once an American Lake is becoming a Socialist sea."[9]

Before the Point Salines airport became the nexus of U.S. fears, the Reagan administration had floated the news that the Soviet Union was constructing a nuclear submarine base on the south coast of Grenada. Widely accepted as fact until 1983, the story fell apart when a *Washington Post* reporter visited the area and found no base under construction and the sea there too shallow for submarines.[10]

Early in February an official at the U.S. Defense Department reported that the Soviet Union had shipped to Grenada assault helicopters, hydrofoil torpedo boats, and supersonic MIG fighters which gave Grenada an air force of 200 modern planes. However, "the whereabouts of this mighty armada have remained a mystery ever since."[11]

CIA agents were busy visiting United States travel agents to discourage tourism, the island's life's blood.[12] Even with all the saber rattling in the background, my wife and I enjoyed a relaxing vacation on a laid back island of great natural beauty among friendly people; visiting the rehearsal of a church choir, attending a school dance, and spending lots of time on the beach. We saw no military officers, trucks, tanks, or planes.

About a week after our arrival I heard a surprising announcement on the local radio: the Cuban workers at Point Salines were inviting everyone on the island to come to the construction site for a huge party to celebrate the July 26 anniversary of the attack on the Moncada barracks in 1953 that signaled the birth of the Cuban Revolution. It seemed the Cubans were throwing open a Soviet base to anyone who wanted to see it. We didn't want to miss that.

On the evening of July 26, 1982, we drove towards Point Salines, passing hundreds of Grenadians on foot, bicycle, and motor scooter heading the same way. The unfinished airport looked disappointingly like any other large construction site. Earth moving equipment stood parked here and there beside huge piles of dirt. But where loomed the barbed wire fences, the guards armed with machine guns, the Soviet officers in black polished boots? Nowhere in sight.

Early arrivals had already started camp fires and whole families were eating and drinking. The entire place was a noisy nighttime picnic. Around one bonfire I ran into a light-skinned middle aged man of 45 or so. I greeted him in Spanish and he replied in kind. Before I realized it I was talking to one of those dangerous Cubans, 800 of whom were on the island, 90 percent of them in construction. He invited us to meet his friends and take a tour of their facilities. Now, finally, a chance to see just what these communists had going on. In one quonset hut he introduced us to four more of his comrades, each as middle-aged and pot bellied as him. Bunk beds filled the hut and photos covered the walls. There were snapshots of families as well as buxom magazine pinups. The men opened their wallets and showed us photos of wives and kids. We drank bottles of the local Carib beer.

The Cubans talked about their homesickness, their hard physical work in the Caribbean sun, and their hope to complete the airport so as to return home soon. We passed a friendly night and for nearly thirty years I have not been able to shake the fear that some of that night's new made friends were among the 24 Cubans who died in the U.S. invasion.

We flew home a few days later. I started doing some research. It turned out that Grenada asked the U.S., Europe, and various South American countries for help building the airport. Only the United States said no.[13] But Reagan went further, launching a covert economic assault on the island, lobbying the World Bank, International Monetary Fund, and other international aid funds to deny Grenada development aid[14] even as we deployed carrier attack groups in naval 'war games' off the coast.

The U.S. invasion began on October 25, 1983, the thirty-fourth, but not the last, U.S. military intervention in the Caribbean.[15] Fifteen thousand U.S. Army, Navy, and Marines attacked some 1,000 Grenada Army regulars and 1,000 militia. The attack, in the planning stages for more than four years,[16] followed an October 13 coup d'etat against Prime Minister Maurice Bishop which ended in his death and a military curfew. It was justified as protecting U.S. students at two Grenada medical schools, who had not been threatened by the new government and had been told they were free to leave the island. President Reagan announced that the Organization of Eastern Caribbean States asked the United States to intervene but never explained how one state asking another state to invade yet at third state provided any legal justification for this violation of international law. Later we learned that Eugenia Charles, Prime Minister of Dominica and head of the OECS, had received covert CIA finding for "a secret support operation."[17]

The United States did mistakenly bomb a mental hospital in the capital, killing 30 inmates, but no U.S. citizen was ever in danger and none sustained any injury. The invasion restored American military morale, capturing headlines from the terrorist bombing two days earlier that had killed 241 U.S. Marines in Lebanon.

The United Nations Security Council voted 11 to 1 to condemn the invasion but the single "no" vote was cast by the United States as a veto and the U.N. could take no further action

From a hotel room in Barbados, Duane "Dewey" Clarridge, chief of the CIA's Latin American division and one of the invasion's main planners, said that Bishop's murder had given "an excuse to go deal with that problem."

Clarridge drew up a list of supporters to lead the new Grenadian government and gave it to his counterpart in the State Department, Tony Gillespie. As Tom Weiner writes in his Pulitzer Prize winning book on the CIA, *Legacy of Ashes*:

> "The CIA had a plan to form a government," Gillespie recalled. "This was a top secret list with all kinds of code words on it." He ran it past the most experienced American diplomats in the region. "They looked at it and then just threw up their hands. They said: 'These are some of the worst people in the Caribbean. You don't want them anywhere near this island.' The list included "the worst crumb-bums ... narcotics traffickers, and crooks." These miscreants were the CIA's paid sources.[18]

In 1984 the Council on Hemispheric Relations issued its annual report on human rights in Grenada saying of the newly installed U.S.–backed government: "Reliable accounts are circulating of prisoners being beaten, denied medical attention and confined for long periods without being able to see lawyers. The country's new U.S. trained police force has acquired a reputation for brutality, arbitrary arrest, and abuse of authority."[19]

A few years later an American construction company completed the Point Salines airport. Its runway stands, as originally planned, at 9,000 feet in length. Grenada named it the Maurice Bishop International Airport in memory of the slain revolutionary leader. A monument planned there to the Cuban construction workers who died in the invasion has yet to be built. Grenadians, however, continue pretty much as before the revolution: mostly poor and unemployed, their beautiful green island underdeveloped and, for most Americans, forgotten.

A Template for Terror

Americans grow up believing that our free country and democratically elected government operates for good in the world. In Grenada I wandered into a situation that opened my eyes to a darker picture and led me, through reading and research, to discover a consistent historical pattern of U.S. intervention and destruction abroad, a template for terror in which the CIA and other U.S. government agencies have repeatedly seized control of the lives of hundreds of millions of people around the world, and ended or impoverished those lives.

Putting the pieces together, a template emerged as a list of ten Theorems of Terror governing U.S. foreign policy. Nine of them look like this:

(1) The United States finds or creates an enemy. It might be a country following its own path to development, like Grenada, or a new movement

deposing one of our old friends, like the Sandinistas overthrowing the Somoza dynasty in Nicaragua, or a democratic uprising as in the Dominican Republic in 1965.

(2) The United States demonizes the enemy at home and abroad. The CIA and other intelligence agencies crank up the propaganda machines to turn the offending maverick into a pariah by condemning it through (often flimsy) association with (take your pick of deviltry) socialism, communism, Cuba, the Soviet Union, in the old days, or jihadism, terrorism, antizionism, radical Islam, etc., today. They lie to the American people (using Americans' own tax money and violating strictures against CIA operations within the United States) about the presence of foreign troops, sub bases, and threatening air bases, as in Grenada, equate land reform with communism as in Guatemala, El Salvador, and Brazil, link neutrality with communism as in Indonesia, or equate sovereignty with despotism as in Venezuela. The disinformation machine works, as Frank Wisner, the CIA's first Assistant Director of Policy Coordination, described it, like a "'mighty Wurlitzer organ' capable of playing any propaganda tune he desired."[20]

(3) The United States engages in covert economic destabilization ("make the economy scream" as Nixon ordered in Chile after Marxist Salvador Allende was democratically elected there in 1970), manipulates international organizations to withhold development money or call in debts, leans on allies to withdraw loans and cancel investments as in Cuba, Grenada, and Nicaragua, all designed to make the lives of ordinary citizens miserable.

(4) The United States manipulates the internal political life of the target country by creating and funding opposition parties, churches, civic organizations, opposition newspapers, books and foundations to convince the population that their government is "radical," "communist," or "socialist" as we did in Chile, Cuba, Brazil, Iran, etc.

(5) The United States uses selective bribery, sabotage. blockades, embargoes, etc. to isolate regimes and undermine domestic tranquility or terrorizes the population with bombs against civilian targets as in Cuba, Nicaragua, Venezuela, or wages secret biological war, such as the CIA introduction of swine flu in Cuba to to kills pigs and reduce the food supply.

(6) The CIA assassinates, or attempts to assassinate, leaders who may challenge U.S. goals as it did with Zhou Enlai in China, Sukarno in Indonesia, Mohammed Mossadegh in Iran, Jawaharlal Nehru in India, Gamal Nasser in Egypt, Jose Figueres in Costa Rica, Patrice Lumumba in Congo, Ngo Dinh Diem in Vietnam, Fidel and Raul Castro in Cuba, Rene Schneider and Salvador Allende in Chile, Omar Torrijos in Panama, Michael Manley in Jamaica, and Miguel d'Escoto in Nicaragua. This constitutes a very partial historical list of CIA murders and attempted murders.[21]

(7) The CIA illegally creates, arms, and trains native mercenary forces to overthrow the offending government as in Nicaragua, Cuba, El Salvador (again a partial list)

(8) If all else fails, the United States reverts to overt military force and sends in the Marines to occupy the country as in Grenada, Haiti, Nicaragua, Panama, Mexico, China, Cuba, the USSR, Honduras (a very partial historical list).[22]

(9) The linchpin of this terror template is the Central Intelligence Agency which plans the moves every step of the way.

There are two key additions I would make to this terror template, but first let me detail how I saw it work in another country I visited many years ago. In 1980 I served as minister of the First Unitarian Church of Los Angeles. One day I got a phone invitation to join a delegation put together by baby doctor Benjamin Spock and educator Jonathan Kozol to observe first hand the national literacy crusade in Nicaragua. I hadn't previously spent much time out of the United States and had never visited Central America. A little research on my part brought me up to speed on a country, no bigger in size than Iowa, and then home to three million people that had just emerged from a revolution ending forty years of Somoza family dictatorship, a dynastic rule which had left the country impoverished and the people uneducated and malnourished. The per capita annual income of Nicaraguans was below $600, life expectancy was only 52 years, and the illiteracy rate was above 50 percent. Eighty percent of the country's homes lacked running water and 60 percent lacked electricity.[23] Yet when Somoza Jr. arrived in exile in Miami in 1979 he claimed a personal fortune of $100 million. *The New York Times* reported his assets as closer to $900 million.[24]

The Somoza clan, an unlovely lot of murderers, thieves, and torturers, clung tightly to U.S. apron strings. From Anastasio Sr. (assassinated 1956) to his children Luis and West Point trained Anastasio Jr. (assassinated 1980) they served as loyal servants of the U.S. government for 46 years. As President Franklin Roosevelt famously said of Anastasio Sr., who had seized power in a coup d'etat in 1933, "He's an S.O.B. but he's our S.O.B."

Somoza Sr. also worked for the CIA, collaborating in the arming of a CIA mercenary force under Castillo Armas to invade Guatemala and overthrow the elected government of Jacobo Arbenz in 1954. In that operation the CIA used one of Somoza's own cattle ranches to set up a "field studio" for the CIA's bogus "Voice of Liberation" station beaming radio propaganda into nearby Guatemala warning that Soviet troops were about to land and that 16-year-old Guatemalan boys and girls would be rounded up and placed in communist indoctrination camps.[25] In 1961 Somoza Jr. followed in his father's

CIA footsteps turning over ports and airbases on the Atlantic Coast around Puerto Cabezas, as staging grounds for the CIA invasion of Cuba. Five freighters and 1400 Cuban mercenaries steamed out of Nicaragua for the Bay of Pigs as CIA planes flew bombing missions against Cuba from Nicaraguan airfields. No wonder the United States turned a blind eye for half a century to the poverty, illiteracy, and desperation of ordinary Nicaraguans.

On my first visit to Nicaragua I encountered a lushly green country of volcanoes and lakes and desperately poor people living in dirt floor shacks and squatting without water or electricity in the crumpled ruins of buildings destroyed in the great earthquake eight years before. Our delegation met newly literate peasants and some of the young people who had been their teachers. One of the first acts of the Sandinista Revolution of July 1979 had been to close the high schools and recruit the students as *brigidistas* in the first ever national literacy crusade.

Given rudimentary literacy training, these teenagers sallied out to the countryside to live with the campesinos where they worked with the peasants in the fields during the day and taught them to read at night by the light of government issued kerosene lanterns. By the end of the five month Literacy Crusade, 420,000 people had learned the rudiments of reading and writing. In one small rural town with dirt streets and hitching posts outside each small cinder block building for folks to tie up their horses, I watched a 75-year-old *campesino* laboriously write his name, which he had learned to do for the first time in his life. At the end of the campaign the newly literate were enrolled in free evening adult education classes.

One of these young boys made an indelible impression on me and I have recounted his story in each of my two previous books. In retrospect I see that my encounter with him may be the reason I began working with at-risk teenagers in the United States and eventually became a teacher.

As I wrote in *After-School Theatre Programs for At-Risk Teenagers*:

> I will never forget meeting little Felix Vijil. Felix was just 11 years old, which means he was too young to join the 12-to-19-year-old brigidistas. But he told me he had run away from home, a comfortable urban home with multiple servants, and "infiltrated" a literacy brigade. Joining late, he got "the ones that were hard to teach," he said, 12 students between the ages of 17 and 62. He planted corn during the day and taught classes in the evening. He suffered from fleas and worms, and in the middle of the course he came down with ricketsia, a type of typhoid, which sent him home for bed rest for two weeks, and yet at the end of the five month campaign, one of his 12 students earned her certificate as literate and the other 11 committed to the follow-up program of adult education. When I asked Felix what he would do if such a campaign were ever necessary again, he replied, "I'll infiltrate again."[26]

Although citizens in the United States take literacy for granted, keep in mind that if you cannot read or write you are excluded from your society:

you cannot write your elected representative, you cannot sign a petition, you cannot write a letter-to-the-editor of the newspaper, you cannot read the newspaper, you cannot read any books on subjects that might be of importance to your work, health or future.

I wasn't the first North American to visit Nicaragua, of course, but many of my predecessors had visited with guns. The United States sent our Marines, Army, or Navy to Nicaragua in 1853, 1854, 1857, 1867, 1894, 1896, 1898, 1899, and 1910 to overthrow governments we didn't like, collect debts, or protect U.S. commercial interests. Troops landed again in 1912 and remained, though in fewer numbers, until 1925, only to return again in force in 1926 to put down a revolution aimed at tossing out our presidential favorite. These forces flew the first aerial bombardment campaign in history, targeting civilians and troops supporting revolutionary General Augusto Sandino and withdrew only in 1933 when Somoza Sr. and his U.S.–trained National Guard seized power, assassinated Sandino, and lorded it over ordinary Nicaraguans for 46 years.

I did visit Nicaragua at a moment of transition, as it moved from despotism to a functioning and more egalitarian civic society. That kind of change, unfortunately, usually calls for another visit from the CIA and/or the Marines.

Let's apply the Terror Template to Nicaragua. For a fuller discussion of the CIA war on Nicaragua I recommend William Blum's book *Killing Hope*, from which I will quote frequently.

First: Find or create an enemy

Presidents Carter and Reagan, and especially Reagan's CIA Chief William Casey, decided Nicaragua and the *Sandinistas* were our enemy. Certainly everything the CIA subsequently did made them our enemies. We had our reasons: our pique at losing our friend Somoza, chagrin at having to forego CIA bases in Central America, fear that the revolution might go too far towards a socialist economy, or that the new Nicaraguan government would aid rebels fighting a civil war in El Salvador against a U.S.–supported government of death squads and oligarchs. In the 1980s the United States still framed world politics in the East-West competition of the Cold War and that left only two categories of friend and foe with little room for ambiguities or even new ideas: "The strategic issue is a simple one," asserted Patrick Buchanan, Reagan's Director of Communications. "Who wants Central America more — the West or the Warsaw Pact."[27]

Felix Vijil was not our enemy. That 75-year-old peasant who just learned to write his name was not our enemy. The new farming cooperatives formed by peasants on the land confiscated from Somoza and his cronies were not our enemies. The health care workers who went into rural areas to offer free medical care to the peasants who had never seen vaccines before were not our enemies. Few of them had ever heard of the Warsaw Pact or ever seen a Russian. The Christians who served at very level of the new government and the three Roman Catholic priests who served in top positions as Foreign Minister, Minister of Culture, and Minister of Education, were not our enemies. Even the nine *Comandantes* who led the revolution and formed the National Directorate, who included intellectuals, trained engineers, political pragmatists, liberals, and Marxists, were not our enemies.

Second: Demonize the enemy

To make the facts fit the theory, the CIA set the propaganda machine (that "mighty Wurlitzer") into overdrive. For domestic consumption they set up the Office of Public Diplomacy, "operating as an arm of the National Security Council," whose "overall theme" was, in the words of its Deputy Director Colonel Daniel Jacobowitz, the "FSLN [Sandinistas] are evil."[28] How were they evil? They were arming the insurgency in El Salvador, housing Cuban bases, practicing genocide against their own people, exporting drugs, indulging in anti–Semitism, developing chemical weapons, training Brazilian guerrillas, linking up to the radical new theocracy in Iran, landing Soviet MiGs, and threatening to invade neighboring Honduras or Costa Rica. Sounds pretty evil if true. It wasn't.

The CIA never lets the truth get in the way of a good story. So they 'created' new facts. Colonel Oliver North colluded with the top CIA employee in Panama, General Manuel Noriega, to ship Soviet-bloc arms to El Salvador that could be fraudulently tied to Nicaragua.[29] Photos of piles of Nicaraguan bodies being burned, proffered by Secretary of Sate Alexander Haig as evidence of genocide, proved to date from 1978 and the reign of Somoza.[30] The U.S.–tagged surveillance photos of Nicaraguan military bases "Cuban" because they had "a standard rectangular configuration like we have seen in Cuba"[31] rather than circular, like the yurts of Mongolia, presumably. The drug-running story had to be withdrawn for lack of evidence and most experts agreed the *Sandinistas* ended material support to the Salvadoran rebels in 1981. There were no chemical weapons and no MiGs. The CIA churned out lies faster than they could be debunked, the media parroted their charges, and Americans swallowed most of them. The 1980 Republican Party platform, on which Reagan won the presidency, opposed "the Marxist Sandinista takeover of Nicaragua."[32]

Third: Wage Economic war on the new enemy

The United States had previously showered loans and economic and military aid on Somoza. These ended. Standard Fruit tore up their contract and withdrew from Nicaragua while Exxon refused to transport Mexican oil to Nicaragua, leaving no more than a ten day supply on hand. The United States cut Nicaraguan sugar imports 90 percent[33] and leaned on international lenders to stay away. But other U.S. money continued to pour into the country: funding the long time CIA front the American Institute for Free Labor Development, the opposition press, and the hierarchy of the Catholic Church, all of which kept up a drumbeat of criticism of the new government.

As Nixon did in Chile, Reagan "made the economy scream." When I returned to Central America for the second time in 1983 our church group delivered a dozen second-hand wheelchairs to disabled Nicaraguans too impoverished to obtain new chairs in a country too undeveloped to manufacture them. I saw the retreats in health and education as funding for development disappeared. I saw a poor people sink into yet deeper poverty and beggars multiply on the streets.

Four: Manipulate public opinion and political life within the target country

As people "scream" about the failing economy the CIA blames it on their own government, builds up the opposition parties, and spreads disinformation. In Nicaragua President Carter began secretly funding opposition political parties, unions, and church groups almost as soon as Somoza boarded a plane into exile.[34] Reagan upped the ante, directing the CIA to pay people to organize anti-government rallies and sending millions of dollars to *La Prensa*, the opposition newspaper. This covert funding snaked its way south through the National Endowment for Democracy and "private" donors. In 1990 the NED poured $11 million into the presidential election campaign while the CIA added additional funds covertly to elect the U.S.–favored candidate Violeta Chamorro.[35] Ironically U.S. law forbids our domestic candidates from accepting foreign campaign money.

Five: Disturb domestic tranquility through bribery, embargo, and sabotage

President Reagan's CIA Chief William Casey chose Duane "Dewey" Clarridge (who also coordinated the Grenada invasion) as his point man:

> Just shy of fifty, hard-drinking and cigar-puffing despite an early heart attack, Clarridge never had worked in Latin America, spoke no Spanish, and knew next to nothing

about the region. Casey said, "Take off a month or two and basically figure out what to do about Central America," Clarridge said. "That was the sum total of his approach. And it didn't take rocket science to understand what needed to be done." Clarridge said he came up with a two point plan: "Make war in Nicaragua and start killing Cubans. This was exactly what Casey wanted to hear and he said, 'Okay, go ahead and do it.'"[36]

Words turned to deeds as the CIA dispatched a "mother ship" to international waters off the Nicaraguan coast from which they launched attacks by helicopter and speed boat, letting the *Contras*, former *Somocistas* and other disaffected Nicaraguans, take the blame for a series of deadly attacks. In 1983, in an effort to cut off Nicaragua's oil and in violation of both international law and the U.S. Congress' Boland Amendment,

> the CIA itself carried out the attacks and mining of the ports. The mother ship acted as a command post and carried raiding parties to distant targets It also had armed helicopters to support raids. Commando parties consisted mostly of Latins and CIA contract agents for underwater demolition and specialized tasks. Contract employees piloted the helicopters while agency officers had complete command.[37]

CIA operatives blew up fuel depots, oil pipelines, and refineries. Foreign ships turned back after CIA mines damaged seven of them. In addition: "Nicaragua's ports were under siege: mortar shelling from high speed motor launches, aerial bombing and rocket and machine-gun attacks were designed to blockade Nicaragua's exports as well as to starve the country of imports."[38]

In January 1984, I returned to Nicaragua for a third time. On sabbatical from my church, I planned to stay six months and write a book about the novel mix of religion and revolution in the *Sandinista* movement. It appeared a year later as a collection of interviews entitled *Nicaragua: A New Kind of Revolution*.

I soon felt that I had a target on my back. I visited San Juan Del Sur, a beautiful lazy beach town on the Pacific for a weekend. Two weeks later CIA speedboats dashed into the bay and shot up the town and set oil storage tanks on fire. I took a boat down the Rio Escondido through lush rain forests from El Rama to Bluefields to interview descendants of African slaves and Miskito Indians on the Pacific Coast. Soon after the CIA/Contra attacked, burned, and sunk the small passenger boat I had taken, cutting this important east-west connection for several weeks. In each case the results were the same: dead and wounded Nicaraguans, lost export income, and a national sense of insecurity and fear. The newspapers I read reported daily on attacks on fishing boats, irrigation projects, grain silos, and farm crops.

On my first visit to Nicaragua in 1980, they were spending one half of their national budget on health and education and only 18 percent on defense. Seven years later the military ate up 50 percent of the Nicaraguan budget as

the country struggled to repulse attacks from the CIA and their Contra surrogates, and they could expend less than 20 percent on health and education.[39]
The people, on whole, poorer, sicker, and desperate, felt ever more hopeless.

Six: Kill selected targets through a CIA program of assassination

Health care workers, teachers, and agronomists became particular targets
in Nicaragua,[40] but *Sandinista* leaders stood in the crosshairs too. William
Blum recounts how the CIA sent a hit team from Honduras to Managua in
1983 hoping to blow up all nine *Sandinista comandantes* at a single meeting. London TV broadcast a documentary, complete with an interview with
one of the assassins, noting the plot unraveled when the explosives failed to
arrive.[41]

Also in 1983, Nicaraguan security forces foiled a plot to assassinate the
Foreign Minister Miguel D'Escoto and expelled the three U.S. Embassy officials responsible, including the CIA Chief of Station. Two months later
another plot against D'Escoto was discovered and another CIA agent fingered
as the ringleader. Perhaps this explains why of the four Catholic priests serving
at the highest levels of the *Sandinista* government, Father Edgard Parrales,
Ambassador to the Organization of American States, Father Ernesto Cardenal,
Minister of Culture, and Father Fernando Cardenal, Minister of Education,
I was able to interview all but D'Escoto in my time there. I finally met him
in 2009 in Monterrey, Mexico when he was serving as Nicaragua's Ambassador
to the United Nations and President of the UN General Assembly.

One CIA assassination target I did meet in Managua was Ben Linder, a
27-year-old, pale, thin man from Portland, Oregon. After graduating from
the University of Washington in 1983 with a degree in engineering Linder
headed for Nicaragua to put his skills to work for some of the poorest people
in our hemisphere.

Many North Americans visiting or working in Nicaragua would gather
each Thursday outside the U.S. Embassy in Managua. There was singing,
and speeches, sometimes street theatre, all directed against Reagan's policies
in Central America. I knew I'd seen it all, however, when a guy wearing a big
red nose and riding a tall unicycle rode through the crowd. Juggler, clown,
and engineer, Ben Linder stole the show that day.

Three years later, helping build a hydroelectric station to bring electricity
to the rural town of El Cua, a Contra hit team ambushed Ben and two
Nicaraguans. Wounded by grenade fragments, Ben fell to the ground. Based
on the autopsy we know what happened next: one of the commandos walked
up to where Ben lay, pressed a gun to his head, and executed him. With my
experiences in San Juan del Sur and El Rama I knew it could have been me.

CBS news anchor Dan Rather responded to the murder of the first North American killed by the Contras:

> Benjamin Linder was no revolutionary firebrand spewing rhetoric and itching to carry a rifle through the jungles of Central America. He was a slight, softspoken, thoughtful young man. When at 23 he left the comfort and security of the United States for Nicaragua, he wasn't exactly sure what he would find. But he wanted to see Nicaragua firsthand, and so he headed off, armed with a new degree in engineering, and the energy and ideals of youth.
>
> This wasn't just another death in a war that has claimed thousands of Nicaraguans. This was an American who was killed with weapons paid with American tax dollars The bitter irony of Benjamin Linder's death is that he went to Nicaragua to build up what his own country's dollars paid to destroy — and ended up the victim of the destruction. The loss of Benjamin Linder is more than fodder for an angry political debate. it is the loss of something that seems rare these days: a man with the courage to put his back behind his beliefs. It would have been easy for this bright young man to follow the path to a good job and a comfortable salary. Instead he chose to follow the lead of his conscience.[42]

George Bush I, then vice president and formerly CIA chief, said, justifying the murder: "Ben Linder 'was on the other side.'"[43]

I've edited this book for America's college students who are being recruited by the CIA at my university and other campuses right now and that is why I have dedicated it to Ben Linder, an American college student just like them, killed by the CIA. You might think I indulge in hyperbole, that a Nicaraguan, a Contra, not a bona fide employee with a paycheck and a pension from the CIA committed this murder. But, as Joan Kruckewitt wrote,

> the CIA resumed day-to-day management of the war, stockpiling weapons and dispatching supply planes from a secret air base on Swan Island, off the Caribbean coast of Honduras. From El Salvador, Honduras, and U.S. ships cruising the Nicaraguan coast, the CIA directed Contra attacks deep into Nicaragua.... Top Contra commanders were sent to U.S. army bases in North Carolina and Florida where Spanish-speaking American instructors taught two-month courses in map theory, navigation, and patrolling and instructed them how to use new weapons including artillery and explosives.
>
> When the Contra leaders returned to their base in Honduras, the CIA supplied them with intelligence data, including blueprints of Nicaraguan government installations and aerial reconnaissance maps that showed Sandinista army bases in such detail that every outhouse was noted. The CIA supplied the Contras with Datotek mini-computers to encode and decode messages, portable solar panes to recharge field radios, and 200-channel scanners to eavesdrop on the Sandinistas. Contra troops received new FAL and Kalishnakov AK-47 automatic rifles and heavier machine guns. Each group was assigned a surface-to-air shoulder-fired missile, either a Soviet-made SAM-7 or a sleek U.S.–made Redeye, worth $30,000 each.[44]

Since the World Court had ruled U.S. efforts to overthrow the Sandinistas through the Contra mercenary army illegal these actions of aiding and abetting the murder of Ben Linder, and many thousands more, themselves rise to the level of Felony Murder. The Felony Murder law, on the books in most states of the U.S., holds that anyone aiding a felony in which a murder occurs becomes equally guilty, whether they are present at the scene or not, of that murder and may, if found guilty, be sentenced to the maximum penalty allowed by law, either death or life imprisonment.

Seven: Recruit, train, arm, and pay a native mercenary force to topple the government

Although many members of Somoza's feared National Guard were taken into custody or demobilized following the dictator's fall in 1979, many followed the example of their chief and fled. Without his millions they only made it as far as neighboring Honduras and Costa Rica where they were happy to take the CIA's money, weapons, training, and food and reconstitute themselves as Contras (for counterrevolutionaries) for infiltration back over the border for new terror attacks on the people. While perhaps only 20 percent of the Contra foot soldiers were former Guardsmen, former National Guard commanders made up the majority of high ranking officers.[45]

For these unreformed terrorists the CIA supplied thousands of copies of an instructional manual entitled *Psychological Operations in Guerrilla Warfare* just in case they weren't prepared to be vicious enough. The manual advocated "hiring professional criminals," creating martyrs for the cause by "arranging deaths of the Contras' own fighters" and "selective violence, as in assassinating Sandinista officials in order to cow villagers."[46] America's Watch (now Human Rights Watch), a non-governmental human rights organization, reported that "the contras systematically engage in violent abuses ... so prevalent that these may be said to be their principal means of waging war."[47] The contras terrorized civilians, destroyed schools, health centers, and community centers while especially targeting health and literacy workers.

The assassinations advocated in the CIA terror manual violated a presidential ban but the CIA never worried about legalities in running the Contra war. When Congress cut off funding for the war through the Boland Amendment, the CIA traded arms to the ayatollahs in Iran, in violation of an arms embargo, for money for the Contras. Nicaragua took its case to the International Court of Justice, the UN's judicial organ, established in the UN Charter of 1945, in 1986 and won a decision against the United States for funding the Contras and mining Nicaraguan ports. The United States withdrew its earlier acceptance of the Court's jurisdiction and refused to pay a multibillion dollar judgment against it. U.S. Ambassador to the UN Jeanne Kirkpatrick explained the International Court was no more than a "semi-legal, semi-juridical, semipolitical body which nations sometimes accept and sometimes don't."[48]

On my third visit to Nicaragua in 1984, I interviewed wounded Sandinista soldiers at the army convalescent center in Las Colinas, a suburb of Managua. Ranging in age from 14 to 27, in wheelchairs and flat on their backs in hospital cots, all had voluntarily enlisted. They showed me captured Contra military equipment stamped "Made in the U.S." As one of the young soldiers, Noel Laguna, told me: "The FALs [rifles] aren't made in Central America, the webbed belts aren't made in Central America, the mines ... aren't made in Central America. None of the arms that the contras are using ... are made in Central America — it's all made in the U.S."[49]

Eight: Invade

In Nicaragua, terror template tactics one through seven worked so well that number eight became unnecessary. But, given the Grenada invasion of 1983, there was not a moment that Nicaraguans I met didn't think the same thing could and would happen to them.

Nine: The CIA runs it all

The CIA is not simply an intelligence gathering agency. For 63 years it has been and remains the go-to network for covert action involving assassinations, torture, destabilization, and invasion. The CIA ran the invasion of Grenada and the mercenary war in Nicaragua.

Ten: The CIA terror template is refined, empowered, and staffed from our campuses

The CIA has always been attracted to covert work on campus to obtain access to the best brains, to skew research, recruit students (1,000 agency employees are recruited from campuses each year), burnish its image, and to spy on faculty. As former CIA Personnel Director F.W.M. Janney wrote: "It is absolutely essential that the Agency have available to it the greatest single source of expertise: the American academic community."[50]

Beginning in the late 1940s and into the early 1950s the CIA paid Yale crew coach "Skip" Walz $10,000 to "spot" likely recruits as the newly organized CIA concentrated on recruiting from the Ivy League. Given names, the CIA conducted secret background checks, investigated the students without their knowledge or approval, and then approached them with job offers.[51] The effort grew and by the late 1970s about 5,000 academics were working with the CIA to identify and recruit students for the Agency.[52] Among them were

William Buckley and Henry Kissinger, recruited at Yale and Harvard, respectively, to both recruit students and to inform on their colleagues at the time of the campus purges and loyalty oaths of the 1950s.

But recruiting wasn't the only CIA outreach on campus. In 1950 the CIA initiated Project Artichoke, a four year series of mind control experiments utilizing "heroin, amphetamines, sleeping pills ... and LSD."[53] Besieged by a fear of double agents, the CIA set up the equivalent of today's "black sites" with secret detention centers in Japan, Germany (think 2006 sites in Poland and Thailand) and the U.S. enclave in the Panama Canal Zone where "like Guantanamo [fifty years later] ... it was anything goes."[54] In cement block cells "bulldozed out of the jungle ... the agency was conducting secret experiments in harsh interrogation, using techniques on the edge of torture, drug-induced mind control, and brainwashing."[55] In 1952 the experiments morphed into Project MKULTRA within the United States. "Under its auspices," writes Tim Weiner,

> seven prisoners at a federal penitentiary in Kentucky were kept high on LSD for seventy-seven consecutive days. When the CIA slipped the same drug to an army civilian employee, Frank Olson, he leaped out of the window of a New York hotel. Like the suspected double agents sent to the secret brig in Panama, these men were expendable conscripts in the battle to defeat the Soviets.[56]

Next the CIA decided to experiment on unknowing American college students. As a result, some experienced psychotic episodes, several committed suicide and others suffered life long psychological problems. Participating in the program were reputable academics like Ewan Cameron, President of the American Psychiatric Association.[57] This occurred not on one campus, nor on a handful. Somehow the CIA found collaborating administrators and faculty at 44 colleges and universities in the United States for these immoral and illegal drug experiments.[58] This was no rogue operation but authorized by the CIA Director himself.[59] As Weiner concludes: "The drive to penetrate the iron curtain had led the CIA to adopt the tactics of its enemies."[60] In 1973, then CIA Director Richard Helms destroyed all files relating to MKULTRA and

> continued to push for an expanded drug testing program, even after it had been terminated. Referring to its usefulness, Helms stated, "While I share your uneasiness and distaste for any program which tends to intrude upon an individual's private and legal prerogatives, I believe it is necessary that the Agency maintain a central role in this activity."[61]

When millions of American college students took to the streets to protest the war in Vietnam, President Lyndon Johnson ordered the CIA Director Helms to find the foreign powers behind the student protests. In violation of U.S. law and its own charter the CIA initiated Operation CHAOS, spying on American citizens, infiltrating student peace groups, tapping phones, and compiling computer files on 300,000 citizens and organizations. Though they found no foreign involvement in the domestic peace movement, the CIA did demonstrate their willingness, through projects MKULTRA and CHAOS, to apply their well-honed terror template against our own college students. Former CIA agent Verne Lyon addresses these abuses of our civil liberties from his inside role as campus spy in essay number 6.

The CIA also recruited academics for adventures abroad. In the late 1950s MIT and Cornell professors at field projects in Indonesia trained military officers who later led the coup that overthrew Indonesian President Sukarno.[62] CIA funding was exposed at Michigan State University in a plan to train South Vietnamese police to prop up that dictatorship in 1969. A year earlier,

the CIA used the Eagleton Institute for Research at Rutgers University in a plan to influence the outcome of the presidential election in Guyana. Through the Institute the CIA helped amend the Guyanese constitution to allow Guyanese and relatives of Guyanese living abroad to vote by absentee ballot. Then 16,000 votes were manufactured in New York City giving the CIA's candidate, Forbes Burnham, a narrow margin over socialist Cheddi Jagan.[63]

Oddly enough Burnham secured 94 percent of this overseas vote while getting only 50 percent of the vote in country. As one Guyanese remarked: "To call it an election is to give it a name it does not deserve; it was a seizure of power by fraud, not election."[64] As with so many other CIA funded adventures this one came back to bite the U.S. in the end when its creature, Burnham, prime minister from 1964 to 1980 and then president from 1980 to 1985, later cooperated with Jim Jones' People's Temple, giving them agricultural land in 1974, allowing their mass migration from San Francisco in 1977, and witnessing their mass suicide that claimed 918 American lives in November 1978.

In 1966, *Ramparts Magazine* uncovered the decades long CIA secret funding of the National Student Association, the largest student organization in the United States. As the largest funding source for the NSA, the CIA required NSA officers to sign secrecy oaths about the CIA relationship:

The CIA had a significant say in NSA operations. Student agents were enjoined against making ... diplomatic overtures without first requesting permission of the Agency. In return for their cooperation, student agents received draft deferments arranged by the CIA.[65]

CIA funding also went to other campus front organizations like The Foundation for Youth and Student Affairs. The CIA used that organization as a "pass through" to fund other youth organizations like the Asia Foundation, the American Friends of the Middle East, The International Student

Conference, the United States Youth Council, and the International Catholic Youth Federation[66] always hiding the CIA connection.

The CIA has historically been interested in getting its hands on university research. In 1984 Professor Richard Mansbach, chair of the Rutgers Political Science Department assigned an undergraduate class to research Western Europe political developments and then secretly passed the student reports on to the CIA without the students' knowledge or permission.[67] Following disclosures that Dr. Nadav Safran, Director of Harvard University's Center for Middle Eastern Affairs, served on the CIA payroll, Harvard removed him in 1986, but only after the CIA had subsidized him to write an academic book on Saudi Arabia and to organize an academic conference on Islam.[68] As a result we read what the CIA wanted us to read about this key U.S. ally and reactionary Kingdom in the Middle East. A few years earlier Samuel P. Huntington, former director of Harvard's Center for International Affairs, was revealed to have been in the employ of the CIA "publishing documents that were both paid for and censored by the CIA."[69]

Revisiting the ploys used to involve U.S. colleges in the Vietnam war, the CIA returned to campus in 1986 at the Northwestern University Traffic Institute to host a CIA program to train Salvadoran police, some of them connected to the death squads then operating in El Salvador.[70]

Since 1985 the CIA has run special seminars for university administrators focusing on campus recruitment[71] and in 1988 the CIA had agents on 10 college campuses as part of its Officers in Residence program where active-duty CIA agents teach academic credit bearing courses,[72] choosing what students read, framing the parameters of discussion of controversial political issues and determining how they are interpreted, and awarding grades.

Publication of a secret memo in 1991 revealed that the Rochester Institute of Technology had signed a Memorandum of Agreement with the CIA in 1985 agreeing that "its curriculum would be 'responsive to certain defined specialties of the CIA.'"[73] In 1988 a CIA agent had become an Institute trustee and in that same year the Federal Programs Training Center opened on campus where students were paid to forge documents, design furniture with secret drawers and picture frames with hidden compartments to hide listening devices.[74]

Today CIA representatives regularly attend academic conferences of "librarians, geographers, anthropologists, mathematicians, statisticians, etc."[75] for recruitment and information. We can understand how CIA spokeswoman Sharon Foster could announce in 1988 that "the CIA has enough professors under Agency contract 'to staff a large university.'"[76] CIA official John Phillips, interviewed by the *Wall Street Journal,* said: "We don't want to turn [academics] into spies.... We want to capture them intellectually."[77] An intellectual captive does its master's bidding without question and without even knowing its will is not its own.

Porter Goss, one of President Bush's CIA directors, delivered the commencement address to the graduating class at Tiffin University in May 2006 and told students: "If this were a graduating class of CIA case workers, my advice would be short and to the point: Admit nothing, deny everything, and make counteraccusations."[78] The CIA has followed this advice for 60 years and wants our campuses, faculty and students to do the same.

Finally it is clear that the CIA terror template has one corollary, unrecognized by its authors but ever present and ultimately fatal to the entire enterprise: application of the template hurts all of us.

Eleven: The CIA terror template undermines U.S. security and democratic values

The CIA war in Nicaragua succeeded so well in ousting the Sandinistas and installing a U.S.–friendly regime that a Pentagon analyst said: It's going right into the textbook."[79] That textbook details the CIA terror template. But what has it gained us? The cost is easy to tally: hundreds of thousands murdered in sixty countries around the world from Indonesia to Iran, Guatemala and Brazil, Grenada and Nicaragua; millions left behind in poverty, illiteracy, and disease; frustrated hopes for democracy, development, and decent lives; rigged elections; assassinated leaders; destabilized economies; and millions of people permanently angry at the U.S. manipulation of their sovereignty.

Iran, after the CIA disposed of democratically elected Prime Minister Mohammed Mossadegh, became Iran under Shah Pahlavi and his Savak secret police, which became Iran under the ayatollahs, President Mahmoud Ahmadinejad, and nuclear weapons. Guatemala after the CIA overthrew democratically elected President Jacobo Arbenz entered a violent downward spiral of genocidal military governments and civil war. The CIA coup in Indonesia against Ahmed Sukarno left 500,000 dead in the first several months and began the 30-year reign of dictator Suharto. The CIA conspiracy to murder Prime Minister Patrice Lumumba in the Congo led inexorably to the 32-year kleptocratic rule of Sese Seko Mobutu.

There is an oft repeated bit of self-serving CIA whimsy that their successes remain secret and only their mistakes become public (see the following list of Major Failures of CIA Intelligence). But I have been discussing CIA "successes" which they celebrated at the time but which have been long term disasters for U.S. interests. Even as the CIA blew the biggest intelligence stories since Pearl Harbor by failing to warn us of the 9/11 attacks on New York City and Washington, D.C., and getting it all wrong about "Weapons of Mass

Destruction" in Iraq, the terror template has made the United States less secure and less free than ever by creating new enemies abroad and weakening democratic rule at home. As Tim Weiner asks in his Pulitzer Prize winning book *Legacy of Ashes*: "How do you run a secret intelligence service in an open democracy? How do you serve the truth by lying? How do ou spread democracy by deceit?"[80] History reveals the answer: You don't.

Major CIA Failures of Intelligence and Security

1949: The CIA tells President Truman the USSR needs at least four more years to develop the atomic bomb. Three days later the USSR explodes an A-bomb.[81]

October 30, 1950: The CIA tells President Truman there is no evidence China will intervene in the Korean War. Two days later 300,000 Chinese troops attack U.S. forces in Korea.[82]

1953: The CIA assures President Eisenhower the USSR will be unable to launch an ICBM at the United States until 1969. The USSR has a working ICBM capable of hitting the United States in 1957.[83]

1953: The USSR explodes an H-bomb. The CIA has no advance warning and President Eisenhower reads about the test in the newspapers.[84]

1956: Hungarians rise in revolt against USSR. The CIA has no station in Hungary and no Hungarian section at CIA headquarters "and almost no one who spoke the language. During the two week life of the Hungarian revolution the agency knew no more than what it read in the newspapers."[85]

1956: The CIA pays millions to Gamal Abdel Nasser, leader of Egypt, who nationalizes the Suez Canal in July 1956. The CIA assures President Eisenhower that reports of a British, French and Israeli invasion of Egypt in retaliation are "absurd." All three countries invade and seize the Canal in October 1956.[86]

1959: CIA station chief in Havana tells headquarters the new Castro government cannot last more than a few months. He's off by 50 years and counting.[87]

1960: CIA tells President Eisenhower the USSR has 500 ICBMs capable of hitting the United States. In reality they have four.[88]

1961: After assuring President Kennedy the CIA-Cuban exile mercenary army can successfully invade and overthrow the new Cuban government the invaders are defeated on the beaches with 114 killed and 1,189 captured. The CIA maps of the Bay of Pigs "suggesting that the swampland would serve as guerrilla country had been drawn in 1895."[89]

August 1962: The CIA tells President Kennedy it does not believe the USSR will base nuclear weapons in Cuba.[90] On September 15, 1962, the first

Soviet missiles arrive in Cuba.[91] On September 19, 1962, the CIA concludes placing Soviet missiles in Cuba is "incompatible with Soviet policy."[92] On October 15, 1962, U-2 flights provide photographic evidence of Soviet missiles in Cuba.[93]

January 31, 1968: 400,000 Vietnamese troops attack cities and bases across South Vietnam in coordinated attacks planned months in advance. The CIA "never saw it coming and had next to no intelligence on the enemy's intent."[94]

1973: Egypt attacks Israel. CIA Chief William Colby reported later: "We predicted the day before the war broke out that it was not going to break out." In fact, a few hours before the war began the CIA informed President Nixon: "Exercises are more realistic than usual. But there will be no war."[95]

1974: A military coup in Portugal and India's test of a nuclear bomb "had come as complete surprises [to the CIA]."[96]

1979: CIA is caught unaware by the USSR invasion of Afghanistan. CIA fails to predict the revolution in Iran. CIA Chief Stansfield Turner admits, "We were just plain asleep."[97]

1985–1992: The head of CIA chief of counterintelligence, Aldrich Ames, on the payroll of the USSR, betrays hundreds of CIA agents and spies in the Soviet Union.[98]

1986–1994: The CIA "knowingly gave the White House information manipulated by Moscow — and concealed the fact."[99]

July 1995: CIA failed to confirm the slaughter of 8,000 Moslems by Serbs at Srebenica until five weeks after first newspaper reports.[100]

1990: CIA station in Sudan issues an entry visa to the United States to Omar Abdel Rahman, soon after his release from an Egyptian prison. Rahman plans the first bombing of the World Trade Center in 1993.[101]

1998: CIA intelligence on nerve gas production at a factory outside Khartoum, Sudan, is the basis for a U.S. cruise missile attack. The facility turns out to be a pharmaceutical factory. Said the former U.S. Ambassador to Sudan: "It was a mistake."[102]

1998 to 2011: The CIA searches for but cannot find Osama bin Laden.

1999: CIA identifies a military depot in Belgrade which is subsequently bombed. The building turns out to be the Chinese Embassy and civilians die.[103]

September 11, 2001: The CIA has no advance warning and is helpless to stop the terrorist attacks on New York and Washington, D.C., "the Pearl Harbor the CIA had been created to prevent."[104]

NOTES

1. Kate Braverman, *Lullaby for Sinners* (New York: Pinnacle, 1980), 99.

2. Catherine Sunshine and Philip Wheaton, eds., *Grenada: The Peaceful Revolution* (Washington, D.C.: EPICA Task Force, 1982), 54.

3. William Blum, *Killing Hope: U.S. Military and CIA Interventions Since World War II* (Monroe, ME: Common Courage, 2004), 273.

4. Ibid., 275.

5. Hugh O'Shaughnessy, *Grenada: An Eyewitness Account of the U.S. Invasion and the Caribbean History that Provoked It* (New York: Dodd, Mead, 1984), 112–113.

6. Ibid., 154.

7. Quoted in Blum, 275

8. Sunshine and Wheaton, 70.

9. Ibid., 118.

10. Blum, 274.

11. Ibid., 275.

12. Ibid., 274.

13. Sunshine and Wheaton, 69.

14. Ibid., 118.

15. O'Shaughnessy, 56.

16. Ibid., 3.

17. Quoted in Blum, 270

18. Tim Weiner, *Legacy of Ashes: The History of the CIA* (New York: Doubleday, 2007), 392.

19. Quoted in Blum, 277.

20. Hugh Wilford, *The Mighty Wurlitzer: How the CIA Played America* (Cambridge, MA: Harvard University Press, 2008), 7.

21. Blum, 463–464.

22. Ibid., 454–462.

23. Joan Kruckewitt, *The Death of Ben Linder: The Story of a North American in Sandinista Nicaragua* (New York: Seven Stories, 1999), 19.

24. Quoted in Blum, 290.

25. Weiner, 99.

26. Philip Zwerling, *After School Theatre Programs for At-Risk Teenagers* (Jefferson, NC: McFarland, 2008), 72.

27. Quoted in Blum, 296.

28. Quoted in Blum, 301.

29. Ibid., 296.

30. Ibid., 301.

31. Quoted in Blum, 296.

32. Quoted in Blum, 291.

33. Blum, 291.

34. Weiner, 380.

35. Blum, 304.

36. Weiner, 380–381.

37. John Prados, *Safe for Democracy: The Secret Wars of the CIA* (Chicago: Ivan R. Dee, 2006), 528.

38. Blum, 292.

39. Ibid., 302.

40. Kruckewitt, 29–30.

41. Blum, 295.

42. Quoted in Kruckewitt, 12.

43. Quoted in Kruckewitt, 11.

44. Kruckewitt, 233.

45. Prados, 518.

46. Ibid., 519.

47. Quoted in Blum, 293.

48. Quoted at http://www.lewrockwell.com/wall/wall33.html, accessed September 19, 2010.

49. Philip Zwerling, *Nicaragua: A New Kind of Revolution* (Chicago: Chicago Review Press, 1985), 225.

50. Quoted in Ami Chen Mills, *CIA Off Campus: Building the Movement Against Recruitment and Research* (Boston: South End, 1991), 29.

51. Ibid., 21.

52. Robert Witanek, "The CIA on Campus," *Covert Action Information Bulletin* (Winter 1989), 4.

53. Weiner, 65.

54. Ibid., 64.

55. Ibid.

56. Ibid., 65.

57. David N. Gibbs, "Academics and Spies: The Silence That Roars," *The Los Angeles Times*, January 28, 2001, M2.

58. Mills, 38.

59. Gibbs.

60. Weiner, 66.

61. Morton Halperin, Jerry Berman, Robert Borosage, and Christine Marwick, *The Lawless State: The Crimes of the U.S. Intelligence Agencies* (New York: Penguin, 1976), 53.

62. Witanek, 2.

63. Ibid., 3.

64. Quoted in Cheddi Jagan, *The West On Trial: The Fight for Guyana's Freedom* (Berlin: Seven Seas, 1971), 391.

65. Mills, 133.

66. Wilford, 137.

67. Mills, 33.

68. Ibid., 32.

69. Ibid.

70. Ibid., 38.

71. Ibid., 23.

72. Ibid., 30.

73. Geoffrey D. White with Flannery Hauck, eds., *Campus, Inc.: Corporate Power in the Ivory Tower* (Amherst, NY: Prometheus, 2000), 180.

74. Ibid., 185.

75. Mills, 37.

76. Ibid.

77. Quoted in Gibbs.

78. Quoted in Weiner, 508.

79. Blum, 305.

80. Weiner, 501.

81. Ibid., 42.

82. Ibid., 52.

83. Ibid., 75.

84. Ibid.

85. Ibid., 129.

86. Ibid., 128.

87. Ibid., 155.

88. Ibid., 158.

89. Ibid., 173.

90. Ibid., 191.

91. Ibid., 195.

92. Ibid.

93. Ibid., 196.

94. Ibid., 287.

95. Ibid., 329.

96. Ibid., 333.

97. Ibid., 370.

98. Ibid., 449.
99. Ibid., 450.
100. Ibid., 457.
101. Ibid. 443.
102. Ibid., 470.
103. Ibid.
104. Ibid., 481.

Works Cited

Blum, William. *Killing Hope: U.S. Military and CIA Interventions Since World War II.* Monroe, ME: Common Courage, 2004.

Braverman, Kate. *Lullaby for Sinners.* New York: Pinnacle, 1980.

Gibbs, David N. "Academics and Spies: The Silence That Roars." *The Los Angeles Times,* January 28, 2001, p. M2.

Halperin, Morton, Jerry Berman, Robert Borosage and Christine Marwick. *The Lawless State: The Crimes of the U.S. Intelligence Agencies.* New York: Penguin, 1976.

Jagan, Cheddi. *The West On Trial: The Fight for Guyana's Freedom.* Berlin: Seven Seas, 1971.

Kruckewitt, Joan. *The Death of Ben Linder: The Story of a North American in Sandinista Nicaragua.* New York: Seven Stories, 1999.

LewRockwell.com. http://www.lewrockwell.com/wall/wall33.html.

Mills, Ami Chen. *CIA Off Campus: Building the Movement Against Recruitment and Research.* Boston: South End, 1991.

O'Shaughnessy, Hugh. *Grenada: An Eyewitness Account of the U.S. Invasion and the Caribbean History that Provoked It.* New York: Dodd, Mead, 1984.

Prados, John. *Safe for Democracy: The Secret Wars of the CIA.* Chicago: Ivan R. Dee, 2006.

Sunshine, Catherine, and Philip Wheaton, eds. *Grenada: The Peaceful Revolution.* Washington, D.C.: EPICA Task Force, 1982.

Weiner, Tim. *Legacy of Ashes: The History of the CIA.* New York: Doubleday, 2007.

White, Geoffrey D., with Flannery Hauck, eds. *Campus, Inc.: Corporate Power in the Ivory Tower.* Amherst, NY: Prometheus, 2000.

Wilford, Hugh. *The Mighty Wurlitzer: How the CIA Played America.* Cambridge, MA: Harvard University Press, 2008.

Witanek, Robert. "The CIA on Campus." *Covert Action Information Bulletin* (Winter 1989), pp. 25–28.

Zwerling, Philip. *After School Theatre Programs for At-Risk Teenagers.* Jefferson, NC: McFarland, 2008.

_____. *Nicaragua: A New Kind of Revolution.* Chicago: Chicago Review Press, 1985.

2

Uninvited Guests:
A Short History of the
CIA on Campus

DAVID PRICE

In the decade since September 11, 2001, the American public's attitudes towards the Central Intelligence Agency have radically changed. Politicians, news reports from corporate news outlets, and fictional media portrayals of brutal superhuman intelligence operatives like *24's* Jack Bauer feed public fears in ways that steadily erode American concerns for due processes, civil rights, rule of law, and the maintenance of traditional boundaries between civil society and the military state.

A national surge of fear following 9/11 brought with it a cultural "memory wipe" that overwrote what had once been broad understandings of the dangers that the FBI, CIA, NSA and other domestic and international intelligence agencies present to the freedom of thought, political discourse and dissent. That fear following the 9/11 attacks spawned the rapid adoption of the PATRIOT Act, and soon the CIA and other American intelligence agencies gained expanded, extrajudicial powers at home and abroad — in some cases having powers restored to them that had specifically been withdrawn after the public airing of past abuses. As the Bush and Obama administrations' terror wars have grown, so have the powers and presence of the CIA; a zeitgeist pressing for allegiance to increased military and intelligence spending overshadows public memories of past agency atrocities while budget cuts gut public services.

These conditions have fostered all of the types of CIA expansions onto our campuses described in this book's essays, but it is vital that students, professors, university staff, administrators and citizens understand the history of *why* American colleges and universities historically developed standards and policies to separate themselves from the CIA and other intelligence agencies.

While current fears make it easy to forget why we our predecessors fought to keep the CIA off our campuses, this history remains vital today because these same past dangers face academic communities today. As the generations of faculty who last struggled against these incursions retire and die off, increasing numbers of professors have only vague understanding of why only a few decades ago so many American universities had strict policies keeping the CIA off campus, and faculty and students broadly opposed *any* CIA presence on campus.

Contemporary academic communities which neglect this history face serious consequences. As sociologist Sigmund Diamond observed: "since historical memory is one of the weapons against abuse and power, there is no question why those who have power create a 'desert of organized forgetting.' But why should those who have been the victims sometimes act as if they, too, had forgotten."[1]

To confront the CIA's rapid incursion onto our campuses and unannounced entrance into our classrooms, faculty meetings, and student political meetings, individuals need to develop the sort of historical memory that Diamond calls for, the sort of memory that illuminates past struggles to keep our campuses open places for learning by working to keep the CIA off campus.

Early Campus Intelligence Roots

American experiences in the Second World War profoundly shaped academic contributions to the Central Intelligence Agency and other appendages of American intelligence agencies during the Cold War. Because the Second World War thrust America into a state of total warfare, academics from all branches of the academy joined the war effort in ways that normalized expectations that academics could and should contribute their skills to military and intelligence efforts.

During the Second World War at the Office of Strategic Services, "Wild Bill" Donovan recruited physicists, chemists, mathematicians, statisticians, biologists geographers, anthropologists, psychologists, sociologists, medievalists, modern literature professors and members of any conceivable academic discipline.[2]

Recognized as "the physics war" for the contributions of academics working on the Manhattan Project, the Second World War also raised awareness of the vital role that deskbound scholars gathering and analyzing vital intelligence could play to win the war.

While the Second World War institutionally alerted military and intelligence agencies of the central roles played by scholars contributing to warfare, the war also profoundly transformed the attitudes of academics and institutions impacted by the war in ways that shaped their responses to the CIA as it reached out for academic assistance during the post-war 1940s and 1950s when they knew little about the Agency. Assisting military and intelligence agencies in the struggle against fascism during the war opened the door for similar requests for very different agendas in the coming Cold War, as a fight against totalitarianism segued into a struggle for the hearts, minds and markets of client nation states throughout the underdeveloped world in a battle pitched as free market capitalism struggling against Soviet style Communism.

The formation of the Central Intelligence Agency in a world still shaken by the devastation of the Second World War, the ripples of decolonization, and the rise of Soviet international power presented the United States with a series of strategic choices that had long term consequences. Some choices involved siding with European allies (like the French, British, Belgians, Dutch, etc.) exploiting neo-colonial control over peoples of Africa and Asia; these alignments placed America in opposition to what once been traditional American anti-colonial beliefs. As the nations of the Third World struggled for independence from European powers, American policy makers' lack of support for these underdeveloped nations empowered Soviet advances. These choices found the CIA bifurcating into an agency charged not simply with collecting and processing intelligence reports, but also undertaking covert actions at the president's discretion. They aligned the CIA's loyalties, not with American values of democracy and freedom, but actively undermining democratically elected leaders not to the liking of American presidents and corporations; as the CIA interfered with elections and toppled democratically elected regimes in the Northern (e.g., Iran, Italy) and Southern Hemispheres (e.g., Guatemala, Chile, etc.). Working with the CIA, academics played their roles in these anti-democratic covert actions.

As an unidentified CIA analyst observed in the pages of the CIA's classified in-house journal, *Studies in Intelligence,* "Close ties between the Central Intelligence Agency and American colleges and universities have existed since the birth of the Agency in 1947."[3] The links between the Ivy League and the CIA born in the early days of the agency, and the institutional overlaps between Yale, Harvard and other elite universities distorted the growth of the agency in ways that had long term institutional impact. The agency nurtured its own elite intellectual mythos, celebrating the literary intellects of scholar spies like

James Jesus Angleton, Cord Meyer, and Norman Holmes Pearson, as if literary intellect signified something more than literary intellect.

If the Central Intelligence Agency simply gathered and analyzed intelligence, it would constitute a natural place for America's greatest scholars to work, drawing on the skills and experiences of humanists, historians and socialists — applying their analytical skills to help gather information needed to develop national policies based on thoughtful analysis. But the CIA's history of mixing in illegal, amoral, anti-democratic covert operations demonstrates how the CIA is so much more than an agency gathering and interpreting intelligence.

The CIA's core over-reliance on secrets makes it necessarily antithetical to normally open academic pursuits of knowledge, and this secrecy presents fundamental risks to the campuses where the CIA operates. Today, the increased corporatization of American university campuses also brings a damaging acceptance of proprietary research to campuses in ways that normalize secrecy and weaken bonds of shared knowledge and trust. While secrecy and intelligence appear to be necessarily linked, assumptions about the necessity of secrecy for most intelligence work need some unpacking.

In *Cloak and Gown: Scholars in the Secret War, 1939–1961,* historian Robin Winks recounts how in 1951, the CIA's Sherwood Kent conducted an experiment in which a handful of Yale historians used nothing but declassified materials in Yale's library to challenge CIA analysts (with access to classified data) to produce competing reports on U.S. military capacities, strengths and weaknesses focusing on a scale of detail down to the level of military divisions.[4] Known as the "Yale Report," the written evaluation of this contest concluded that over 90 percent of material in the CIA's analysis existed in public documents in the Yale library. Kent further estimated that of the remaining 10 percent of "secret" materials, only half would remain secret for any length of time. President Truman, furious with the results of the Yale Report, suppressed its distribution, arguing that the press needed more restrictions governing the release of such sensitive materials, while Republican pundits joined the furor claiming that Yale liberals were trying to leak state secrets.

The implications of the Yale Report strike profound chords today, yet the CIA continues to shroud itself in an intense secrecy that shields public inspection of its everyday activities, successes and blunders; however, today the majority of the intelligence developed by the Agency overwhelmingly comes from open sourced intelligence available in a first rate research library. Conducting one's business in private allows a wide range of errors to propagate without external review and critique in ways that run counter to fundamental academic principles. Working in such secrecy encourages the sorts of serious CIA intelligence failures (i.e., erroneous intelligence estimates during the

Vietnam War, not predicting the collapse of the Soviet Union, Iraq failures, etc.) which only make headlines after the fact.

Early Cold War Campus Recruiting

The CIA did little to hide its contacts with university professors during the agency's first years. In reading through old issues of academic journals and professional association newsletters from the late 1940s and first years of the 1950s I find numerous mentions of academics going to work for the CIA. Given how many social scientists worked for agencies like the OSS during the Second World War, and public perceptions that the agency collected information for analysis, such connections did not seem unnatural. And the CIA did not earn its reputation as a nefarious outfit, until later, when the public learned of its covert paramilitary illegal activities in places like Iran, Guatemala and Cuba.

Yet even during these early years, the CIA already covertly funded, or more directly coopted domestic academic activities. In 1949, the CIA secretly funded and influenced the Cultural and Scientific Conference for World Peace held at New York City's Waldorf-Astoria Hotel; a venue organized and packed with intellectuals from the radical and Communist left, but subtly controlled by the CIA. CIA money secretly channeled through fellow NYU philosopher James Burnham, and Americans for Intellectual Freedom (AIF) funded an anti–Stalinist group organized by New York University philosophy professor and ex-communist Sidney Hook; this group pestered Soviet conference delegates and others seen as allied with Soviet positions.[5]

As one CIA historian observed, because so many members of the OSS and early CIA came from elite Ivy League universities, in the 1950s

> it is not surprising that a disproportionate number of the new recruits came from the same schools. Similarly, professors who had joined the Agency often turned to their former colleagues still on campuses for consultation and assistance. This "old Boy" system was quite productive in providing new employees in the professional ranks. Thus, there was an early linkage between Agency and the Ivy League, or similar schools.[6]

As the CIA established close, quiet, contacts on American university campuses in the 1950s, the ethos of the successes and the strong sense of national unity supporting the military purpose of the Second World War remained an important part of the national psyche. This central support for World War II era militarization remained vital even as the American military and intelligence mission shifted from one of defense and fighting totalitarianism, to one more linked with American expansionism and neo-colonialism;

few Americans criticized the CIA's exploits until the 1960s. Even as the CIA undermined democratically elected regimes in 1953 Iran and 1954 Guatemala, engaged in undeclared counterinsurgency operations in the Philippines, or in Indochina, most academics, like other Americans, remained supportive of the CIA's activities. When an occasional CIA operative appeared on campus seeking consultations with professors or doing some targeted recruiting: administrators, faculty, and students saw this as an honored visit, not a raid from an organization that hired shady thugs or arranged kidnappings, murder, bribes, gun running, and fixed elections.

In 1951 the CIA quietly launched its "University Associates Program" establishing a network of covert contacts between the agency and professors teaching at fifty elite American universities. The CIA referred to these professors as "consultant-contacts who would receive a nominal fee for spotting promising students, steering them into studies and activities of interest to the Agency, and eventually nominating them for recruitment."[7] Connecting with the right professors took on an increased importance for the CIA, and this same year, the CIA covertly approached the Executive Board of the American Anthropological Association (AAA) and established a secret relationship wherein the AAA gathered details on members' expertise, travel, linguistic competence, military background, overseas connections, etc. for a professional roster which the CIA compiled on the agency's computers and then handed over as a collated index to the AAA, which filed the data for its own uses.[8] The CIA highly valued these covert campus contacts, known as "P-Sources" (professor sources) in CIA reports, yet the agency generally consulted only professors already ideologically aligned with the agency's institutional perspective, thereby excluding critical voices and rarely expanding the forms of analysis already found within the agency.

The CIA emerged as a silent partner in the establishment of key area study centers and think tanks during the early Cold War. Harvard's Russian Research Center maintained a public face of an academically independent scholarship, yet between McCarthyism's ability to purge, or better yet, to instruct scholars in the virtues of self-censorship and conformity, certain narrow forms of scholarship emerged in these Centers.[9] During the early 1950s, MIT's Center for International Studies (CENIS) mixed classified CIA sponsored research with publicly funded research projects. In this CIA nurtured environment economists Max Millikan, himself a CIA assistant director of Central Intelligence, and Walt Rostow developed economic development models that served as important tools in the Cold War's economic competition for the hearts and minds of the underdeveloped world. Rostow developed Modernization Theory, a crudely simplistic theory underlying the economic development policies of USAID and other agencies during the Cold War, in this intellectually constrained CIA nurtured environment. The forms of analysis secretly sponsored by the CIA at CENIS took their place as strategic Cold War weapons, as the CIA secretly funded a variety of skewed research projects designed to provide rationalizations for CIA favored policies as if they resulted from academically independent inquiry. In an ironic partisan attack, in 1957, the conservative journal *The National Review* exposed the CIA's relationship with CENIS in an article arguing that the CIA had violated its charter by using their relationship with CENIS to advocate for foreign policy. *The National Review* accused CENIS CIA funded scholars of producing a report for the CIA advocating for "a permanent foreign aid program to give underdeveloped nations a 'sense of progress'—without regard of course, to U.S. political or strategic interests."[10]

During the early days of the Cold War, as Harvard and Columbia University opened Russian Study Centers, the CIA quietly moved among these programs, privately contacting students and professors as they altered the nature of the academic work produced by secretly funding and encouraging specific types of studies, even as the FBI monitored and persecuted scholars believed to be engaging in research, writing, or activism (most commonly, anti-racial segregation activism) that Hoover's FBI believed aligned with Communist ideology. In some cases, the CIA got professors to covertly steer the research questions students pursued in ways that aligned with the Agency's intelligence needs.[11]

In the 1950s future Secretary of State Henry Kissinger used covert CIA funds to establish Harvard's International Summer School, a program that brought future world leaders to Harvard, where they mixed with other international students as well as scholars secretly linked to the CIA in ways designed to establish contacts, steer loyalties and indenture ongoing patron relationships. During the 1960s, the CIA provided $135,000 in covert funds for the International Summer School.[12]

Though federal programs such as the Fulbright scholarship programs explicitly forbid recipients from having ties to intelligence agencies, some scholars with CIA connections have entered these programs from its earliest days. Though he later maintained a convoluted story claiming he joined, resigned, then rejoined the CIA—1949 Fulbright scholar Frank Bessac entered the CIA as a contract employee in 1947, later claiming he resigned before traveling to Shanghai as a foreign student traveling on a Fulbright scholarship, only later to be contacted by a CIA operative in China, where Bessac and his CIA contact would later flee the Communists and travel overland to Tibet with secret information on the Soviet's first nuclear weapons detonation in August 1949.[13]

As the Cold War came to dominate American foreign policy and spawned increased military spending, the growing National Security State had needs for academics and intellectuals who could produce and maintain the hardware and ideology needed to sustain decades of competition against the Soviets. Engineers, chemists, physicists and other divisions within the "hard sciences" received federal funds from agencies ranging from the National Science Foundation, as well as more secretive arrangements from the CIA, NSA, Department of Defense and its surrogates. Historians, political scientists, and a range of sociologists, psychologists, anthropologists, literary scholars and artists found funds available to study not only America's enemy states, but also to study a variety of potential client states who hosted the military and economic battle grounds of the Cold War.[12]

In 1954 President Truman appointed a panel led by General James Doolittle to undertake a secret accounting of the range and scope of the CIA's activities and accomplishments. The panel produced "The Doolittle Report," classified secret, which described a range of CIA intelligence gathering and covert operations, and recommended that the CIA should cut some of its historic ties to the 1940s OSS and CIG (Central Intelligence Group) by revising its existing CIA campus recruitment program beyond the connections established from World War II era good old boy networks, noting failures in the current recruitment program:

> In part, this is due to the general shortage of technically trained people *vis-à-vis* heavy current demands by industry in practically all fields. On the other hand we have heard criticism from scholastic sources that the C.I.A. approach, both to the school and to the individual, is not what it should be, and furthermore, that many potentially good people are lost because of the very great length of time that now elapses between initial contact and entry into the job.[15]

The Doolittle Report led the CIA to change its campus recruiting program, focusing more on identifying specific professors who could recommend known students. Scattered literature records how the CIA routinely recruited (mostly white, male) students from America's finest colleges and universities throughout the 1950s and early '60s. In the late 1950s, Philip Agee a bright young graduate of Notre Dame University, where he had majored in philosophy, received a message from the university's job placement bureau informing him that the CIA was sending someone from Washington to meet with him on campus in a week. Agee met with a man named Gus who said Agee "had been recommended for the CIA's most important training program, the one through which they recruited the future executive leadership of the agency." After an abortive effort at law school Agee drew on this university recruitment effort and joined the agency.[16]

More efficiently and commonly than the cumbersome formality of using a campus job placement center, the CIA used established and respected university professors to identify and approach students for CIA recruitment.

Anthropologist Michael Coe described his decision to join the CIA as the result of being approached by Clyde Kluckhohn, regarded as "surely the most brilliant social anthropologist at Harvard" who took him to lunch one day in 1950 and asked him: "'How would you like to work for the government in a really interesting capacity?'" "I grasped his meaning pretty quickly, as I knew that he had been instrumental in setting up an inter-university Russian studies program that was known to be linked to the Central Intelligence Agency," Coe explained, "and that was how I came to be a CIA case officer."[17]

The CIA's covertly funded academics and intellectuals in the 1950s on a massive scale. Between 1955 and 1959, the CIA secretly funded Michigan State University (MSU) with $25 million to establish the false appearance of a legitimate academic training center for a range of counterinsurgency and "policing" operations supporting Ngô Đình Diệm in Vietnam. The MSU program provided needed academic cover for several CIA agents operating in South Vietnam. When public revelations of this program occurred in 1966, massive campus protests followed.[18]

As Frances Stonor Saunders documents in *The Cultural Cold War*, the CIA covertly sponsored a wide range of avant-garde artistic movements in the 1950; secretly supporting abstract impressionist painters and symphonic works condemned by the Soviets as decadent — including Igor Stravinsky's *The Rite of Spring* Paris premiere.[19]

In 1958, the Independent Research Service, a foundation with secret CIA funding, hired future feminist icon Gloria Steinem as director of the Independent Service for Information (ISI). Steinem oversaw the ISI's financing of hundreds of American college students attending the 1958 World Youth Festival of Vienna, a festival designed to showcase accomplishments of the Soviet-aligned world. When revelations of the CIA's financing leaked in 1967, the *New York Times* quoted Steinem as surprised, saying that "almost all of the young persons who received aid from the foundation did not know about the relationship with the intelligence agency."[20] Steinem later put a positive spin on the CIA operation, claiming that the CIA actually sent many students sympathetic to Communists, but this ignores her role in assisting the CIA in choreographing the students participation in ways that stressed racial segregation, oppression and inequality in the Communist world — even organizing a bus tour where students could see armed communist guards at the Hungarian border.[21]

CIA Campus Research Programs and Funding Fronts

Although the public had no knowledge of these programs until revealed by the Church Hearings in 1975, the CIA had in 1953 initiated the MKULTRA program, which used funding fronts to sponsor unknown numbers of unwitting professors and graduate students to conduct individual pieces of research that contributed to larger CIA projects. These projects gathered information on the varieties of and limits of human mental experiences in hopes of developing the CIA's understanding of interrogation, brainwashing and torture techniques. The CIA's interest in these topics grew from claims that the Chinese had taken U.S. soldiers captured during the Korean War into Manchuria to torture, interrogate and brainwash them.[22] The CIA wanted to understand the possibilities of breaking individuals through harsh interrogation, torture, extreme forms of deprivation, or a host of psychotropic substances. Using a mixture of in-house researchers and unwittingly outsourced researchers on university campuses across the country, they funded individual projects that contributed to the CIA's larger understanding of questions relating to the manipulation of human behavior.

The range of hundreds of witting and unwitting university professors the CIA funded under these projects is stunning. Scholars financed by these CIA funds included social and behavioral scientists like B.F. Skinner, Karl Rogers, Erwin Goffman, and Jay Schulman.[23] Initially, the CIA wanted to explore the possibility of "brainwashing" or torturing individuals so that they would perform acts, make confessions, or reveal secrets that they would otherwise not do; and to produce data that could be used to teach agents and members of the armed forces to resist such efforts by enemy forces. While the CIA did not discover any radical forms of "mind control" through its MKULTRA research projects, it did refine some forms of effective interrogation, harsh interrogation and torture that it compiled in its 1963 Classified Secret *KUBARK Counterintelligence Interrogation Manual.* The *KUBARK* Manual drew heavily on MKULTRA research, and detailed techniques for CIA interrogations which relied upon disruptions of sleep, feeding and other bodily comforts that shifted control of wellbeing and the environment from prisoners to captors and used stress and relief of stress as tools to crack uncooperative prisoners.[24] I have interviewed and corresponded with several researchers who unknowingly took CIA funds to work on projects secretly connected with MKULTRA and the KUBARK Interrogation Manual, and to a person each of these scholars feels violated by the CIA's abuse of their work for such ends.

The CIA funding front, the Society for the Investigation of Human Ecology (which later changed its name to the Human Ecology Fund), channeled CIA funds as grants to unwitting scholars researching topics ranging from academic studies of "brainwashing"[25] to interviews by Rutgers sociologists Jay Schulman and Richard Stephenson with anti–Communist Hungarian refugees.[26] In 1977, Stephenson discovered that the CIA had secretly funded research he had done interviewing Hungarian refugees since the 1950s. While not an anti–CIA scholar, Stephenson resented not being told about what was being done with his research, writing:

> When I first heard of the role the CIA had played in the research I participated in, my feelings were mixed. On the one hand, I felt offended and resentful, if not actually angry, I had "been had," and by people I respected and with whom I had enjoyed a congenial and stimulating association. On the other hand, in view of the nature of the sociological data and its undirected and unclassified status, the idea that the CIA was involved and the Society was its "cover" assumed a cloak and dagger staging closer to comic opera that serious drama.[25]

With the absurdity and incompetence of the CIA's actions, these projects damaged the credibility and reputations of scholars and disciplines involved in this and similar other CIA funded projects.

The CIA's bungled Bay of Pigs operation not only brought public awareness to the CIA's key role as a covert arm of the presidency operating without congressional oversight, but the negative publicity associated with the Bay of Pigs also created problems for the agency on American campuses. To counter these negative public reactions, the agency's

> Office of Personnel in 1962 established the Hundred Universities Program in which recruiters and senior officials of CIA made presentations before selected faculty members and placement officers in an effort to publicize the CIA's role in national security and to emphasize the Agency recruitment personnel needs.[28]

But because public critiques of the CIA were mounting, the CIA kept these presentations quiet for select faculty only.

In response to a growing awareness that the CIA lacked the needed personnel capable of following the rapid political developments in China, in 1966 the CIA's deputy director forintelligence hired former University of Virginia professor and CIA analyst John Kerry King to establish the office of Coordinator for Academic relations (CAR), which selectively established contacts between CIA and American universities specializing in China. Under CAR, King organized China conferences, which brought top scholars from academic setting to discuss political developments with "agency experts in low-profile and informal discussions;" sometimes scholars were shown non-classified CIA documents and asked for comments.[29] CIA analysts also enrolled as graduate students in Harvard's East Asian Research Center without publicly acknowledging their status as CIA employees; but in 1967 when members of Students for a Democratic Society discovered the CIA presence, the CIA analysts fled and public criticism of the CIA's presence on campus grew.

In 1999 Bruce Cumings observed of these massive though unacknowledged CIA campus connections, "CIA-connected faculty were so influential that they made critics who stood for academic principle look like wild-eyed radicals in the 1960s; today, critics merely appear to be naifs who didn't know what was going on."[30]

CIA Campus Revelations

In 1967, *Ramparts* magazine published an exposé disclosing how the CIA had infiltrated the National Student Association since the early 1950s and hijacked the organization's agenda. The *Ramparts* revelations led to broad inquiries concerning a range of illegal CIA operations infiltrating domestic organizations. These disclosures revealed vast networks of CIA operations undermining numerous domestic political organizations.

Sol Stern introduced an ingenious method of tracing money through foundations serving as funding fronts for CIA sources: he first learned of the CIA's use of foundations after reading reports that Texas Congressman Wright Patman had accidentally stumbled across CIA funds in 1964 while investigating American non-profit foundations being used as tax dodges. While investigating irregularities at the J.M. Kaplan Fund, Patman discovered it served as a CIA front, and after Patman's initial discovery, the CIA and IRS met with Patman privately and quietly acknowledged its role with no further follow up in the media. Stern picked up the trail from this public record, and found that five foundations (the Borden Trust, Price Fund, Edsel Fund, Beacon Fund and Kentfield Fund) had been identified by Patman as contributing to the Kaplan Fund during the early 1960s. Stern worked outward patiently piecing together a network of funding fronts and pass-through organizations used by the CIA to fund unwitting scholars.[31] With this information, Stern connected the Borden, Price, Beacon, Kentfield and Edsel Funds with the National Student Association — and from there he uncovered further uses of CIA funds to limit the production of what could have otherwise been free academic inquiry.[32] Stern's revelations showed the CIA controlling academic inquiry in ways supporting the CIA's stilted political world view.

Ramparts' revelations led more mainstream media outlets to report previously withheld stories on the CIA's interference with domestic political activities, and this coverage fed public calls for investigations of the CIA's domestic activities.[33] Heading off possible congressional investigations that would be difficult to control, President Johnson appointed a small committee chaired by his Undersecretary of State, Nicholas Katzenbach, with a narrow charge of investigating the CIA and other governmental agency activities that could "endanger the integrity and independence of the educational community." While the Katzenbach Commission produced some criticism of the CIA, because Johnson appointed DCIA Richard Helms (along with Secretary of Health, Education and Welfare John Gardner) to the Commission, no real possibility ever existed that it would issue findings castigating the CIA or recommend criminal proceedings with prison sentences for CIA personnel violating the agency's charter and the civil rights of Americans. These CIA revelations provided the White House with leverage over the agency. As historian Rhodri Jeffreys-Jones observes, after President Johnson chose to have the Katzenbach Commission conduct only a light investigation of CIA misconduct "then, having 'saved' the Agency, he demanded its loyalty on the Vietnam issue. His demand produced further cosmetic exercises, including an attempt to discredit political protest against the war and the suppression of dissent within the CIA."[34] Through such political deal making, the CIA established institutional policies of cooking intelligence estimates to meet political expectations. The Katzenbach findings, coupled with a growing opposition to the Vietnam War, created serious difficulties for CIA activities on campuses. The CIA observed that

> picketing of recruiters began in 1966, rapidly spread across the nation, and peaked in 1968 when 77 incidents or demonstrations occurred. Procedures were changed with interviews held off campus and, whenever it appeared that a visit might precipitate incidents, the visit was canceled.[35]

The CIA increasingly met with professors off campus, either in neutral locations, or at CIA Headquarters.

The year 1967 brought disturbing revelations that the CIA had covertly funded the publication of thousands of books from apparently mainstream American presses. Many of these secret CIA programs funded progressive analyses that undermined or attacked communism or communist positions. Articles in the *New York Times* and *Ramparts* revealed Praeger Press as a secret CIA publishing conduit and exposed *Encounter* magazine (linked to the Conference for Cultural Freedom), *Partisan Review*, and other liberal magazines as supported with CIA funds.[36]

A 1968 confidential internal CIA memo on "Student Reaction to CIA Recruitment Activities" recorded an increase in anti–CIA activities on the campuses of Grinnell, CCNY, San Jose State and Harvard, but the CIA believed that in 1966, a series of positive CIA articles in *The New York Times* "did much good" and that "on the whole, the publicity and free advertising did more good than harm for the recruitment effort — inspiring a great many write-in candidates whom we might never have heard otherwise."[37]

But after 1966 the CIA recognized a steep decline in the Agency's standing on college campuses, with a total of seventy-seven anti–CIA campus incidents in 1968.

The early 1970s brought a growing awareness that a wide variety of U.S. intelligence operations had exceeded their mandates and illegally interfered with domestic political processes. Other governmental agencies besides the CIA illegally spied on American citizens; in January 1970, Christopher Pyle, a political science professor at Mt. Holyoke College, disclosed that while serving in the Army he had learned of a secret program in which the Army used over 1,500 plainclothes operatives to monitor anti-war demonstrations across the country. Congressional investigation verified Pyle's claims, and found continuities between these programs and CIA programs monitoring legal political dissent.[38] In the summer of 1971 Daniel Ellsberg released the *Pentagon Papers*, and the break-in of the regional FBI office in Media, Pennsylvania, brought the release of documents establishing the FBI's COINTELPRO operation illegally monitoring, spying on, and harassing U.S. citizens. Attitudes towards the CIA soured as increasing numbers of citizens came to understand how American intelligence agencies were undermining domestic democratic movements.

In 1973, DCI James Schlesinger commissioned a secret CIA internal accounting of past illegal activities undertaken since its creation. The report became known as the "Family Jewels" and detailed a broad range of CIA illegal and immoral activities including assassination plots targeting foreign leaders, elaborate poison and drug programs, kidnappings, undermining elections, coups, gun running, illegal domestic wiretaps and surveillance of reporters deemed hostile to the Nixon Administration, illegal break-ins of private residences, illegal mail opening, etc. Summaries of the Family Jewels Report leaked to the press, and a swell of public outrage rose from the American public as they learned the broad range of illegal activities their government had engaged in.

From 1967 to 1973 the CIA and FBI collaborated on a massive covert program which illegally monitored and at times interfered with the legal political activities of hundreds of thousands of American citizen under a program (disclosed to the public in 1974) known as Operation CHAOS[39], described from the inside by Verne Lyon in essay number 6 of this book. The FBI and CIA monitoring of New York's central mail intercept, illegal wire taps, and infiltration of political meetings, generated "watch lists" of citizens, and the governmental report found that "approximately 300,000 names of American citizens and organizations were thus stored in the CHAOS computer system."[40] Most of the groups monitored by Operation CHAOS involved students, such as the SDS, Women's Liberation Movement, Student Non-Violent Coordinating Committee, U.S. Committee to Aid the National Liberation Front of South Vietnam, etc. In CHAOS and other domestic operations the CIA criminally violated its charter and illegally interfered in domestic political processes. Seymour Hersh's revelations of CHOAS and other elements of the Family Jewels led President Ford to appoint a commission, led by his Vice President

Nelson Rockefeller, to investigate and report on these matters. The Rockefeller Commission found that

> although the stated purpose of the Operation was to determine whether there were any foreign contacts with American dissident groups, it resulted in the accumulation of considerable material on domestic dissidents and their activities.
>
> During six years, the Operation compiled some 13,000 different files including files on 7,200 American citizens. The documents in these files and related materials included the names of more than 300,000 persons and organizations, entered in a computerized index.
>
> This information was kept closely guarded within the CIA. Using this information, personnel of the [Special Operations] Group prepared 3,500 memoranda for internal use; 3,000 memoranda for dissemination to the FBI; and 37 memoranda for distribution to White House and other top level officials in the government.[41]

The CIA indexed 7,000,000 individuals under their Operation CHAOS, a list that included approximately 115,000 U.S. citizens.[42]

Some claims about CIA campus activities from this period remain difficult to evaluate without further verification. For example, William Corson, a historian, professor and lieutenant colonel in the Marine Corps, wrote in his 1977 book, *The Armies of Ignorance* (a claim repeated elsewhere), that CIA campus recruitments of foreign nationals lead to the suicides of some of these students once they returned home. Corson wrote,

> Without rendering final judgment on the temerity of America's academic leaders in failing to face the relationship of their institutions and its faculty members to the intelligence community, there is a final aspect of the recruiting situation which needs mention. Since 1948, more than 40 of the agents so recruited have committed suicide in response to the fear of exposure of their relationships with America's intelligence services. These deaths have largely gone unnoticed in the United States, but in several countries — some of which are essential to the United States' international and national security — suicide notes detailing the United States' perfidy are in the hands of those countries' leaders; and unknown to presidents since Kennedy, these have been a factor in souring American relations with those countries.[43]

Corson estimated that in 1977 the CIA was working with 5,000 academics, who recruited between 200 and 300, foreign students studying in the U.S., each year. Corson believed that about 60 percent of the university professors and staff involved in this recruiting were contract CIA employees who knew what they were doing.[44]

The CIA was a common presence on campus, seeking out professors doing international research. Anthropologist Theodore Graves described how the CIA in the 1960s and 1970s roamed about the campuses of UCLA and the University of the University of Colorado looking for a graduate students or professors needing research funds with an understanding that they would provide the CIA with special information. Graves wrote,

Beginning as soon as I held a faculty position at the University of Colorado, I was visited each year by representatives of the CIA with offers of funding for graduate students to conduct field research in sensitive parts of the world. The funds would be channeled through "respectable" agencies, of course, and their true source kept confidential. Although I always ushered these visitors to the door with an admonition about what this could do to the principle of open scholarship and relations with academics and other citizens of a host community, they persisted in returning with such offers each year. I presume my colleagues were similarly approached, though we never talked about it. Nan and I ran into "respectable funding" of this kind during our first year in East Africa (1967–1968), and one of the tenured faculty at UCLA apparently recruited students for research in politically sensitive areas of the world for many years, with secret financial support from our government. This was the focal issue which set some of my junior colleagues at UCLA against some of their senior colleagues during the student strikes of 1970.[45]

With the accumulating revelations of misconduct by the FBI and CIA in the Watergate Affair, the revelations of the Family Jewels, COINTELPRO, and media exposés in *The New York Times, Washington Post* and *Ramparts*, in 1975, the U.S. Senate Select Committee to Study Governmental Operations with Respect to Intelligence Activities held hearings investigating CIA activities. The committee, chaired by Sen. Frank Church, produced fourteen reports, documenting hundreds of illegal activities ranging from kidnapping, murder, drugging of unsuspecting civilians, and the widespread infiltration and subversion of domestic academic institutions.

Book One, Section Ten of the Church Committee Report described the hearings' findings on "The Domestic Impact of Foreign Clandestine Operations: The CIA and Academic Institutions." This report described how the CIA's Office of Personnel and the Domestic Collection Division secretly worked with university administrations to locate American academics traveling abroad to countries of interest to the CIA. The CIA contacted these academics and "consulted on the subject of their expertise" and that these contacts ranged "from the occasional debriefing to a continuing operations relationship — with many thousands of United States academics at hundreds of U.S. academic institutions."[46] The Church Committee's questioning of CIA agent E. Howard Hunt, revealed that the CIA had secretly funded the publication of over a thousand academic books. Under questioning, Hunt admitted that these CIA funded books, including some published by Praeger Press, had been read by unsuspecting Americans — not knowing they were reading CIA propaganda, a criminal violation of the CIA charter.[47] The Committee concluded that

the Central Intelligence Agency has long-developed clandestine relationships with the American academic community, which range from academics making introductions for intelligence purposes to intelligence collection while abroad, to academic research and writing where CIA sponsorship is hidden.[48]

The Church Committee's investigation of the *Ramparts* revelations that the CIA had used foundations as fronts to direct the work of unwitting academics, found that these illegal CIA activities had gone much further than had previously been imagined. The Committee found

> the CIA's intrusion into the foundation field in the 1960s can only be described as massive. Excluding grants from the "Big Three"— Ford Rockefeller, and Carnegie — of the 700 grants over $10,000 given by 164 other foundations during the period 1963–1966, at least 108 involved partial or complete CIA funding. More importantly, CIA funding was involved in nearly half the grants the non-"Big Three" foundations made during this period in the field of international activities. In the same period more than one-third of the grants awarded by non-"Big Three" in the physical, life and social sciences also involved CIA funds.... A 1966 CIA study explained the use of legitimate foundations was the most effective way of concealing the CIA's hand as well as reassuring members of funding organizations that the organization was in fact supported by private funds. The Agency study contended that this technique was particularly effective for democratically-run membership organizations, which need to assure their own unwitting members and collaborators, as well as their hostile critics, that they have genuine, respectable, private sources of income.[49]

The Church Committee recognized that the academic community needed to protect itself from future efforts by the CIA to encroach on university campuses. Recognizing that the CIA had repeatedly demonstrated its inability to follow even basic ethical standards, it recommended that "the American academic community ... set the professional and ethical standards of its members. This report on the nature and extent of covert individual relationships with the CIA is intended to alert [universities, professors and students] that there is a problem."[50] The outrage in the academic community over the extent of the CIA's interference with free academic inquiry rose so high that William van Alstyne, present of the American Association of University Professors called for public prohibitions against the CIA using academics for intelligence gathering — prohibitions which existed for missionaries and journalists; but the CIA would not agree to any such limits.[51]

Congressman Otis Pike (D, New York) chaired the House Select Intelligence Committee's 1975 to 1977 inquiry into CIA wrongdoing. The Pike Commission demonstrated more hostility to the CIA than the Church Committee or any of the previous commissions investigating CIA activities. Even though the CIA stonewalled Pike's inquiries, his Committee amassed an impressive report of CIA covert actions taken between 1965 and 1975. Pike concluded that the CIA was far from the "Rogue Elephant" organization imagined by the Church Committee and others. Pike showed that the CIA instead functioned as a covert arm of the presidency, taking orders from the Executive Branch. Pike found that the CIA had intentionally kept its involvement in influencing the outcomes of foreign elections, assassination program, media propaganda operations, covert arms deals and paramilitary guerrilla training and other programs from congressional scrutiny and oversight.[52] The Pike Commission established that the CIA had used the USAID, in counterinsurgency programs such as the one run at Michigan State University, for "police training" and "public safety" campus programs. The report found:

> In the early 1960's the Agency for International Development's Office of Public Safety (AID-OPS) became actively involved in foreign police training. OPS' 14 week course was augmented by an additional four weeks of training at IPS, pursuant to a contractual arrangement with AID. Students were not made aware that they were being trained at a CIA facility, and only a handful of AID officials, including the Director of OPS, knew of IPS' CIA status.
>
> Instructors were asked to record names of students who demonstrated a pro–American attitude. It does not appear, however, that the CIA attempted to recruit students while in the United State, although CIA documents indicate that with the cooperation of OPS, lists of OPS and IPS students were made available, along with biographical information, to CIA components for operational use.
>
> As many as 5,000 foreign police officers from over 100 countries, many of whom have become high officials, unwittingly received training from the CIA.[53]

Because the Pike and Church Committees found a wealth of evidence establishing the CIA engaged in a wide range of illegal and morally depraved activities, the cumulative evidence of the CIA's deep infiltration of campuses as covert recruiting stations meant these universities bore the damages of these other associations. As an outcome of these hearings, some university communities established guidelines denying access to their campuses. Some of these policies were like those established by Harvard's President Derek Bok, requiring the CIA and professors notify the administration of any contractual relationships, but DCI Stansfield Turner flatly refused to agree with Bok's basic request.

Because of the findings of the Church and Pike Committees, the House and Senate created permanent intelligence oversight committees, and enacted legislation creating legal firewalls protecting the American people from CIA and FBI interference in a wide range of domestic activities. The signing of the PATRIOT Act destroyed these legal firewalls; as a Congress acting in fear once again allowed the CIA and FBI to secretly infiltrate American religious meetings, political organizations and our university classrooms.

The CIA on Campus After Church and Pike

As the years passed after the Church and Pike Committees, the CIA decreasingly worried about protests at campus recruitment sessions. Things had improved for campus recruitment since the low points of the 1960s and 70s. Beginning in 1977 the CIA began secretly bringing in a stream of scholars, usually on sabbatical, to the Agency as contract employees to assist analysts through an exchange of ideas, a review of written reports, and the production of finished intelligence for dissemination to policy makers. In exchange, these 'Scholars-in-Residence' are, for one or two years, privy to information that would never be available to them on campus.[54]

The CIA brought university presidents to CIA Headquarters at Langley for flattering audiences with the DCI, and developed a range of outreach campaigns such as providing limited briefings to campus and public groups. In the 1980s, the CIA's Office of Personnel had active connections with 300 campus placement centers.[55]

Some CIA-contract professors used students as unwitting research mules, unknowingly working on portions of CIA research contracts. In 1984, *Counter Spy* magazine reported how Rutgers University political science professor Richard Mansbach had assigned a graduate research seminar to study and gather data on different components of the growing political crisis in Western Europe over the U.S. installation of Pershing II missiles. *Counter Spy* claimed that Manbach had planned on compiling elements of the data generated by the unwitting students and producing his own analytical report from the students' work.[56]

Anti-CIA campus activities remained somewhat mainstream in the 1980s. In 1986 police arrested President Carter's daughter Amy along with Abbie Hoffman and thirteen University of Massachusetts students on for trespassing and disorderly conduct. The resulting trial allowed the defense to present testimony from former CIA agent Ralph McGehee, former CIA sponsored Nicaraguan Contra Edgar Chamoro, Howard Zinn, Daniel Ellsberg, Ramsey Clark and other CIA critics as they testified about CIA atrocities and violations of international law in support of a necessity defense, which successfully led to Carter and the other defendants' acquittal.[57]

The 1980s saw the growth of campus CIA "Officer in Residence" programs, as the CIA loaned openly identified CIA personnel to elite campuses free of charge, as part of an effort to rehabilitate the Agency's image, and as a recruitment tool. Former CIA agency John Stockwell described CIA campus recruitment operations in this period as widespread and active, with the CIA working

the campuses from covert offices in its Foreign Resources Division, the euphemistic title for its *domestic* covert operations division. Case officers in this division work out of branch offices scattered about the nation.... There are enough of them that they keep in touch with every major campus in the nation. They work with professors, using aliases on various programs. Their activities include building files on students whom the professors help them target.[58]

Widespread public moral outrage over exposed CIA abuses limited CIA campus activities. Ami Chen Mills' book *CIA Off Campus* provides good summaries of the variety and scope of CIA connections with American campuses in the 1980s, with incidents such as Nadav Safran's disclosed CIA contract forcing him to step down from Harvard's Center for Middle Eastern Affairs, Samuel Huntingon exposed as another Harvard CIA contractor, and a wide range of students and faculty identified as working with the Agency.[59]

In 1991 Congress enacted the National Security Education Act, more commonly known as the Boren Act. The Boren Act funded the National Security Education Program (NSEP), the first program in a coming generation of payback educational programs which link the receipt of funds with contractual obligations to work for the federal government after graduation — with the program requiring recipients to circulate resumes with national security related agencies. For many academics, the CIA's presence on NSEP's Board raised concerns about the independence of the academic work of scholars funded under the program. NSEP's requirement for future national security employment brought objections from area studies associations such as the Middle East Studies Association, the African Studies Association, and the Latin American Studies Association. Standard scholarship programs of Boards of mainstream bodies like the Social Science Research Council and American Council of Learned Societies expressed concerns over NSEP's mixing of academic enquiry with national security funding.

Post 9/11 CIA Campus Campaigns

After 9/11, the intelligence community developed new programs expanding upon NSEP's principles of tying students to contractual agreements for future work with governmental agencies. Programs like the Pat Roberts Intelligence Scholars now fund undisclosed students as they work on research projects unidentified as having ties to intelligence agencies. With history as a guide we have good reason for concerns that some of these students will collect dossiers of information on students with whom they share classes, seminars and political discussions; activities that poison the atmosphere of open discourse needed for free academic enquiry.

The CIA's bold move back onto American university campuses remains underreported in the corporate media. While *CounterPunch, Democracy Now, Mother Jones, In These Times* and other progressive news sources have covered some of the developments bringing the CIA onto American campuses, and conservative publications like *The New Republic* have occasionally written approvingly of these campus invasions, mainstream media have missed out on reporting on these revolutionary campus activities. As of this writing (late 2010), the *New York Times* has yet to write a single word about the Pat Roberts Intelligence Scholars Program, the Intelligence Community Scholarship Program, or the Intelligence Community Centers for Academic Excellence.[60]

These Intelligence Community Centers for Academic Excellence (IC/

CAE) constitute bold new CIA intrusions onto American university campuses that bring federal funds and CIA employees onto campuses. Beginning in 2005, the CIA established prototypes of their "Intelligence Community Centers for Academic Excellence" (IC/CAE) on ten public and private universities across the United States. These first ten ICCAE programs began on the campuses of California State University San Bernardino, Clark Atlanta University, Florida International University, Norfolk State University, Tennessee State University, Trinity University, University of Texas El Paso, University of Texas Pan American, University of Washington, and Wayne State University. During the next five years (a period which coincided with radical budget cuts on university campuses — leaving many budgets in shambles and making universities desperate for any new sources of funds) the CIA established IC/CAE programs on eleven more university campuses: Carnegie Mellon, Clemson, North Carolina A&T State, University of North Carolina Wilmington, Florida A&M, Miles College, University of Maryland College Park, University of Nebraska, University of New Mexico, Pennsylvania State University, and Virginia Polytechnic Institute.[61]

IC/CAE provides operational funds to university hosts and it staffs these campus centers with a mixture of CIA and non–CIA linked personnel. IC/CAE offers opportunities for universities to take advantage of a CIA in residence program where CIA analysts spend a term or a year on campus without charge to their host university. IC/CAE sets its goals for these campus programs to "systematic long-term program at universities and colleges to recruit and hire eligible talent for IC agencies and components," and to "increase the [intelligence recruiting] pipeline of students ... with emphasis on women and ethnic minorities in critical skill areas."[62]

While the media ignored the friction these IC/CAE programs generate when university administrators attempt to foist these programs on unwilling faculty, many faculty at campuses with IC/CAE programs expressed grave concerns over the damage these Centers pose to academic freedom, and worried that faculty and students from IC/CAE universities studying or working abroad might face danger because of assumed links with the CIA. At the University of Washington, the Faculty Senate publicly raised such concerns, and faculty from the departments of Anthropology and History, the International Studies Fund Group Librarians, the Latin American Studies Division in the Henry M. Jackson School of International Studies, and Southeast Asian Studies Center wrote impassioned objections to the university administration opposing establishment of these intelligence centers on campus.[63] But as on other IC/CAE campuses, the administration ignored these concerns and made a deal with the IC/CAE, as new forms of secrecy interfere with the establishment and maintenance of an environment of open academic inquiry.

Since 2001, American intelligence agencies have increasingly violated laws establishing the limits of intelligence methods. In 2008, ABC reported that "in an apparent violation of U.S.policy, Peace Corps volunteers and a Fulbright scholar were asked by a U.S. Embassy official in Bolivia 'to basically spy on Cubans and Venezuelans in the country.'"[64] The Fulbright scholar, John Alexander van Schaick said he was "told to provide the names, addresses and activities of any Venezuelan or Cuban doctors or field workers" he encountered while working in Bolivia. The previous summer, Peace Corps volunteers had reported that the same U.S. Embassy official had also asked them to spy on Cubans and Venezuelans they met in Bolivia.[65] Other examples of Fulbright scholarships used by the CIA to gather intelligence occur in Lindsay Moran's book *Blowing My Cover: My Life as a CIA Spy* detailing how after being recruited and cleared to work for the CIA, she delayed her official start date while a Fulbright scholar in Bulgaria under an agreement that she would "begin" her CIA spy work once she returned from Bulgaria.[66]

The terror attacks of September 11, 2001, provided opportunities for the CIA and supporters trying to overcome deeply held institutional resistance to the CIA presence on American university campuses. The CIA made itself clearly understood in the post–Church Committee meetings with Harvard President Bok that it would not enter into agreements that curtailed their effort to gain footholds on university campuses and it continued to fund ways onto our campuses; and 9/11 provided hundreds of such footholds across the country. It has become a cliché to say with 9/11 "everything changed," and while many American attitudes towards intelligence agencies radically shifted after 9/11, one thing that did not change was the historical record of the CIA's abuses of human rights, violations of international law, and problems created for independent scholarship and academic freedom when the CIA and a climate of secrecy moves onto our university campuses. Revelations of the CIA's involvement in extreme renditions (the illegal kidnapping of terror suspects and moving them to secret detention centers where the kidnapped are interrogated and tortured), illegal assassinations, the crimes of Abu Ghraib, the Obama Administration's authorization of CIA assassinations of U.S. citizens suspected of ties to Al-Qaeda, etc. provide good practical and moral reasons for academics to resist allowing the CIA on our campuses, but other reasons also exist.

It makes sense that the CIA wants to use university professors and students; campuses are fertile grounds for the production and analysis of knowledge and analysis. But scholars familiar with the history of the CIA's recurrent problems with CIA campus activities do not want their work linked with an agency repeatedly tied to lawlessness, dishonesty, murder and violations of human rights.

The levels of secrecy and duplicity accompanying any CIA presence on college campuses run counter to fundamental principles of academic inquiry, and limit students' and professors' academic freedom. Academic inquiry demands honesty, open discussions and debates, disclosure of sponsorship, meaningful informed consent from all involved in research projects, and forms of openness that the CIA will not countenance. Whether secretly sending undisclosed CIA linked students to campuses through PRISP and other post–9/11 programs, or secretly funding professors to undertake specific forms of research; the CIA interferes with free and open academic inquiry. While the CIA argues these moves will expand the agency's limited perspectives, because of the ways that these programs covertly link professors and students with agency culture, the most significant results will instead be the spread of CIA culture and limited means of analysis to our university campuses. The great irony exists that the CIA says it wants to come on campus to learn to think differently, yet its presence will inevitably lead the CIA to spread the limitations it wishes to overcome onto American university campuses.

As a generation of academic opponents to CIA campus infiltrations retire or die out, the informed opposition to CIA campus intrusions risks evaporation at rates that seemed unimaginable just a few years earlier. If the CIA succeeds in its current campaigns to enmesh the agency into our university fabrics, we can expect foreign countries will stop hosting American researchers. And who can blame them? This will have devastating consequences for geologists, political scientists, anthropologists, language scholars, and any scholar working in medicine, or the sciences, or any other discipline engaged in research linked with scholars in other countries.

Just as American society increasingly embraces what anthropologist Cathy Lutz refers to as the new "military normal," our culture normalizes the CIA as an acceptable, necessary component of American empire.[67] Just as Russia had its retired-KGB-director-president (Vladimir Putin), the United States had its retired-CIA-director-president (George H. Bush). With only minor discomfort expressed from concerned faculty and students, Texas A & M University installed former CIA DCI Robert Gates as university president as if some continuity exists between running an agency flaunting international law and running massive international espionage operations, and leading scholarly pursuits of knowledge. We are asked to accept Murder Inc. into polite company by accepting arguments about differences between analysts and operations, and such moves on university campuses require the muting of critical voices that still remember the CIA atrocities of yesterday and today.

We live in an age where the once clear dangers of linking the CIA and our academic institutions no longer seem obvious to many citizens: university administrators and increasing numbers of students and professors. With increased corporatization of American university campuses, professors have increasingly learned to accept external forces limiting elements of academic inquiry and making demands upon forms of produced knowledge; factors that contribute, along with tight budgetary conditions, to many universities' decisions to coalesce with intelligence agency desires. As cuts to higher education continue, universities will find themselves under increasing pressure to accept any available funding sources. These economic conditions and a culture of growing American militarism now embolden the CIA to openly move onto our university campuses and expand Agency links into academia.

The global economic crises and the rise of neoliberalism, massive military deficit spending, and collapsing tax revenues leave our public universities especially vulnerable to CIA expansions as soaring tuition increases cannot keep up with universities' financial needs. Even with strong faculty and student opposition to CIA campus programs like IC/CAE, market forces will press administrators and Regents or Trustees to welcome the CIA in much the same way that corporations have gained free passage in the last two decades. While these economic arguments for an increased CIA campus presence will continue to sway non-academics, whatever shreds of shared governance still exist on our campuses demand faculty input on a move that can so quickly undermine the independence and legitimacy of academic inquiry. Faculty and students must understand the CIA historical opposition to democratic movements; they must understand why American academics have historically struggled in opposition to CIA intrusions on our campuses and the threats the agency presents to our campuses' culture of free and open academic inquiry.

The CIA's own history provides the best arguments for keeping the agency off our campuses. Its history of training death squads, suppressing democratic movements at home and abroad, cooking intelligence to best suit government policy needs, and lawless spying on American citizens undermines basic principles of academia. Those who wish to bring the CIA on campus must confront this history of lawlessness, interference with free academic inquiry, and spying that will destroy the academic settings the CIA seeks to join.

NOTES

1. Sigmund Diamond, *Compromised Campus: The Collaboration of Universities with the Intelligence Community, 1945–1955* (New York: Oxford University Press, 1992).

2. David Price, *Anthropological Intelligence: The Deployment and Neglect of American Anthropology in the Second World War* (Durham: Duke University Press, 2008).

3. Studies in Intelligence [Author's name classified by CIA]. "The CIA and Academe." *Studies in Intelligence* (Winter 1983): 33. [Originally classified Confidential.]

4. Robin Winks, *Cloak and Gown: Scholars in the Secret War, 1939–1961,* 2d ed. (New York: Morrow, 1996), 457–459.

5. Hugh Wilford, *The Mighty Wurlitzer: How the CIA Played America* (Cambridge, MA:

Harvard University Press, 2008), 75–82; Frances Stonor Saunders, *The Cultural Cold War: The CIA and the World of Arts and Letters* (New York: New, 1999).

6. Studies in Intelligence, 34.

7. Ibid., 8. David H. Price, "Anthropology *Sub Rosa*: The AAA, the CIA and the Ethical Problems Inherent in Secret Research," in *Ethics and the Profession of Anthropology*, 2d ed., ed. Carolyn Fluehr-Lobban (Walnut Creek, CA: AltaMira, 2003), 29–49.

9. Diamond.

10. "Did CIA Take the Senate?" *National Review,* February 2, 1957, 103.

11. Diamond.

12. Wilford, 127.

13. Thomas Laird, *Into Tibet: The CIA's First Atomic Spy and His Secret Expedition to Lhasa* (New York: Grove, 2002).

14. Noam Chomsky, et al., *The Cold War and the University* (New York: New, 1997); Saunders.

15. James H. Doolittle, William B. Franke, Morris Hadley and William Pawley, with S. Paul Johnston, "Report on the Covert Activities of the Central Intelligence Agency," 25. [Classified, Top Secret, 1954]. http://www.foia.cia.gov/helms/pdf/doolittle_report.pdf, accessed November 18, 2010.

16. Philip Agee, *On the Run* (Secaucus, NJ: Lyle Stuart, 1987), 13

17. Michael D. Coe, *Final Report* (New York: Thames and Hudson, 2006), 64.

18. John Ernst, *Forging a Fateful Alliance: Michigan State University and the Vietnam War* (East Lansing: Michigan State University Press, 1998).

19. Saunders.

20. "CIA Subsidized Festival Trips," *New York Times* February 21, 1967.

21. Willford, 141–148.

22. John Marks, *The Search for the "Manchurian Candidate": The CIA and Mind Control* (New York: Times, 1979).

23. Marks.

24. Alfred McCoy, *A Question of Torture: CIA Interrogation from the Cold War to the War on Terror* (New York: Henry Holt, 2006); David Price, "Buying a Piece of Anthropology" (Parts One and Two), *Anthropology Today* 23.8(2007):8–13 and 23.5:17–22.

25. Society for the Investigation of Human Ecology, *Brainwashing, a Guide to the Literature: A Report* (Forest Hills, NY: Society for the Investigation of Human Ecology), 1960.

26. Society for the Investigation of Human Ecology, *The Hungarian Revolution of October 1956, Second Seminar,* June 6, 1958 (New York: Society for the Investigation of Human Ecology); Richard M. Stephenson, "The CIA and the Professor: A Personal Account," *The American Sociologist* (1978) 13:128–133.

27. Stephenson, 130.

28. Studies in Intelligence, 34.

29. Studies in Intelligence, 35.

30. Bruce Cumings, *Parallax Visions* (Durham: Duke University Press, 1999), 191.

31. Sol Stern, "A Short Account of International Student Politics and the Cold War with Particular Reference to the NSA, CIA, etc," *Ramparts*, March 1967, pp. 29–38.

32. Ibid.

33. "The Administration: House of Glass," *Newsweek,* March 6, 1967, pp. 28–30.

34. Rhodi Jeffreys-Jones, *The CIA and American Democracy* (New Haven: Yale University Press: 1989), 156.

35. Studies in Intelligence, 35.

36. Wilford.

37. CIA, 1968. http://www.foia.cia.gov/docs/DOC_0001468660/DOC_0001468660.pdf.

38. http://www.mtholyoke.edu/offices/comm/oped/spying2.shtml, accessed December 21, 2010.

39. Seymour Hersh, "Huge CIA Operation Reported in U.S. Against Antiwar Forces, Other Dissidents in Nixon Years," *New York Times,* December 22, 1974.

40. Rockefeller Commission, Report to the President by the Commission on CIA Activities within the United States, Final Report (Washington, D.C.: Government Printing Office, June 1975), 142–144.

41. Rockefeller Commission, 23–24.

42. Rockefeller Commission, 41.

43. William R. Corson, *The Armies of Ignorance: The Rise of the American Intelligence Empire* (New York: Dial, 1977), 313.

44. Corson, 312.

45. Theodore D. Graves, *Behavioral Anthropology: Toward an Integrated Science of Human Behavior* (Walnut Creek, CA: AltaMira, 2004), 314–315.

46. Church Committee, Final Report of the Select Committee to Study Governmental Operations with Respect to Intelligence Activities, Senate Report, 94 Cong. 2 SESS., No. 94–755 (Washington, D.C.: Government Printing Office, 1976), Book 1, p. 189; Chris Mooney, "Back to Church," *The American Prospect*, November 5, 2001, http://prospect.org/cs/articles?article=back_to_church, accessed November 22, 2010.

47. Church Committee, 198–199.

48. Church Committee, 181.

49. Church Committee, 182–183, emphasis added.

50. Church Committee.

51. Studies in Intelligence, 37.

52. Pike Report, *The Unexpurgated Pike Report: Report of the House Select Committee on Intelligence*, ed. Gregory Andrade Diamond (New York: McGraw-Hill, 1976 [1991]).

53. Pike Report, 157–158.

54. Studies in Intelligence, 39.

55. Studies in Intelligence, 39 and 40.

56. Ege Konrad, "Rutgers University: Intelligence Goes to College," *CounterSpy*, June–August 1984.

57. Ami Chen Mills, *CIA Off Campus: Building the Movement Against Agency Recruitment and Research*, 2d ed. (Boston: South End, 1991).

58. John Stockwell, *The Praetorian Guard: The U.S. Role in the New World Order* (Boston: South End, 1991), 102–103.

59. Mills, 32–37.

60. David Price, "The CIA's Campus Spies," *CounterPunch* (2005), 12(1):1–15, http://www.counterpunch.org/price03122005.html; David Price, *Weaponizing Anthropology: Social Science in Service of the Militarized State* (Oakland, CA: CounterPunch/AK, 2011).

61. Price.

62. http://www.dni.gov/cae/.

63. Price.

64. Jean Friedman-Rudovsky and Brian Ross, "Peace Corps, Fulbright Scholar Asked to 'Spy' on Cubans, Venezuelans," *ABC News*, February 8, 2008, http://abcnews.go.com/Blotter/story?id=4262036&page=1, accessed November 20, 2010.

65. Friedman-Rudovsky and Ross.

66. Lindsay Moran, *Blowing My Cover: My Life as a CIA Spy* (New York: Penguin, 2005).

67. Catherine Lutz, "The Military Normal," in *The Counter-Counterinsurgency Manual*, Network of Concerned Anthropologists, ed. (Chicago: Prickly Paradigm, 2009), 23–38.

Works Cited

"The Administration: House of Glass." *Newsweek*, March 6, 1967, pp. 28–30.

Agee, Philip. *On the Run*. Secaucus, NJ: Lyle Stuart, 1987.

Chomsky, Noam, et al. *The Cold War and the University*. New York: New, 1997.

Church Committee. Final Report of the Select Committee to Study Governmental Operations with Respect to Intelligence Activities, Senate Report, 94 Cong. 2 SESS., No. 94-755. Washington, D.C.: Government Printing Office, 1976.

"CIA Subsidized Festival Trips." *New York Times*, February 21, 1967.

Coe, Michael D. *Final Report*. New York: Thames and Hudson, 2006.

Corson, William R. *The Armies of Ignorance: The Rise of the American Intelligence Empire*. New York: Dial, 1977.

Cumings, Bruce. *Parallax Visions*. Durham: Duke University Press, 1999.

Demanchick, Stephen P., and Howard Kirschenbaum. "Carl Rogers and the CIA." *Journal of Humanistic Psychology* 48.6(2008):6–31.

Diamond, Sigmund. *Compromised Campus: The Collaboration of Universities with the Intelligence Community, 1945–1955*. New York: Oxford University Press, 1992.

Doolittle, James H., William B. Franke, Morris Hadley and William Pawley, with S. Paul Johnston. "Report on the Covert Activities of the Central Intelligence Agency," Classified, Top Secret, 1954. http://www.foia.cia.gov/helms/pdf/doolittle_report.pdf.

Ernst, John. *Forging a Fateful Alliance: Michigan State University and the Vietnam War*. East Lansing: Michigan State University Press, 1998.

Friedman-Rudovsky, Jean, and Brian Ross. "Peace Corps, Fulbright Scholar Asked to 'Spy' on Cubans, Venezuelans." *ABC News*, February 8, 2008. http://abcnews.go.com/Blotter/story?id=4262036&page=1.

Graves, Theodore D. *Behavioral Anthropology: Toward an Integrated Science of Human Behavior*. Walnut Creek, CA: AltaMira, 2004.

Hersh, Seymour. "Huge CIA Operation Reported in U.S. Against Antiwar Forces, Other Dissidents in Nixon Years." *New York Times*, December 22, 1974.

Human Ecology Fund. "Society for the Investigation of Human Ecology." Report. New York: Human Ecology Fund, 1961/63.

Jeffreys-Jones, Rhodi. *The CIA and American Democracy*. New Haven: Yale University Press, 1989.

Konrad, Ege. "Rutgers University: Intelligence Goes to College." *CounterSpy*, June–August 1984.

Laird, Thomas. *Into Tibet: The CIA's First Atomic Spy and His Secret Expedition to Lhasa*. New York: Grove, 2002.

Marks, John. *The Search for the "Manchurian Candidate": The CIA and Mind Control*. New York: Times, 1979.

McCoy, Alfred. *A Question of Torture: CIA Interrogation from the Cold War to the War on Terror*. New York: Henry Holt, 2006.

Mills, Ami Chen. *CIA Off Campus: Building the Movement Against Agency Recruitment and Research*, 2d ed. Boston: South End, 1991.

Mooney, Chris. "Back to Church." *The American Prospect*, November 5, 2001, http://prospect.org/cs/articles?article=back_to_church.

Moran, Lindsay. *Blowing My Cover: My Life as a CIA Spy*. New York: Penguin, 2005.

Pike Report. *The Unexpurgated Pike Report*. Report of the House Select Committee on Intelligence. Gregory Andrade Diamond, ed. New York: McGraw-Hill, 1976 [1991].

Price, David. *Anthropological Intelligence*. Durham: Duke University Press, 2008.

_____. "Anthropology *Sub Rosa*: The AAA, the CIA and the Ethical Problems Inherent in Secret Research." In *Ethics and the Profession of Anthropology: The Dialogue Continues*, 2d ed., ed. Carolyn Fluehr-Lobban, pp. 29–49. Walnut Creek, CA: Altamira, 2003.

_____. "The CIA's Campus Spies." *CounterPunch* 12.1(2005):1–15. http://www.counterpunch.org/price03122005.html

_____. *Weaponizing Anthropology: Social Science in Service of the Militarized State*. Oakland, CA: CounterPunch/AK, 2011.

Saunders, Frances Stonor. *The Cultural Cold War: The CIA and the World of Arts and Letters*. New York: New, 1999.

Society for the Investigation of Human Ecology. *The Hungarian Revolution of October 1956, Second Seminar*, June 6, 1958. New York: Society for the Investigation of Human Ecology, 1958.

Stephenson, Richard M. "The CIA and the Professor: A Personal Account." *The American Sociologist* 13(1978):128–133.

Stern, Sol. 1967. "A Short Account of International Student Politics and the Cold War with Particular Reference to the NSA, CIA, etc." *Ramparts,* March 1967, pp. 29–38.

Stockwell, John. *The Praetorian Guard: The U.S. Role in the New World Order.* Boston: South End, 1991.

Studies in Intelligence [author's name classified by CIA]. "The CIA and Academe." *Studies in Intelligence* (Winter 1983): 33–42. [Originally classified Confidential.]

U.S. Senate. *Foreign and Military Intelligence: Book I, Final Report of the Select Committee to Study Governmental Operations With Respect to Intelligence Activities.* (Church Committee) April 26, 1976, Report No. 94-755. Washington, D.C.: Government Printing Office, 1976.

U.S. Senate. (Senate Select Committee on Intelligence). "Project MKULTRA, The CIA's Program of Research in Behavioral Modification," Joint Hearing Before the Select Committee on Intelligence and the Subcommittee on Health and Scientific Research of the Committee on Human Resources United States Senate. Ninety-Fifth Congress, First Session, August 3, 1977. Washington, D.C.: Government Printing Office, 1977.

Vidal, Gore. "The Day the American Empire Ran out of Gas." In *At Home,* pp. 105–114. New York: Vintage, 1988.

Wilford, Hugh. *The Mighty Wurlitzer: How the CIA Played America.* Cambridge, MA: Harvard University Press, 2008.

Winks, Robin. *Cloak and Gown: Scholars in the Secret War, 1939–1961,* 2d ed. New York: Morrow, 1996.

Witanek, Robert. "Students, Scholars and Spies: The CIA on Campus." *Covert Action Information Bulletin* 31(1989):25–28.

3

South of the Border:
The CIA in Latin America

DAVID CARLSON

> The C.I.A. taught us everything — everything...they taught us explosives, how to kill, bomb, trained us in acts of sabotage. When the Cubans were working for the C.I.A. they were called patriots...now they call it terrorism. The times have changed.
> — Luis Posada Carriles, *New York Times*, 13 July 1998

> Historical amnesia is a dangerous phenomenon, not only because it undermines moral and intellectual integrity, but also because it lays the groundwork for crimes that lie ahead.
> — Noam Chomsky[1]

Slogans of the diverse Central American solidarity movements of the 1980s and early 1990s in North American communities and college campuses included "Hands Off Central America!" and "CIA Off Campus!" That was then. At many universities and colleges, the battle against Central Intelligence Agency recruitment and involvement within academe won important, if temporary, successes against a secretive part of the United States foreign policy apparatus tainted by long association with Latin American anti-communist dictatorships and appalling human rights abuses including torture and mass murder.[2] These struggles against the "Company" or "la CIA" often over-determined the power and influence of the agency. Certainly exposure and publicity of the CIA's frequently sordid history of duplicity, skullduggery, "dirty tricks," and of ignoring or even abetting grave abuses in Latin America, ensured that scholars of the region — even those policy-oriented intellectuals who aspired to government service — were chary of the agency, if not actively critical or hostile to it.

In the post–September 11 United States, vastly different political circumstances swiftly eroded this earlier skepticism and active opposition. Defenders of a new close relationship between intelligence agencies and scholars frequently relegated this past record to the "dustbin of history" and in so doing remained willfully blind even as evidence mounted of a continuity of patterns rooted in past practices.[3] This is now.

Turning to the epigraphs above to explain how the intelligence agencies have largely evaded past wrong-doing amid a general societal retreat into Gore Vidal's "United States of Amnesia" during the current ongoing wars in Central Asia and the Middle East, one might agree with Chomsky who aptly noted that such forgetting is often deliberate, providing "the groundwork for crimes that lie ahead." This chapter argues that the history of the CIA in Latin America remains relevant to the contemporary moment and should inform critical scrutiny of the Agency as it re-insinuates itself into areas of the world and within academe. Many U.S. actions in the world after 9/11 are quite different from past foreign policy experience. Yet many other actions repeat the errors of the past, particularly the maintenance of U.S. super-power hegemony vis-à-vis Central America and the Caribbean.

Two September Elevens

The 1991 end of the Cold War and collapse of the socialist bloc also saw the end of "two, three, many" hot wars in the so-called Third World, especially in Central America, thought of as Soviet-U.S. proxy conflicts by many North Americans. This historical watershed had the effect of removing Central America from sustained North American scrutiny and popular consciousness over the intervening decades. For many North Americans, historical erasure of U.S. involvement in these conflicts became complete with the terrorist attacks of 11 September 2001 and the onset of the "Global War on Terror": 9/11 as the day "everything changed."

Latin Americanists pointed to the "first 11 September," that of 1973, when a brutal CIA-abetted Chilean coup d'état overthrew the elected Marxist president, Salvador Allende and the Popular Unity socialist government and ushered in the 17-year dictatorship of General Augusto Pinochet. Often such comparisons of state terrorism with Islamist acts of terror, or introspections on political violence were rejected as false equations. To critics, such views invoked a now mostly irrelevant Cold War history only of interest to Chileans and other Latin Americans.[4]

The tragedy of 9/11 exonerated neoconservative exponents of militarism and American hard power. The Middle East would be democratized, so policy-makers urged, transformed through social engineering and regime change using the Pentagon as an efficient crusading Wilsonian instrument of "liberation."

Open-ended wars of occupation and avowed "state building" in Afghanistan and Iraq ensued. A political cartoon in which a perplexed college student asks a mortified and exhausted history teacher "Why do we need to learn the lessons of Vietnam? It seems no one else has" encapsulated the feelings of many critics of empire and opponents of President George W. Bush's national security strategy and the decision to invade Iraq on pretexts of "gathering threats" and "weapons of mass destruction."

American exceptionalism and Eurocentrism have shaped policy makers' traditional views that Europe and Asia (and now, ever increasingly, the Middle East) should be the primary focus for U.S. policymakers. Latin America is still distinctly a backburner issue thought of as a poor province or variant "other path" of the "West." As historian Grandin noted in *Empire's Workshop* on how Latin America, specifically Central America, was early on a laboratory of the new imperialism, President Richard M. Nixon told Donald Rumsfeld, "Latin America doesn't matter.... Long as we've been in it, people don't give one damn about Latin America."[5]

This collective ignorance and inattention after 9/11 persisted even after the early–twenty-first century economic crisis discredited the neoliberal Washington Consensus, and a resultant rise in Latin American left-populist politics and new models of development.

Those who followed such trends included film director Oliver Stone, who made *South of the Border* about populist leaders, and writer Oscar Guardiola-Rivera, in *What if Latin America Ruled the World? How the South Will Take the North through the 21st Century.*[6] The disjuncture between public discourse in the Americas — North and South — suggested to observers the decline of U.S. hegemony and slipping regard in the South for North American "soft power." Preoccupations in the North lay elsewhere. PBS documentary director Ofra Bikel, who made a 2008 *Frontline* episode on president Hugo Chávez in Venezuela, began her career during the 1980s civil wars in Central America, when "people were very interested" in the region. Today "that's changed. The U.S. is involved in the Middle East ... China is sexy, but certainly not Latin America. So people here in the U.S. don't know very much about it and don't care to."[7] She asserted that Chávez's often boorish and demagogic behavior, his anti–American invective, and the "insane things [he said] about President [George W.] Bush, calling him 'donkey,' 'Mr. Danger,' the 'devil'" and so on attracted North American attention to the region, but little else.[8]

One might add that the politicized framing of drug war violence in México and Colombia, and undocumented immigration from the Global South complete a pastiche of media-derived images for many North Americans that seemingly urge militarized responses.[9] Cautionary tales about the origin of the murderous drug and human-smuggling gang *los Zetas* from among U.S.-trained

GAFES antinarcotics special forces, and ex-soldiers from Central America, as well as the lengthy regional record of malfeasance and destructiveness of the CIA, even in recent cases like the April 2002 failed coup against Chávez, often make little headway as a result.[10] North Americans within academe and without are therefore often surprised at the level of ire the CIA arouses among many of their neighbors, "south of the border."

"Why Do They Hate Us" and Historical Amnesia

Consignment of the role of the CIA in Latin American history to irrelevance portended this widening disjuncture in understanding. Historical amnesia allows the CIA to continually reemerge amid declamations that it has changed the error of its past ways. After the terrorist attacks of September 11, 2001, various commentators castigated restrictions imposed after the 1975 Church Committee hearings revealed CIA involvement in coups, acts of aggression, and assassination plots against foreign leaders.[11] The "first September 11" 1973 coup against Allende and the onset of the Pinochet regime, together with Vietnam-era skepticism toward the agency's often nefarious roles, underlay the Church Committee investigations. After 9/11, pundits urged that the "gloves come off" insofar as restrictions on executive power and the use of intelligence agencies as, in effect, clandestine branches of the armed forces to engage in "plausibly deniable" covert operations.[12] Amid the palpable societal desire to wreak vengeance on the perpetrators — however broadly construed or ill defined by policymakers — others grappled with how to understand and thereby effectively combat such atrocious criminal actions and those terrorist groups — Islamists in this case — who organized them.

The call went up: "Why do *they* hate *us?*" A few concluded, in agreement with Los Angeles journalist John Powers, that "they hate us because we don't even know why they hate us."[13] Historian of Brazil John D. French wrote that our North American collective ignorance about the rest of the planet of six billion people, "profoundly divided by power, wealth, culture, and ideology" — and, it must be said, by historical memory — has deepened from saturation in manipulated media-generated images that reassure us that globalization is making that bafflingly complex "other" world more like us.[14] One tragedy of the early–twenty-first century included such introversion and lack of perspicacity: "citizens of the United States are a generous people who will do anything for the rest of the world, except learn about them."[15]

Another tragedy arising from militarism and aggression lay in the explicit turn away from legal norms and the promotion of untrammeled executive power in an imperial presidency. It was not long before reinforced and greatly expanded intelligence agencies with fewer checks on their power, intrusiveness, impunity and secrecy, overthrew restrictions and firewalls established after exposure of the abuses of the 1950s, 1960s, and 1970s. The CIA and kindred agencies of presidential power returned to the university as the nation undertook a reassertion of empire and militarism in a "Long War" likened by some critics as "permanent war."[16] The changed political circumstances, and above all, fear prompted by a direct physical attack on the United States, offered justification to shunt aside past qualms. As sociologist Kim Scipes suggested in a recent book on the AFL-CIO's labor imperialist foreign policy "the conscious political project of the elites of" the United States "has been the continual effort" throughout the nation's history "to get Americans to 'fear' others" so that the "post 9/11 ... U.S. world has focused on President Bush's 'global war on terrorism,' the idea is the same: be afraid, be very afraid."[17] The replacement of the Cold War now appears to be "permanent war," described by journalist Chris Hedges as "a kind of surrogate religion, whether it is against the Hun, the Bolshevik, the fascist, the communist, or the Islamic terrorist."[18]

For Latin Americanists opposed to the CIA, including not a few who cut their political teeth in activist efforts within Central American solidarity groups prior to entering the ranks of graduate students and the professoriate, the amply detailed and uniformly grim record was dispelled by what Chomsky has called the "doctrine of the change of course"— pushing all of past history into the dustbin as essentially irrelevant minutiae. "Yes," we may say, "in the past we did some wrong things because of innocence or inadvertence. But now that's all over, so let's not waste any more time on this boring, stale stuff."[19] Such a posture negates critical histories of past wrong-doing and refocuses attention on a desired future result, even toward those "crimes that lie ahead."

As a result, when historians and critics of CIA involvement in Latin American nation's internal politics, civil wars, attempts to subvert or influence labor unions, the media and press, civic associations, and other institutions, as well as complicity in human rights abuses, point to the results of the CIA's defense of reactionary sectors in the name of "stability," they find many North American audiences disinclined to contemplate and ponder the ramifications of something that happened so long ago.

A litany of CIA transgressions in Latin America often starts with the well-known example of the 1954 Operation PBSUCCESS overthrow of the elected nationalist and reformist government of Jacobo Arbenz. This coup had grave ramifications for Guatemala, leading to polarization and militarization of politics resulting in civil war.[20] It also radicalized nationalist reactions to the United States throughout the hemisphere, informing the uncompromising vision of Cuban July 26th Movement (M-26-7) leaders, and the Argentine doctor Ernesto "Ché" Guevara. The implications of curtailing reform for short-term political gain included not stability but fomenting armed conflict between states and revolutionary challenges. As Richard H. Immerman observed in 1982, Washington policy makers frequently faced dilemmas of their own making. He quoted a "State Department official" who "conceded, 'what we'd give to have an Arbenz now. We are going to have to invent one, but all the candidates are dead.'"[21] Present-day U.S. disputes with Iran, similarly rooted in the 1953 CIA and British overthrow of Mohammed Mossadegh, who had nationalized Iran's oil, installing the autocratic Shah, followed by the 1979 Iranian revolution point to kindred dilemmas in the Middle East in a pattern described as "blowback."

Historical amnesia dispelled not only any "lessons of Vietnam" but even those of "El Salvador — Spanish for Vietnam" as the old 1980s activist bumper sticker put it. By 2004, calls to quash the insurgency in Iraq via the "Salvador Option" of death squads, and by implication dirty war methods of torture, kidnapping, extrajudicial executions and murder, could be advanced as plausible propositions, and considered defensible given their apparent "success" in the 1980–1992 Salvadoran counterinsurgency and civil war.

Exposure in 2004 and 2005 of U.S. military and CIA practice of "enhanced interrogation" techniques — euphemisms for torture — within prisons and detention facilities at Guantánamo Bay, Cuba, in Iraq and Afghanistan, immediately recalled Vietnam and Central America. CIA agents and other U.S. "operators" kidnapped terrorist suspects or persons with established or presumed ties to militant Islamist groups, then transported them in a drugged or sedated state to a global network of so-called "black sites" in Eastern Europe, Central Asia, the Indian Ocean, and Southeast Asia or to nations such as Egypt, Morocco, Uzbekistan, Syria, and Jordan. This clandestine prison network, called "extraordinary rendition," evoked "disappearance," and past abusive practices in Latin America as well. The difference lay in who carried out the actual torture of captives: U.S. personnel or contractors in the former scenario, a mix of CIA and foreign secret police in the latter.

Prisoners snatched from various locales, then handed over to security services notorious for their use of torture, reminded not a few historians of Latin America of the internationalization of torture and state terrorism by the Southern Cone National Security States in Operation Condor and the "Dirty Wars" in the 1970s.[22] Ex-CIA agent Robert Baer characterized the arrangement, ostensibly rooted in the administration of President Bill Clinton, as one whereby if the CIA wanted "a serious interrogation, [it would] send a prisoner to Jordan. If you want them to be tortured, you send them to Syria. If you want someone to disappear — never to see them again — you send them to Egypt."[23]

Disappearance, of course, was emblematic of counterinsurgency and dirty wars in Central America and the Southern Cone. In disappearance, security forces abducted or captured members of armed movements, guerrillas, dissidents, and opponents of anti-communist national security states — typically labeled communists — held them incommunicado, tortured them to extract information and to terrorize the civil population, and ultimately murdered the captives while concealing the role of the state. State agents blamed paramilitary groups or criminal networks for these deeds.

For many years activists pointed to the roles of the CIA and the Pentagon's School of the Americas (SOA) — later renamed the Western Hemisphere Institute for Security Cooperation (WHISC) — in globalizing American counterinsurgency methods, and the prominence of SOA graduates in various egregious human rights abuses in Latin America. A.J. Langguth's 1978 investigation, *Hidden Terrors,* brought to light U.S. security and police aid and training for the secret police in Brazil and Uruguay, and advanced claims of direct U.S. participation in torture and intelligence assistance.[24] Jennifer K. Harbury, whose Guatemalan guerrillero husband Everardo (Efraín) Bámaca Velásquez was disappeared, tortured, and murdered by security officials employed as CIA assets, furthered these lines of inquiry by connecting how U.S. programs and training imparted counterinsurgency methods throughout the hemisphere.[25]

The internationalization of torture and state terror regimes within the U.S. ambit had a longer history, one that included the CIA and U.S. military and security aid in Latin America. This complex post–World War II process of intelligence organization and counterinsurgency planning coincided with systemic political and economic crises throughout Latin America and anti-communist politics. Myriad programs offered advice, support, training, and a pro–U.S. orientation under the general rubric of imparting professionalization. Political elites in several Latin American states sought to counter leftist and nationalist political projects they considered subversion. This ensured that oppositional politics often assumed a militarized and clandestine cast. So these alliances between the U.S. CIA and Latin American counterparts included a mix of local, regional, and international strategic objectives for the states involved. The CIA aspired to establish a wider reach through cooperation and cooptation and by the cultivation of paid assets within Latin American state institutions, all occurring amid, and legitimated by, the overarching Cold War ideological conflict.[26]

The international features of the relationship created complex patterns. Anti-communism created an overarching East vs. West Manichean struggle but consideration must be given to how various western states responded to threats posed by nationalist and decolonization movements, in other words, North-South conflicts. Various hot wars underscored the Cold War itself — frequently viewed by the superpowers as proxy conflicts, including the Korean War, the Vietnam War, and the French wars fought in Indochina/

Vietnam and Algeria. Throughout Latin America, counter-revolutionary political sectors grew concerned in the wake of the Cuban Revolution, and the concomitant rise of movements dedicated to armed struggle against entrenched
systems of inequality.[27]

Vietnam and Algeria constituted two sites for the development and promulgation of global counterinsurgency designed to defeat the prospect of "wars
of national liberation." French investigative journalist Marie-Monique Robin's
documentary film and book, *Escuadrones de la muerte*, traced the role of French
counterinsurgency and *guerre revolutionnaire* theorists experienced in fighting
the Viet Minh and Algerian FLN in imparting their repertoire of practices —
including savage and systemic torture — to Argentine military officers directly,
and to their North American counterparts at the SOA.[28]

The example of Cuba, where the July 26th Movement (M-26-7) overthrew
a squalid U.S.-supported dictator, Fulgencio Batista, in turn, gave a sense of
urgency to counterinsurgent prerogatives and the application of state building
strategies influenced by modernization theory. These theories typically presented Latin American societies riven with profound inequality as particularly
vulnerable and susceptible to left-wing subversive threats in much the same
fashion that rhetoric about "failed states" appeals to discourses about terrorism.
The theories acknowledged a need for reform, but also urged state building
carried out by powerful institutions — particularly the armed forces. As noted
by Michael McClintock and other scholars, in reaction to the onset of foco
theories of rural guerrilla warfare articulated by Ché Guevara, and later in the
1960s the spread of urban guerrilla and terrorist movements in Brazil and
Uruguay, some regional militaries implemented counterinsurgency strategies
prior to the actual emergence of an active insurgency.

At various times Latin American allied militaries and intelligence agencies
formed an internationalized counter-revolutionary system. In the case of El Salvador, for example, officials of the paramilitary group ORDEN visited South
Vietnam in the 1960s to observe U.S. state building and counterinsurgency
operations first-hand.[29] During the 1980s, the Reagan administration decided
to destabilize the revolutionary government of Nicaragua. U.S. officials tapped
allies including Israel and Argentina to assist the effort. The CIA organized
a proxy army of Contras to attack Nicaragua through terrorist tactics: destroying the programs of the revolutionary state, including clinics, schools, and
village-level organizations with considerable cruelty, rape, and torture. At the
outset, Argentine military and intelligence officials of the junta lent assistance
in the endeavor as contractors and auxiliaries. Harbury wrote that

> although it has been reported that the U.S. advisors did not teach extreme measures
> of physical torture on the grounds that it was counterproductive, it was the United
> States that paid the Argentines, despite their abysmal human rights record, to carry

out the training as well. The Argentines, of course, did not hesitate on the issue of torture. In fact, the Argentines and the CIA worked very closely indeed in Honduras, with Argentine officials acting as surrogates for the CIA's Contra actions. In short, the CIA contracted out torture in Honduras just as it often does today in Iraq and Afghanistan.[30]

CIA assistance in the 1970s enabled the Argentine and Chilean military dictatorships to create an international program of secret police cooperation and state terrorism between the regimes of Chile, Argentina, Paraguay, Brazil, Uruguay, and Bolivia known as Operation Condor.

Political Scientist J. Patrice McSherry has demonstrated that Operation Condor formed part of an overarching "inter–American counterinsurgency strategy"—an unrecognized earlier "global war on terror"—facilitated, financed, and overseen by Washington.[31] Officials implicated in murder, torture, and international terrorism — including the 1976 car bomb assassination of former Chilean ambassador Orlando Letelier and U.S.-citizen Ronni Moffitt in downtown Washington, D.C.— have sought to portray the operation as analogous to Interpol or similar international police operations. McSherry notes that Condor, however, "was a criminal operation that used terrorist practices" to assassinate, kidnap, and eliminate a range of political opponents utilizing "parallel, or parastatal, structures ... concealed from domestic and international view" that included "secret detention centers and clandestine killing machinery" beyond the reach of national and international law.[32]

If "extraordinary rendition" actually began under President Bill Clinton, not George W. Bush, it is certain that both the "Pentagon and especially the CIA ferociously resisted compliance" with Clinton's 2002 order to disclose further records related to Argentina's Dirty War "Process of National Reorganization" from 1976 to 1983, and McSherry shows that the repertoire of U.S. counterinsurgency "in Afghanistan and Iraq included the methods of disappearance, torture, extrajudicial transfer across borders, incommunicado detention, extrajudicial execution, and military rule to achieve counterterror objectives" while internally "agencies rounded up and imprisoned thousands of immigrants, and several U.S. citizens, without the right to counsel; set up vast new domestic surveillance programs; and planned the use of military tribunals."[33]

Alfred W. McCoy's history of CIA research into a panoply of actual U.S. psychological torture techniques emphasizing sensory bombardment (strobe lights, blaring music and jarring sounds, freezing temperatures), short-shackling, "stress positions," sensory and sleep deprivation, isolation, and drowning or so-called "water boarding" shows how the agency consciously emulated techniques employed by totalitarian states.[34] Many of these tortures appear in any number of human rights reports from Cold War–era Latin American National Security States.[35] The transmission belt of such torture techniques appears simply to reflect application of what some military personnel undergo as "SERE" or "Survival Evasion Resistance and Escape" training. Students face possible techniques of coercion and torture that might be used against them if captured by the enemy.[36] As a result, the CIA 1960s KUBARK manual contained torture techniques later de-emphasized in the 1983 *Human Resource Exploitation Training Manual* distributed to Central American militaries and through the SOA.[37] Instructors demonstrated torture techniques culled from vicious secret police, and even copied from human rights reports, ostensibly to educate pupils of what they might conceivably face, and these same methods were then redirected against prisoners.

Belief in torture's efficacy in interrogation relies on ideology. The enemy is dehumanized and caricatured as an inhuman monster deserving to be tortured. Imagined sacralized "ends" justify any means adopted. Journalist Joshua E. S. Phillip's *None of Us Were Like This Before: American Soldiers and Torture* suggests that views of the appropriateness and effectiveness of torture among many North Americans apparently relied on cultural fantasy.[38] A steady diet of TV shows and films rehabilitate the archetypal "bad cop" willing to use the "third degree" on criminal suspects. Others indulge sadistic revenge fantasies. Sophomoric philosophical myths, like the so-called "ticking bomb" scenario, imply that torture may be necessary in some instances to save lives. Thus, if one valorizes one's comrades-in-arms or citizens, and believes that brutalizing an enemy who has knowledge of an impending attack or ambush will save them, then torture becomes legitimated. Of course, war breeds hate and those who intend to function as soldiers in a combat zone must cultivate an abiding hatred of the enemy. It is a common psychological mechanism. Racist, nationalist, or ideologically-constructed views of the "other"— in this case, the enemy other — serve to dehumanize victims as beneath contempt. In the mind of the torturer, the victim of torture thereby deserves torture. One of the questions related to CIA practice in Latin America, and the application of similar processes in contemporary U.S. wars of occupation in the Islamic world, is that of how systems of mass detention and abusive interrogations and torture generate a pool of "actionable intelligence," while swept-up hapless victims unrelated to the insurgency or movement being repressed become written-off as mere "collateral damage."

After 9/11 the Pentagon organized screenings of Gillo Pontecorvo's 1966 film, *Battle of Algiers*, portraying French urban counterinsurgency operations against the Algerian FLN that included the systematic use and philosophical defense of torture as an important weapon against the nationalist movement. Given that Argentinean navy personnel who later made up the counter-subversive task forces in the Dirty War apparently also watched the film in the late 1960s to prepare them for war with a segment of their own people and that the French effort ultimately failed to defeat Algerian decolonization, one wonders what viewers were expected to take away from the film.

Alistair Horne, author of a book about Algeria's war of national liberation, met President Bush twice, finding him in 2007 having "read attentively" and eager to discuss "parallels between Iraq and Algeria."[39] Horne spoke of the difficulty of combating insurgents, porous borders, the "ruthless targeting of local police forces" and indigenous collaborators and the problems of "extrication" noting that war in Algeria lasted eight years and cost Charles de Gaulle his career. Horne "omitted a fifth point, on which" he "felt most strongly: the vile issue of torture (or, in Iraq, read 'abuse')" apparently because he believed President Bush had "already got the message, and was heeding the clamor ... and was going to lead to the closing down of Guantánamo."[40] Or not. The clandestine prisons remain, and Guantánamo as an off-shore prison beyond the reach of U.S. law — an "anti–Statue of Liberty" in Thomas Friedman's evocative phrase — has not been shuttered by President Barack Obama, in spite of campaign pledges to do so.

It should be clear that anyone interested in the ongoing dilemmas and conflicts of the "war on terror" and the wars of occupation in Iraq and Afghanistan ignores the history of the CIA, and the history of political violence in Latin America itself at her/his peril. Operation Condor once saw U.S. intelligence officials encouraging Latin American counterparts to coordinate policing and intelligence functions of their states against internal threats within an overarching Cold War ideological framework of hemispheric defense from internal subversion. The global war on terror simultaneously outsourced torture so that North Americans would not dirty their hands, but also replicated a similar architecture of covert warfare and "ghost detention" with salient similarities to the National Security States in Latin America. It should be clear that we are hardly over this dated Cold War history and its implications. Turning to the earlier history of the CIA in Latin America suggests that its "successes" and failures as a clandestine foreign policy tool and quasi-military intervention arm of presidential power have been fraught with enduring deleterious consequences.

More "Blowback": From the CIA's PBSUCCESS in Guatemala to ZAPATA in Cuba

Former CIA National Intelligence Estimate author and self-confessed "spear carrier for Empire," the late historian Chalmers Johnson presciently wrote *Blowback: The Costs and Consequences of American Empire,* followed after 9/11 by *The Sorrows of Empire* and *Nemesis* as a trilogy against proponents of a Pax

Americana. He urged North Americans to understand that the culture of secrecy and illegal covert actions carried out in their names will foment retaliations and unexpected consequences that the public will be unable to contextualize or contemplate as related to past subterfuge and misdeeds.[41] Restricting our gaze to just Guatemala and Cuba reveals much of the tangled and portentous themes he described for Asia, both sites of recurring "blowback" that has had lasting consequences for both nations.

Before Americans became inured to perpetual war, they first grew accustomed to the "never-ending national security crisis" framed by the Cold War with the Soviet Union.[42] To neo-revisionist historian Andrew Bacevich, this framework constituted a dyad of U.S. power at the end of World War II: the CIA and Strategic Air Command (SAC) as a "yin-yang": the nuclear bombs of SAC as the ultimate deterrent and umbrella for U.S. power and force projection, and with the national security state and the CIA as a clandestine paramilitary arm of an increasingly imperial presidency to wage covert operations. Thus, the CIA and SAC existed in a "reciprocal relationship, the existence and actions of one justifying the existence and actions of the other."[43] The CIA's predilection for operations, frequently undertaken to influence the internal politics of nations thought to be moving in nationalist, neutralist, or pro-socialist directions during the East vs. West ideological struggle, absorbed ever-greater portions of its classified budget. This covert warfare function of the CIA arose from the last item in its charter, namely performance of "such other functions and duties related to intelligence affecting the national security as the President ... may direct."[44]

Under the Presidency of Dwight D. Eisenhower, "such other functions and duties" within the original 1947 CIA charter included regime change. In August 1953, in cooperation with British intelligence, the CIA assisted the Shah of Iran and monarchists in Operation TPAJAX: the overthrow of the democratically elected nationalist Prime Minister Mohammed Mossadegh because he had nationalized the nation's oil. Britain rejected offers of compensation, and U.S. officials took a dim view of Mossadegh's nationalism, his government's toleration of the Tudeh, the Iranian communist party, and given the nation's sheer proximity to both the USSR and the Arabian peninsula with its oil resources, opted to conspire against Mossadegh. Kermit "Kim" Roosevelt (a grandson of President Theodore Roosevelt), who headed the operation, wrote a book about it the same year the Iranian Revolution toppled the shah and ushered in a vehemently anti–American Islamic Republic. In it he advanced the proposition that it was a "countercoup" to forestall impending communist takeover.[45] This formulation would be reiterated in several other subsequent cases of "regime change," including the 1954 CIA Operation PBSUCCESS in Guatemala against the democratically elected reformist government of Jacobo Arbenz.[46]

Arbenz became President of Guatemala in the 1950 elections made possible after a 1944 revolution that overthrew the 13-year dictatorship of Jorge Ubico, the "Little Napoleon of the Tropics." This democratic period, 1944 to 1954, is sometimes referred to as the "Guatemalan Spring" during which a reformist coalition sought to implement policies designed to stimulate Guatemalan industry and the national economy through competition with U.S.-owned firms, and an ambitious land reform project to create the conditions for a rural middle-class of farmers in a nation where 2.2 percent of the population owned 70 percent of the arable land.[47] Arbenz turned to members of Guatemala's small communist party to help implement the reform, and a handful of communists took sub-cabinet level positions in the government. The United Fruit Company, which had acquired vast tracts of land for its banana growing operations, defended its property from expropriation by the Guatemalan state. One principal concern was Arbenz's use of tax receipts to assess the value of the lands at over half a million dollars, while the Boston-based corporation insisted that the value was not less than 16 million dollars.[48]

United States government officials, including John Foster Dulles, Secretary of State, and his younger brother Allen Dulles, Director of the CIA, had considerable personal financial interest in United Fruit, but historian Piero Gleijeses agreed with the analysis of a member of the PGT, that the United States would have overthrown "us even if we produced no bananas."[49] The United States isolated Guatemala, and pulled out its military mission while halting the transfer of equipment and supplies to the army. Arbenz had increased army salaries to maintain their support but when the Arbenz government purchased a shipment of World War II–vintage weapons from socialist Czechoslovakia, the United States denounced it as an attempt to create a "communist beachhead" in Central America. For a combination of strategic rationales — Guatemala lies between Texas and the Panama Canal — anticommunism, and U.S. economic interests, Arbenz had to go.

The CIA organized a rebel force in nearby Honduras led by Colonel Carlos Castillo Armas and attacked. When the army refused to defend the government, Arbenz fled. This action, carried out for short-term gain, and re-imposition of U.S. hegemony in the hemisphere, had lasting repercussions for Guatemala. By 1960 the nation plunged into 36 years of civil war between the left and right, while a succession of army dictators ruled with a heavy hand. The United States offered overt security assistance of all kinds, until Guatemala's egregious human rights record rendered this politically unfeasible by the late 1970s. U.S. allies like Israel then stepped in.

In the early 1980s, the Guatemalan armed forces carried out a scorched earth campaign directed at mostly indigenous rural villagers thought a base of support for several leftist guerrilla movements organized into the URNG —

Unidad Revolucionaria Nacional Guatemalteca/ Guatemalan National Revolutionary Unity. In the course of this campaign, the military destroyed over 440 villages and committed over 600 massacres in a population removal strategy to "drain the sea in which the rebel fish swam" accompanied by shocking and widespread human rights abuses. By the end of the conflict, up to 200,000 Guatemalans had been killed, with 40,000 "disappeared."[50]

In the shorter term, many Latin Americans reacted with fury to CIA intervention. By its actions, the United States implicitly rejected anti-interventionist principles contained in treaties from the 1930s. Franklin Delano Roosevelt's legacy of the "Good Neighbor Policy" appeared at an end. In its place, the coup in Guatemala augured a return to overt interventionism to defend U.S. hegemony, now equipped with the CIA as a secret paramilitary wing to augment its overwhelming economic "soft power." The CIA proved a lasting source of rancor and anti–American grievance. Vice President Richard Nixon's 1958 reception in his Latin American tour represented the depths of popular ire. In Perú and Venezuela in particular, Nixon met with scorn and popular fury.[51] The conclusion of the South American tour in Venezuela was an infamous fiasco: spat upon by angry *peruanos* and *venezolanos*, assaulted by anti–American mobs in Caracas just five months after dictator Marcos Pérez Jiménez and his chief of police fled to exile in the United States, and four years after the CIA's overthrow of Arbenz. Cuban rebels, organizing against the U.S.-backed dictatorship of Fulgencio Batista, who had seized power in a 10 March 1952 putsch, took note of the CIA's Guatemalan "success" too.

A clear implication to ambitious revolutionaries like Fidel Castro and his Argentine friend Ernesto "Ché" Guevara, who had fled Guatemala during the coup against Arbenz, was that the United States would respond negatively to reforms harmful to economic and broadly construed strategic interests. Any future revolutionary solution to social problems in the region would have to defend land reforms or other wealth-redistribution programs from the United States, according to this nationalist viewpoint. The lesson proved instructive in the case of Cuba's revolutionary movement. It is impossible to extricate the history of the CIA from other manifestations of hegemonic U.S. "soft power" and "hard power" in dependent relationships with pre-revolutionary Cuba.

The island gained putative independence on 20 May 1902, at the end of an 1899–1902 U.S. occupation after the 1898 war with Spain but with Cuba's exercise of sovereignty subject to U.S. veto on foreign relations and debt policy through the Platt Amendment. The United States required adoption of this rider to the Army Appropriation bill without modification into the Cuban Constitution. If not, the occupation would continue. Stipulations included authorization for the United States to intervene in certain circumstances. After bitter debate, Cuban legislators adopted it by a 16 to 11 vote with four abstentions.

Before departure back to the United States, the military governor, General Leonard Wood, candidly wrote Theodore Roosevelt: "There is, of course, little or no independence left Cuba under the Platt Amendment."[52] Cuba became beholden to the economic and political power of the United States throughout the first half-century of national "independence."

By the late 1940s, North American capital controlled 40 percent of the Cuban sugar industry, fully 90 percent of telephone and electric utilities, 50 percent of railways and 23 percent of non-sugar industries.[53] U.S. hegemony seemed assured, and when strongman Batista seized power in 1952, State Department officials extended recognition because he had been previously amenable to North American prerogatives. Many were not happy to see an undemocratic transition, but stability trumped those considerations. Therein lies one of the main props of U.S. exceptionalism, and one that opponents of the CIA often must argue against: the deep-seated belief that the United States means well, and if it errs, it represents an aberration, a mistake, but not an intention. The unfortunate fact of the matter is that many top-level U.S. policy makers typically view the society in question, whether Nicaragua from the 1930s through the mid–1970s, or Cuba or Guatemala in the 1950s with indifference or even disdain.

U.S. military, diplomatic, and economic support for Batista continued, and came to include the input of the recently founded CIA. The "Great White Case Officer" Allen Dulles, who had urged since 1953 that "the CIA must reach into every corner of the world" with stations in every U.S. diplomatic post, assisted Batista in setting up a new secret police, the BRAC, *Buró de Represión de las Actividades Comunistas*, whose badge would include the "all seeing eye" first used by the original private security contractors of the nineteenth-century, the Pinkertons.[54] The Bureau would augment the work of the FBI-assisted SIM military secret police. A net of CIA agents operated under flimsy cover reminiscent of Graham Greene's *Our Man in Havana*, reporting on the activities of the M-26-7 rebel movement, Batista's government and the armed forces, and the Cuban communist party. Some agents, immersed in the 1956–1959 guerrilla war, and fully cognizant of the Batista regime's brutality and declining repute among the civil population, became sympathizers of M-26-7. There is evidence that the Agency began to hedge its bets and offer support to both sides as Batista's crisis worsened, and the M-26-7 gained strength. Indeed, strongly pro–Batista U.S. Ambassador Early E.T. Smith thought that CIA Station Chief William Caldwell secretly supported Fidel Castro.[55]

Throughout the Cuban Revolution the United States openly backed Batista until the odious criminality of the regime could no longer be plausibly defended. An arms embargo cut off U.S.-supplied armaments in 1958. The CIA at the time never offered an intelligence analysis that demonstrated Fidel Castro was a Marxist-Leninist, but U.S. opposition remained firmly implacable because of his nationalism. U.S. policy makers struggled to find an alternative between Batista and Castro, and when the increasingly despotic Batista finally fled the country on 1 January 1959, they faced the one grim alternative that they had refused to contemplate: the victory of a rebel movement led by a popular and charismatic leader, described later that same year in a National Intelligence Estimate as appearing "inspired by a messianic sense of mission to aid his people."[56]

Castro moved against the internal mechanisms of U.S. control in Cuba. When the revolutionary regime presided over a series of show trials and executions of former Batista supporters, the United States complained on human rights grounds.[57] In televised addresses, Castro responded that Batista's henchmen had conducted many atrocities, and complained of U.S. hypocrisy and double standards given the period of past support, which included 28 military advisors with the pre-revolutionary army. Castro's revolutionary government expropriated and nationalized American-owned properties. A series of tit for tat reprisals led to a lasting Cuban-U.S. rift. The United States could not respond favorably to the seizure of North American assets and refused compensation as inadequate. When U.S. citizens complained about Cuban revolutionaries targeting their holdings, Cubans defended such actions with vituperative anti–American rhetoric. Ché Guevara and others frequently responded: "This is not Guatemala."[58]

Eventually, amid much recrimination, U.S. and Cuban policy makers severed relations. The stage was shortly set for the April 1961 Bay of Pigs invasion — one of the biggest debacles in the CIA's history — perhaps the defining fiasco that set the problems of covert operations in starkest relief. U.S. responses to the "perfect failure" ushered in an unusual, but not entirely unpredictable, turn of events that led to the brink of nuclear war between the U.S. and Soviets in October 1962. Lasting damage and enduring enmity resulted — half a century of no official relations and economic embargo — between the United States and a defiant revolutionary Cuban state. The CIA's attempt to depose or assassinate revolutionary leaders brought about a worst-case scenario for U.S. strategists and policymakers: from 1961 to 1991 Cuba as an avowedly communist regime that hewed to the Soviet orbit.

The Bay of Pigs — Operation Mongoose — The October 1962 Cuban Missile Crisis

By November 1959 President Dwight Eisenhower, amid imputations of Castro's madness in his pugnacious conflict with American leaders, directed the CIA to support anti–Castro groups. By March 1960, after trade agreements between Cuba and the USSR, Eisenhower directed the CIA to train a brigade of Cuban exiles for a PBSUCCESS-style invasion, while the CIA began covert sabotage and other provocations.[59] On 4 March 1960, a French cargo ship *La Coubre* carrying a large shipment of Belgian munitions destined for the Revolutionary Armed Forces (FAR) exploded in Havana harbor during unloading, killing between 75 and 100 Cubans and six crew members.[60] For *habaneros,* the implications resembled the popular outrage of North Americans after the USS Maine blew up in the same harbor in 1898. Accusations of deliberate sabotage leveled at the CIA, however, appeared to have greater weight than the earlier tragedy: The ship made port in the United States after U.S. diplomats blocked any European nation from supplying armaments to revolutionary Cuba. Ongoing sabotage and acts of terrorism by counter-revolutionaries and the CIA lent additional context that the explosion of *La Coubre* was by design.

The United States prepared to replicate PBSUCCESS in Cuba using the CIA as a clandestine branch or adjunct to the military. The CIA's paramilitary operations allowed the Executive branch the ability to carry out "plausibly deniable" covert operations skirting international law and Constitutional procedure. It did not fool people in the target nation. Castro moved to defend his regime, informed by the example of Guatemala. Many Cubans responded to his summons, motivated by nationalism and disdain for CIA dirty tricks.

A revealing 24 November 1959 British memo from Ambassador Sir H. Caccia to Foreign Secretary recorded a conversation of the Ambassador with CIA Director Dulles. Declassified in early 2001, on the 40-h anniversary of the 17–19 April 1961, Bay of Pigs invasion — the climax of CIA attempts at Cuban "regime change"— the memo offers a view of the CIA's machinations and use of PBSUCCESS as something of a template. In late 1959, the Cuban revolutionary government requested delivery of weapons purchased previously by Batista. Initially, before the turn toward the Soviets for arms, the revolutionary state sought weapons from Europe, and as the successor government, would take delivery of equipment bought by the previous regime, such as a shipment of propeller-driven Hawker Sea Fury fighter aircraft from Britain. Cuban officials asked for the planes to be upgraded to Hawker Hunter jets. Although a relatively straightforward request, the British consulted with their U.S. ally, mindful of the Cuban-U.S. friction and growing U.S. hostility at Cuban defiance and policies viewed as provocations.

In the memo, Allen Dulles urged the British not to go through with it. He was quoted as hoping that refusal "might lead the Cubans to ask for Soviet or Soviet bloc arms" and the British ambassador wrote "it was, of course, a fact that in the case of Guatemala," i.e., the overthrow of Jacobo Arbenz in 1954 Operation PBSUCCESS, "it had been a shipment of Soviet arms that had brought the opposition elements together and created the occasion for what was done." Dulles also mentioned "that there was, of course, always the chance that Castro would get shot."[61]

So CIA director Dulles, thinking of assassination months before any known plot — and there would be many — expressed the wish that the Cuban government would acquire Soviet weapons, because this would replicate the necessary pretext to legitimate U.S. aggressive action, or in the antiseptic language of the British document, create "the occasion for what was done" in Guatemala. In a historical irony, a similar but much more recent 23 July 2002 approach to finding appropriate pretexts to foregone policy decisions arose with the 2005 release of the "Downing Street Memo" that revealed the Bush administration set on invading Iraq without UN authorization eight months before in a course of aggressive action that would be "justified by the conjunction of terrorism and WMD" with "intelligence and facts ... being fixed around the policy."[62] It might be tempting to think of this rather Machiavellian document as betraying a high level of cynicism, but the defeat of the CIA's invasion force, made up of Cuban counterrevolutionaries led to President John F. Kennedy and his brother Robert embarking on new schemes to overthrow Castro and the revolution with an elevated sense of urgency. Witnesses to some of the high-level White House meetings after the Bay of Pigs defeat described the atmosphere as "almost savage." In the words of CIA executive officer Sam Halpern of one such meeting: "And when I asked Dick [Richard Helms, CIA director after Dulles was fired] what does 'Get rid of [Castro]' mean, he said, 'Sam, use your imagination.' That was it.... You haven't lived until you've had Bobby Kennedy rampant on your back."[63]

The defeat of the CIA invasion force prompted a decision to engage in economic warfare, sabotage, and what would be considered state-sponsored terrorism today: Operation Mongoose. In the midst of Mongoose, the United States military establishment prepared incredible — even outlandish — pretexts that might possibly justify direct use of U.S. force to overthrow the Castro regime, and by the autumn of that year prepared OPLAN 314–61, a nearly complete invasion template.[64] These provocations did not occur. There was no Cuban analog to the Gulf of Tonkin incident prior to U.S. escalation in Vietnam. Nonetheless, the level of cynical cloak and dagger operations and CIA and other agencies' pursuit of presidential policies should give American citizens pause. A declassified 12 March 1962 program, "Operation Northwoods," included wild pretexts of manufacturing a "Remember the Maine incident" blowing up a ship at Guantánamo, or development of an ostensibly communist terror campaign in Miami or Washington, disguising aircraft as Cuban MiGs, and so on, all so the United States might use its overwhelming military might against a small neighboring nation that while constituting a source of vexation had neither attacked nor threatened the United States.[65]

Small wonder that such U.S. behavior pushed the Castro brothers, Fidel and Raúl, closer to the Soviets. During the run-up to the Bay of Pigs invasion, the day after CIA bombers made preparatory air strikes, Castro thundered the revolution's goals were explicitly socialist, and would be pursued "under the very noses of the Yankees." Largely unknown to North Americans (and certainly Cubans), U.S. diplomats rebuffed exploration of some kind of rapprochement or modus vivendi. Such furtive back-channel discussions included the possibility of a Cuban version of small-power relationship to a superpower neighbor reminiscent of Finland's cool but correct relationship with the USSR (one of the only nations arrayed against the Soviet Union in World War II not subsequently incorporated as a buffer-state with a client regime installed). It was not to be.

Cuban defiance of the United States fed American ambitions to bring about the revolution's downfall. The efforts of the CIA and high-level planning for overt intervention in turn convinced the Cuban revolutionary leaders to align even more solidly with the USSR, the United States' superpower rival. The escalation resulted in the October 1962 Missile Crisis, which profoundly shocked North Americans.[66] Ever after, U.S. citizens, who often cannot (or perhaps refuse to) draw the thread of causation linking the Bay of Pigs to Mongoose and thence to the 1962 Missile Crisis, have viewed their nation as victim of outrageous and reckless Cuban and Soviet behavior. As Louis A. Pérez wrote, explication of U.S. policy toward Castro and Cuba lies "within the realm of trauma."[67] The Missile Crisis very nearly led to direct superpower confrontation. The experience presented the United States as victim of Soviet and Cuban threat, and remained seared into the memories of a generation. It completely personalized responses to Cuba in the person of Fidel Castro. Any and all discussion of Cuba — an island nation of 11½ million inhabitants, with a further 1½ million to 2 million in a diaspora, principally in the United States inevitably arouses the figure of Castro as bogeyman, even after ten U.S. presidencies and several years into his dotage. That the actions of the CIA at the Bay of Pigs and after led to the very outcomes such intervention sought to prevent — a base for a hostile superpower within the Western Hemisphere — elicits no introspection, merely an enduring enmity against an island that defied the United States.

Rarely has there been a clearer case of Chalmers Johnson's "blowback" than the ramifications of the CIA's biggest debacle: the April 1961 Bay of Pigs led directly to the October 1962 Missile Crisis. Perhaps only recent scandals have eclipsed it: CIA failure to prevent "another Pearl Harbor" on 11 September 2001 — when missed intelligence about Al-Qaeda plots did not alert security about the prospect of suicide hijackers — further compounded by a compliant willingness to "stove-pipe" cherry-picked intelligence that suited White House fixations in what the Downing Street Memo described as "intelligence and facts ... being fixed around the policy" to propel the United States into war with Iraq.

Conclusion

In rekindling anti–CIA campus activism in post–PATRIOT Act America amid the ongoing wars of occupation and proliferating terrorist threats, perhaps one last aspect of the tragedy of the CIA's role in Cold War Latin America might be germane to the contemporary scandals of continued CIA illegality, torture, and impunity in pursuit of untrammeled presidential policy in the name of national security. Simply, permanent war will not result in peace. Political solutions remain paramount. No amount of maladroit U.S. covert action will redeem the underlying environmental and political challenges the present generation faces.

At the time of writing, a Cuban-exile terrorist Luis Posada Carriles trained by the CIA belatedly went on trial in El Paso. Accused of blowing up a Cubana airlines passenger jet over the Caribbean in 1976, killing all 73 passengers and crew aboard — the worst act of air terrorism in the hemisphere prior to September 11, 2001— and of planting bombs in Havana hotels during the late 1990s, Posada served as a covert operative in El Salvador during the 1980s. Imprisoned in 2000 in Panama for plotting Castro's assassination during a visit with students, Posada received amnesty from the outgoing president, and illegally entered the United States from a private yacht. His U.S. trial concerns his lying about that entry, and not the violent crimes he is accused of, and for which he received training from the CIA and U.S. Army. He does not face deportation to either Cuba, or Venezuela, where he escaped prison in 1985. The rationalization proffered included statements that should he be sent to Venezuela, he might face torture. Given the ongoing extraordinary renditions of prisoners to allied nations precisely to suffer torture, U.S. double-standards would seem to be utterly hypocritical.

Cold War–era professor of political science, Cole Blasier, founder of the Latin American Studies program at the University of Pittsburgh — began his career in the 1950s as a foreign service official in Eastern and Central Europe, as well as Moscow. By the 1960s, he worked as an academic, and visited Colombia at the behest of the Rockefeller Foundation, placing him in a unique position to comment on Soviet Latin American policy, and Latin American attitudes toward the United States' super-power rival. His complex book explained that vis-à-vis revolutionary change in Latin America, the United States historically exerted a mildly to vehemently counterrevolutionary role —

always hostile to disruptions of the status quo.[68] In *The Giant's Rival: The USSR and Latin America* he offered the following claim about the power of communist ideology among Latin Americans in 1983, at a time when the Cold War was being fought as a brutal hot war throughout Central America:

> Most Latin Americans concluded the local Communists were more consistently loyal to the interests of Moscow than to those of the nation ... the Soviet model as a whole rarely dominates, and it is attractive only to a very few. A non–Soviet position, however, is not necessarily accompanied by any enthusiasm for U.S. institutions or policies. Certainly the incessant anti–American propaganda in the region has taken its toll. But U.S. behavior in the area — postwar interventions in Guatemala, Cuba, and the Dominican Republic, interference in Chile, clumsy maneuvering in Central America in the 1980s — has probably done the American image far more harm than the USSR ever could: the Soviet apparatus is experienced in capitalizing on these errors.[69]

Substitute the appeal, or lack thereof, of extreme Islamist ideology — today's "evil doers" — free of U.S. hegemony, authoritarianism in the Middle East, and the ongoing Israeli rejection of Palestinian claims, in short, an underlying lack of justice, and one might agree that the historical parallels are unsettling. The wars of occupation in Iraq and Afghanistan, the attempts at nation building using the Pentagon system as a tremendous engine of social reengineering — for which it is eminently unsuited — and the constant attempts to bolster the hegemony of the United States using the CIA when overt power cannot wielded, are leading to financial insolvency and provoking resistance to maladroit imperial missteps. The shameful record of the CIA in Latin America should be widely known, and it must surely militate against maintaining such an agency that has abetted and perpetrated such a lengthy list of duplicitous, cynical, vile, criminal, and murderous acts.

NOTES

1. Noam Chomsky, *Hopes and Prospects* (Chicago: Haymarket, 2010), 268. See also "The Torture Memos and Historical Amnesia," *The Nation* (1 June 2009), http://www.thenation.com/article/torture-memos-and-historical-amnesia.

2. William Blum, *Killing Hope: U.S. Military and CIA Interventions Since World War II* (Monroe, ME: Common Courage, 1995).

3. So-called "no touch torture" emphasizing psychological techniques such as isolation, sensory and sleep deprivation, "stress positions," and drowning or so-called "water boarding" — about which, more later — for example, relied on past CIA collaboration with academics and participation in Cold War–era counterinsurgencies. See Jennifer Harbury, *Truth, Torture, and the American Way* (Boston: Beacon, 2005); Alfred W. McCoy, *A Question of Torture: CIA Interrogation from the Cold War to the War on Terror* (New York: Metropolitan, 2006); Stephen Soldz, "CYA at the CIA," Z Net (Monday, 7 June 2010) http://www.zcommunications.org/cya-for-the-cia-by-stephen-soldz.

4. Ariel Dorfman, Pilar Aguilera, Ricardo Fredes, eds., *Chile: The Other September 11* (Melbourne: Ocean, 2002). For differing recent interpretations of the U.S. role in the 1973 coup see Jonathan Haslam, *The Nixon Administration and the Death of Allende's Chile: A Case of Assisted Suicide* (London: Verso, 2005) and Peter Kornbluh, *The Pinochet File: A Declassified Dossier on*

Atrocity and Accountability (New York: New, 2003). On the Pinochet regime's international reach and state terrorism connected to it, see John Dinges, *The Condor Years: How Pinochet and His Allies Brought Terrorism to Three Continents* (New York: New, 2004) and http://www.John Dinges.com/Condor; J. Patrice McSherry, *Predatory States: Operation Condor and Covert War in Latin America* (Lanham, MD: Rowman and Littlefield, 2005).

    5. Cited in Grandin, *Empire's Workshop* (New York: Owl, 2006), 1.

    6. Oscar Guardiola-Rivera, *What if Latin America Ruled the World? How the South Will Take the North through the 21st Century* (New York: Bloomsbury, 2010).

    7. "An Interview with Producer Ofra Bikel," PBS *Frontline*, available online at http://www. pbs.org/wgbh/pages/frontline/hugochavez/etc/bikel/.html.

    8. Ibid.

    9. For a decadent Pax Americana as Imperial Rome historical analogy with the Rio Grande as the Rhine, see Caleb Carr, "Storm Warning," *Lapham's Quarterly* States of War (Winter 2008), http://www.laphamsquarterly.org/essays/storm-warning.php.

    10. There is much literature about the abortive 2002 golpe de estado in Venezuela, but for a Chavista perspective, see Eva Golinger, "The Proof is in the Documents: The CIA was Involved in the April 12 Coup d'état Against Venezuelan President Chávez," V Headline (17 June 2004) www.vheadline.com/readnews.asp?id=37984, and "Colored Revolutions: A New Form of Regime Change, Made in U.S.A.," Postcards from the Revolution (15 February 2010) www.venezuelanalysis.com/pring/5139.

    11. Church Committee Assassination Report, *Alleged Assassination Plots Involving Foreign Leaders*, 94th Congress, 1st Session, Senate Report No. 94–465 (Washington, D.C.: GPO, 1975).

    12. Andrew Bacevich, *Washington Rules: America's Path to Permanent War* (New York: Metropolitan, 2010) deftly contrasts the CIA under Allen Dulles, director from 1953 to 1961 and Strategic Air Command (SAC) under Curtis LeMay from 1948 to 1957 as two sides of U.S. power: the former by "guile and trickery" the latter by "brute force."

    13. Quoted in Morris Berman, *Dark Ages America: The Final Phase of Empire* (New York: W.W. Norton, 2006), 299.

    14. John D. French, "Beyond Words, without Words, and Finding Words: Responding to the Catastrophe," in Timothy W. Crusius and Carolyn Channell, eds., *The Aims of Argument: A Text and Reader,* 4th ed. (Boston: McGraw Hill, 2004), 429–30.

    15. French, 430.

    16. David N. Gibbs, "The CIA Is Back on Campus: Spying Secrecy and the University," *CounterPunch* (7 April 2003); Michael Gould-Wartofsky, "Repress U: How to Build a Homeland Security Campus in Seven Steps," *CounterPunch* (10 January 2008); David Price, "Silent Coup: How the CIA is Welcoming Itself Back Onto American University Campuses," *CounterPunch* (9–11 April 2010); "The CIA's Campus Spies: Exposing the Pat Roberts Intelligence Scholars Program," *CounterPunch* (12–13 March 2005). On "permanent war" see Chris Hedges, *Death of the Liberal Class* (New York: Nation, 2010), chapter 2; Bacevich.

    17. Kim Scipes, *AFL-CIO's Secret War Against Developing Country Workers: Solidarity or Sabotage?* (Lanham, MD: Lexington, 2010), 87–88.

    18. Hedges, 19.

    19. Noam Chomsky, "Selective Memory and False Doctrine," Z Magazine (21 December 2003) http://www.zcommunications.org/selective-memory-and-false-doctrine-by-noam-chomsky.

    20. On PBSUCCESS see Blum, 72–82; Nick Cullather, *Secret History: The CIA's Classified Account of its Operations in Guatemala, 1952–1954* (Stanford: Stanford University Press, 1999); Piero Gleijeses, *Shattered Hope: The Guatemalan Revolution and the United States, 1944–1954* (Princeton: Princeton University Press, 1991); Greg Grandin, *The Last Colonial Massacre: Latin America in the Cold War* (Chicago: University of Chicago Press, 2004), 66–67, 76–78, 82–86; Richard H. Immerman, *The CIA in Guatemala: The Foreign Policy of Intervention* (Austin: University of Texas Press, 1982).

    21. Immerman, 197.

    22. American Civil Liberties Union, "Fact Sheet: Extraordinary Rendition," http://www. aclu.org/national-security/fact-sheet-extraordinary-rendition; Chomsky, *Hopes and Prospects*;

Dinges; Stephen Grey, *Ghost Plane: The True Story of the CIA Rendition and Torture Program* (New York: St. Martin's, 2007); Harbury.

23. ACLU, "Fact Sheet."

24. A.J. Langguth, *Hidden Terrors: The Truth About U.S. Police Operations in Latin America* (New York: Pantheon, 1978). See also, Dinges; Michael McClintock, *Instruments of Statecraft* (New York: Pantheon, 1990); McSherry.

25. See Blum; Dinges; KateDoyle, "The Atrocity Files: Deciphering the Archives of Guatemala's Dirty War," *Harper's* (December 2007) http:www.harpers.org/archive/2007/12/0081831; Grandin, *The Last Colonial Massacre;* Langguth; LeoGrande; Michael McClintock, *The American Connection,* 2 vols.: *El Salvador and Guatemala* (London: Zed, 1985), McClintock, *Instruments of Statecraft;* Allan Nairn, "Behind the Death Squads: An Exclusive Report on the U.S. Role in El Salvador's Official Terror," *The Progressive* (May 1984).

26. See, for example, Harbury; Michael McClintock, *Instruments of Statecraft;* for a longer history of political violence in Central America, and the beginning of U.S. military missions, see Robert Holden, *Armies Without Nations: Public Violence and State Formation in Central America, 1821–1960* (Oxford: Oxford University Press, 2004).

27. On the post–Cuban Revolution U.S. Alliance for Progress program, see Stephen G. Rabe, *The Most Dangerous Area in the World: John F. Kennedy Confronts Communist Revolution in Latin America* (Chapel Hill: University of North Carolina Press, 1999).

28. Marie-Monique Robin, *Escuadrones de la muerte: La escuela francesa* (Buenos Aires: Sudamericana, 2005).

29. Harbury, 46; Nairn, "Behind the Death Squads," *The Progressive* (May 1984). On explicit comparisons of Salvadoran COIN with the CORDS program and Operation Phoenix in Vietnam, see McClintock, *The American Connection,* vol. 1: *El Salvador,* 322–325.

30. Harbury, 52.

31. McSherry, 241.

32. McSherry, 241–42.

33. McSherry, 247.

34. McCoy, *A Question of Torture.*

35. For example, Servicio Paz y Justicia Uruguay, *Uruguay Nunca Más: Human Rights Violations, 1972–1985* trans. Elizabeth Hampsten (Philadelphia: Temple, 1992), which includes a list of torture methods.

36. Katherine Eban, "Rorschach and Awe," *Vanity Fair* (17 July 2007) http://www.vanityfair.com/politics/features/2007/07/torture200707?printable=true&currentPage=all; Soldz.

37. Harbury, 103.

38. Joshua E.S. Phillips, *None of Us Were Like This Before: American Soldiers and Torture* (New York: Verso, 2010).

39. Alistair Horne, "My History Lesson in the Oval Office," *The Telegraph* (15 July 2007) http://www.telegraph.co.uk/comment/personal-view/3641318/My-history-lesson-in-the-Oval-Office.html.

40. Ibid.

41. Chalmers Johnson, *Blowback: Costs and Consequences of American Empire* (New York: Holt, 2004); *The Sorrows of Empire: Militarism, Secrecy, and the End of the Republic* (New York: Metropolitan, 2004); *Nemesis: The Last Days of the American Republic* (New York: Metropolitan, 2007).

42. Bacevich, 55, 57.

43. Bacevich, 56.

44. The Central Intelligence Agency, "About CIA," https://www.cia.gov/about-cia/index.html.

45. Blum, 71.

46. On Guatemala, 1954, see Blum, Chapter 10; the CIA's own history of PBSUCCESS, Cullather; Gleijeses, *Shattered Hope*; Grandin, *The Last Colonial Massacre,* 52, 66–67 and 76–78; Harbury, 33–35; Immerman.

47. Blum, 74; Harbury, 33.

48. Blum, 75.

49. Gleijeses, *Shattered Hope*, 7.

50. Grandin, *Last Colonial Massacre*, 3; Harbury, 35. See also Piero Gleijeses "Afterword: The Culture of Fear" in Cullather, pp. xix–xxxii.

51. On the Nixon trip, see Alan L. McPherson, *Yankee No! Anti-Americanism in U.S.-Latin American Relations* (Cambridge, MA: Harvard University Press, 2003), "Nixon Must Get Stoned" and Peter H. Smith, *Talons of the Eagle: Latin America, the United States, and the World 3rd edition* (Oxford: Oxford University Press, 2008), 128–131, 152.

52. Lars Schoultz, *That Infernal Little Cuban Republic: The United States and the Cuban Revolution* (Chapel Hill: University of North Carolina Press, 2010), 24.

53. Julia Sweig, *Cuba: What Everyone Should Know* (Oxford: Oxford University Press, 2009), 19.

54. Bacevich, 38; Thomas G. Paterson, *Contesting Castro: The United States and the Triumph of the Castro Revolution* (Oxford: Oxford University Press, 1994), 63–65.

55. Paterson, 105.

56. Piero Gleijeses, *Conflicting Missions: Havana, Washington, and Africa, 1959–1976* (Chapel Hill: University of North Carolina Press, 2003), 366.

57. Paterson, 255; Schoultz, 87–88; Sweig, 39–40.

58. Paterson, 242.

59. Paterson, 258; Schoultz 114–117.

60. Keith Bolender, *Voices from the Other Side: An Oral History of Terrorism Against Cuba* (London: Pluto, 2010), chapter 10; Schoultz, 115.

61. Document No. 6: Ciphered Telegram from British Ambassador in Washington to British Foreign Secretary Selwyn Lloyd Regarding Conversation with Allen Dulles on Cuba, November 24, 1959. *Girón 40 años después/ Bay of Pigs 40 Years After*, Briefing Book of International Documentation from Brazilian, British, Canadian, Czech and Russian Archives for an international conference Havana, Cuba — March 22–24, 2001. Full collection housed at the National Security Archive, Gelman Library at the George Washington University, Washington, D.C. See also Schoultz, 116.

62. Mark Danner, *The Secret Way to War: The Downing Street Memo and the Iraq War's Buried History* (New York: NYRB, 2006).

63. Quoted in PBS, *The American Experience: RFK,* online at "Get Rid of Castro," http://www.pbs.org/wgbh/amex/rfk/peopleevents/e_mongoose.html.

64. Bacevich, 84–5.

65. Chairman, Joint Chiefs of Staff, "Justification for U.S. Military Intervention in Cuba" (includes cover memoranda, March 13, 1962) available online at http://www.gwu.edu/~nsarchiv/news/20010430/docl.pdf>.

66. Louis A. Pérez, Jr., "Fear and Loathing of Fidel Castro: Sources of U.S. Policy Toward Cuba" *JLAS* 34, no. 2 (May 2002): 227–254.

67. Ibid.

68. Cole Blasier, *The Hovering Giant: U.S. Responses to Revolutionary Change in Latin America* (Pittsburgh: University of Pittsburgh Press, 1976) and *The Giant's Rival: The USSR and Latin America* (Pittsburgh: University of Pittsburgh Press,1983).

69. Blasier, *The Giant's Rival*, 14–15.

Works Cited

American Civil Liberties Union. "Fact Sheet: Extraordinary Rendition." http://www.aclu.org/national-security/fact-sheet-extraordinary-rendition.

Armony, Ariel C. *Argentina, The United States, and the Anti-Communist Crusade in Central America, 1977–1984.* Athens: Ohio University Press, 1997.

Armstrong, Fulton, and Thomas Powers. "The CIA and WMDs: The Damning Evidence." *The New York Review of Books* LVII, no. 13 (19 August 2010): 53–4.

Bacevich, Andrew J. *Washington Rules: America's Path to Permanent War.* New York: Metropolitan, 2010.

Bamford, James. *Body of Secrets: Anatomy of the Ultra-Secret National Security Agency from the Cold War Through the Dawn of a New Century.* New York: Doubleday, 2001.

Berman, Morris. *Dark Ages America: The Final Phase of Empire.* New York: W.W. Norton, 2006.

Blasier, Cole. *The Giant's Rival: The USSR and Latin America.* Pittsburgh: Pittsburgh University Press, 1983.

_____. *The Hovering Giant: U.S. Responses to Revolutionary Change in Latin America.* Pittsburgh: Pittsburgh University Press, 1976.

Blum, William. *Killing Hope: U.S. Military and CIA Interventions Since World War II.* Monroe, ME: Common Courage, 1995.

Bolender, Keith. *Voices from the Other Side: An Oral History of Terrorism Against Cuba.* London: Pluto, 2010.

Brown, Jonathan. "Contrarevolución en el Caribe: La CIA y los paramilitares cubanos en los 60." *Temas* Havana 55 (July–September 2008): 57–72.

Carr, Caleb. "Storm Warning." *Lapham's Quarterly* States of War (Winter 2008), http://www.laphamsquarterly.org/essays/storm-warning.php.

Chomsky, Noam. *Hopes and Prospects.* Chicago: Haymarket, 2010.

_____. "The Torture Memos and Historical Amnesia." *The Nation* (1 June 2009), http://www.thenation.com/article/torture-memos-and-historical-amnesia.

Church Committee Assassination Report. *Alleged Assassination Plots Involving Foreign Leaders.* 94th Congress, 1st Session, Senate Report No. 94–465. Washington, D.C.: GPO, 1975.

Cockburn, Alexander, and Jeffrey St. Clair. *Whiteout: The CIA, Drugs and the Press.* New York: Verso, 1998.

Cullather, Nick. *Secret History: The CIA's Classified Account of its Operations in Guatemala, 1952–1954.* Stanford: Stanford University Press, 1999.

Danner, Mark. *The Secret Way to War: The Downing Street Memo and the Iraq War's Buried History.* New York: NYRB, 2006.

Dinges, John. *The Condor Years: How Pinochet and His Allies Brought Terrorism to Three Continents.* New York: New, 2004.

Dorfman, Ariel, Pilar Aguilera, and Ricardo Fredes, eds. *Chile: The Other September 11.* Melbourne: Ocean, 2002.

Doyle, Kate. "The Atrocity Files: Deciphering the Archives of Guatemala's Dirty War." *Harper's* (December 2007), http://www.harpers.org/archive/2007/12/0081831.

Eban, Katherine. "Rorschach and Awe." *Vanity Fair* (17 July 2007), http://www.vanityfair.com/politics/features/2007/07/torture200707?printable=true&currentPage=all.

Feldman, Jonathan. *Universities in the Business of Repression: The Academic-Military-Industrial Complex in Central America.* Boston: South End, 1989.

Fletcher, Laurel E., and Eric Stover. *The Guantánamo Effect: Exposing the Consequences of U.S. Detention and Interrogation Practices.* Berkeley: University of California Press, 2009.

French, John D. "Beyond Words, without Words, and Finding Words: Responding to the Catastrophe." In Timothy W. Crusius and Carolyn Channell, eds., *The Aims of Argument: A Text and Reader,* 4th ed. Boston: McGraw Hill, 2004.

Gibbs, David N. "The CIA Is Back on Campus: Spying, Secrecy and the University." *CounterPunch* (7 April 2003).

Gleijeses, Piero. *Conflicting Missions: Havana, Washington, and Africa, 1959–1976.* Chapel Hill: University of North Carolina Press, 2002.

_____. *Shattered Hope: The Guatemalan Revolution and the United States, 1944–1954.* Princeton: Princeton University Press, 1991.

_____. "Ships in the Night: The CIA, the White House and the Bay of Pigs." *JLAS* 27, no.1 (February 1995): 1–42.

Golinger, Eva. "Colored Revolutions: A New Form of Regime Change, Made in U.S.A." Postcards from the Revolution (15 February 2010), www.venezuelanalysis.com/pring/5139.

_____. "The Proof is in the Documents: The CIA Was Involved in the April 12 Coup d'état

Against Venezuelan President Chávez." V Headline (17 June 2004), www.vheadline.com/readnews.asp?id=37984.

Grandin, Greg. *Empire's Workshop: Latin America, the United States, and the Rise of the New Imperialism*. New York: Owl, 2006.

_____. "It Was Heaven That They Burned." *The Nation* (27 September 2010), http://www.thenation.com/article/154582/it-was-heaven-they-burned.

_____. *The Last Colonial Massacre: Latin America in the Cold War*. Chicago: University of Chicago Press, 2004.

Grey, Stephen. *Ghost Plane: The True Story of the CIA Rendition and Torture Program*. New York: St. Martin's, 2007.

Guardiola-Rivera, Oscar. *What if Latin America Ruled the World?* New York: Bloomsbury, 2010.

Harbury, Jennifer K. *Truth, Torture, and the American Way: The History and Consequences of U.S. Involvement in Torture*. Boston: Beacon, 2005.

Haslam, Jonathan. *The Nixon Administration and the Death of Allende's Chile*. London: Verso, 2005.

Hedges, Chris. *Death of the Liberal Class*. New York: Nation, 2010.

Holden, Robert H. *Armies Without Nations: Public Violence and State Formation in Central America, 1821–1960*. Oxford: Oxford University Press, 2004.

Immerman, Richard H. *The CIA in Guatemala: The Foreign Policy of Intervention*. Austin: University of Texas Press, 1982.

Johnson, Chalmers. *Blowback: The Costs and Consequences of the American Empire*. New York: Holt, 2004.

_____. *Nemesis: The Last Days of the American Republic*. New York: Metropolitan, 2006.

_____. *The Sorrows of Empire: Militarism, Secrecy, and the End of the Republic*. New York: Metropolitan, 2004.

Jones, Howard. *The Bay of Pigs*. Oxford: Oxford University Press, 2008.

Kornbluh, Peter. "Former CIA Asset Luis Posada Goes to Trial." *The Nation* (24 January 2011), http://www.thenation.com/article/157510/former-cia-asset-luis-posada-goes-trial.

_____. *The Pinochet Files: A Declassified Dossier on Atrocity and Accountability*. New York: New, 2003.

_____, ed. *Bay of Pigs Declassified: The Top Secret Report of the CIA Inspector General on the Invasion of Cuba*. New York: New, 1998.

Langguth, A. J. *Hidden Terrors*. New York: Pantheon, 1978.

LeoGrande, William M. *Our Own Backyard: The United States in Central America, 1977–1992*. Chapel Hill: University of North Carolina Press, 1998.

McClintock, Michael. *The American Connection. Volume 1: State Terror and Popular Resistance in El Salvador. Volume 2: State Terror and Popular Resistance in Guatemala*. London: Zed, 1985.

_____. *Instruments of Statecraft: U.S. Guerrilla Warfare, Counter-Insurgency, Counter-Terrorism, 1940–1990*. New York: Pantheon, 1992.

McCoy, Alfred W. *The Politics of Heroin: CIA Complicity in the Global Drug Trade*, 3d ed. Chicago: Lawrence Hill, 2003.

_____. *A Question of Torture: CIA Interrogation, From the Cold War to the War on Terror*. New York: Metropolitan, 2006.

McPherson, Alan L. *Yankee No! Anti-Americanism in U.S.–Latin American Relations*. Cambridge, MA: Harvard University Press, 2003.

McSherry, J. Patrice. *Predatory States: Operation Condor and Covert War in Latin America*. Lanham, MD: Rowman and Littlefield, 2005.

Nairn, Allan. "Behind the Death Squads: An Exclusive Report on the U.S. Role in El Salvador's Official Terror." *The Progressive* (May 1984).

_____. "Confessions of a Death Squad Officer." *The Progressive* (March 1986).

Nocella, Anthony J. II, Steven Best, and Peter McLaren, eds. *Academic Repression: Reflections from the Academic Industrial Complex*. Oakland: AK, 2010.

Paterson, Thomas G. *Contesting Castro: The United States and the Triumph of the Cuban Revolution*. Oxford: Oxford University Press, 1994.

Pérez, Louis A., Jr. *Cuba: Between Reform and Revolution,* 3d ed. Oxford: Oxford University Press, 2006.

_____. "Fear and Loathing of Fidel Castro: Sources of U.S. Policy Toward Cuba." *JLAS* 34 Issue 2 (June 2002): 227–254.

Philips, Joshua E. S. *None of Us Were Like This Before.* New York: Verso, 2010.

Price, David. "Silent Coup: How the CIA is Welcoming Itself Back Onto American University Campuses." *CounterPunch* (9–11 April 2010).

Rabe, Stephen G. *The Most Dangerous Area in the World: John F. Kennedy Confronts Communist Revolution in Latin America.* Chapel Hill: University of North Carolina Press, 1999.

Robin, Marie-Monique. *Escuadrones de la muerte: la escuela francesa.* Buenos Aires: Sudamericana, 2005.

Rodríguez, Juan Carlos. *The Bay of Pigs and the CIA.* Melbourne: Ocean, 1999.

Schou, Nick. *Kill the Messenger: How the CIA's Crack-Cocaine Controversy Destroyed Journalist Gary Webb.* New York: Nation, 2006.

Schoultz, Lars. *That Infernal Little Cuban Republic: The United States and the Cuban Revolution.* Chapel Hill: University of North Carolina, 2009.

Scipes, Kim. *AFL-CIO's Secret War Against Developing Country Workers: Solidarity or Sabotage?* Lanham, MD: Lexington, 2010.

Servicio Paz y Justicia Uruguay. *Uruguay nunca más: Human Rights violations, 1972–1985.* Trans. Elizabeth Hampsten. Philadelphia: Temple University Press, 1992.

Smith, Peter H. *Talons of the Eagle: Latin America, the United States, and the World,* 3d ed. Oxford: Oxford University Press, 2008.

Soldz, Stephen. "CYA for the CIA." *Z Net* (7 June 2010), http://www.zcommunications.org-/cya-for-the-cia-by-stephen-soldz.

Sweig, Julia. *Cuba: What Everyone Should Know.* Oxford: Oxford University Press, 2009.

U.S. Senate. *Allegations of Connections Between CIA and the Contras in Cocaine Trafficking to the United States.* 2 vols. Washington, D.C.: GPO, 1996–1998.

Warner, Michael. "The CIA's Internal Probe of the Bay of Pigs Affair" *Studies in Intelligence* (Winter 1998–1999), https://www.cia.gov/library/center-for-the-study-of-intelligence/kent-csi/vol42no5/pdf/v42i5a08p.pdf.

Weiner, Tim. *Legacy of Ashes: The History of the CIA.* New York: Anchor, 2008.

Weisbrot, Mark. "CIA and Venezuela: CIA Documents Cast New Light on Washington's Role in Venezuela." *Z Net* (12 December 2004) http://www.zcommunications.org/cia-and-venezuela-by-mark-weisbrot.

4

The Spooks in the Stacks:
Academic Libraries and the
National Security State Since 9/11

DEIRDRE MCDONALD

In late 2010, Wikileaks dominated the news. The whistleblower website had just begun to release thousands of classified U.S. diplomatic cables. These leaked documents, published simultaneously by major world newspapers, corroborated previous evidence that the U.S. used its diplomatic corps both to gather intelligence and to act at odds with foreign policy rhetoric emanating from the White House and State Department. The raw and unflattering reports provoked the U.S. government to exert damage control, which included suppression of access to the Wikileaks website. On December 3, the Library of Congress, following a White House Office of Management and Budget directive, banned staff and patron access to Wikileaks.[1] The leading American research library's decision to support government censorship of already widely available documents marked the capstone of a decade-long national security state effort to exert increasingly intrusive control over information retrieval by researchers, students, and the general public in the post–9/11, post–PATRIOT Act United States.

By banning access to Wikileaks sites, the Library of Congress took the political position that it would adhere to government efforts to withhold and censor information needed to understand U.S. policy decisions, a stance in contravention to the Library of Congress' mission and purpose as well as long-standing professional ethics within the field of librarianship. In doing so, it distanced itself from librarians' decade-long struggle to preserve civil liberties and privacy in an increasingly intrusive state. This essay argues that libraries, as the site of an ongoing contest over constitutional and civil rights issues concerning information access, control, and surveillance, challenge the anti-democratic direction that the post–9/11 U.S. government and its national intelligence agencies are taking us. As institutions resistant to the prerogatives of the national security state and, in particular, the encroachment of intelligence agencies such as the CIA into academe and society— the "spooks in the stacks" snooping and eavesdropping with little oversight over the means employed to surveil and invigilate in the name of lofty national security ends — libraries pose a small but real opposition to the complete destruction of civil liberties in twenty-first century America.

Since the beginning of the Cold War, libraries have stood as one of the primary institutional safeguards of civil liberties in the U.S., both a threat and a temptation to the national security apparatus. By providing access to multiple, conflicting viewpoints, libraries ideally function as access points where people can become self-educated and develop nuanced understandings of events, moving beyond the black and white rhetoric of a country at war. In an academic environment, students and faculty use the library to support research in diverse subjects, including those not aligned with existing government policy. These patrons' records, normally protected by library privacy codes and state laws, have the potential to enhance already existing data-mining practices used by national security agencies to track and profile those who question prevailing ideologies or the imperial project of the post–9/11 security state.[2]

Today, librarians find it increasingly difficult to maintain their patrons' privacy, but also vitally important. As the intelligence agencies become more and more entrenched in academia, the ability of students and faculty to explore new, controversial ideas is threatened both overtly, through legal measures like the USA PATRIOT Act, and more subtly, through the inevitable self-censorship that comes about when one knows that one could always be spied upon. While librarians have been at the forefront of the struggle for the right to privacy and the freedom to read in the post–9/11 era, new dangers are evolving with the creation and maintenance of intelligence agency-sponsored programs on university campuses. These programs have contributed to a chilling intellectual climate on campus, and, with the integration of prestigious library schools into the funding mechanisms of the security state, threaten the directions that librarianship will take in the future.

The Development of Libraries as First Amendment Institutions

A hallmark of the national security state is control over information through a combination of overt censorship, disinformation, misinformation, and propaganda. Since the mid-twentieth century, the library has emerged as a site of struggle over information control and access. Even earlier, in the 1930s when concerns about totalitarianism motivated many citizens, libraries started to stake their claim as all–American democratic institutions based on their ability to protect and preserve First Amendment rights. Recent scholarship explains library reaction to specific crises in recent U.S. history — the Depression, World War II, McCarthy-era repression — as progressive moves towards an anti-censorship position, showing that

> each crisis compelled librarians to evolve and question their ethical stance. With each of these moments, this professional group developed new ways to respond to the State's requests for its participation in the collective efforts to root out designated enemies and facilitate the operations of security agencies.[3]

The development of these responses over time, especially during the anti–Communist hysteria of the Cold War, would prepare librarians to fight the twenty-first century attacks on civil liberties in the wake of 9/11.

Earlier public and university libraries did not have universal ethical codes, and operated under the model of helping to shape their patrons' ideas, values, and beliefs through selection of the best possible literature, typically as defined by the librarians themselves. Industrialists like Andrew Carnegie strongly supported their didactic mission as a way to control the militant aspects of the growing labor movement by offering educational opportunities and limited social services. Libraries also provided the space and materials to help new immigrant workers assimilate as part of "Americanization" programs.[4] During World War I, librarians participated in the U.S. government's war effort, providing reading materials for servicemen through the American Library Association's Library War Services Committee.[5] While the decision to provide reading material to servicemen was not in and of itself problematic, the blind patriotism and invocations of national emergency of the day caused librarians to support aspects of Woodrow Wilson's Espionage Act (May 1917), the Alien Act (October 1918) and the Sedition Act (May 1918) that impacted library services. In an early precursor to USA PATRIOT Act provisions, "military intelligence issued an order to remove from libraries any materials on explosives, as well as to report the names of requestors to the Army. Libraries readily complied," even in some extreme cases, burning German-language books.[6]

The Depression, coupled with unfolding events and the rise of fascism in Europe and Asia, saw libraries begin to promote themselves as institutes of civil liberties and democratic values. In an oft-quoted essay, social scientist Bernard Berelson wrote, "Librarianship must stand firmly against social and political and economic censorship of book collections; it must be so organized that it can present effective opposition to this censorship and it must protect librarians who are threatened by it."[7] This article, and the discussions it provoked among librarians, led to the creation of the American Library Association Code of Ethics and Library Bill of Rights, both adopted by the organization in 1939, the first year of World War II.

The 1939 Code of Ethics for Librarians laid the foundation for creating a library community that would fight against censorship and governmental intrusions into personal matters. It was the first official statement from the organization that compelled professional librarians to respect reader privacy above any intrusive pretext. Specifically, it stated in the section "The Relation of the Librarian to His [*sic*] Constituency" that "it is the librarian's obligation to treat as confidential any private information obtained through contact with library patrons."[8] This ethical imperative remains an important precept in librarianship today. Librarians strive to keep information about individual reading habits, internet searches, and reference questions confidential. This allows the patron to feel safe researching controversial subjects or those that fall outside of community or familial norms.

The Code of Ethics provided the librarian the guidance to serve the public; its partner document, the Library Bill of Rights, outlined what the public could expect from their libraries. The first Bill of Rights included the rights to access materials with conflicting points of view, to use the library without being discriminated against, to challenge censorship, and the understanding that the library's role is to provide the space to do this.[9] This document

> marked the entrance of librarians into the political realm. The Bill of Rights was composed of three separate statements that advocated for the selection of books based on their own value and interest to the community, not on criteria of race, nationality or religion. The second recommended that libraries represent all sides of an issue while the last one addressed the issue of racial segregation and declared that in a democratic society, library rooms should be equally opened to all community groups. With this resolution, the American Library Association had turned a page of its history. From a weak professional group concerned about its image and role in the eye of the government in time of crisis, it had become a group mobilized around the defense of ethical values.[10]

By World War II, librarians had begun to internalize their new roles as protectors of civil liberties and democratic values, even in times of war. While the American Library Association's war-time policy statements of 1942 included elements of the patriotic program of World War I, they encouraged a more pedagogical, informational, and inquisitive role for library services:

> Officially or unofficially, every library must become a war information center in which are currently available the latest facts, reports and instructions for public use; The library must supply technical information to industrial defense workers and students; The library must disseminate authentic information and sound teachings in the field of economics, government, history and international relations; The library must make available valid interpretations of current facts and events.[11]

Although libraries in both periods supported the war effort, World War I actions uncritically followed government policy and directives, even when those went against democratic access to information and catered to nationalist xenophobia. By World War II, librarians had initiated an agenda for taking their place as active agents promoting information use as a key to victory against Nazi Germany. At the same time, some of the older patterns of compliance with national security directives also took place. In 1942, the War Department demanded again that libraries remove materials on explosives — considered of value only to saboteurs — as well as those in the growing field of cryptology, and therefore only useful to potential spies. Librarians were also asked to contact the Federal Bureau of Investigation to report those who tried to access such materials. Unfortunately for the emergent civil libertarian librarianship code of ethics, "compliance was common."[12] Then, as now, national security seemingly trumped democratic values.

From the 1930s on, then, librarians intermittently and gradually developed their ethical code. However, librarians' active resistance against government encroachments on the rights of the public to freely access information without fear of reprisal began after World War II. As the Cold War progressed, and with it various "culture wars" internal to American society, libraries began to position themselves as democratic institutions in contrast to those in Communist nations — again, in similar fashion to the anti-totalitarian politics of wartime. But this counter to the perceived dangers of conformity, censorship, and control of speech and thought now often put libraries at odds with the growing anti-communist movement in the Unites States that itself threatened democratic access to information and sought to replace it with propaganda of its liking. The American Library Association took a strong stand against this movement, creating a revised Library Bill of Rights in 1948. This strengthened the idea that libraries were "forums of information and ideas" and stressed that they "should provide materials and information presenting all points of view on current and historical issues" while crucially urging that books "should not be proscribed or removed because of partisan or doctrinal disapproval."[13]

In 1953, the American Library Association and the American Book Publishers' Council issued a joint "Freedom to Read" statement defending readers' rights. It urged publishers and librarians to take responsibility to uphold dissemination of a multiplicity of viewpoints and ideas to the American public. "Freedom to Read" contained seven basic principles that librarians used to defend their collection development choices, including the imperative to "make available the widest diversity of views and expressions" regardless of political climate, to try to avoid use of "their own political, moral, or aesthetic views as a standard for determining what should be published or circulated," to protect the reading public against attempts of censorship both by the community and by the government, and to create a free space for intellectual inquiry "by providing books that enrich the quality and diversity of thought and expression."[14]

Widely read and distributed though publications like the *New York Times*, this statement strongly appealed to many liberals and some conservatives, particularly of the wartime generation, concerned about the direction of public discourse as Senator Joseph McCarthy and his ilk gained power and prestige.[15] In reaction to news reports that overseas American libraries censored and burned politically-oriented books, even President Dwight D. Eisenhower took notice. He alluded to the anti-democratic nature of the incidents in his commencement address at Dartmouth, and followed this up with a letter to the American Library Association in which he stated:

> Libraries of America are and must ever remain the homes of free, inquiring minds. To them, our citizens — of all ages and races, of all creeds and political persuasions — must ever be able to turn with clear confidence that there they can freely seek the whole truth, unwarped by fashion and uncompromised by expediency.[16]

The idea that within the local or academic library one should be able to "freely seek the whole truth" had finally come of age.

Since 1953, the consensus within the profession, namely that the library would provide access to many, varied types of materials so people could form their own conclusions on matters of import, sometimes created conflicts between libraries, citizens groups, and the government. Some such conflicts resulted in compromises; for example, although many public libraries kept sexually explicit or otherwise sensitive materials — even certain political tracts subject to defacement, theft, or impromptu censorship by community residents — behind the desk or in closed stacks, patrons could still request access to them. Academic libraries, serving adult learners and faculty almost exclusively, operated with less concern about the corruption of the morals or values of patrons. The adoption of this anti-censorship ethos evidenced itself in a 1953 *New York Times* poll that asked academic and public librarians about patron access to communist texts such as the works of Karl Marx and similar materials. In a survey of 30 cities, *The Times* found that only a small segment of religious colleges and universities either banned outright, or limited access to, writers such as Marx. Columbia University's library director stated succinctly, "Our job as a research library ... is to support objective research and instruction. To that end, materials are made freely available to students."[17] Public and academic libraries largely accepted the new role as protectors of the rights of patrons to read freely and without fear. During the next decades, libraries faced repeated challenges posed by community organizations seeking to limit access to or even ban materials. In general, librarians frequently used their newfound power as champions of public rights, individual privacy, and civil liberties more broadly to fight off these attempts at censorship.[18]

Cold War Hysteria and the Library Awareness Program

Until the 1950s, much of the struggle within libraries took place in the public library setting, where the debates centered around citizen and immigrant access to information. With the Cold War, the attention shifted to academic and research libraries. From the turbulent 1960s to the 1980s, in the eyes of many agents within the federal government, the library's mission, materials, and patrons all constituted a potential national security threat. To combat it, they regularly attempted to turn librarians into informants and to engage in surveillance against library patrons.

Perhaps the most notorious use of the domestic intelligence apparatus to investigate potential threats to national security in libraries occurred under the Library Awareness Program of the 1980s.[19] However, a number of earlier incidents marked the development of surveillance practices against library users. The FBI operated on college campuses in the 1960s, both recruiting student, staff, and faculty informants and also infiltrating student organizations directly.[20] The Senate's Subcommittee on Investigation provides the first documentation available for direct interaction between libraries and the state security during this period.[21] In 1970, Arkansas Senator John L. McClellan importuned the Bureau of Alcohol, Tobacco, and Firearms (ATF) to "initiate a broad program to investigate suspected users of explosives."[22] The ATF obliged, requesting library records of people not under any investigation, but who had simply checked out books on topics related to explosives, mining, demolition, and guerrilla warfare. Both individual librarians and the American Library Association protested these open-ended fishing expeditions as intrusions into patron confidentiality and the right to read freely. Apparently librarians' vocal counter-claims prompted a July 1970 change in ATF investigative technique; the Bureau decided to only seek records of library users subject to prior ongoing investigations.[23]

The ATF investigations primarily concerned public library users, but created palpable threats to academic research as well. Many academic researchers employ controversial materials in order to effectively carry out their work. Undergraduate students often find sensationalistic research projects attractive, irrespective of their political motivations or objectives. The idea that agents of the U.S. government could mine data on the reading habits of the American public in order to uncover hidden subversives or detect plots stood as antithetical to all that post–World War II–era libraries had come to mean. Librarians did not unhesitatingly comply with state prerogatives, and at times resisted with the means at their disposal, refusing to release patron information and critically publicizing the ATF's actions in terms of First Amendment rights. At the same time, the American Library Association proved itself willing to work with legitimate and legally-conducted government investigations. A 1970 joint statement from the Treasury Department/IRS and the ALA acknowledged that

> an attempt will be made to identify areas of reconciliation that would give the Government access to specific library records in justifiable situations but would unequivocally proscribe "fishing expeditions" in contradistinction to the investigation of a particular person or persons suspected of a criminal violation.[24]

In other words, librarians would support concrete official criminal investigations, but only once investigators obtained court orders on specific individuals and suspects. This stance, positioning libraries as watchdogs of civil liberties but also as good citizens, ready to assist legitimate investigations, remains an important precept even as intelligence agencies seek to subvert it in the name of countering proliferating threats and global terrorism.

The Library Awareness Program first came to the attention of the public in September 1987 with the publication of *The New York Times* article "F.B.I. in New York Asks Librarians' Aid in Reporting on Spies."[25] The story described a June incident at Columbia University where FBI agents visited the Mathematics and Science Library and confronted a library clerk, asking to get information about "foreign library users."[26] A professional librarian on duty immediately understood the implications of this request and told the agents to talk with the Acting University Librarian, Paula Kaufman. The agents told her

> that they were doing a general "library awareness" program in the city and that they were asking librarians to be alert to the use of their libraries by people from countries "hostile to the Unites States, such as the Soviet Union," and to provide the F.B.I. with information about these activities.[27]

Once the story broke, more information appeared that documented similar programs in multiple cities since the 1970s.[28]

The Columbia University incident clearly demonstrated how the FBI planned to use the Library Awareness Program to track foreign nationals accessing publicly available, scientific information, and it revealed how national security agencies envisioned using library information prior to 11 September 2001. When agents first arrived at the library, they went directly to a library clerk. Clerks, often student-workers, have none of the training and education in library ethics that professional librarians receive. Yet, they often work in circulation and reference departments, some of the most sensitive areas of the library in terms of information privacy. These workers have access to patron records, including what books are checked out, as well as personal information such as home addresses and phone numbers, and even, in some older systems, social security numbers. Without training in correct library procedures for police investigations, library clerks may willingly give out confidential information to authoritative, badge-wielding government or university officials. FBI or other intelligence agents could thereby receive requested information without having to go through required legal channels and processes.

The FBI had two different goals with the Library Awareness Program: to gain access to records and information on foreign library users requesting specific types of materials and to recruit library workers as informants. In the former objective, they could gather information within extant legal procedures, such as obtaining a search warrant for the records of a specific suspect. However, rather than investigating anyone in particular, the agents sought to create "awareness" of the perceived problem of foreign nationals accessing scientific information in American libraries.[29] The latter, and more sinister second goal, to enlist librarians as informants for the FBI, directly conflicted with librarianship's ethical code. Librarian informants, cultivated by agents to proffer leads and information, would create a climate of fear in any research library. If librarians reported foreign nationals for "suspicious behaviors," real or imagined, it required no great leap to imagine that U.S. citizens were next. If researchers could not examine materials needed for their projects without fear of investigation, then innovative and important studies would likely be impeded or prevented. Kaufman, recognizing the threat raised by this visit, reported to *The New York Times* that she "told them we were not prepared to cooperate with them in any way, described our philosophies and policies respecting privacy, confidentiality and academic freedom, and told them they were not welcome here."[30]

Stories continued to turn up that showed the Columbia encounter not as an isolated incident, but rather as part of a larger FBI strategy of seeking information through library use records. In the same *New York Times* article the FBI revealed that "fewer than 20 libraries, most of them academic rather than public, had been asked to cooperate with agents in a Library Awareness Program that is part of a national counterintelligence effort."[31] That just under 20 libraries in New York City had been approached did little to calm librarians' fears or keep them silent. They continued to report their concerns to the American Library Association, the media, and their Congressional representatives, hoping to raise public awareness of the FBI's interest in patron records and behaviors.

By 1988, the House Subcommittee on Civil and Constitutional Rights launched an inquiry into the Library Awareness Program. While the hearings did not stop the program, they succeeded in keeping the issue in the media and allowed librarians a platform to express their concerns.[32] The overall library position on the program focused on the adverse effects that Library Awareness would have on intellectual inquiry and freedom of speech. C. James Schmidt, chair of the American Library Association's Intellectual Freedom Committee, summed up the issues involved in his testimony to the committee:

> The requests of the FBI that library staff monitor and report the use of the library by any patron chills the First Amendment freedoms of all library and database users. The Library Awareness Program is a threat to the fundamental freedom of this nation. If continued, it will seriously and unnecessarily invade the intellectual life of citizens.[33]

The negative publicity caused the FBI to state that they would narrow the scope of the program to New York City.[34] However, this limitation proved disingenuous on the part of the FBI, as illustrated by FOIA documents requested by the National Security Archive showing that the FBI continued running background checks on hundreds of librarians and did little to modify the Library Awareness Program after this agreement.[35]

The full extent of the FBI interest in libraries and their patrons remains unknown. In the only full-length book about the program, librarian Herbert N. Foerstel outlines all reported FBI attempts to recruit librarians as part of the Library Awareness Program. He provides evidence that it operated from 1973 to 1976 and again from 1985 to at least 1989.[36] Although the FBI stated that it ran the program only in New York, FBI agents dropped by universities and research libraries nationwide throughout the 1980s. In addition to libraries, the FBI also targeted database companies providing library access to research materials.[37] In these interactions, the FBI invoked issues of national security, sometimes appealing to patriotic impulses, and at other times employing threats and intimidation. Concerned libraries documented the cases that appear in Foerstel's work; it is impossible to say how many other libraries were contacted where the librarians or other staff members complied and cooperated.

In general, the 1980s saw more incidents of the FBI overstepping its reach, conducting illegal or quasi-legal surveillance activities against activists and dissenters, for example, against the Committee in Solidarity with the People of El Salvador (CISPES).[38] Like library patrons targeted by the Library Awareness Program, CISPES members were exercising their First Amendment rights, and, like the foreign library patrons using scientific sources, they were under investigation for acting as presumed agents of foreign movements or governments.[39] The timing of these investigations was not coincidental; under the leadership of first FBI Director William H. Webster (1978–1987, later to become CIA Director from 1987 to 1991, and currently serving as Chair of the Homeland Security Advisory Council) and then FBI Director William S. Sessions

(1987–1993), the Bureau engaged in surveillance activities and investigations that directly violated or threatened to violate the constitutional rights of U.S. citizens and others protected by civil rights laws.[40] Unfortunately, this would not be the last time that U.S. national security agencies engaged in anti-constitutional surveillance practices.

With the pattern in place, all that was needed was the opportunity to revitalize the programs. On the morning of September 11, 2001, that opportunity presented itself in the form of the devastating terrorist attacks on the World Trade Center and the Pentagon and the growing realization that incriminating information about the plotters was neither analyzed correctly, nor shared with other agencies, nor acted on. From that point on, national security concerns served as a ready, and constantly invoked, justification for a trampling of civil liberties not seen since the Red Scares of the early 1920s and the 1950s.

The USA PATRIOT Act: When Reading Habits Are a National Security Concern

In the immediate aftermath of 9/11, national security agencies in the United States, still reeling from their massive intelligence failures leading up to the terrorist attacks, began to pull together a wish list of surveillance methods and other forms of information gathering, many of which had been refused by Congress in the past.[41] These were bundled together into Public Law 107–56, the "Uniting and Strengthening America by Providing Appropriate Tools Required to Intercept and Obstruct Terrorism" Act of 2001, better known by the acronym USA PATRIOT Act. The act's stated purpose — to facilitate better communication between national and local security agencies and to provide for more comprehensive information gathering to prevent future terrorist attacks — frequently gave constitutional safeguards short shrift. Two sections apply to library records. Section 215 amended the Foreign Surveillance Intelligence Act (FISA) to broaden the scope of what types of records agencies could acquire in a terrorism or intelligence investigation. Specifically, it let national security agencies obtain a FISA warrant to not only gain access to library and bookstore transactions, but to put a gag order on the parties served with the warrant. In other words, under threat of legal prosecution, no one could comment that agents accessed and viewed requested records. Another section, 505, allowed use of National Security Letters, administrative subpoenas issued without a court order, to obtain library patron records, again placing a gag order on the librarians while the investigation proceeded.

No one knows — by design — exactly how often security agencies used the Act to obtain library records. This information remains classified, a matter of national security. Multiple organizations have tried to get access, drawing up lawsuits in hope of gaining some statistical break-downs of the application of the law, but to date without much success.[42] An informal, anonymous survey conducted in early 2002 showed at least 85 libraries had been contacted in the first six months following September 11, 2001.[43] Gag orders prevent a wider dissemination of the system's contours.

Congress conceived of the USA PATRIOT Act as a way to catch terrorists before they strike, through closer surveillance, improved tracking, and streamlined investigative and communication methods by state agencies. The act modified current laws and statutes to make it easier for federal law enforcement and intelligence agents to gain information about suspected terrorists.[44] The Act has vast civil liberties implications generally, but two elements directly impact libraries: (1) agents' access to personal Internet records and electronic communications and (2) their ability to obtain personal patron information from library records. The FBI, or any other federal law enforcement agency, can swiftly obtain a court order or a National Security Letter to view patron records, check who uses public internet terminals, and monitor e-mail, social networking sites, and chat services. They can even monitor Internet use of all computers using a particular Internet service provider, including what sites the patrons visit and how long they spend on each site. Combined with patron records, the agencies can use this information to trace individuals through e-mail and chat rooms, show patrons' interaction with suspected terrorists through electronic media, and monitor who accesses "terrorist"-oriented websites.[45] The FBI and other intelligence agencies need no solid evidence to begin these searches, nor do they need to define terrorist activity.

Librarians sometimes found ways to get around the letter of the law in order to keep personal data safe from unwarranted searches. With the adoption of the USA PATRIOT Act, libraries moved swiftly to review their confidentially policies and their patron records retention schedules. Under the Act, agencies like the FBI could request patron records, but libraries did not have any requirements for record retention. Soon libraries using paper-based computer logs began shredding these daily to protect patron privacy. Popular library magazines published articles on how to avoid divulging patron information. *Library Journal* suggested that librarians become more "privacy literate" by gaining a command of the technology that the FBI used to monitor internet activity and by making sure that they kept patron records only long enough to allow the library circulation system to function properly. Some suggested that libraries should conduct periodic "privacy audits," viewing all aspects of data collection in the library within the scope of the USA PATRIOT Act.[46] Libraries posted signs warning patrons about the possible privacy breeches that could occur under the Act. Although small-scale, these actions helped bring the USA PATRIOT Act to the attention of a terrified and often quiescent public and showed that librarians were willing to lead the fight for the protection of basic civil liberties.

Along with small acts of daily resistance, librarians also challenged the legality of the USA PATRIOT Act directly through the courts. *Doe vs. González*, involving a Connecticut library consortium, emerged as the best known example of this effort. In July 2005, George Christian of Library Connection consortium received a National Security Letter (under Section 505 of the USA PATRIOT Act) requesting information on computer logs related to an IP address used by one of the consortium libraries. The NSL came with an automatic gag order making it illegal for Christian to let patrons know about the letter or the investigation. After consulting with the consortium's lawyer and the Executive Committee of the Library Connection, he decided that the only way to protect patron privacy would be to file suit against then — U.S. Attorney General Alberto González to remove the gag order so that the librarians could inform their patrons that their records were under investigation.

Ironically, due to relative incompetence of the government, publicly available documents revealed the librarians' identities. Yet, even after *The New York Times* published their names, the four remained under gag order.[47] Just like the current Library of Congress censorship decision to suppress publically available information only to those that work at or use the library, this case continued to require silence on the part of the consortium librarians even when the entire reading public could find their names in a variety of media sources.

Ultimately the FBI dropped the case. This prevented the librarians from finishing their constitutional challenge against National Security Letters and the gag orders. The NSL provision, with minor revisions to the gag order provisions, remains. However, *Doe vs. González* showed that librarians could successfully stand up and defend their patrons' privacy and civil rights.

Though often overlooked, the USA PATRIOT Act also impacts academic freedom and research. As in public libraries, security agencies may request patron records with a FISA warrant or National Security Letter. Unlike the Library Awareness Program, this time most of the requests come with gag order restrictions that keep the library director from informing either staff members or patrons about records requests. Although privacy protection laws in almost every state apply to library records, the USA PATRIOT Act trumps those state laws, perhaps rendering them as "quaint" and out-of-date as members of the Bush Administration viewed the Geneva Conventions concerning the treatment of prisoners. The U.S. Department of Justice (DoJ) continues to insist that the ability to access library records is a matter of national security.

In their rebuttal to American Civil Liberties Union charges that the act is unconstitutional and an anti-democratic intrusion of the state into people's personal reading habits, the DoJ stated, without qualification,

> Historically, terrorists and spies have used libraries to plan and carry out activities that threaten our national security. If terrorists or spies use libraries, we should not allow them to become safe havens for their terrorist or clandestine activities.[48]

In reality, the historical record does not support the DoJ's claims. Little evidence exists that libraries have been particularly attractive to either terrorists or spies. With the commercial availability of almost all material housed in or provided by libraries, foreign governments and well-financed terrorist organizations can easily purchase any desired information or access it through pre-paid smartphones and similar technology.

Many large research libraries, both academic and public, also provide access to official government reports, studies, and similar information. Since 1813, when Congress decided that, as part of the democratic process, congressional materials should be available to the voting public, U.S. government agencies have been required to deposit important documents in what would become Federal Depository Libraries.[49] These libraries have the responsibility for maintaining current and historical collections of government documents, a record of the workings of the federal government which the public can access at any time and for any reason.

Under the William J. Clinton presidency, the government moved towards a more electronic format, publishing online much of the information that used to be available in print form. The material remained available to the public, but the difference was permanence. The U.S. government has been active in creating stable, permanent web addresses (called PURLs), arguing that these addresses would ensure that web-based information would not disappear over time. While these PURLs do allow websites of defunct agencies to exist beyond the life of the organizations themselves, they do not stop conscious and deliberate website changes.

On September 11, 2001, most important government agencies closed their websites to review them for sensitive materials. These materials included data that, in a hard copy form, would typically go to the depository libraries. In the electronic environment, however, there remained no hard copy on deposit to back up the information. Suddenly no longer available to the public, this non-classified information had existed in an easily accessible, open format just days earlier, before it was removed from the websites because of national security concerns.

In October 2001, depository libraries received a letter from the U.S. Geological Survey requiring them to destroy an unclassified CD-ROM about large water sources in the USA, again due to national security.[50] This is the most highly documented example of the daily destruction of public access to sensitive, but not classified, government information. Government documents librarians warned of three major consequences of the censoring of these types of documents: that current, needed information would not be available to the public, that there would be less accountability because of less documentation of governmental actions, and that the historical record would have gaps due to the lack of a hard copy.[51] The removal and destruction of government documents in the wake of 9/11 severely restricted access to current and historical data freely available only months, or even days, before.

As many librarians and academics have observed, the USA PATRIOT Act and the removal of government information stifles research and discovery in our universities. The threat of surveillance creates a self-censorship that causes researchers to question whether they should use or view controversial materials.[52] The gag order restrictions prevent public debate over specific information requests and add to a climate of anxiety and suspicion. The reappearance of national security agencies on academic campuses, including libraries, only strengthens those fears.

Bringing It to Campus: Centers of Academic Excellence, Spies in the Libraries, and Academic Freedom

Since the 1950s, national security and intelligence agencies like the CIA and the FBI have been operating on university campuses, both overtly through sponsored programs and grant-funding and covertly through faculty and student recruitment and intelligence gathering. However, publicized excesses of the CIA and the FBI during the 1970s helped to foster a healthy critique of their presence on campuses, giving rise to CIA-off-campus movements in the 1980s.[53] Covert activities remained, such as the monitoring and infiltration of student activist groups, especially those involved in Central American Solidarity work, but funding sources shifted to other governmental organizations and private donors. Yet, the temptation of using the university and its resources as a base for agent recruitment and research remained. Again, the specter and shock of 9/11, especially the intelligence failures that led up to it, provided the opportunity to re-legitimate campus-based intelligence programs. In this context, the Office of the Director of National Intelligence (ODNI) looked for ways to increase on campuses nationwide the influence of national security agencies, including the CIA and the FBI, by creating Intelligence Community Centers of Academic Excellence (IC/CAEs).[54] Not to be outdone, the Department of Homeland Security and the National Security Agency, both also part of the

ODNI structure, designed their own National Centers for Academic Excellence in Information Assurance Education and Research (CAE/IAE or CAE-Rs) in addition to those already sponsored by ODNI.[55] (See a list of the campus-based NSA CAEs at the end of essay number 8 in this book.)

While the university-ODNI collaboration raises many issues of academic integrity and freedom, a few pertain specifically to libraries. The ODNI guidelines for IC/CAE programs require that universities maintain and fund a Resource Reading Room as part of the institution's obligations under the grant.[56] While the grant itself does not specify where to locate these reading rooms, campus libraries seem a logical place. For example, when the University of Texas–Pan American (UTPA) received its IC/CAE grant, the program coordinator asked the library to provide a room for use by the Center. The grant set aside funding for specific databases, books, and journals that the IC/CAE program's representatives would select and housed them within this dedicated resource room inside the library.

Collection development constitutes a key area where librarians, in keeping with the Library Bill of Rights and Freedom to Read statement, should create balanced selections based on a multiplicity of viewpoints. The intrusion of the IC/CAE into library collection development activities posed a direct threat to the ability for librarians to provide the services required of them both as ethical professionals and as experts in research methods and materials. It took away autonomy in collection development, effectively politicizing the collection, and set a precedent for additional outside agency influence on library collection development. More broadly, the involvement of intelligence agency interests in collection development at IC/CAE schools removed the neutrality that libraries, especially academic libraries, need to maintain to create an environment that makes research and a free exchange of ideas possible. At UTPA, the creation of a room dedicated to security interests put all library staff in a position of seemingly supporting the program and its goals both materially and politically, the opposite of the intellectual environment that academic libraries traditionally try to provide for their patrons — students, faculty, and community members.

As long as the grants continue, institutions must "ensure that books, magazines, softcopy (e.g., web content, CD ROMs, etc.) and material about each of the IC agencies and components are readily available for students."[57] Program guidelines do not state the funding sources, leaving it to individual institutions whether this support will be grant-funded or come from reappropriating existing funds. The external pressure to support these programs, especially within funding guidelines, removes the autonomy of the library staff and undercuts attempts to provide fair access to information. Like the IC/CAE, CAE/IAE and CAE-R programs must prove that the institution supports the programs materially in their library or resource center's collections. To qualify as a CAE program, for example, institutions must show "evidence that subscription-based IA [Information Assurance] journals are available for student and faculty use."[58] Academic libraries must provide these journals, even as they cut important journal subscriptions in other fields due rapidly rising costs.

Another troubling aspect of the Centers of Academic Excellence is the potential role their students could play in intelligence gathering activities on campus. IC/CAE programs prepare students for careers in the burgeoning national security state, intelligence services, or proliferating private intelligence and private security contracting sector. Anthropologist David Price (author of essay number 2 in this book) has uncovered multiple examples of students who have informed on their professors for political reasons.[59] It is not entirely unreasonable to suspect that some students in the IC/CAE programs would also report on faculty activities to highlight their keen observational skills to potential employers in security agencies (Verne Lyon speaks from personal experience in this area in essay number 6.) Additionally, students in work-study or graduate assistant positions may use their access to personal and sensitive information to gain favors from potential employers or faculty members in the IC/CAE programs.

The FBI has a pattern of using student and part-time library workers as potential information sources. As shown earlier, they approached student workers during the Library Awareness Program to gain access to patron information during the 1980s. Even more alarming, perhaps, in 1970 FBI agents made use of a part-time library worker in an attempt to frame a librarian accused of supporting terrorist acts.[60] In that incident, agents recruited a prisoner, Boyd Douglas, from the federal penitentiary in Lewisburg, Pennsylvania, as an informant against Father Phillip Berrigan, an outspoken anti-war activist and Roman Catholic Priest serving a prison sentence for civil disobedience against the Vietnam War. They secured Douglas a work-release position in the library at Bucknell University so that he could infiltrate local anti-war groups. Douglas, presenting himself as an anti-war activist, befriended the librarian Zoia Horn and began attempts to embroil her in the Berrigan case.[61] Eventually, Douglas set up meetings between a group of Berrigan's friends, then under surveillance for conspiracy to commit kidnapping and acts of violence, and Horn. After the meetings, FBI agents visited Horn at home to attempt to debrief her, and also interviewed her reference assistant and two student workers. Horn refused to answer their questions, and found herself hauled in front of a grand jury convened for the conspiracy case against Berrigan and his friends. When asked to testify at their trial the following year, she refused, stating:

I cannot in my conscience lend myself to this black charade. I love and respect this country too much to see a farce made of the tenets upon which it stands. To me it stands on: Freedom of thought — but government spying in homes, in libraries and universities inhibits and destroys this freedom. It stands on freedom of association — yet in this case gatherings of friends, picnics, parties have been given sinister implications, made suspect. It stands on freedom of speech — yet general discussions have been interpreted by the government as advocacies of conspiracy.[62]

The judge cited Zoia Horn for contempt of court; she served 20 days in jail.[63]

The Horn case demonstrates the FBI used library assistants to wreak havoc with civil liberties. Douglas may also have accessed student and faculty records for his FBI handlers. Horn certainly believed "he was in a position to do so."[64] How many other student workers, library clerks, and assistants have security agencies used to gain access to sensitive information or to commit acts of provocation or entrapment? While we may never know, acknowledging that these incidents happened in the past permits observation that the potential exists for them to happen again today. As security and intelligence agencies make further inroads in universities, they create a climate where fear and suspicion reign. Anyone who has access to sensitive data who is also connected with on-campus security agency programs must be considered a potential asset of these agencies.

IC/CAE programs have met with resistance on many campuses, especially major research institutions like the University of Washington in Seattle. At the University of Washington, social scientists recognized that receiving funding from the CIA and other national security agencies could compromise their ability to do research in their fields. Many members of the history department and the international school strongly opposed the program both due to the historical legacy of the CIA and its current use of torture and other forms of inhuman punishment and the general secrecy of its actions.[65] In smaller schools, agencies found it relatively easy to place these programs in colleges of social science, engineering, or computer science. At the University of Washington, none of the traditional departments would house the program. It ended up being assigned to the Information School and headed by an iSchool assistant professor.[66]

The implications of this decision for librarians are stunning. Information schools, also known as "iSchools," are an outgrowth of traditional library school programs. Most information schools, including that of the University of Washington, maintain an American Library Association-accredited Masters of Library and Information Science program. With the decision to place the IC/CAE program in the Information School, the University of Washington created a situation where faculty working with the very agencies that trampled civil rights with the USA PATRIOT Act would train librarians. Whether by accident or design, an important library school in the United States would now be beholden to ODNI funding and feel its influence on curriculum decisions, collection development, and research topics and design. In a particularly cynical statement from their website, the Information School states the

> goal is to guide practice that shapes real world decisions in both public and private sectors within the scope of public safety and national security. Areas of application include: Civil liberties and ethics, Collaborative practices in organizations and communities, Decision making and knowledge management, Social interactions in virtual worlds.[67]

With the strong history of librarians' ethics and positions on civil liberties getting in the way of surveillance practices, it is useful to ask what particular interests the ODNI agencies would have in guiding practice for librarians. Perhaps the interest lies in guiding new librarians away from the pro-civil liberties stance and getting them on board for the information control demanded by the national security state? It is too early to tell what effects this program will have on the acculturation of librarians into their profession, but it will clearly have a chilling effect on the program's faculty and students who disagree with collaboration with programs that support secrecy, closed records, duplicity, disinformation, and silence.

The University of Pittsburg and Syracuse University have Centers of Academic Excellence in the form of CAE/IAE programs in their iSchools. These schools also house traditional library science programs. There is an inherent conflict of interest between the goals of modern librarianship to create democratic access to information and that of Information Assurance, which aims to monitor and control data and to use data mining and other collection techniques "to reduce vulnerability in our national information infrastructure."[68] One path allows people to freely access information as they wish, without fear of surveillance or punishment. The other controls information access and uses any data acquired to track and profile information users in the name of national security or commercial interests. By combining these two programs into one school, future librarians may no longer receive the same training in ethics that they would have independent of these types of funding sources.

Looking Forward

Within the current political context in the U.S., academic libraries still stand as beacons of hope for the re-establishment of civil rights in the twenty-first century. Most librarians hold firm to the belief that patrons have the right to privacy in their reading habits and internet use, and continue to revise privacy statements and record retention policies to ensure that library users have as much freedom as possible within the national security state. Legal actions, such as that of Doe vs. González, have the potential to challenge the constitutionality of surveillance methods in use today by intelligence and policing agencies.

In the university, libraries continue to provide a relatively safe research environment within the constraints of the USA PATRIOT Act. Today, though, the academic library finds itself under assault not only from the overt legal issues brought up by the USA PATRIOT Act, but also from local university policies and procedures. As libraries come to rely more heavily on internet-based resources, they struggle with these issues while at the mercy of institutional Information Technology departments' information management policies. Again in the name of security, many academic libraries have been forced to comply with IT departments' demands to have internet users tracked via secure sign-in processes. IT departments, not the library, keep and maintain the usage logs and back-up tapes. In the electronic research environment, the librarians can do little more than alert patrons to the lack of confidentiality inherent in the use of online resources.

Since the beginning of the Cold War, while universities and colleges played a central role in what President Eisenhower termed the "military-industrial complex," academic libraries nonetheless performed an important duty to the public as institutional protectors of First Amendment rights. University libraries have had the role of not only protecting those rights, but of providing a research environment that would operate in support of, but separate from, university programs of study. However, the changes in curriculum, outside influences on collection development, grant requirements such as that of the IC/CAE programs, institutional IT policies, and the move to electronic resources all threaten the autonomy of the modern academic library. When librarians can no longer guarantee the privacy of researchers, it creates an intellectual climate where many students and faculty will self-censor or tailor their research questions and agendas in exchange for their personal safety or to gain the emoluments and favor of the outside agencies.

With the growing relationship between national security agencies and library schools, and the focus on the methods of data acquisition and analysis rather than the ethics of data use, the strong possibility exists that the next generation of librarians as a whole will no longer have the same commitment to the defense of civil liberties developed in the earlier post–World War II generations. The data collection and analysis needs of the new national security state fit naturally into the changes in the profession from a patron-oriented, privacy-based approach to that of information management. Libraries contain tremendous amounts of information useful to data-mining operations designed to identify dissent within U.S. society, and, as reported recently in the *Washington Post*'s investigative series "Top Secret America," the FBI is creating new analysis programs to capture the remarkable amount of electronic information available today.[69]

As we move towards the future, librarians will increasingly find themselves in situations where they must choose whether they will serve the intrusive and repressive intelligence apparatus of the state or stand up for their patrons' privacy and rights. For the past ten years, librarians have overwhelmingly supported civil liberties. Yet, as exemplified by the Library of Congress' endorsement of the censorship of Wikileaks, for the first time since 9/11 a major American research library decided to side with state power and authority at the expense of its patrons and longstanding professional practice. Whichever direction librarians choose in the future, the library, with its mission to provide information and materials from multiple viewpoints and political orientations, will remain a site of contestation over issues of privacy, access, and freedom well into the twenty-first century.

NOTES

1. Matt Raymond, "Why the Library of Congress is Blocking Wikileaks," Library of Congress Blog (3 December 2010), http://blogs.loc.gov/loc/2010/12/why-the-library-of-congress-is-blocking-wikileaks/.

2. For a discussion on the political and economic aspects of the imperial project of post–9/11 American policies, see Chalmers Johnson, *Blowback: The Costs and Consequences of American Empire*, rev. ed. (New York: Metropolitan, 2004) and Andrew J. Bacevich, *American Empire: The Realities and Consequences of U.S. Diplomacy* (Cambridge, MA: Harvard University Press, 2002). For the cultural aspects, see Chris Hedges, *Empire of Illusion: The End of Literacy and the Triumph of Spectacle* (New York: Nation, 2009).

3. Florent Blanc, "Dissent after September 11: Mobilization of Librarians, ACLU, Cities and Lawyers" (PhD diss., Northwestern University, 2010), 162.

4. Plummer A. Jones, *Still Struggling for Equality: American Public Library Services with Minorities* (Westport, CT: Libraries Unlimited, 2004), 15–17.

5. Joan Starr, "Libraries and National Security: An Historical Review," *First Monday* 9, no. 12 (6 December 2004), http://firstmonday.org/htbin/cgiwrap/bin/ojs/index.php/fm/rt/printerFridendly/1198/1118.

6. Starr.

7. Ibid.

8. "Code of Ethics for Librarians," American Library Association, http://www.ala.org/ala/issuesadvocacy/proethics/history/index5.cfm.

9. "Library Bill of Rights," American Library Association, http://www.ala.org/ala/issuesadvocacy/intfreedom/librarybill/lbor.pdf.

10. Blanc, 166.

11. Ibid.

12. Starr.

13. "Library Bill of Rights."

14. "Freedom to Read Statement," American Library Association, http://www.ala.org/ala/aboutala/offices/oif/statementspols/ftrstatement/freedomreadstatement.cfm.

15. American Library Association, "Texts of Librarians' Manifesto and Resolution on Book Curbs," *New York Times*, June 26, 1953, 8.

16. Dwight D. Eisenhower, "Text of Letter by the President," *New York Times*, June 27, 1953, 1.

17. "Poll of Libraries Shows Free Choice," *New York Times*, June 16, 1953, 22.

18. For a discussion of community-based book banning in the United States, see Herbert N. Foerstel, *Banned in the U.S.A: A Reference Guide to Censorship in Schools and Public Libraries* (Westport, CT: Greenwood, 2002).

19. Herbert N. Foerstel, *Surveillance in the Stacks: The FBI's Library Awareness Program* (New York: Greenwood, 1991).

20. For examples of FBI investigations, see Ward Churchill and Jim Vander Wall, *The COINTELPRO Papers: Documents from the FBI's Secret Wars Against Dissent in the United States* (Boston: South End, 1990).

21. Foerstel, *Surveillance in the Stacks*, 5.

22. Ibid.

23. Ibid.

24. Ibid., 6.

25. Robert D. McFadden, "F.B.I. in New York Asks Librarians' Aid In Reporting on Spies," *New York Times*, September 18, 1987, A1.

26. Starr.

27. McFadden, B2.

28. David Cole and James X. Dempsey, *Terrorism and the Constitution: Sacrificing Civil Liberties in the Name of National Security* (New York: New, 2006), 61.

29. This fear continues today in the rhetoric over intellectual property rights and foreign espionage. See, for example, the discussion on open access publications funded by U.S. government grants in Barbara Fister, "Liberating Knowledge: A Librarian's Manifesto for Change," *Thought and Action* 26 (Fall 2010): 86.

30. McFadden, B2.

31. McFadden, A1.

32. Herbert Mitgang, "Library Spy Hunt Is Curbed By F.B.I.," *New York Times*, November 11, 1988, A24.

33. Foerstel, *Surveillance in the Stacks*, 29.

34. Mitgang.

35. Foerstel, *Surveillance in the Stacks*, 113.

36. Ibid., 14.

37. Ibid., 72.

38. Ross Gelbspan, "More Probes Found of Latin Policy Foes: FBI Surveillance Called Pervasive," *Boston Globe*, June 18, 1988, 1.

39. Cole and Dempsey, 26–28.

40. Gelbspan, 1.

41. "Surveillance Under the USA PATRIOT Act," American Civil Liberties Union, http://www.aclu.org/national-security/surveillance-under-usa-patriot-act.

42. Ed Nawotka, "ABFFE files FOI Suit Over Patriot Act," *Publisher's Weekly* 249, no. 34 (26 August 2002): 10. See also, Norman Oder and Andrew Albanese, "Patriot Act Stats Won't Be Revealed," *Library Journal* 127, no.15 (15 September 2002): 17.

43. News From Washington, *American Libraries*, August 2002, 19.

44. Mary Minow, "The USA PATRIOT Act," *Library Journal* 127, no. 16 (1 October 2002): 52.

45. Scott Carlson and Andrea L. Foster, "Colleges Fear Anti-Terrorism Law Could Turn Them into Big Brother," *Chronicle of Higher Education*, 1 March 2002, 31–32.

46. Karen Coyle, "Make Sure You Are Privacy Literate," *Library Journal* 127, no. 16 (1 October 2002): 56.

47. Barbara M. Jones, "Librarians Shushed No More: The USA Patriot Act, the 'Connecticut Four,' and Professional Ethics," *Newsletter on Intellectual Freedom*, 58, no. 6 (2009): 195–223.

48. "Dispelling Some of the Major Myths about the USA PATRIOT Act," United States Department of Justice, http://www.justice.gov/archive/ll/subs/u_myths.htm.

49. Anne Heanue, "In Support of Democracy: The Library Role in Public Access to Government Information," in *Libraries and Democracy: The Cornerstones of Liberty*, ed. Nancy Kranich (Chicago: American Library Association, 2001), 122.

50. Ann Miller, "Popular Government, Popular Information," *Duke University Libraries* 16, no. 1 (Fall 2002): 12.

51. Ibid., 13.

52. David Price, "Librarians as FBI Extension Agents," *CounterPunch*, March 5, 2003, http://www.counterpunch.org/price03062003.html.

53. Ami C. Mills, *CIA Off Campus: Building the Movement Against Agency Recruitment and Research* (Boston: South End, 1991).

54. "About the Intelligence Community," Office of the Director of National Intelligence, http://www.dni.gov/faq_intel.htm.

55. "National Centers of Academic Excellence," National Security Agency, http://www.nsa.gov/ia/academic_outreach/nat_cae/index.shtml.

56. "Guidance and Procedures," Office of the Director of National Intelligence, http://www.nsu.edu/iccae/pdf/IC-CAEGuidanceAndProcedures.pdf, 4.

57. Ibid., 6.

58. "Criteria for Measurement for CAE/IAE," National Security Agency, http://www.nsa.gov/ia/academic_outreach/nat_cae/cae_iae_program_criteria.shtml.

59. Dave Price, "The CIA's Campus Spies," *CounterPunch*, March12/13, 2005, http://www.counterpunch.org/price03122005.html.

60. Foerstel, *Surveillance in the Stacks*, 7.

61. Ibid., 7–8.

62. Faye Chadwell, "Actions Speak Louder Than Words: The Courage of Zoia Horn," *LSA News* 67 (August 2005), http://lsa.uoregon.edu/newsletter05/0508news.html.

63. Foerstel, *Surveillance in the Stacks*, 9.

64. Ibid., 8.

65. David Price, "Silent Coup," *CounterPunch*, April 9–11, 2010, http://www.counterpunch.org/price04092010.html.

66. UW Information School eNews Bulletin, Spring, 2007, http://www.washington.edu/alumni/partnerships/ischool/200703/desouza.html.

67. For an overview of the University of Washington's IC/CAE program, see http://inser.ischool.uw.edu/.

68. "National Centers of Academic Excellence, National Security Agency. http://www.nsa.gov/ia/academic_outreach/nat_cae/index.shtml.

69. Dana Priest and William M. Arkin, "Monitoring America," *Washington Post*, December 20, 2010, http://projects.washingtonpost.com/top-secret-america/articles/monitoring-america/.

Works Citied

American Library Association. "Code of Ethics for Librarians." http://www.ala.org/ala/issuesadvocacy/proethics/history/index5.cfm.

_____. "Freedom to Read Statement." http://www.ala.org/ala/aboutala/offices/oif/statementspols/ftrstatement/freedomreadstatement.cfm.

_____. "Library Bill of Rights." http://www.ala.org/ala/issuesadvocacy/intfreedom/librarybill/lbor.pdf.

_____. "Texts of Librarians' Manifesto and Resolution on Book Curbs." *New York Times*, June 26, 1953.

Bacevich, Andrew J. *American Empire: The Realities and Consequences of U.S. Diplomacy*. Cambridge, MA: Harvard University Press, 2002.

Blanc, Florent. "Dissent after Sept 11: Mobilization of Librarians, ACLU, Cities and Lawyers." Ph.D. diss., Northwestern University, 2010.

Carlson, Scott, and Andrea L. Foster. "Colleges Fear Anti-Terrorism Law Could Turn Them into Big Brother." *Chronicle of Higher Education*, 1 March 2002, 31–32.

Chadwell, Faye. "Actions Speak Louder Than Words: The Courage of Zoia Horn." LSA News 67 (August 2005), http://lsa.uoregon.edu/newsletter05/0508news.html.

Churchill, Ward, and Jim Vander Wall. *The COINTELPRO Papers: Documents from the FBI's Secret Wars Against Dissent in the United States*. Boston: South End, 1990.

Cole, David, and James X. Dempsey. *Terrorism and the Constitution: Sacrificing Civil Liberties in the Name of National Security*. New York: New, 2006.

Coyle, Karen. "Make Sure You Are Privacy Literate." *Library Journal* 127, no.16 (2002): 55–57.

Eisenhower, Dwight D. "Text of Letter by the President." *New York Times*, June 27, 1953.

Fister, Barbara. "Liberating Knowledge: A Librarian's Manifesto for Change." *Thought and Action* 26 (Fall 2010): 83–90.

Foerstel, Herbert N. *Banned in the U.S.A: A Reference Guide to Censorship in Schools and Public Libraries*. Westport, CT: Greenwood, 2002.

_____.*Surveillance in the Stacks: The FBI's Library Awareness Program*. New York: Greenwood, 1991.

Golden, Daniel. "In From the Cold: After Sept. 11, The CIA Becomes A Force on Campus." *Wall Street Journal*, October 4, 2002.

Heanue, Anne. "In Support of Democracy: The Library Role in Public Access to Government Information." In *Libraries and Democracy: The Cornerstones of Liberty*, ed. Nancy Kranich, 121–128. Chicago: American Library Association, 2001.

Hedges, Chris. *Empire of Illusion: The End of Literacy and the Triumph of Spectacle*. New York: Nation, 2009.

Johnson, Chalmers. *Blowback: The Costs and Consequences of American Empire*, rev. ed. New York: Metropolitan, 2004.

Jones, Barbara M. "Librarians Shushed No More: The USA Patriot Act, the 'Connecticut Four,' and Professional Ethics." *Newsletter on Intellectual Freedom* 58, no. 6 (2009): 195–223.

Jones, Plummer A. *Still Struggling for Equality: American Public Library Services with Minorities*. Westport, CT: Libraries Unlimited, 2004.

McFadden, Robert D. "F.B.I. in New York Asks Librarians' Aid in Reporting on Spies." *New York Times*, September 18, 1987.

Miller, Ann. "Popular Government, Popular Information." *Duke University Libraries* 16, no. 1 (Fall 2002): 12–13.

Mills, Ami C. *CIA Off Campus: Building the Movement Against Agency Recruitment and Research*. Boston: South End, 1991.

Minow, Mary. "The USA PATRIOT Act." *Library Journal* 127, no. 16 (2002): 52–55.

Mitgang, Herbert. "Library Spy Hunt Is Curbed by F.B.I." *New York Times*, November 11, 1988.

Nawotka, Ed. "ABFFE Files FOI Suit Over Patriot Act." *Publisher's Weekly* 249, no. 34 (26 August 2002): 10.

News from Washington. American Libraries, August 2002, 19.

Oder, Norman, and Andrew Albanese. "Patriot Act Stats Won't Be Revealed." *Library Journal* 127, no. 15 (2002): 17.

Price, Dave. "The CIA's Campus Spies." *CounterPunch*, March 12–13, 2005, http://www.counterpunch.org/price03122005.html.

_____. "Librarians as FBI Extension Agents." *CounterPunch*, March 5, 2003, http://www.counterpunch.org/price03062003.html.

_____. "Silent Coup." *CounterPunch*, April 9–11, 2010, http://www.counterpunch.org/price04092010.html.

Priest, Dana, and William M. Arkin. "Monitoring America." *Washington Post*, December 20, 2010, http://projects.washingtonpost.com/top-secret-america/articles/monitoring-america/.

Raymond, Matt. "Why the Library of Congress Is Blocking Wikileaks." Library of Congress Blog (3 December 2010) http://blogs.loc.gov/loc/2010/12/why-the-library-of-congress-is-blocking-wikileaks/.

Starr, Joan. "Libraries and National Security: An Historical Review." *First Monday* 9, no. 12 (6 December 2004), http://firstmonday.org/htbin/cgiwrap/bin/ojs/index.php/fm/rt/printerFridendly/1198/1118.

UW Information School. eNews Bulletin, Spring 2007, http://www.washington.edu/alumni/partnerships/ischool/200703/desouza.html.

AGENCY/ PROGRAM WEBSITES

National Security Agency, http://www.nsa.gov/.

Office of the Director of National Intelligence, http://www.dni.gov/.

Syracuse University, Center of Academic Excellence in Information Assurance, http://ischool.syr.edu/prospective/graduate/washingtonconnection/coeia.aspx.

University of Pittsburgh, Laboratory for Education and Research on Security Assured Information Systems, http://www.sis.pitt.edu/~lersais/.

University of Texas–Pan American, Integrated Global Knowledge and Understanding Collaboration, http://portal.utpa.edu/utpa_main/daa_home/csbs_home/csbs_research/igknu_home.

University of Washington, Institute for National Security Education and Research, http://inser.ischool.uw.edu/.

5

Deception Detection and Torture:
The American Psychological Association
Serves the Intelligence Services

Stephen Soldz

It is now well known that the Bush administration engaged in a systematic program of torture and prisoner abuse as part of its so-called "war on terror." The CIA picked up alleged terrorists around the world and rendered them into secret prisons and tortured.[1] Sent to the prison at Guantánamo Naval Base, other individuals found themselves abused or tortured despite, in many cases, having little or no intelligence value. CIA operatives, Special Forces, and ordinary soldiers doing what they believed their commanders and the Commander-In-Chief wanted them to do tortured other detainees at various prisons in Iraq and Afghanistan.[2]

Although some of this torture resulted from inadequate training and supervision combined with ambiguous instructions, in many cases the abuse followed deliberate policy decisions made at the highest levels of the U.S. government. The Principals Committee-consisting of the vice president, the secretaries of Defense, State, and Justice, the directors of National Security and the CIA, and the National Security Advisor-carefully briefed on the CIA's "enhanced interrogation" torture program, gave the authorization demanded by the CIA.[3]

Concomitant with this authorization, the Office of Legal Counsel in the Justice Department — the government office which forms legal judgments regarding how laws are interpreted — issued a series of secret memos redefining "torture" and "cruel, inhuman, and degrading treatment and punishment" to exclude the tactics included in the "enhanced interrogation" program.[4] These memos made clear that psychologists and other health professionals played key roles in the administration's plans to legalize behavior previously defined as torture. The memos claimed that since the legal definition of torture requires an intent to cause severe harm, not just actual harm, assessments by health professionals that severe harm would not result could be used as a defense against torture charges. Illustrating the participation of academic psychologists in the CIA's program from the beginning, the CIA obtained judgments "from a number of psychologists and knowledgeable academics in the area of psychopathology" that severe long-term harm would not result from their "enhanced Interrogation techniques."[5] The identity of these psychological experts remains unknown.

Governments often torture.[6] But the extent to which the U.S. government's "enhanced interrogation" torture program relied upon psychologists and other social and behavioral scientists who lobbied, recruited, provided theoretical rationales, designed, implemented, supervised, researched, and provided legal cover and ethical protections for this program of systematized abuse rises to new levels. This process involved a confluence of psychological professionals from the military and civilians in the Defense Department and CIA, along with those in corporate consulting firms and universities, all supported and encouraged by the leadership of the American Psychological Association (APA), the world's largest organization of psychologists. In a previous series of articles I have explored the various ways that psychological practitioners, aided by the APA, helped design and implement the torture program.[7] Space precludes my retelling that story here.

In this essay I focus upon a different aspect of psychologists' involvement in the past decade's war on terror through examining roles of academic and research psychologists in the torture program and in related intelligence operations. While much of this story focuses upon the CIA, I cast my net wider because, in a country with over 1,000 agencies devoted to intelligence,[8] one cannot isolate the CIA from the broader range of government intelligence activities.

In telling this story, I suffer from the difficulties of investigating contemporary events. Only a few of the principal actors have spoken publicly, sometimes offering self-serving partial or inaccurate accounts. Many of the relevant documents remain secret and we, undoubtedly, do not even know of the existence of some of the most important ones. Here I uncover pieces of information and place them into patterns. Certain elements of those patterns may prove incomplete or even incorrect when more material becomes available. Therefore, although the data I provide are carefully referenced and most are incontrovertible, readers will have to evaluate my interpretations for themselves.

MKULTRA

The collaboration between psychologists, social scientists and the military-intelligence establishment began decades ago. Psychologists and the

APA played important roles in both World Wars I and II, leading to greater acceptance of psychology as a profession.[9]

During the Cold War, the CIA engaged in an immense behavioral science research program aimed at discovering the secrets of mind control and successful interrogation.[10] We now know these efforts by the CIA code name MKULTRA, though they occurred as part of a number of discrete programs.[11] Over 20 years the CIA experimented with hypnosis, LSD, sensory deprivation, and other putative mind-altering techniques. These experiments frequently involved unwitting subjects, including mental patients,[12] prisoners, soldiers,[13] men lured into CIA-run brothels by agency-employed prostitutes, children,[14] and defectors.[15]

The CIA destroyed most records from these efforts, successfully hiding the identities of many cooperating researchers. But we know that it involved well over 100 academic institutions, and hundreds of psychologists, along with physicians and other behavioral and social researchers. Among them many prominent names in psychology, including Donald Hebb, Carl Rogers, Lauretta Bender, Charles Osgood, Martin Orne, Hans Eysenck, and George Kelly, can be found. Leading behaviorist B. F. Skinner also received money from the CIA but may not have known its source.[16]

The details of how this CIA program involved academic researchers — as well as clinicians and numerous universities, hospitals, and other institutions of our society — remain to a great degree successfully hidden. We may never know the extent of APA involvement in these CIA efforts, though we know that the APA served as a conduit for the CIA to send a team of psychologists to tour the Soviet Union, resulting in an APA-published book while at least three APA presidents participated in CIA efforts.[17]

This CIA research program produced an American model of psychological torture, based on the basic principle of creating debility, dependency, and dread in prisoners.[18] Despite the CIA's extensive research, their psychological torture model largely derived from the brainwashing techniques used by the Communist Soviet Union, China, and North Korea — were designed to induce false confessions. The U.S. government then exported these techniques to U.S. allies over several decades until largely dismantling the program at the end of the Cold War.[19]

Reverse Engineering

When the CIA launched its "enhanced interrogation" program, the agency no longer had direct operational experience with its own psychological torture model. They therefore turned to psychologists from the military's Survival,

Evasion, Resistance, Escape (SERE) program.[20] SERE trains service members judged to be at high risk of capture, briefly subjecting trainees to a variety of abuses they may experience if captured by forces that do not obey the Geneva Convention's ban on torture. Such exposure, the military hoped, would inoculate soldiers from breaking under torture. SERE was developed in the wake of the Korean War when a number of POWs cooperated with their captors, making propaganda statements condemning U.S. actions and "confessing" to false claims generated by their captors. The CIA's debility, dependency, dread psychological torture model formed the basis of SERE.

Not long after 9/11, SERE psychologists James Mitchell and Bruce Jessen retired from the military, forming a consulting company — Mitchell, Jessen & Associates — to reverse-engineer the SERE techniques for use in breaking down alleged Al-Qaeda terrorists in CIA custody. They developed a set of techniques designed to induce a state of "learned helplessness" in prisoners, leading, it was claimed, to cooperation with their captors.

Most attention has focused upon the CIA's use of waterboarding, which forces a person to breathe water until he starts to drown before being pulled back from death. For decades the U.S. and other governments condemned it as torture. But waterboarding was just the extreme of an incredibly brutal and inhumane regime to which unknown numbers of prisoners were subjected. The Mitchell-Jessen treatment involved keeping prisoners in total isolation, often for months, initially keeping them naked, in cold and total darkness, with constant white noise or blaring music designed to disrupt their senses. Sometimes they were chained to the ceiling for days on end, defecating and urinating into diapers or on themselves, allegedly as a form of "sleep deprivation." At times interrogators slammed prisoners against the wall and stuffed at least one prisoner into a tiny box where he could neither stand nor sit for hours on end.[21] These techniques, alone or when used together, had long been known to cause severe psychological harm, even in milder form than used by the CIA — a fact the CIA and Justice Department studiously ignored.[22]

Academic Psychologists

While Mitchell and Jessen had been employed by the military, the development of the torture program also had input from academic psychologists. Among them was former American Psychological Association (APA) President and emeritus professor at Oregon Health Services University Joseph D. Matarazzo, a founding board member of Mitchell, Jessen & Associates.[23] Matarazzo reportedly had long-term connections with the CIA. Sources report that he talked of doing work for the CIA in the early 1990's. *The New Yorker's*

Jane Mayer reports that Matarazzo served on the CIA's Professional Standards Board "during the time the interrogation program was set up."[24]

Former Navy SERE psychologist Bryce Lefever told National Public Radio that Joseph Matarazzo was recruiting military psychologists, prior to 9/11. As NPR host Alix Spiegel described:

> At a meeting just before 9/11/01 military psychologists were visited by former APA President Joseph Matarazzo, whose words "crystallized their sense of mission." They determined that their "marching orders" were to "help America and use our skills in any way we possibly can as a psychologist," according to military psychologist and SERE instructor Bryce Lefever.[25]

Similarly, another psychologist shared with me Matarazzo's attempts to recruit him for CIA work in the immediate aftermath of the 9/11 attacks. Matarazzo told him that psychologists had important roles in the War Against Terrorism, but "we would have to get our hands dirty."[26]

While Matarazzo apparently helped the CIA with the recruitment of psychologists and played some still unspecified role in Mitchell, Jessen & Associates, another prominent psychologist, University of Pennsylvania professor and 1998 APA President Martin Seligman apparently contributed to the CIA's program, though controversy remains as to the degree of Seligman's awareness of his role. Seligman first became prominent as the developer of the "learned helplessness" model of depression that became the theoretical foundation of the CIA's torture program. Seligman based this model on dog experiments in which they were repeatedly shocked while restrained in a harness. Eventually a state of learned helplessness was induced in which the dogs would no longer try to escape shocks even when the harness was removed.

In December 2001, three months after the 9/11 attacks, Seligman hosted a meeting on the "Psychology of Capitulation" at his home, inviting academics and personnel from intelligence agencies, including the FBI, CIA, and Israeli intelligence.[27] Kirk Hubbard, a top CIA psychologist then working on setting up the "enhanced interrogation" program, and James Mitchell, soon to be a principal of Mitchell, Jessen & Associates, participated. Reportedly, during a break Mitchell lavished praise upon Seligman's theory of learned helplessness.[28]

Seligman again interacted with torture psychologist Mitchell and his partner Jessen in May 2002, when, organized by CIA's Kirk Hubbard, he lectured on learned helplessness to the Navy SERE school in San Diego.[29] According to Seligman, both Mitchell and Jessen attended. However, Seligman explained: "I was told then that since I was (and am) a civilian with no security clearance that they could not discuss American methods of interrogation with me."[30] The very fact that Seligman discussed U.S. interrogation tactics, even to be told they were off limits for discussion, should have alerted him to the possibility that his lecture might be used in the refinement of those techniques, especially once public reports of the brutality of these techniques surfaced in late 2002.[31] Nonetheless, Seligman claimed to be shocked when this possibility was suggested in 2008.

In 2010 Seligman was awarded a $31 million no-bid contract by the Army to conduct resilience training with soldiers, raising the possibility of payback for services to the intelligence community.[32] The circumstances surrounding the awarding of the contract remain murky, with Salon reporting that Brig. Gen. Rhonda Cornum on behalf of Army Chief of Staff Gen. George Case "rammed [the contract] ... through the Army bureaucracy." In response, both Physicians for Human Rights and the Coalition for an Ethical Psychology, of which I am a cofounder, issued a call for an investigation of the circumstances surrounding the awarding of the contract: "We are especially concerned that a psychologist who apparently instructed CIA interrogators is alleged to have received special treatment from the Defense Department," emphasized the Coalition.[33]

CIA Torture Research

In developing its torture program, the CIA did not rely solely upon prior research, whether from the MKULTRA era or from the SERE program. Rather, it engaged in new studies. Some of this research focused on the physiological and psychological effects of their interrogation efforts, while a second line of research, supported by numerous federal agencies and the APA, concerned the detection of deception, including, apparently, deception in prisoners subjected to "enhanced interrogation" techniques.

A Physicians for Human Rights report, which I coauthored, provides strong evidence that the CIA engaged in research on detainees in its custody.[34] The report points to several instances where medical personnel — physicians and psychologists — monitored the detailed administration of torture techniques and its effects. The CIA then used both as a legal rationale for the use of the techniques and to refine them.

For example, the Office of Medical Services (OMS) guidelines emphasize how important it is "that every application of the waterboard be thoroughly documented" by medical personnel, including: how long each application (and the entire procedure) lasted,

> how much water was applied (realizing that much splashes off), how exactly the water was applied, if a seal was achieved, if the naso- or oropharynx was filled, what sort of volume was expelled, how long was the break between applications, and how the subject looked between each treatment.[35]

The OMS used this documentation to best inform future medical judgments and recommendations on how to abuse people. This systematic monitoring aimed to modify how these techniques were implemented — to develop generalizable knowledge to be utilized in the future, which fits the generally accepted definition of research.

The report also describes instances in which OMS staff investigated the degree to which severe pain arose from a specific or from combinations of individual techniques. The Office of Legal Counsel drew upon this research in its torture memos to argue that these techniques did not cause pain sufficient or long-lasting enough to count as "torture."

One might misinterpret these documents as suggesting that the CIA engaged in this research to avoid harming the detainees, to keep the interrogations "safe and ethical." Rather, the Justice Department torture memos argued that torturers could be protected from prosecution if they demonstrated a "good faith" effort to avoid causing the "severe pain" involved in legal definitions of torture irrespective of how much suffering and harm the torturers actually caused. One way they could demonstrate such a good faith effort was to consult with health professionals, including researchers, who could assure them that their actions would not cause harm. Another way to demonstrate good faith was to collect and analyze evidence of prior interrogations demonstrating, allegedly, that they did not cause severe harm. Thus, the quality of the research did not matter. Its very existence would provide CIA torturers and responsible officials with a get-out-of-jail-free card.

Deception Detection

A second line of research by several intelligence agencies, including the CIA, focused on the detection of deception as a major concern of both U.S. intelligence officials and psychologists cooperating with them. Reportedly, plans for a top-secret Special Access Plan (SAP) involving research on deception detection by studying and experimenting upon Guantánamo detainees began almost immediately after 9/11. A recent article reported that top members of the Senate Defense Appropriations Committee received a briefing in late 2001 regarding the plan; those briefed included Senator Daniel Inouye and his chief of staff, psychologist Patrick DeLeon,[36] then the immediate Past-President and Board member of the APA.[37] These authors note:

> A July 16, 2004, Army Criminal Investigation Division (CID) report obtained by Truthout shows that between April and July 2003, a "physiological warfare specialist" attached [*sic*] to the military's Survival, Evasion, Resistance and Escape (SERE) program was present at Guantanamo. The CID report says the instructor was assigned to a top-secret Special Access Program.

While details on this SAP remain sparse, it appears to have applied to the often abusive interrogations occurring at the prison. Reportedly a former

Pentagon official stated: "A dozen [high-value detainees] were subjected to interrogation methods in order to evaluate their reaction to those methods and the subsequent levels of stress that would result." One wonders if the presence of hundreds of detainees known from early on to be innocent may have provided a convenient control group for these studies.[38]

APA Workshops

During this same period, the APA held two invitation-only workshops, together with the CIA and the Rand Corporation, on the psychology of deception as part of a larger series of workshops between the APA and the national security establishment. The workshops brought together a carefully selected group of academics with "operational staff working in the intelligence community," as one workshop description by APA staff put it.[39] The first of this series occurred in February 2002 as a joint APA-FBI workshop on "Countering Terrorism: Integration of Practice and Theory." Attending was torture psychologist James Mitchell, identified in the conference report as being from the CIA.[40] We see the intertwining of academics, law enforcement personnel, and "operational staff" in the workshop proceedings' description of the composition of discussion groups:

The ten or so discussants in each small group were likely to be

- scholars or researchers from psychology or political science or medical science;
- an attorney with expertise in immigration laws;
- someone from the Office of Science and Technology Policy or from the National Academy of Sciences or the National Science Foundation;
- a member of a training or operational unit of the FBI;
- personnel from the CIA, the U.S. Secret Service, the National Security Agency, the Department of Defense, the U.S. Marine Corps, or the State Department;
- someone on staff at the Office of Homeland Security or the new Transportation Security Administration;
- officers from the New Mexico State or Stafford or Arlington, VA, Washington, D.C., Philadelphia, or New York City police or sheriff's Departments.[41]

Many of the discussion topics, not unreasonably, concerned how to get cooperation from Muslim communities in the U.S. in reporting potential terrorist activity. However, they also discussed the possibility of psychologists becoming informers if their clients mentioned possible "terrorist" suspicions about others:

There is a need for the American Psychological Association and state psychological associations to develop an ethical code for practitioners for instances where a client may have information relevant to terrorism (similar to other mandates that already exist, such as those for instances of abuse of children and the elderly and a client's intention to harm himself or another person).[42]

The proceedings do not reveal that any of the psychologists present expressed concern about the dangers of turning therapists into informers without their client's consent. Rather, an APA ethics committee member present described legal changes that would help overcome APA ethics code provisions on maintaining confidentiality.

The second of these workshops, entitled "The Science of Deception: Integration of Theory and Practice," appears related to the theme of the deception detection SAP. Torture psychologists James Mitchell and Bruce Jessen and their CIA Project Officer and later employee Kirk Hubbard participated.[43] The APA's description of this workshop in one of its newsletters described it in a way that emphasizes the close connections being built between academics and the intelligence community:

RAND Corp. and the APA hosted a workshop entitled the "Science of Deception: Integration of Practice and Theory" with generous funding from the Central Intelligence Agency (CIA). The workshop provided an opportunity to bring together individuals with a need to understand and use deception in the service of national defense/security with those who investigate the phenomena and mechanisms of deception.... [T]he workshop drew together approximately 40 individuals including research psychologists, psychiatrists, neurologists who study various aspects of deception and representatives from the CIA, FBI and Department of Defense with interests in intelligence operations. In addition, representatives from the White House Office of Science and Technology Policy and the Science and Technology Directorate of the Department of Homeland Security were present.[44]

The participation of the White House in this workshop suggests that the deception detection subject, and potentially the APA connection, were important to the top levels of the U.S. government.

We glean the content of this workshop from the scenarios discussed.[45] Though originally posted on the APA web site, they, and all links to them, have since disappeared from the web site and from Google and Yahoo search engines, though they remain available from the Internet Archive Wayback Machine.[46] The workshop report included more information regarding discussion of these scenarios, was marked "Not for Distribution" and was never made publicly available nor was it provided to reporters who requested it. An APA senior staff member replied to a reporter that it was "lost."[47]

Among these scenarios four represented different intelligence and law enforcement situations in which detection of deception would be useful. Among these was "Law Enforcement Interrogation and Debriefing," in which determining if a suspect is telling the truth is an essential aspect of the interrogation process. The description of this scenario raises two issues which suggest that the conference likely addressed certain "enhanced interrogation" techniques. Listed under "Research Challenges" are "What pharmacological agents are known to affect apparent truth-telling behavior?" and "What are sensory overloads on the maintenance of deceptive behaviors? How might we overload the system or overwhelm the senses and see how it affects deceptive behaviors?"

Sensory overload, in the form of blaring music for hours or days on end[48] and strobe lights[49] constituted standard techniques used in U.S. interrogations, while the use of drugs as an interrogation tool at Guantánamo has long been suspected.[50] Given the presence of Mitchell, Jessen, and Hubbard from the CIA's "enhanced interrogation" program at the workshop, it seems likely that the use of these techniques as interrogation tools was discussed there, helping explain why the workshop report was kept hidden and the scenarios removed from the web.

A second workshop on "Interpersonal Deception: Integration of Theory and Practice," also sponsored jointly by the APA, CIA, and Rand Corporation, occurred in June 2004. APA also removed the announcement of this workshop[51] from its website and only one reference to it, from an APA critic, can be found in Google, Yahoo, or the Internet Archive.[52] The announcement reports attendees from academia, the CIA, the military's Special Operations, the Department of Homeland Security, the British Home Office and Scotland Yard, as well as several defense contractors. One participant, listed as "Andy Morgan" from the CIA, is also listed as having a Yale email address and is Charles "Andy" Morgan of the Yale Medical School Department of Psychiatry, giving a sense of the overlap between the intelligence agencies and academia.

According to a brief description in an APA newsletter, this meeting aimed to create close ties between the academics and intelligence professionals as it was "designed to forge collaborations between operational staff working in the intelligence community and scientists conducting research on interpersonal deception."[53] In addition to eight researchers, the meeting included about 25 others, including both APA and intelligence officials.

This workshop apparently focused upon means of perpetrating deception, the inverse of detecting deception. As the conference announcement stated, "How to deceive (on an interpersonal level) is the topic of this meeting." The announcement listed three questions among the foci of the meeting: "What are the most effective methods for deceiving? What are the key personal and environmental variables for success or failure? What factors shorten/prolong or amplify the effect of deception?"[54]

The organizing team for these two deception conferences consisted of

Geoff Mumford of the APA's Science Directorate, Scott Gerwehr of the Rand Corporation, Kirk Hubbard of the CIA, and Susan Brandon. Brandon's career illustrates the way in which academia, intelligence agencies, health policy, private defense contractors, and the APA intertwine. She started at Yale (1985– 2001), where she remained despite publishing only 12 papers over these years and being first author on only six of these. Brandon left Yale to become a Fellow and Senior Scientist at the APA, where she helped promote psychology's role in counterintelligence efforts. From the APA there followed in swift succession stints at the National Institutes of Mental Health; the Bush White House Office of Science and Technology Policy, where she played a large role in creating a major report on the role of social, behavioral, and economic sciences in countering terrorism; defense contractor Mitre Corporation; the Defense Department Counterintelligence Field Activity (CIFA); and the Defense Counterintelligence and Human Intelligence Center (DCHC). She currently serves as Director of Research for President Obama's High Value Detainee Interrogation Group. During much of her post–Yale career at these various organizations Brandon has focused on the area of detection deception.[55]

> In summer 2005, a series of six workshops also devoted to deception detection followed the APA-CIA-Rand workshops. Congress mandated the workshops and the National Science Foundation and the White House Office of Science and Technology Policy sponsored them, ostensibly on "Behavioral, Psychological, and Physiological Aspects of Security Evaluations." Yet much of the material had broader implications regarding the detection of deception in a variety of settings, including interrogations. As the report stated: although the security evaluations backlog for worker clearances is a critical operational challenge, the kinds of problems, relevant behavioral, psychological, and physiological variables, and scientific issues identified in the context of clearance evaluations *extended across a wide range of situations*[56] [emphasis added].

Similarly, in presenting various "security evaluation contexts" as "Federal and private security clearance," the report lists the rather mysterious phrase "difficult intelligence problems."[57]

The planning of the workshops illustrates the synergistic efforts of academia and the intelligence community. An Interagency Advisory Group that included the National Science Foundation, the White House Office of Science and Technology Policy, Departments of Defense, State, Justice, Energy, and Homeland Security, CIA, FBI, and National Counterintelligence Executive organized the workshop project, chose topics and issues for the six workshops and selected academic researchers to organize each of them. The selected researchers included faculty from five universities as well as the defense consultant MITRE Corporation. As observers to each of the workshops, the Advisory Group used the workshops to develop a set of recommendations for this emerging research area.

Many of their recommendations involve closer ties–called "embedding researchers and practitioners"—between academic researchers and the intelligence community.[58] Having identified the need for researchers to gain access to real world data, they recommended much closer relationships between academic researchers and intelligence personnel: "Researchers and practitioners will need to develop strong partnerships to overcome the present legal, political, social, practical and financial constraints of using real-world data."[59] It was also suggested that new collaborative arrangements between intelligence personnel and academic researchers be developed where members of each group could spend time in the other's settings.

While the workshops undertook the task of examining the social, ethical, and legal issues involved in deception research, they apparently discussed ethics only as an impediment. The workshop report makes no recommendations in this area other than to note "privacy and confidentiality are inherently at risk as public and private behaviors are scrutinized, and rights are given up for the privilege of crossing borders or flying on airplanes."[60] In contrast to the lack of attention to privacy and confidentiality concerns, the workshop planners exhibited a passion for loosening the constraints that research ethics place upon the ability to conduct deception research:

> [T]here are requirements to operate experiments in accordance with the Common Rule (the standard for regulating human research), but also a clear need for deception experiments that must use human subjects. On some campuses, research is hampered by Institutional Review Boards (IRB)[61] that may not fully understand the risks and benefits of this work, and thus may limit security evaluation research in ways not called for by the Common Rule. For example, some IRBs are reluctant to waive informed consent ... even though the Common Rule gives them the flexibility to do so.[62]

Informed consent for all but the minimally intrusive research has stood as the keystone of research ethics in this country for decades. The workshop planners are apparently claiming that the "benefits" of deception research to society warrant sidelining this bedrock principle since "the ends justify the means."

The workshop sponsors clearly had interests broader than the narrow area of security evaluations for employment as they raised the possibility of the development of a new multidisciplinary field they titled "security science." The quite extensive list of disciplines they foresee as contributing to this new field gives a sense of the scope of the field as well as the potential extensive impacts that the development of this field might have upon academia:

> clinical psychology; cognitive neuroscience; communications; computer and information science; criminal justice/criminal science; decision science; developmental psychology; geography; human cognition and perception psychology; industrial organization psychology; laws, ethics, and society; linguistics and computational linguistics; physical and cultural anthropology; psychophysiological psychology; risk and risk management; social psychology; sociology.[63]

In addition to contributing to the new "security science" field, each of these disciplines would in turn be transformed by their involvement in the field, and by their partnerships with the intelligence establishment. They would be affected by the disturbing effects of the availability of significant funding for work of interest to intelligence agencies, likely to the detriment of other lines of inquiry.

One Participant's Perspective

Further understanding of how these workshops affected the relationship between the intelligence community and academic researchers can be obtained from the reflections of one of the participants, Martha Davis, at two APA conferences in 2004, the FBI on intuition and law enforcement and the second APA-CIA-Rand conference on interpersonal deception. Davis spent forty years studying nonverbal behavior and over a decade investigating cues to deception, eventually applying her work in consultations with New York Police. Davis, since turned APA critic, describes how these workshops appeared to have an agenda hidden from at least some of the attendees — "a screening of work that would be of value for intelligence agents." As Davis explained about the CIA-Rand meeting, "The meeting felt like an audition for Department of Homeland Security funds."[64]

Davis further suggests that during the CIA-Rand workshop, in participants' excitement to apply academic deception research, they often ignored cautions regarding this research's validity and appropriateness to the security setting, increasing the possibility of serious misuse of the work with potential resultant civil liberties abuses. Further, she expresses concerns that they sidetracked major research efforts in the pursuit of national security funding. Davis also emphasizes the lack of attention to potential ethical complications involved in academics contributing to intelligence research, complications that she raised with a conference organizer, the APA ethics office, and APA forensic psychology division to no avail. As a result of these experiences, Davis decided to abandon this line of research after four decades.

CIFA and DCHC

It appears that the intelligence community's interest in behavioral science research on deception detection expanded in later years to research initiatives by the Defense Department's Counterintelligence Field Activity (CIFA) and its successor Defense Counterintelligence and HUMINT Center (DCHC).[65]

Former APA staff member, and CIFA and DCHC employee, Susan Brandon's role in organizing the APA-CIA-Rand conferences indicates that these new efforts extended prior efforts in the workshops, and potentially elsewhere.

In 2007 CIFA expressed an interest in funding:

> (1) to develop, test and evaluate the application (translation) of known principles and findings of the behavioral and social sciences to enhancing capabilities relevant to current and future intelligence, counter-intelligence, and human intelligence collection; and (2) to understand threats to national security in terms of the principles and methods of the social and behavioral sciences.[66]

Similarly, in 2009 DCHC requested behavioral and social science research proposals on three topics: field validation of evidence-based HUMINT collection; application of behavioral science to current human intelligence collection methods; and effects of interpreters on information collected from human intelligence targets.[67] The description of desired research in the first area is especially interesting:

> At present the methods for collecting information from human sources via screening, elicitation, debriefing and interrogation are not evidence-based. Effective methods for the collection of valid information from human sources have been developed in laboratory settings. The need here is to conduct field validation of the evidence-based methods to test the efficacy of these methods for application in operational contexts.[68]

While the CIFA proposal did not specify who is eligible to apply, the DCHC proposal made clear that university researchers were welcome.

Interestingly, we have reports of interrogation research being conducted by DCHC at a secret prison, referred to as the "Black Jail" by released detainees, on the outskirts of the Bagram Air Base in Afghanistan.[69] This facility uses techniques from Appendix M of the Army Field Manual on interrogations, which allows such abusive interrogation techniques as isolation and sleep deprivation, and does not forbid a number of other abusive techniques.[70] As Ambinder reported about the Black Jail in his *Atlantic* blog:

> From what information I've been able to gather, the interrogation environment is much like a social science laboratory, with psychologists and experts in human behavior looking for clues to see who might know more than they do, alternating with interrogators trained to ferret out actionable intelligence information.[71]

Other sources informed me that research on interrogation strategies goes on in U.S. detention facilities in Iraq. One may wonder if the Black Jail and the Iraq facilities are sites for the DCHC research program involving "field validation of the evidence-based methods to test the efficacy of these methods for application in operational contexts." One may also wonder if any academic researchers are obtaining field experience studying interrogations at these sites.

National Security Psychology

Simultaneous with government efforts to create a field of security science, the APA and psychologists from the military-intelligence establishment were working to create a field of "national security psychology." While these efforts were active prior to the 9/11 attacks, those attacks gave new urgency and opened up new opportunities for psychology to wed itself to the growing national security state. As early as September 19, 2001, the APA Board of Directors discussed terrorism on a conference call and established a Subcommittee on Psychology's Response to Terrorism.[72] This subcommittee contained several members who later played pivotal roles in assuring the APA's support, often through manipulation, of psychologist participation in Bush-era interrogations.[73] APA then threw itself behind the War on Terror, promising to mobilize psychology to defeat terrorism. As the Board expressed in a 2002 resolution, APA "encouraged increased support for behavioral research that will produce greater understanding of the roots of terrorism and the methods to defeat it, including earlier identification of terrorists and the prevention of the development of terrorism and its related activities."[74]

APA staff and elected officers started actively lobbying the intelligence agencies, the Executive Branch, and Congress for increased funding for psychological research aimed at terrorism while promising close collaboration with the intelligence agencies. A group composed of prominent academic psychologists and APA staff met in March 2002 with senior staff from Congressional science committees "to raise awareness of how psychological research might be used to understand, prepare for and counter terrorism."[75] Also in 2002, an academic psychologist joined APA public policy staff in meeting with a special assistant to the President "to discuss how behavioral and social science research could inform the mission of homeland security."[76] Another academic testified that year for APA before the Senate Appropriations subcommittee on Defense, asking for more psychological research money in the Defense budget. APA responded to a call from the President's Science Advisor by collecting examples of research applicable to counterterrorism efforts.[77] Then APA President Philip Zimbardo also met with National Security Council officials in spring 2002 to discuss psychology's contributions. While the APA report on the discussion claimed that it occurred "to discuss the contributions of psychology to ameliorate the repercussions of the Sept. 11 terrorist attacks," it is hard to believe that such a high-level meeting did not discuss broader contributions of psychology to the anti-terrorism fight.

The focus on deception detection apparent in the previously discussed workshops continued over the ensuing years, becoming a major priority of APA's science lobbying. APA and other organizations organized a presentation in 2004 on lying and deception for Congressional staff and administration officials.[78] The APA's various newsletters featured a number of articles on lying, deception, and deception detection, many more than this area warranted to most psychological researchers or practitioners.[79]

A couple of years after 9/11, the APA started emphasizing its ties to CIFA. In October 2004, APA staff met with CIFA officials "to discuss possible areas of collaboration."[80] In its description of the meeting, the APA stressed that two APA psychologist members, Scott Shumate and Kirk Kennedy, held senior positions at CIFA, giving psychology and the APA influence in the agency. Interestingly, both these psychologists previously worked at the CIA and played roles in the black sites and "enhanced interrogation" program. Shumate was present at the torture of Abu Zubaydah, the first high value detainee tortured by the CIA, but claims to have left the interrogation in disgust,[81] though he remained with the CIA's Counterterrorism Center for another year before moving to CIFA. However, Scott Shane in the *New York Times* cast doubt upon Shumate's disgust claim.[82] In any case, Shumate's disgust didn't prevent him from bragging about his proximity to the high value detainees held, and tortured, by the CIA when he moved from government employee to private consulting.[83] Despite, or because of, his involvement in the CIA torture program, the APA appointed him to its 2005 taskforce on Psychological Ethics and National Security (PENS).[84]

Also in 2004, the APA implemented the embedding of psychologists in intelligence agencies as later recommended for other scholars by the NSF–White House workshops. APA initiated a research fellowship program, placing academic psychologists and graduate students in CIFA for a year, supervised by Shumate.[85] One of those fellows continued her work on deception detection through employment by the Defense Intelligence Agency after her fellowship ended.[86] APA fellows were placed in CIFA at least through 2007. Other fellows worked at the CIA and the White House Office of Science and Technology Policy, one of the agencies behind the 2005 deception detection workshops.[87]

While the APA was lobbying for CIFA funding, the agency got caught up in controversy by revelations that it had spied on peaceful antiwar activists and others in the U.S., in violation of rules restricting domestic spying by the Defense Department; this spying involved the use of scandal-associated consultants.[88] While the mainstream press reported on CIFA scandals, no mention of them made it into APA publications touting the association's close relationship to the agency. As late as 2008, when CIFA was being abolished, or rather "reorganized" into DCHC in the Defense Intelligence Agency due to the scandals, APA ignored those scandals as they asked Congress to preserve CIFA's psychology funding. As the APA described its testimony for CIFA/DCHC:

Dr. Boehm-Davis concluded her testimony by noting another APA concern — the potential loss of invaluable behavioral science programs within DoD's Counterintelligence Field Activity (CIFA) as it reorganizes and loses personnel strength. APA's testimony urged Congress to provide ongoing funding in the next fiscal year for CIFA's behavioral research programs on cyber security, insider threat, and other counter-terrorism and counter-intelligence operational challenges.[89]

No evidence exists that those testifying for APA mentioned, much less expressed concern about the rampant civil rights abuses that led to CIFA's transfer; it appears that the APA gave greater priority to increased funding for its members than it did to the protection of civil rights.

Ethics Code Changes

As an organization with many health providers as members, the APA had long committed itself to the "do no harm" ethic common to virtually all health providers for centuries, as delineated in Principle A of the APA's ethics code: "Psychologists strive to benefit those with whom they work and take care to do no harm."[90] Yet this ethic conflicted with many of the activities of psychologists working for national security agencies.

This problem had not gone unnoticed. Two psychologists, Ewing and Gelles, published a 2003 paper on psychologists and psychiatrists in the national security sector. They concluded that many activities of these professionals might well be considered unethical by colleagues, including, they feared, the ethics committees of professional associations and/or state licensing authorities. They called for exempting psychologists (and psychiatrists) in national security work from the standards incumbent upon other members of these professions.

> [W]e cannot continue to place them in situations where the ethics of their conduct will be judged, post hoc, either by rules that have little if any relevance to their vital governmental functions or by professional organizations or licensing authorities.[91]

The authors understood these dangers from firsthand experience. Gelles, in fact, had previously had a complaint filed against him for prisoner abuse — when interviewing an American sailor wrongly suspected of spying — with the APA ethics committee by prominent human rights attorney Jonathan Turley. That committee reportedly exonerated Gelles without investigation, outraging Turley.[92] Notwithstanding these charges of prisoner abuse, and Gelles' public position that the APA ethics code posed a danger to psychologists in national security, the APA appointed him to its 2005 taskforce on Psychological Ethics and National Security formed to judge the ethics of psychologist participation in national security interrogations.[93]

While the Ewing and Gelles paper appeared in 2003, given the long lags involved in scholarly publication in psychology, Ewing and Gelles must have written the article at least a year earlier, around the time that the APA was revising its ethics code. In any case, the APA revised the code in such a manner as to provide exactly the protection demanded by Ewing and Gelles for their national security colleagues. APA modified three ethics standards in problematic ways. Most familiar is standard 1.02, which allows psychologists to ignore the provisions of the code when it conflict with "law, regulations, or other governing legal authority."[94] With its echoes of the universally reviled Nuremberg Defense — "I was just following orders" — of the Nazi doctors and others tried for war crimes after World War II[95], this standard deeply disturbed many APA members and others. For years APA critics, human rights organizations, and some members of APA's Council of Representatives feared that this standard could protect psychologists aiding Bush-era torture and called for its revision.[96] But the APA Board, staff, and ethics committee failed to act to remove this clause until February 2010, long after the Bush administration left the scene.

When the APA did act to modify 1.02 they left unmodified two other problematic standards with potentially greater relevance to CIA and other intelligence research, making one wonder if they are still protecting DCHC, High Value Detainee Interrogation Group, or CIA interrogation research.[97] These are Section 8.05 of the Code, which dispenses with informed consent in research "where otherwise permitted by law or federal or institutional regulations," and Section 8.07, which sets an unacceptably high threshold of "severe emotional distress" — akin to the threshold of required suffering in the definition of psychological torture in the UN Convention Against Torture — for when deception is unacceptable in the design of a research study.[98] These sections, still in the APA ethics code despite protest, avoid placing the code in opposition to CIA and DCHC prisoner research.

While APA was actively promoting the contributions of psychological research to national security and changing the ethics code in ways consistent with the needs of the intelligence agencies, the APA took no steps to alert its members or other researchers to possible ethical complications when working on intelligence research. Just as when APA promoted psychologists as interrogation consultants,[99] the long record of ethical lapses in such work went unacknowledged and unexamined — and the association took no preventive steps to prevent recurrences. Instead, the APA regularly chose psychologists like Gelles and Shumate, with questionable records in dealing with prisoners, as its ethics consultants.[100]

Why It Matters

Close ties between academic psychologists and intelligence agencies are problematic for several reasons. Some of the issues have to do with the academic and research endeavors themselves, while others connect to unique aspects of psychology as a profession.

Academia, and the research undertaken by academics, traditionally rests upon an ethic of openness, transparency, and peer review. Thus, academic researchers are expected to reveal the details of their hypotheses, methodologies, and findings so that others may judge, and build upon, them. Increasingly, we expect them to allow other researchers to access their data.

Intelligence work has quite different traditions and values, operating largely in secret. When aspects of operations leak to the public, a much larger whole remains unrevealed. When academics engage in work for or with intelligence agencies, they often lose their freedom to communicate freely about their work. Perhaps more disturbingly, work done for intelligence agencies adds to a larger body of activity which the academic cannot know in its totality. Thus, much research on detection deception may appear unproblematic, such as studies of facial expression when lying, which approximate studies traditionally undertaken by academic psychologists. However, the academic may never know where his or her work fits into a broader spectrum of research and operations by the intelligence agency.[101] They may never know, for example, if, in fact, their findings get applied at Guantánamo or at a secret CIA or DCHC prison. They may never know if prisoners face incarceration, or "enhanced techniques" to overcome supposed deception on the basis of intriguing yet preliminary findings that are statistically significant but not necessarily robust predictors. They also may never know if their research becomes part of a vast secret effort to unlock the mystery of mind control and develop techniques for coercive interrogations, as happened to hundreds of behavioral scientists and others in the decades of the CIA's MKULTRA and other Cold War behavioral science initiatives. Academics aware of intelligence agency secrets, are knowingly colluding in keeping professional secrets from colleagues, often by lying to them, thereby undermining the basic ethic of academia.

While other forces, such as the large influx of corporate money into academic research along with various confidentiality and nondisclosure agreements, also weakens the academy's commitment to transparency, work with intelligence agencies potentially generates problems of a greater order of magnitude. When a university researcher violates an agreement with a corporation, she may face financial consequences but individuals who reveal classified information may face imprisonment. Further, the intelligence agencies possess far greater powers than large corporations to punish those they view as transgressors.

For psychologists, working with intelligence agencies creates additional ethical problems. Many psychologists act as practitioners, serving the public as psychotherapists and other types of helping professionals. Ethical principles based upon the Nuremberg Code — developed in response to horrific experimentation by Nazi doctors — which begins with "The voluntary consent of the human subject is absolutely essential" guides psychological research.[102] The combination of practitioner and researcher ethics has led the psychology profession to define itself as one based upon a "do no harm" ethic. Intelligence work, as Ewing and Gelles correctly acknowledge, focuses rather on identifying and defeating enemies, a goal often diametrically opposed to the "do no harm" ethic.

APA's collaboration with the intelligence establishment damages psychological ethics. The APA changed its ethics code to accommodate the concerns of those working in the national security sector. Many of the foremost proponents among APA leaders of psychologist involvement in national security pose as experts in psychological ethics. These include a former chair of the APA ethics committee, the association's ethics director,[103] and a former association President who edits *Ethics & Behavior,* the only journal exclusively dedicated to psychological ethics.[104]

Furthermore, neither the APA ethics committee nor any state licensing board has investigated and adjudicated a single complaint among a number filed against psychologists accused of detainee abuse.[105] Evidently the disciplinary institutions that police therapists sleeping with their patients support or refuse to address potential torture collusion.

The failure — and indeed, the collusion — of so much of the psychological ethics establishment to confront the profession's leading role in our government's torture program undermines the profession. It interferes with the profession's learning lessons from this experience. To learn those lessons the profession needs a thorough investigation of and a reckoning with its response to 9/11 and its active collusion with or blind eye turned toward our government's torture regime.

After exposure of the CIA's KUBARK and other Cold War abuses, there was no accountability. Congress held hearings, but most of the hundreds of researchers and institutions involved remained unnamed. The APA flagship magazine published one article on the CIA program which involved hundreds of its members and no one faced sanctions.[106] No protections arose to prevent a repetition — no penalty existed for collaborating with the intelligence establishment in even the most horrific of abuses.

So far, the message remains the same for the past decade of psychology's collusion with government torture. As citizens and as psychologists, we cannot let that be the final lesson of this sordid period. As noted last year by 13 health, religious, and human rights organizations, we desperately need an independent investigation focused on the roles of psychologists in the torture program and APA collusion in that program, as well major reforms in APA itself.[107] The future of the profession and its capacity to act a force for human betterment is at stake, along with the values of openness, transparency, and free inquiry that guided academia for decades.

NOTES

1. Central Intelligence Agency Inspector General, Special Review: Counterterrorism Detention and Interrogation Activities (September 2001–October 2003), (Washington, D.C.: Central Intelligence Agency, 2004), August 29, 2009 http://luxmedia.com.edgesuite.net/aclu/IG_Report.pdf; International Committee of the Red Cross, ICRC Report on the Treatment of Fourteen "High Value Detainees" in CIA Custody, *New York Review of Books*, February 2007 http://www.nybooks.com/icrc-report.pdf; Jane Mayer, *The Dark Side: The Inside Story of How the War on Terror Turned into a War on American Ideals* (New York: Doubleday, 2008).

2. Senate Armed Services Committee, Documents Released at the Senate Armed Services Committee Hearing "The Origins of Aggressive Interrogation Techniques" (United States Senate, 2008), June 17 http://levin.senate.gov/newsroom/supporting/2008/Documents.SASC.061708.pdf; Senate Armed Services Committee, Inquiry into the Treatment of Detainees in U.S. Custody, April 21, 2009, http://armed-services.senate.gov/Publications/Detainee%20Report%20Final_April%2022%202009.pdf, April 21 2009; Seymour M. Hersh, *Chain of Command: The Road from 9/11 to Abu Ghraib* (New York: HarperCollins, 2004); Karen J. Greenberg and Joshua L. Dratel, eds., *The Torture Papers: The Road to Abu Ghraib* (New York: Cambridge University Press, 2005); Tony Lagouranis and Allen Mikaelian, *Fear Up Harsh: An Army Interrogator's Dark Journey through Iraq* (New York: NAL Caliber, 2007).

3. Jan Crawford Greeenburg, Howard L. Rosenberg and Ariane de Vogue, "Sources: Top Bush Advisors Approved 'Enhanced Interrogation,'" ABC News, April 13, 2008, http://abcnews.go.com/print?id=4583256; Jan Crawford Greeenburg, Howard L Rosenberg and Ariane de Vogue, "Bush Aware of Advisers' Interrogation Talks: President Says He Knew His Senior Advisers Discussed Tough Interrogation Methods," ABC News, April 11, 2008, http://abcnews.go.com/TheLaw/LawPolitics/Story?id=4635175&page=1.

4. David Cole, *The Torture Memos: Rationalizing the Unthinkable* (New York: New, 2009).

5. Central Intelligence Agency Inspector General, Special Review: Counterterrorism Detention and Interrogation Activities (September 2001–October 2003).

6. Darius M. Rejali, *Torture and Democracy* (Princeton: Princeton University Press, 2007).

7. Stephen Soldz, "Psychologists, Guantanamo and Torture: A Profession Struggles to Save Its Soul," August 1, 2006, *CounterPunch*, http://www.counterpunch.org/soldz08012006.html, January 19, 2007; Stephen Soldz, "Aid and Comfort for Torturers: Psychology and Coercive Interrogations in Historical Perspective," April 13, 2007, *CounterPunch*, http://www.counterpunch.org/soldz04132007.html, April 20, 2007; Stephen Soldz, "Closing Eyes to Atrocities: U.S. Psychologists, Detainee Interrogations, and Response of the American Psychological Association," in *Interrogations, Forced Feedings, and the Role of Health Professionals: New Perspectives on International Human Rights, Humanitarian Law and Ethics*, eds. Ryan Goodman and Mindy Roseman (Cambridge, MA: Harvard Human Rights Program at Harvard Law School, 2009); Stephen Soldz, "Healers or Interrogators: Psychology and the United States Torture Regime," *Psychoanalytic Dialogues* 18 (2008); Stephen Soldz, "Psychologists, Torture, and Civil Society: Complicity, Institutional Failure, and the Struggle for Professional Transformation," in *United States and Torture: Interrogation, Incarceration, and Abuse*, ed. Marjorie Cohn (New York: New York University Press, 2010); Stephen Soldz, "Psychologists Defying Torture: The Path Traveled and the Path Ahead," in *First Do No Harm: The Paradoxical Encounters of Psychoanalysis, Warmaking and Resistance*, eds. Adrienne Harris and Stephen Botticelli (New York: Routledge, 2010); Brad Olson and Stephen Soldz, "Positive Illusions and the Necessity of a Bright Line Forbidding Psychologist Involvement in Detainee Interrogations," *Analyses of Social Issues and Public Policy* 7 (June 28, 2007), http://www.asap-spssi.org/default.htm; Brad Olson, Stephen Soldz and Martha Davis, "The Ethics of Interrogation and the American Psychological Association: A Critique of Policy and Process," *Philosophy, Ethics, and Humanities in Medicine* 3 (February 14, 2008), http://www.peh-med.com/content/3/1/3.

8. Dana Priest and William M. Arkin, "A Hidden World, Growing Beyond Control," *Washington Post*, July 31, 2010, http://projects.washingtonpost.com/top-secret-america/articles/a-hidden-world-growing-beyond- control/1/.

9. James H. Capshew, *Psychologists on the March: Science, Practice, and Professional Identity in America, 1929–1969* (New York: Cambridge University Press, 1999); Frank Summers, "Making Sense of the APA: A History of the Relationship between Psychology and the Military," *Psychoanalytic Dialogues* 18.5 (2008).

10. John D. Marks, *The Search for the "Manchurian Candidate"* (New York: Norton, 1991), Patricia Greenfield, "CIA's Behavior Caper," *APA Monitor* (1977).

11. H. P. Albarelli Jr., *A Terrible Mistake: The Murder of Frank Olson and the Cia's Secret Cold War Experiments* (Walterville, OR: Trine Day, 2009).

12. Louis Porter, "Evidence Suggests CIA Funded Experiments at State Hospital," *Rutland Herald*, December 1, 2008, http://www.rutlandherald.com/apps/pbcs.dll/article?AID=/2008 1130/NEWS/811300299.

13. Bruce Falconer, "Uncle Sam's Human Lab Rats," *Mother Jones*, May 25, 2010, http://motherjones.com/politics/2009/05/uncle-sams-human-lab-rats.

14. H. P. Albarelli Jr. and Jeffrey S. Kaye, "The Hidden Tragedy of the CIA's Experiments on Children," *Truthout* (2010), August 13, 2010 http://www.truth-out.org/the-hidden-tragedy-cias-experiments-children62208.

15. H. P. Albarelli Jr. and Jeffrey S. Kaye, "The Real Roots of the CIA's Rendition and Black Sites Program," *Truthout* (2010), February 18, 2010 http://www.truthout.org/the-real-roots-cias-rendition-black-sites-program56956..\

16. Marks, "Manchurian Candidate."

17. Ibid.

18. I. E. Farber, Harry F. Harlow and Louis Jolyon West, "Brainwashing, Conditioning, and DDD (Debility, Dependency, and Dread)," *Sociometry* 20.4 (1957); Alfred W. McCoy, *A Question of Torture: CIA Interrogation, from the Cold War to the War on Terror, The American Empire Project* (New York: Metropolitan /Henry Holt, 2006); Michael Otterman, *American Torture: From the Cold War to Abu Ghraib and Beyond* (Ann Arbor, MI: Pluto, 2007).

19. Otterman, *American Torture*; McCoy, *A Question of Torture*.

20. Senate Armed Services Committee, Inquiry into the Treatment of Detainees, Central Intelligence Agency Inspector General, Special Review: Counterterrorism Detention and Interrogation Activities (September 2001–October 2003). The Defense Department's torture program as seen at Guantánamo and Abu Ghraib was also designed based upon SERE.

21. Mayer, *The Dark Side;* International Committee of the Red Cross, ICRC Report; Cole, *Torture Memos*.

22. Physicians for Human Rights and Human Rights First, *Leave No Marks: Enhanced Interrogation Techniques and the Risk of Criminality* (Physicians for Human Rights, 2007), August 10, 2008 http://physiciansforhumanrights.org/library/documents/reports/leave-no-marks.pdf.

23. Bill Morlin, "Expert Has Stake in Cryptic Local Firm," August 12 2007, *Spokesman Review*, http://www.spokesmanreview.com/tools/story_pf.asp?ID=204358, September 5, 2007.

24. Jane Mayer, "The Secret History: Can Leon Panetta Move the C.I.A. Forward without Confronting Its Past?" *New Yorker* (2009), http://www.newyorker.com/reporting/2009/06/22/090622fa_fact_mayer?printable=true.

25. Alix Spiegel, "Military Psychologist Says Harsh Tactics Justified," May 4, 2009, account of radio interview, National Public Radio, http://www.npr.org/templates/story/story.php?storyId=103787285&sc=emaf, May 4, 2009.

26. Personal communication, October 21, 2010.

27. Mark Benjamin, "'War on Terror' Psychologist Gets Giant No-Bid Contract," Salon (2010), November 15, 2010 http://www.salon.com/news/torture/index.html?story=/politics/war_room/2010/10/14/army_contract_seligman.

28. Scott Shane, "2 U.S. Architects of Harsh Tactics in 9/11's Wake," *New York Times* (2009), December 9, 2009 http://www.nytimes.com/2009/08/12/us/12psychs.html?_r=5&hp=&pagewanted=all.

29. Mayer, *The Dark Side.*

30. Martin Seligman, "Former APA President Martin Seligman Denies Involvement in Developing CIA Tactics," July 14 2008, *Psyche, Science, and Society,* http://psychoanalystsopposewar.org/blog/2008/07/14/former-apa-president-martin-seligman-denies-involvement-in-developing-cia-tactics/, July 25 2008.

31. Stephen Soldz, Brad Olson, Steven Reisner, Jean Maria Arrigo and Bryant Welch, "Torture after Dark: Torture and the Strategic Helplessness of the American Psychological Association," July 22, 2008, *CounterPunch,* http://www.counterpunch.org/soldz07232008.html; Dana Priest and Barton Gellman, "U.S. Decries Abuse but Defends Interrogations," *Washington Post* (2002), April 8, 2009 http://www.washingtonpost.com/wp-dyn/content/article/2006/06/09/AR2006060901356_pf.html.

32. Benjamin, "'War on Terror' Psychologist Gets Giant No-Bid Contract."

33. Coalition for an Ethical Psychology, "Coalition for an Ethical Psychology Calls for Investigation of Allegations Concerning Martin Seligman, Denounces APA Inaction," October 15, 2010, Coalition for an Ethical Psychology, http://www.ethicalpsychology.org/resources/press-release-10-14-10.php, November 15, 2010.

34. Nathaniel Raymond, Scott Allen, Vincent Iacopino, Allen Keller, Stephen Soldz, Steven Reisner and John Bradshaw, "Experiments in Torture: Evidence of Human Subject Research and Experimentation in the 'Enhanced' Interrogation Program" (Cambridge, MA: Physicians for Human Rights, 2010), June 6, 2010 http://phrtorturepapers.org/?dl_id=9; L.S. Rubenstein and S.N. Xenakis, "Roles of CIA Physicians in Enhanced Interrogation and Torture of Detainees," *Journal of the American Medical Association* 304.5 (2010); Renée Llanusa-Cestero, "Unethical Research and the CIA Inspector General Report of 2004: Observations Implicit in Terms of the Common Rule," *Accountability in Research: Policies and Quality Assurance* 17.2 (2010).

35. Raymond, Allen, Iacopino, Keller, Soldz, Reisner and Bradshaw, "Experiments in Torture: Evidence of Human Subject Research and Experimentation in the 'Enhanced' Interrogation Program."

36. Inouye's staff never responded to repeated requests for comment from Leopold and Kaye, though, after their story appeared, DeLeon denied ever being briefed on the plan.

37. Jason Leopold and Jeffrey Kaye, "Wolfowitz Directive Gave Legal Cover to Detainee Experimentation Program," *Truthout* (2010), October 14, 2010 http://www.truth-out.org/wolfowitz-directive-legal-cover-human-experimentation-detainees64184?print.

38. Mayer, *The Dark Side.*

39. American Psychological Association Science Directorate, "Lies and the Lying Liars Who Tell Them," *Science Policy Insider News* (2004), December 10, 2010 http://www.apa.org/about/gr/science/spin/2004/07/also-issue.aspx.

40. American Psychological Association and FBI Academy, "Countering Terrorism: Integration of Practice and Theory" (American Psychological Association and FBI Academy, 2002).

41. Ibid., 6.

42. Ibid., 17.

43. Susan E. Brandon, "The Science of Deception: Integration of Theory and Practice" (American Psychological Association, 2004), July 6, 2008 http://www.apa.org/ppo/deception.pdf.

44. American Psychological Association Science Directorate, "APA Works with CIA and Rand to Hold Science of Deception Workshop," *Science Policy Insider News* (July 2003), December 10, 2010 http://web.archive.org/web/20051127200936/http://www.apa.org/ppo/spin/703.html.

45. American Psychological Association, "Science of Deception: Integration of Practice and Theory: Scenarios," 2003, American Psychological Association, http://web.archive.org/web/20060211185145/www.apa.org/ppo/issues/deceptscenarios.html, December 10, 2010.

46. Jeffrey Kaye, "APA Scrubs Pages Linking It to CIA Torture Workshops," *Firedoglake* (2010), http://my.firedoglake.com/valtin/2010/05/16/apa-scrubs-pages-linking-it-to-cia-torture-workshops/.

47. Brandon, "The Science of Deception: Integration of Theory and Practice." This report, like the scenarios, has since been scrubbed from the web site.

48. Andy Worthington, "Hit Me Baby One More Time: A History of Music Torture in

the War on Terror," *CounterPunch* (2008), December 15, 2008 http://counterpunch.org/worthington12152008.html; Suzanne G. Cusick, "Music as Torture / Music as Weapon," *Transcultural Music Review* 10 (2006), July 8, 2008 http://www.sibetrans.com/trans/trans10/cusick_eng.htm.

49. Lagouranis and Mikaelian, *Fear Up Harsh*; Katherine Eban, "Rorschach and Awe," *Vanity Fair* July 17, 2007 http://www.vanityfair.com/politics/features/2007/07/torture200707?printable=true&currentPage=all; Associated Press, "FBI Details Possible Guantanamo Bay Abuse: Newly Released Documents Focus on Harsh Interrogation Techniques," January 3, 2007, MSNBC, http://www.msnbc.msn.com/id/16444296/, January 3, 2007.

50. Jeff Stein, "Evidence Grows of Drug Use on Detainees," April 4, 2008, *CQ Homeland Security,* http://public.cq.com/docs/hs/hsnews110-000002697912.html, April 4, 2008; Joby Warrick, "Detainees Allege Being Drugged, Questioned," April 22, 2008, http://www.washingtonpost.com/wp-dyn/content/article/2008/04/21/AR2008042103399.html?hpid=topnews2008.

51. American Psychological Association Science Directorate, Preliminary Agenda: Interpersonal Deception: Integration of Theory and Practice, 2004, American Psychological Association, http://old.apa.org/ppo/issues/deceptionagenda.html, October 11, 2010.

52. The APA's newsletter notice stated that they would later report on the meeting, but this report apparently was never publicly released.

53. American Psychological Association Science Directorate, "Lies and the Lying Liars Who Tell Them."

54. American Psychological Association Science Directorate, Preliminary Agenda: Interpersonal Deception: Integration of Theory and Practice.

55. Subjecta Bhatt and Susan Brandon, "Review of Voice Stress Technologies for Detection of Deception," December 12, 2008, American Polygraph Association, http://www.polygraph.org/files/Bhatt__Brandon_2008_voice.pdf, October 11, 2010.

56. National Science Foundation and White House Office of Science and Technology Policy, "Behavioral, Psychological and Physiological Aspects of Security Evaluations: Reports on a Series of Workshops" (Washington, D.C.: National Science Foundation and White House Office of Science and Technology Policy, 2007), 5; emphasis added.

57. National Science Foundation and White House Office of Science and Technology Policy, "Behavioral, Psychological and Physiological Aspects of Security Evaluations: Reports on a Series of Workshops," 7. After visiting the prison at Guantánamo Bay, 2005 APA President Ronald Levant described the interrogations there that his members were aiding as "national security investigations," American Psychological Association, "APA President Ronald F. Levant Visits Naval Station at Guantanamo Bay," October 23, 2005, American Psychological Association, http://www.apa.org/releases/gitmo1023.html, June 12, 2006, consistent with the expanded usage I am suggesting Levant's odd language, conveyed in an official APA press release, also suggests that he was adopting language used by others, presumably his hosts from the Pentagon.

58. National Science Foundation and White House Office of Science and Technology Policy, "Behavioral, Psychological and Physiological Aspects of Security Evaluations: Reports on a Series of Workshops,"16.

59. Ibid., 11.

60. Ibid., 12.

61. IRBs are the committees to evaluate the ethics and human subject protections of organizations conducting research on people. All institutions which receive funds from the federal Department of Health and Human Services, among others, are required to have all human subject research reviewed by an IRB.

62. National Science Foundation and White House Office of Science and Technology Policy, "Behavioral, Psychological and Physiological Aspects of Security Evaluations: Reports on a Series of Workshops," 10–11.

63. Ibid., 9.

64. Martha Davis, "Recruiting Research Psychologists for National Security Applications," February 27, 2009, The Psychology and Military Intelligence Casebook on Interrogation Ethics, http://www.pmicasebook.com/PMI_Casebook/Case_-_Davis.html, December 13, 2010.

65. HUMINT = "Human Intelligence" in the intelligence community's lingo.

66. Department of Defense Counterintelligence Field Activity, "Presolicitation Notice. Broad Agency Announcement: Applied Research in Social and Behavioral Science," (2007), December 27, 2010, http://www.dodtechmatch.com/DOD/Opportunities/FedBizView.aspx?id=BAA-CIFA-DB-07-01.

67. Defense Counterintelligence and HUMINT Center, "Broad Agency Announcement: Behavior Science Research and Development," (2009), December 27, 2010, https://www.fbo.gov/utils/view?id=96fa7fc75692998e4f2082a1flea3f34.

68. Ibid., 2.

69. Stephen Soldz, "The 'Black Jail': Obama's Afghan Torture Center and the American Psychological Association," *CounterPunch* (2010), May 22, 2010 http://counterpunch.org/soldz 05212010.html; Marc Ambinder, "Inside the Secret Interrogation Facility at Bagram," *Atlantic* (2010), May 15, 2010 http://www.theatlantic.com/politics/archive/2010/05/inside-the-secret-interrogation-facility-at-bagram/56678/; Alissa J. Rubin, "Afghans Detail Detention in 'Black Jail' at U.S. Base," *New York Times* (2009), November 29, 2009, http://www.nytimes.com/2009/11/29/world/asia/29bagram.html?r=2&pagewanted=print; Joshua Partlow and Julie Tate, "2 Afghans Allege Abuse at U.S. Site," *New York Times* (2009), November 29, 2009 , http://www.washingtonpost.com/wp-dyn/content/article/2009/11/27/AR2009112703438_pf.html.

70. United States Department of the Army, Human Intelligence Collector Operations, September 6, 2006, United States Department of the Army, http://www.army.mil/references/FM2-22.3.pdf, September 17, 2006; Marc Ambinder, "Bagram: What Appendix M Says About Interrogation," *Atlantic* (2010), May 15, 2010, http://www.theatlantic.com/politics/archive/2010/05/bagram-what-appendix-m-says-about-interrogation/56772/; Matthew Alexander, "Torture's Loopholes," *New York Times* (2010), Op Ed, January 24, 2010 http://www.nytimes.com/2010/01/21/opinion/21alexander.html; Jeffrey S. Kaye, "How the U.S. Army's Field Manual Codified Torture — and Still Does," (2009), January 7, 2009, http://www.alternet.org/rights/117807/how_the_u.s._army%27s_field_manual_codified_torture_—_and_still_does/.

71. Ambinder, "Bagram: What Appendix M Says About Interrogation."

72. Ronald F. Levant, Laura Barbanel and Patrick H. DeLeon, "Psychology"s Response to Terrorism," in *Understanding Terrorism: Psychosocial Roots, Consequences, and Interventions*, eds. Anthony J. Marsella and Fathali M. Moghaddam (Washington, DC: American Psychological Association, 2003).

73. Jean Maria Arrigo, "APA Interrogation Task Force Member Dr. Jean Maria Arrigo Exposes Group's Ties to Military," *Democracy Now!* (2007), August 20, 2007, http://www.democracynow.org/article.pl?sid=07/08/20/1628234; Coalition for an Ethical Psychology, Analysis of the American Psychological Association's Frequently Asked Questions Regarding APA's Policies and Positions on the Use of Torture or Cruel, Inhuman or Degrading Treatment During Interrogations, January 16, 2008, Coalition for an Ethical Psychology, http://psychoanalystsopposewar.org/blog/wp-content/uploads/2008/01/apa_faq_coalition_comments_v12c.pdf, February 9, 2008; Bryant Welch, "The American Psychological Association and Torture: The Day the Tide Turned," July 21, 2009, Huffington Post, http://www.huffingtonpost.com/bryant-welch/the-american-psychologica_b_242020.html, July 21, 2009.

74. American Psychological Association, Board of Directors Resolution on Terrorism, 2002, American Psychological Association, http://www.apa.org/about/governance/council/policy/chapter-4b.aspx, December 19, 2010.

75. American Psychological Association Public Policy Office, "Hats Off to Our Psychology Advocates," *Monitor on Psychology* 33 (2002), December 12, 2010, http://www.apa.org/monitor/dec02/ppup.aspx.

76. Ibid.

77. American Psychological Association Science Directorate, "Combating Terrorism: Some Responses from the Behavioral Sciences," *Science Policy Insider News* (2002), December 27, 2010 http://www.apa.org/about/gr/science/spin/2002/04/terrorism.aspx.

78. American Psychological Association Science Directorate, "Researchers Discuss Lying on Capitol Hill," *Science Policy Insider News* (2004), November 13, 2010 http://www.apa.org/about/gr/science/spin/2004/04/deception.aspx.

79. Sadie F. Dingfelder, "To Tell the Truth: Psychologists in the Field of Deception Detection Consult with the Department of Homeland Security and Other Federal Agencies," *Monitor on Psychology* 35 (2004), November 13, 2010 http://www.apa.org/monitor/mar04/consulting. aspx; Rachel Adelson, "Detecting Deception: Some Research Links Lying with Such Facial and Bodily Cues as Increased Pupil Size and Lip Pressing but Not with Blinking or Posture," *Monitor on Psychology* 35 (2004), November 13, 2010 http://www.apa.org/monitor/julaug04/detecting.aspx; John G. Capps and Andrew Ryan, "It's Not Just Polygraph Anymore: Within the Behavioral Sciences Community, the Polygraph Is a Controversial Device That Has Often Generated a Polarizing Reaction," *Psychological Science Agenda* (2005), December 13, 2010 http://www.apa. org/science/about/psa/2005/09/polygraph.aspx.

80. American Psychological Association Science Directorate, "Science Policy Staff Meet with Psychologists in Counterintelligence," *Science Policy Insider News* (2004), December 13, 2010 http://www.apa.org/about/gr/science/spin/2004/10/also-issue.aspx.

81. Eban, "Rorschach and Awe."

82. Shane, "2 U.S. Architects of Harsh Tactics in 9/11's Wake."

83. Stephen Soldz, "Member of APA Pens Task Force Brags of Being with Tortured Prisoners," April 27, 2007, *Psyche, Science, and Society*, http://psychoanalystsopposewar. org/blog/2007/04/27/member-of-apa-pens-task-force-brags-of-being-with-tortured-prion ers/.

84. Coalition for an Ethical Psychology, Analysis of the APA's FAQ; Mark Benjamin, "Psychological Warfare," Salon (2006), July 26, 2006, http://www.salon.com/news/feature/2006/ 07/26/interrogation/print.html.

85. Z. Stambor, "APA's First Department of Defense Summer Fellows Examine Counterintelligence," *gradPSYCH* 3 (2005), October 11, 2010 http://www.apa.org/gradpsych/2005/09/ defense.aspx.

86. Armed with Science, Podcast #24: "The Neuroscience of Deception Detection," 2009, http://science.dodlive.mil/2009/07/15/podcast-24-the-neuroscience-of-deception-detection/, October 11, 2010.

87. American Psychological Association Science Directorate, "Applications Due in January for APA Science Policy Fellowship," *Science Policy Insider News* (2007), December 13, 2010 http:// www.apa.org/about/gr/science/spin/2007/11/also-issue.aspx.

88. Jonathan S. Landay, "Pentagon Hired Contractor to Advise on Collecting Information on Churches, Mosques, Other U.S. Site," *Common Dreams* (2006), July 19, 2008 http://www. commondreams.org/headlines06/0318- 02.htm.

89. American Psychological Association Science Directorate, "Advocating on Capitol Hill for Psychological Research at DoD," *Science Policy Insider News* (2008), May 15, 2010 http:// www.apa.org/about/gr/science/spin/2008/06/advocating.aspx.

90. American Psychological Association, "Ethical Principles of Psychologists and Code of Conduct," 2002, American Psychological Association, http://apa.org/ethics/code/index.aspx, January 10 2010.

91. Charles Patrick Ewing and Michael G. Gelles, "Ethical Concerns in Forensic Consultation Regarding National Safety and Security," *Journal of Threat Assessment* 2.3 (2003): 106.

92. Jeffrey S. Kaye, "Former Top Navy Psychologist Involved in Pre–9/11 Prisoner Abuse Case," *Public Record 2009* (2009), http://pubrecord.org/special-to-the-public-record/2722/ former-psychologist-involved-pre–911/, Jonathan Turley, Testimony in Senate Intelligence Committee on Abuses by Naval Intelligence and the Daniel King Case, 2001, Federation of American Scientists, December 11, 2009, http://jonathanturley.org/2007/08/20/testimony-in-senate-intelligence-committee-on-abuses-by-naval-intelligence-and-the-daniel-king-case/.

93. Coalition for an Ethical Psychology, "Analysis of the APA's FAQ."

94. While the APA claims that their change in 1.02 was in process prior to the 9/11 attacks, the Ewing and Gelles paper shows that the issue of removing ethics code liability for national security psychologists likely was raised prior to the attacks. Further, APA continued with the revision post–9/11 and refused to change the ethics standard for many years after its dangers were pointed out to them. The leadership even ignored several mandates from the associations

Council of Representatives requiring examination of changes to 1.02 to forbid participation in human rights abuses.

95. Lawrence Rockwood, *Walking Away from Nuremberg: Just War and the Doctrine of Command Responsibility* (Amherst: University of Massachusetts Press, 2007).

96. Stephen Soldz, "Will the American Psychological Association Renounce the Nuremberg Defense?," *CounterPunch* (2009), July 28, 2009 http://counterpunch.org/soldz07272009.html; Coalition for an Ethical Psychology, Physicians for Human Rights, Psychologists for Social Responsibility, Amnesty International USA, Center for Constitutional Rights, National Lawyers Guild, Bill of Rights Defense Committee, Network of Spiritual Progressives, Program for Torture Victims — Los Angeles, American Friends Service Committee — Pacific Southwest Region, Physicians for Social Responsibility — Los Angeles, Massachusetts Campaign Against Torture (MACAT) and New York Campaign Against Torture (NYCAT), Open Letter in Response to the American Psychological Association Board, June 29, 2009, Psyche, Science, and Society, http://psycho-analystsopposewar.org/blog/wp-content/uploads/2009/06/Response-to-the-APA-Board-Letter-v10c.pdf; Kenneth S. Pope and Thomas G. Gutheil, "The American Psychological Association and Detainee Interrogations: Unanswered Questions " *Psychiatric Times* 25 (2008), October 10, 2008 http://www.psychiatrictimes.com/display/article/10168/1166964; Kenneth S. Pope and Thomas G. Gutheil, "Psychologists Abandon the Nuremberg Ethic: Concerns for Detainee Interrogations," *International Journal of Law and Psychiatry* 32 (2009), Kenneth S. Pope, "Why I Resigned from the American Psychological Association," February 10, 2008, kspope.com, http://kspope.com/apa/index.php.

97. Stephen Soldz, "American Psychological Association Removes Infamous 'Nuremberg Defense' from Ethics Code, Leaves Other Ethics Loopholes," March 1, 2010, ZNet, http://www.zcommunications.org/apa-removes-its-infamous-nuremberg-defense-by-stephen-soldz.

98. Office of the United Nations High Commissioner for Human Rights, Convention against Torture and Other Cruel, Inhuman or Degrading Treatment or Punishment, 1984, Office of the United Nations High Commissioner for Human Rights, http://www.unhchr.ch/html/menu3/b/h_cat39.htm, August 23, 2006.

99. Arrigo, "Arrigo Exposes Military Ties"; Gerald Koocher, "Speaking against Torture," *Monitor on Psychology,* February 2006, http://www.apa.org/monitor/feb06/pc.html; Ronald F. Levant, "Visit to the U.S. Joint Task Force Station at Guantanamo Bay: A First-Person Account," *Military Psychology* 19.1 (2007), Psychological Ethics and National Security Task Force, Email Messages from the Listserv of the American Psychological Association's Presidential Task Force on Psychological Ethics and National Security: April 22, 2005 — June 26, 2006 (ProPublica, 2009), May 5, 2009 http://s3.amazonaws.com/propublica/assets/docs/pens_listserv.pdf, American Psychological Association, Report of the American Psychological Association Presidential Task Force on Psychological Ethics and National Security (Washington, DC: American Psychological Association, 2005), March 17, 2010 http://www.apa.org/ethics/resources/position-/pens-report.pdf.

100. Coalition for an Ethical Psychology, "Analysis of the APA's FAQ"; Benjamin, "Psychological Warfare."

101. Philip G. Zimbardo, "Thoughts on Psychologists, Ethics, and the Use of Torture in Interrogations: Don't Ignore Varying Roles and Complexities," *Analyses of Social Issues and Public Policy* 7 (2007), August 27, 2007 http://www.asap-spssi.org/pdf/0701Zimbardo.pdf.

102. Nuremberg Code, National Institutes of Health, http://ohsr.od.nih.gov/guidelines/nuremberg.html, June 17, 2010.

103. Stephen Behnke, "Professional Associations and the Ethics of Interrogation: Review of McCoy. A Question of Torture: CIA Interrogation, from the Cold War to the War on Terror," July 26, 2006, PsycCRITIQUES, http://psycinfo.apa.org/psyccritiques/display/?uid=2006-09446-001, November 8, 2006; Stephen Behnke, "The APA Responds," November 22, 2007, *Harpers,* http://www.harpers.org/archive/2007/11/hbc-90001724, February 12, 2008; Stephen Behnke, Thomas G. Gutheil and Kenneth S. Pope, "Detainee Interrogations: American Psychological Association Counters, but Questions Remain," *Psychiatric Times* 25 (2008), October

20, 2008 http://www.psychiatrictimes.com/display/article/10168/1285473; Stephen Behnke and Gerald Koocher, Commentary on "Psychologists and the Use of Torture in Interrogations," November 18, 2007, http://www.asap-spssi.org/pdf/0701Behnke.pdf; Stephen Soldz, "American Psychological Association Supports Psychologist Engagement in Bush Regime Interrogations: A Critique of Stephen Behnke's Letter to the ACLU," May 27, 2008, *CounterPunch*, http://www.counterpunch.org/soldz05272008.html; Stephen Behnke, Letter to Amrit Singh of the American Civil Liberties Union, May 15, 2008, American Psychological Association, www.aclu.org/pdfs/safefree/2008_0515_apa_lettertoaclu.pdf, December 10, 2008.

104. Behnke and Koocher, Commentary on "Psychologists and the Use of Torture"; Koocher, "Speaking against Torture"; Gerald P. Koocher, Open Letter to Amy Goodman, 2007, http://psychoanalystsopposewar.org/blog/wp-content/uploads/2007/09/koocher_open_letter_to_amy_goodman.pdf, August 30, 2007; Gerald P. Koocher, "Twenty-First Century Ethical Challenges for Psychology," *American Psychologist* 62.5 (2007); Gerald P. Koocher, "Ethics and the Invisible Psychologist," *Psychological Services* 6.2 (2009).

105. Trudy Bond, "If Not Now, When? An Open Letter to Dr. Stephen Behnke on Psychologists Engaged in Torture," *CounterPunch* (2008), May 19, 2008, http://counterpunch.org/bond05192008.html; Associated Press, "Court Asked to Order Probe of Gitmo Psychologist," *Wall Street Journal* (2010), November 24, 2010 http://online.wsj.com/article/APb5fba66db06c46db8fc47fe01ae98597.html; Misti Crane, "Ohio Psychologist Faces License Fight over Work at Guantanamo," *Columbus Dispatch* (2010), July 9, 2010 http://www.dispatch.com/live/content/local_news/stories/2010/07/08/military-prison-duty-spurs-challenge.html?sid=101; James Gill, "Tortured Logic," *New Orleans Times-Picayune* (2010), May 20, 2010 http://www.nola.com/opinions/index.ssf/2010/05/tortured_logic_james_gill.html.

106. Greenfield, "CIA's Behavior Caper."

107. Coalition for an Ethical Psychology, Physicians for Human Rights, Psychologists for Social Responsibility, Amnesty International USA, Center for Constitutional Rights, National Lawyers Guild, Bill of Rights Defense Committee, Network of Spiritual Progressives, Program for Torture Victims — Los Angeles, American Friends Service Committee — Pacific Southwest Region, Physicians for Social Responsibility — Los Angeles, Massachusetts Campaign Against Torture (MACAT) and New York Campaign Against Torture (NYCAT), Open Letter in Response to APA Board.

Works Cited

Adelson, Rachel. "Detecting Deception: Some Research Links Lying With Such Facial and Bodily Cues as Increased Pupil Size and Lip Pressing but Not with Blinking or Posture." *Monitor on Psychology* 35.7 (2004). November 13, 2010 http://www.apa.org/monitor/julaug04/detecting.aspx.

Albarelli, H. P., Jr. *A Terrible Mistake: The Murder of Frank Olson and the CIA's Secret Cold War Experiments*. Walterville, OR: Trine Day, 2009. Print.

_____, and Jeffrey S. Kaye. "The Hidden Tragedy of the CIA's Experiments on Children." *Truthout*, August 11, 2010. August 13, 2010 http://www.truth-out.org/the-hidden-tragedy-cias-experiments-children62208.

_____. "The Real Roots of the CIA's Rendition and Black Sites Program." *Truthout*, February 17, 2010. February 18, 2010 http://www.truthout.org/the-real-roots-cias-rendition-black-sites-program56956.

Alexander, Matthew. "Torture's Loopholes." *New York Times*, January 21, 2010. January 24, 2010 http://www.nytimes.com/2010/01/21/opinion/21alexander.html.

Ambinder, Marc. "Bagram: What Appendix M Says About Interrogation." *Atlantic*, May 15, 2010 http://www.theatlantic.com/politics/archive/2010/05/bagram-what-appendix-m-says-about-interrogation/56772/.

_____. "Inside the Secret Interrogation Facility at Bagram." *Atlantic*. (2010). May 15, 2010 http://www.theatlantic.com/politics/archive/2010/05/inside-the-secret-interrogation-facility-at-bagram/56678/.

American Psychological Association. "APA President Ronald F. Levant Visits Naval Station at Guantanamo Bay." American Psychological Association, October 23, 2005. June 12, 2006, http://www.apa.org/releases/gitmo1023.html.

_____. "Board of Directors Resolution on Terrorism." American Psychological Association, 2002. December 19, 2010, http://www.apa.org/about/governance/council/policy/chapter- 4b.aspx.

_____. "Ethical Principles of Psychologists and Code of Conduct." American Psychological Association, 2002. January 10, 2010, http://apa.org/ethics/code/index.aspx.

_____. Report of the American Psychological Association Presidential Task Force on Psychological Ethics and National Security. American Psychological Association, 2005. March 17, 2010, http://www.apa.org/ethics/resources/position/pens-report.pdf.

_____. "Science of Deception: Integration of Practice and Theory: Scenarios." American Psychological Association, 2003. December 10, 2010, http://web.archive.org/web/200602 11185145/www.apa.org/ppo/issues/deceptscenarios.htm.

American Psychological Association and FBI Academy. Countering Terrorism: Integration of Practice and Theory: American Psychological Association and FBI Academy, 2002. Print.

American Psychological Association Public Policy Office. "Hats Off to Our Psychology Advocates." Monitor on Psychology 33.11 (2002). December 12, 2010, http://www.apa.org/monitor/dec02/ppup.aspx.

American Psychological Association Science Directorate. "Advocating on Capitol Hill for Psychological Research at DoD." Science Policy Insider News, June 2008. May 15, 2010, http://www.apa.org/about/gr/science/spin/2008/06/advocating.aspx.

_____. "APA Works with CIA and RAND to Hold Science of Deception Workshop." Science Policy Insider News, July 2003. December 10, 2010, http://web.archive.org/web/2005 1127200936/http://www.apa.org/ppo/spin/703.html.

_____. "Applications Due in January for APA Science Policy Fellowship." Science Policy Insider News, October 2007. December 13, 2010, http://www.apa.org/about/gr/science/spin/2007/ 11/also-issue.aspx.

_____. "Combating Terrorism: Some Responses from the Behavioral Sciences." Science Policy Insider News, April 2002. December 27, 2010, http://www.apa.org/about/gr/science/ spin/2002/04/terrorism.aspx.

_____. "Lies and the Lying Liars Who Tell Them." Science Policy Insider News, 2004. December 10, 2010 http://www.apa.org/about/gr/science/spin/2004/07/also-issue.aspx.

_____. "Preliminary Agenda: Interpersonal Deception: Integration of Theory and Practice." 2004. Workshop agenda. American Psychological Association. October 11, 2010, http:// old.apa.org/ppo/issues/deceptionagenda.html.

_____. "Researchers Discuss Lying on Capitol Hill." Science Policy Insider News, April 2004. November 13, 2010 http://www.apa.org/about/gr/science/spin/2004/04/deception.aspx.

_____. "Science Policy Staff Meet with Psychologists in Counterintelligence." Science Policy Insider News, October 2004. December 13, 2010, http://www.apa.org/about/gr/science/ spin/2004/10/also-issue.aspx.

Armed With Science. "Podcast #24: The Neuroscience of Deception Detection." 2009. October 11, 2010, http://science.dodlive.mil/2009/07/15/podcast-24-the-neuroscience-of-deception-detection/.

Arrigo, Jean Maria. "APA Interrogation Task Force Member Dr. Jean Maria Arrigo Exposes Group's Ties to Military." Democracy Now! September 9, 2007. http://www.democracynow.org/art icle.pl?sid=07/08/20/1628234.

Associated Press. "Court Asked to Order Probe of Gitmo Psychologist." Wall Street Journal, November 24, 2010. November 24, 2010, http://online.wsj.com/article/APb5fba66db0 6c46db8fc47fe01ae98597.html.

_____. "FBI Details Possible Guantanamo Bay Abuse: Newly Released Documents Focus on Harsh Interrogation Techniques." January 3, 2007. MSNBC. January 3, 2007, http://www. msnbc.msn.com/id/16444296/. Behnke, Stephen. "The APA Responds." November 22, 2007. Harpers, February 12, 2008, http://www.harpers.org/archive/2007/11/hbc-90001724.

_____. "Letter to Amrit Singh of the American Civil Liberties Union." May 15, 2008. American

Psychological Association. December 10, 2008, www.aclu.org/pdfs/safefree/2008_0515_
apa_lettertoaclu.pdf.

_____. "Professional Associations and the Ethics of Interrogation: Review of McCoy. A Question
of Torture: CIA Interrogation, From the Cold War to the War on Terror." July 26, 2006.
PsycCRITIQUES. November 8, 2006, http://psycinfo.apa.org/psyccritiques/display/?uid=
2006-09446-001.

Behnke, Stephen, and Gerald Koocher. Commentary on "Psychologists and the Use of Torture
in Interrogations." *Analyses of Social Issues and Public Policy* 7 (2007)1-7, http://www.asap-
spssi.org/pdf/0701Behnke.pdf.

Behnke, Stephen, Thomas G. Gutheil, and Kenneth S. Pope. "Detainee Interrogations: American
Psychological Association Counters, but Questions Remain," *Psychiatric Times* 25.10 (2008).
October 20, 2008, http://www.psychiatrictimes.com/display/article/10168/1285473.

Benjamin, Mark. "Psychological Warfare." *Salon*, July 26, 2006. http://www.salon.com/news/
feature/2006/07/26/interrogation/print.html.

_____. "'War on Terror' Psychologist Gets Giant No-Bid Contract." *Salon* (2010). November
15, 2010, http://www.salon.com/news/torture/index.html?story=/politics/war_room/2010/
10/14/army_contract_seligman.

Bhatt, Subjecta, and Susan Brandon. "Review of Voice Stress Technologies for Detection of
Deception." December 12, 2008. American Polygraph Association. October 11, 2010, http://
www.polygraph.org/files/Bhatt__Brandon_2008_voice.pdf.

Bond, Trudy. "If not now, when? An Open Letter to Dr. Stephen Behnke on psychologists engaged in torture." CounterPunch 2008.May 19 (2008). May 19 http://counterpunch.org/
bond05192008.html.

Brandon, Susan E. "The Science of Deception: Integration of Theory and Practice." 2004. July
6, 2008, http://www.apa.org/ppo/deception.pdf.

Capps, John G., and Andrew Ryan. "It's Not Just Polygraph Anymore: Within the Behavioral
Sciences Community, the Polygraph is a Controversial Device That Has Often Generated
a Polarizing Reaction." Psychological Science Agenda.September, 2005. December 13, 2010,
http://www.apa.org/science/about/psa/2005/09/polygraph.aspx.

Capshew, James H. *Psychologists on the March: Science, Practice, and Professional Identity in America, 1929–1969.* New York: Cambridge University Press, 1999. Print.

Central Intelligence Agency Inspector General. Special Review: Counterterrorism Detention
and Interrogation Activities (September 2001-October 2003). 2004. Counterterrorism
Detention and Interrogation. August 29, 2009, http://luxmedia.com.edgesuite.net/aclu/
IG_Report.pdf.

Coalition for an Ethical Psychology. "Analysis of the American Psychological Association's Frequently Asked Questions Regarding APA's Policies and Positions on the Use of Torture or
Cruel, Inhuman or Degrading Treatment During Interrogations." January 16, 2008. Coalition for an Ethical Psychology. February 9, 2008, http://psychoanalystsopposewar.org/blog-
/wp-content/uploads/2008/01/apa_faq_coalition_comments_v12c.pdf.

_____. "Coalition for an Ethical Psychology Calls for Investigation of Allegations Concerning
Martin Seligman, Denounces APA Inaction." October 15, 2010. Coalition for an Ethical
Psychology. November 15, 2010, http://www.ethicalpsychology.org/resources/press-release-
10-14-10.php.

Coalition for an Ethical Psychology, et al. "Open Letter in Response to the American Psychological Association Board." *Psyche, Science, and Society*, June 29, 2009. http://psychoana-
lystsopposewar.org/blog/wp-content/uploads/2009/06/Response-to-the-APA-Board-Letter
-v10c.pdf.

Cole, David. *The Torture Memos: Rationalizing the Unthinkable.* New York: New, 2009. Print.

Crane, Misti. "Ohio Psychologist Faces License Fight Over Work at Guantanamo." *Columbus
Dispatch*, July 9, 2010, http://www.dispatch.com/live/content/local_news/stories/2010/
07/08/military-prison-duty-spurs-challenge.html?sid=101.

Cusick, Suzanne G. "Music as Torture / Music as Weapon." *Transcultural Music Review* 10 (2006).
July 8, 2008, http://www.sibetrans.com/trans/trans10/cusick_eng.htm.

Davis, Martha. "Recruiting Research Psychologists for National Security Applications." February 27, 2009. The Psychology and Military Intelligence Casebook on Interrogation Ethics. December 13, 2010, http://www.pmicasebook.com/PMI_Casebook/Case_-_Davis.html.

Defense Counterintelligence and HUMINT Center. "Broad Agency Announcement: Behavior Science Research and Development." 2009. December 27, 2010, https://www.fbo.gov/utils/view?id=96fa7fc75692998e4f2082a1flea3f34.

Department of Defense Counterintelligence Field Activity. "Presolicitation Notice: Broad Agency Announcement: Applied Research in Social and Behavioral Science." (2007). December 27, 2010, http://www.dodtechmatch.com/DOD/Opportunities/FedBizView.aspx?id=BAA-CIFA-DB-07-01.

Dingfelder, Sadie F. "To Tell the Truth: Psychologists in the Field of Deception Detection Consult with the Department of Homeland Security and Other Federal Agencies." *Monitor on Psychology* 35.3 (2004). November 13, 2010, http://www.apa.org/monitor/mar04/consulting.aspx.

Eban, Katherine. "Rorschach and Awe." *Vanity Fair,* July 2007.September 5, 2007, http://www.vanityfair.com/politics/features/2007/07/torture200707?printable=true&currentPage=all.

Ewing, Charles Patrick, and Michael G. Gelles. "Ethical Concerns in Forensic Consultation Regarding National Safety and Security." *Journal of Threat Assessment* 2.3 (2003): 95–107. Print.

Falconer, Bruce. "Uncle Sam's Human Lab Rats." *Mother Jones,* May 18, 2010. May 25, 2010, http://motherjones.com/politics/2009/05/uncle-sams-human-lab-rats.

Farber, I.E., Harry F. Harlow, and Louis Jolyon West. "Brainwashing, Conditioning, and DDD (Debility, Dependency, and Dread)." *Sociometry* 20.4 (1957): 271–85. Print.

Gill, James. "Tortured Logic." *New Orleans Times-Picayune,* May 19, 2010. May 20, 2010, http://www.nola.com/opinions/index.ssf/2010/05/tortured_logic_james_gill.html.

Greeenburg, Jan Crawford, Howard L. Rosenberg, and Ariane de Vogue. "Bush Aware of Advisers' Interrogation Talks: President Says He Knew His Senior Advisers Discussed Tough Interrogation Methods." ABC News, April 11, 2008. http://abcnews.go.com/TheLaw/LawPolitics/Story?id=4635175&page=1.

_____. "Sources: Top Bush Advisors Approved 'Enhanced Interrogation.'" ABC News, April 9 2008. http://abcnews.go.com/print?id=4583256.

Greenberg, Karen J., and Joshua L. Dratel, eds. *The Torture Papers: The Road to Abu Ghraib.* New York: Cambridge University Press, 2005. Print.

Greenfield, Patricia. "CIA's Behavior Caper." *APA Monitor* (1977): 1, 10–11 Print.

Hersh, Seymour M. *Chain of Command: The Road from 9/11 to Abu Ghraib.* New York: HarperCollins, 2004. Print.

International Committee of the Red Cross. ICRC Report on the Treatment of Fourteen "High Value Detainees" in CIA Custody. February 2007. http://www.nybooks.com/icrc-report.pdf.

Kaye, Jeffrey. "APA Scrubs Pages Linking It to CIA Torture Workshops." Firedoglake, December 10, 2010. http://my.firedoglake.com/valtin/2010/05/16/apa-scrubs-pages-linking-it-to-cia-torture-workshops/.

Kaye, Jeffrey S. "Former Top Navy Psychologist Involved in Pre-9/11 Prisoner Abuse Case." *Public Record* July 24, 2009. http://pubrecord.org/special-to-the-public-record/2722/former-psychologist-involved-pre-911/.

_____. "How the U.S. Army's Field Manual Codified Torture — and Still Does." January 7, 2009. http://www.alternet.org/rights/117807/how_the_u.s._army%27s_field_manual_codified_torture_—_and_still_does/.

Koocher, Gerald. "Speaking Against Torture." *Monitor on Psychology,* February 2006. http://www.apa.org/monitor/feb06/pc.html.

Koocher, Gerald P. "Ethics and the Invisible Psychologist." *Psychological Services* 6.2 (2009): 97–107. Print.

_____. "Open letter to Amy Goodman." August 30, 2007. http://psychoanalystsopposewar.org/blog/wp-content/uploads/2007/09/koocher_open_letter_to_amy_goodman.pdf.

_____. "Twenty-First Century Ethical Challenges for Psychology." *American Psychologist* 62.5 (2007): 375–84. Print.

Lagouranis, Tony, and Allen Mikaelian. *Fear Up Harsh: An Army Interrogator's Dark Journey Through Iraq*. New York: NAL Caliber, 2007. Print.

Landay, Jonathan S. "Pentagon Hired Contractor to Advise on Collecting Information on Churches, Mosques, Other US Site." *Common Dreams* (2006). July 19, 2008, http://www.commondreams.org/headlines06/0318-02.htm.

Leopold, Jason, and Jeffrey Kaye. "Wolfowitz Directive Gave Legal Cover to Detainee Experimentation Program." *Truthout* (2010). October 14, 2010, http://www.truth-out.org/wolfowitz-directive-legal-cover-human-experimentation-detainees64184?print.

Levant, Ronald F. "Visit to the U.S. Joint Task Force Station at Guantanamo Bay: A First-Person Account." *Military Psychology* 19.1 (2007): 1–7. Print.

Levant, Ronald F., Laura Barbanel, and Patrick H. DeLeon. "Psychology's Response to Terrorism." *Understanding Terrorism: Psychosocial Roots, Consequences, and Interventions*. Eds. Anthony J. Marsella and Fathali M. Moghaddam. Washington, D.C.: American Psychological Association, 2003. 265–82. Print.

Llanusa-Cestero, Renée. "Unethical Research and the CIA Inspector General Report of 2004: Observations Implicit in Terms of the Common Rule." *Accountability in Research: Policies and Quality Assurance* 17.2 (2010): 96–113. Print.

Marks, John D. *The Search for the "Manchurian Candidate."* New York: Norton, 1991. Print.

Mayer, Jane. *The Dark Side: The Inside Story of How the War on Terror Turned into a War on American Ideals*. New York: Doubleday, 2008. Print.

_____. "The Secret History: Can Leon Panetta Move the C.I.A. Forward without Confronting its Past?" *New Yorker* (2009), http://www.newyorker.com/reporting/2009/06/22/090622fa_fact_mayer?printable=true.

McCoy, Alfred W. *A Question of Torture: CIA Interrogation, from the Cold War to the War on Terror. The American Empire Project*. New York: Metropolitan /Henry Holt, 2006. Print.

Morlin, Bill. "Expert has Stake in Cryptic Local Firm." *Spokesman Review* (Spokane, WA), August 12, 2007, September 5, 2007, http://www.spokesmanreview.com/tools/story_pf.asp?ID=204358.

National Science Foundation and White House Office of Science and Technology Policy. Behavioral, Psychological and Physiological Aspects of Security Evaluations: Reports on a Series of Workshops. Washington, D.C.: National Science Foundation and White House Office of Science and Technology Policy, 2007. Print.

Office of the United Nations High Commissioner for Human Rights. "Convention Against Torture and Other Cruel, Inhuman or Degrading Treatment or Punishment." 1984. Office of the United Nations High Commissioner for Human Rights, August 23, 2006, http://www.unhchr.ch/html/menu3/b/h_cat39.htm.

Olson, Brad, and Stephen Soldz. "Positive Illusions and the Necessity of a Bright Line Forbidding Psychologist Involvement in Detainee Interrogations." *Analyses of Social Issues and Public Policy* 7.1 (2007): 1–10 pp. http://www.asap-spssi.org/default.htm.

Olson, Brad, Stephen Soldz, and Martha Davis. "The Ethics of Interrogation and the American Psychological Association: A Critique of Policy and Process." *Philosophy, Ethics, and Humanities in Medicine* 3.3 (2008). February 14, 2008, http://www.peh-med.com/content/3/1/3.

Otterman, Michael. *American Torture: From the Cold War to Abu Ghraib and Beyond*. Ann Arbor, MI: Pluto, 2007. Print.

Partlow, Joshua, and Julie Tate. "2 Afghans Allege Abuse at U.S. Site." *New York Times*, November 28, 2009. November 29, 2009, http://www.washingtonpost.com/wp-dyn/content/article/2009/11/27/AR2009112703438_pf.html.

Physicians for Human Rights, and Human Rights First. "Leave No Marks: Enhanced Interrogation Techniques and the Risk of Criminality." 2007. August 10, 2008, http://physiciansforhumanrights.org/library/documents/reports/leave-no-marks.pdf.

Pope, Kenneth S. "Why I Resigned from the American Psychological Association." February 10, 2008. kspope.com. February 10, 2008, http://kspope.com/apa/index.php.

_____., and Thomas G. Gutheil. "The American Psychological Association and Detainee Interrogations: Unanswered Questions " *Psychiatric Times* 25.8 (2008). October 10, 2008, http://www.psychiatrictimes.com/display/article/10168/1166964.

_____. "Psychologists Abandon the Nuremberg Ethic: Concerns for Detainee Interrogations." *International Journal of Law and Psychiatry* 32 (2009): 161–66. Print.

Porter, Louis. "Evidence Suggests CIA Funded Experiments at State Hospital." *Rutland Herald*, November 30, 2008. December 1, 2008, http://www.rutlandherald.com/apps/pbcs.dll/article?AID=/20081130/NEWS/811300299.

Priest, Dana, and William M. Arkin. "A Hidden World, Growing Beyond Control." *Washington Post*, July 19, 2010. July 31, 2010, http://projects.washingtonpost.com/top-secret-america/articles/a-hidden-world-growing-beyond-control/1/.

Priest, Dana, and Barton Gellman. "U.S. Decries Abuse but Defends Interrogations." *Washington Post*, December 26, 2002. April 8, 2009, http://www.washingtonpost.com/wp-dyn/content/article/2006/06/09/AR2006060901356_pf.html.

Psychological Ethics and National Security Task Force. Email Messages from the Listserv of the American Psychological Association's Presidential Task Force on Psychological Ethics and National Security: April 22, 2005-June 26, 2006. May 5, 2009, http://s3.amazonaws.com/propublica/assets/docs/pens_listserv.pdf.

Raymond, Nathaniel, et al. Experiments in Torture: Evidence of Human Subject Research and Experimentation in the "Enhanced" Interrogation Program. 2010. June 6, 2010, http://phrtorturepapers.org/?dl_id=9.

Rejali, Darius M. *Torture and Democracy*. Princeton: Princeton University Press, 2007. Print.

Rockwood, Lawrence. *Walking Away from Nuremberg: Just War and the Doctrine of Command Responsibility*. Amherst: University of Massachusetts Press, 2007. Print.

Rubenstein, L.S., and S.N. Xenakis. "Roles of CIA Physicians in Enhanced Interrogation and Torture of Detainees." *Journal of the American Medical Association* 304.5 (2010): 569. Print.

Rubin, Alissa J. "Afghans Detail Detention in 'Black Jail' at U.S. Base." *New York Times*, November 29, 2009. November 29, 2009, http://www.nytimes.com/2009/11/29/world/asia/29bagram.html?_r=2&pagewanted=print.

Seligman, Martin. "Former APA President Martin Seligman Denies Involvement in Developing CIA Tactics." *Psyche, Science, and Society* (July 14, 2008). July 25, 2008, http://psychoanalystsopposewar.org/blog/2008/07/14/former-apa-president-martin-seligman-denies-involvement-in-developing-cia-tactics/.

Senate Armed Services Committee. Documents released at the Senate Armed Services Committee hearing "The Origins of Aggressive Interrogation Techniques," June 17, 2008. http://levin.senate.gov/newsroom/supporting/2008/Documents.SASC.061708.pdf.

_____. "Inquiry into the Treatment of Detainees in U.S. Custody." April 21, 2009. Senate Armed Services Committee. April 21, 2009, http://armed-services.senate.gov/Publications/Detainee%20Report%20Final_April%2022%202009.pdf.

Shane, Scott. "2 U.S. Architects of Harsh Tactics in 9/11's Wake." *New York Times* (2009). December 9, 2009, http://www.nytimes.com/2009/08/12/us/12psychs.html?_r=5&hp=&pagewanted=all.

Soldz, Stephen. "Aid and Comfort for Torturers: Psychology and Coercive Interrogations in Historical Perspective." *CounterPunch*, April 13, 2007. April 20, 2007, http://www.counterpunch.org/soldz04132007.html.

_____. "American Psychological Association Removes Infamous "Nuremberg Defense" from Ethics Code, Leaves Other Ethics Loopholes." March 1, 2010. ZNet. March 1, 2010, http://www.zcommunications.org/apa-removes-its-infamous-nuremberg-defense-by-stephen-soldz.

_____. "American Psychological Association Supports Psychologist Engagement in Bush Regime Interrogations: A Critique of Stephen Behnke's Letter to the ACLU." *CounterPunch,* May 27, 2008. May 27, 2008, http://www.counterpunch.org/soldz05272008.html.

_____. "The "Black Jail": Obama's Afghan Torture Center and the American Psychological Association." *CounterPunch,* May 21–23, 2010. May 22, 2010, http://counterpunch.org/soldz05212010.html.

_____. "Closing Eyes to Atrocities: U.S. Psychologists, Detainee Interrogations, and Response of the American Psychological Association " *Interrogations, Forced Feedings, and the Role of Health Professionals: New Perspectives on International Human Rights, Humanitarian Law and Ethics.* Eds. Ryan Goodman and Mindy Roseman. Cambridge, MA: Harvard Human Rights Program at Harvard Law School, 2009. 103–42. Print.

_____. "Healers or Interrogators: Psychology and the United States Torture Regime." *Psychoanalytic Dialogues* 18 (2008): 592–613. Print.

_____. "Member of APA PENS Task Force Brags of Being with Tortured Prisoners." *Psyche, Science, and Society* (April 27, 2007). http://psychoanalystsopposewar.org/blog/2007/04/27/member-of-apa-pens-task-force-brags-of-being-with-tortured-prioners/.

_____. "Psychologists Defying Torture: The path Traveled and the Path Ahead." *First Do No Harm: The Paradoxical Encounters of Psychoanalysis, Warmaking and Resistance.* Eds. Adrienne Harris and Stephen Botticelli. New York: Routledge, 2010. 67–105. Print.

_____. "Psychologists, Guantanamo and Torture: A Profession Struggles to Save Its Soul." *CounterPunch* (August 1, 2006). January 19, 2007, http://www.counterpunch.org/soldz0801 2006.html.

_____. "Psychologists, Torture, and Civil Society: Complicity, Institutional Failure, and the Struggle for Professional Transformation." *United States and Torture: Interrogation, Incarceration, and Abuse.* Ed. Marjorie Cohn. New York: New York University Press, 2010. 177–202. Print.

_____. "Will the American Psychological Association Renounce the Nuremberg Defense?" *CounterPunch* (July 27, 2009). July 28, 2009, http://counterpunch.org/soldz07272009.html.

Soldz, Stephen, et al. "Torture after Dark: Torture and the Strategic Helplessness of the American Psychological Association." *CounterPunch* (July 22, 2008). http://www.counterpunch.org/soldz 07232008.html.

Spiegel, Alix. "Military Psychologist Says Harsh Tactics Justified." Account of National Public Radio interview, May 4, 2009, http://www.npr.org/templates/story/story.php?storyId=103787285&sc=emaf.

Stambor, Z. "APA's First Department of Defense Summer Fellows Examine Counterintelligence." *gradPSYCH* 3.3 (2005). October 11, 2010, http://www.apa.org/gradpsych/2005/09/defense.aspx.

Stein, Jeff. "Evidence Grows of Drug Use on Detainees." CQ Homeland Security, April 4, 2008. http://public.cq.com/docs/hs/hsnews110-000002697912.html.

Summers, Frank. "Making Sense of the APA: A History of the Relationship Between Psychology and the Military." *Psychoanalytic Dialogues* 18.5 (2008): 614–37. Print.

Turley, Jonathan. "Testimony in Senate Intelligence Committee on Abuses by Naval Intelligence and the Daniel King Case." 2001. Federation of American Scientists. December 11, 2009. http://jonathanturley.org/2007/08/20/testimony-in-senate-intelligence-committee-on-abuses-by-naval-intelligence-and-the-daniel-king-case/.

United States Department of the Army. "Human Intelligence Collector Operations." September 6, 2006. United States Department of the Army. September 17 2006, http://www.army.mil/references/FM2-22.3.pdf.

Warrick, Joby. "Detainees Allege Being Rugged, Questioned." 2008. *Washington Post*, April 22, 2008. http://www.washingtonpost.com/wp-dyn/content/article/2008/04/21/AR200804210 3399.html?hpid=topnews.

Welch, Bryant. "The American Psychological Association and Torture: The Day the Tide Turned." Huffington Post, July 21, 2009. http://www.huffingtonpost.com/bryant-welch/the-american-psychologica_b_242020.html.

Worthington, Andy. "Hit Me Baby One More Time: A History of Music Torture in the War on Terror." *CounterPunch* (December 15, 2008). http://counterpunch.org/worthington1215 2008.html.

Zimbardo, Philip G. "Thoughts on Psychologists, Ethics, and the Use of Torture in Interrogations: Don't Ignore Varying Roles and Complexities." *Analyses of Social Issues and Public Policy* 7.1 (2007): 1–9. August 27, 2007, http://www.asap-spssi.org/pdf/0701Zimbardo.pdf.

6

CHAOS on Campus:
I Spied for the CIA

Verne Lyon

I spied for the CIA back in the mid 1960s. As the eyes and ears of the government on my Midwest campus I spied on my fellow students, TAs, and professors. The government paid me a monthly stipend and kept me out of the draft. I attended anti-war rallies and took notes on who said what. I volunteered for office work in peace organizations and copied down membership and sponsor lists for my handlers. I befriended campus leaders and foreign exchange students and then filed secret reports on them. I believed I was doing my patriotic duty and serving my country. Only years later did I realize I had made a terrible mistake and I resigned while I was serving in a hard target overseas. I may have quit the Agency but the government didn't quit spying on campus. We know that as recently as just two years ago the FBI secretly investigated anti-war protestors in my home state at the University of Iowa in Iowa City.

That covert investigation ran for about nine months, between March and December of 2008, and included the documenting of the comings and goings of the protesters at such places as a food store, the public library, a popular local restaurant, a local tavern and a campus religious out-reach center. It seems that the FBI special agents, in cooperation with local law enforcement officers as well as campus security went through garbage cans, reviewed cell phone logs, examined motor vehicle records, photographed and video taped the activists and developed intelligence files on them during this period. According to documents, the probe focused on an organization called The Wild Rose Rebellion. One of the anti-war protesters had filed a Freedom of Information Act request which ended with the disclosure of the operation and the publication of more than 300 heavily censored documents related to the case. Apparently the FBI feared that the anti-war activists formed part of a radical national network bent on disrupting both the Republican and Democratic National conventions scheduled for that year. To facilitate the intelligence operation, the FBI planted a paid informant within the group of about 25 activists with orders to attend meetings, obtain activity plans, dates, etc., and forward them on to the FBI. This *modus operendi* was strikingly familiar to me as it basically mirrored what I had done many years ago for a different federal agency.

While one group of protesters did cause a confrontation at the convention in St. Paul and many were arrested and await trial, none hailed from Iowa. Statements from former members of the Iowa group show that everything they did was open to the public, non-violent, and aimed to exercise their rights under the First Amendment's freedom of expression clauses. These Iowans accuse the government of wasting time, money and resources monitoring them while diverting resources from the search for real terrorists. Of course, the FBI and all Iowa law enforcement officials deny they did anything illegal, maintaining that everything they did was authorized under guidelines established by the U.S. Attorney General and that all of their actions were necessary to resolve the allegations.

The arguments used by the government to justify their actions remain the same as those used 45 years ago. The justifications claimed by the student groups also remain the same as 45 years ago — the provisions of the First Amendment. So, apparently nothing has really changed in this game of government distrusting its citizens. Unchanged too, is the lure of the almighty dollar to convince university and college officials to "cooperate" with these types of investigations in exchange for federal monies. Local law enforcement bellies up to the same feeding trough and relies on their faith that if the fed orders it, it must be legit. They have learned nothing and still cannot discern the difference between true terrorists and legitimate protesters. These events serve as a vivid reminder of how it all began for me some 45 years ago.

Early September of 1965 found me on campus at Iowa State University registering for classes for my senior year. Pre-computers, this process approached organized chaos but after waiting in long lines and completing mountains of paperwork in Beardshere Hall, I exited through the back door and headed for the small brick building hidden in the shadow of Marsten Hall, the hub of most engineering activities on campus.. This one story building housed the offices and classroom of the Aerospace Engineering Department in the College of Engineering. Though relatively small and its resources limited, the Department's reputation placed it within the five best such departments in North American academia. By most measures, other students held us in awe for the rigorous class work and difficult subject matter in our chosen field of study. They easily identified us by the two slide rules we carried along with our briefcase full of thick math, science, and engineering textbooks.

Entering the building I greeted some of the staff and several of my fellow students. The famous "tally board," prominently displayed in the front of the classroom, listed each senior's name, number of job offers they'd received and the name of the company making the offer. I noticed that after my name the number 31 appeared and that swelled my pride to say the least. After saying hello and exchanging pleasantries, talk turned to missing classmates and future plans. Several of our peers had dropped out of school, been drafted, enlisted in one of the branches of the armed services, changed their major, or transferred to another school. All male students had to enroll in one of the three Reserve Officers Training Corp (ROTC) programs for a minimum of two years and if accepted by their particular ROTC group (Army, Navy, and Air Force), they could go on to complete the officer training program and, upon graduation, be inducted into the armed services. As an additional incentive the respective ROTC units paid a partial scholarship for the final two years of school. I had chosen the Air Force program because of my interest in aviation and the fact that I was learning to fly at a local airport when I had the time and money to do so.

Our nation's growing involvement in Vietnam impacted almost every aspect of our lives. We each feared the pending letter from our local draft boards informing us of our classification and telling us to report for a physical examination and, perhaps, military duty later. The local draft boards monitored each student from their district and knew very quickly of any status change. The very fact that one attended school made little or no difference to one's classification or draft status. Anyone could be drafted at the discretion of the draft board so we all played the lottery and the waiting game. Those of us in the College of Engineering had a slight edge in avoiding the draft because many engineering disciplines qualified as "defense related" and this almost guaranteed a draft deferment. The rules did not always apply equally. Many of the large aerospace firms with an interest in hiring us flaunted the fact that they had an "in" with the Pentagon and the Defense Department and could almost assure us a draft deferment if we would only go to work for them.

My fellow Aero-E students understood the importance of making the right employment choice. It's not that we lacked patriotism, but after years of study, living at near poverty levels and generally denying ourselves a social life, we felt we deserved better than carrying a rifle through a rice paddy half way around the world fighting a war we didn't understand. Required to take ROTC our first two years at ISU, many of us did not continue on the track towards a commission in the Air Force, Army or the Navy after graduation.

My two years in the Air Force ROTC program taught me to march to orders, maintain a dress uniform in spotless condition, and prepare myself to fly Phantom F-4 fighters over Hanoi. While I loved to fly, doing it in a small Cessna over our midwest cornfields suited me just fine.

I had just settled into the familiar academic routine of rising early and going to class when I received a letter from Brown Engineering located in Huntsville, Alabama, asking for a follow-up interview. I had flown to Huntsville previously for an interview with this company that built ground support equipment for NASA. I had gone for two reasons, first for a free trip to the city that housed the Redstone Arsenal where Dr. Werner Von Braun had developed America's rocket programs after World War II and secondly out of curiosity about the whole hiring process. After returning home from that trip, I sent them a nice letter turning down their offer. As a propulsion engineer I had little interest in structural engineering. Their request for a follow-up interview pricked my interest so I agreed to meet with their representatives a couple of weeks later in one of the private rooms in the Memorial Union building on campus.

When the agreed on date arrived, I went to the meeting not knowing quite what to expect. I anticipated a better employment offer with a higher starting salary but I knew I probably wouldn't accept as it would still be tied to the structures aspect of engineering. When I arrived the door stood open and two individuals greeted me. They reminded me of the Mutt and Jeff cartoon: one tall and the other short. The taller one introduced himself as William Harris and the younger one claimed to be "Gus." After saying hello, "Gus" closed the door and Mr. Harris asked me if I had decided where to go after graduation. I said I hadn't and he began to tell me that Brown Engineering Company had taken a second look at my credentials after receiving my letter declining their original offer and had put together a new offer uniquely suited to my situation. Harris went on to say that the offer was so unique that before they could present it to me, and regardless of whether I accepted it or not, I would be required to sign a document stating that I would not disclose the nature of the offer to anyone without prior approval. This seemed strange indeed but I remember fantasizing that maybe they wanted to make me president of the company or something like that. After only a moment's hesitation, I signed the documents. The shorter of the two, "Gus," who had been inactive and silent up to that moment immediately whipped out a notary seal, and signed, dated, and stamped the document right then and there. Harris also signed the document.

I sat there in silence wondering what was going on. I had never experienced anything like this. Harris then told me that they did not really represent the Brown Engineering Company; they were representatives of a branch of the U.S. Government. He also told me that I had been selected from a very small group of students to be approached in this manner and then he apologized for the subterfuge. He explained that without my knowledge or consent, a background investigation had been performed on me and that it resulted in my being selected for this type of interview. He shared no other information they had obtained through this investigation.

Harris went on to paint a scenario based on the current political situation in the U.S. He stated that protests against the nation's involvement in Vietnam were increasing and that the federal government had reason to believe that outside forces were promoting these protests; that they were not home grown. He explained that although various agencies were working to ascertain the truth of these allegations, the government would welcome any additional independent confirmation.

Then he informed me that both he and Gus worked for the Central Intelligence Agency (CIA), an independent intelligence branch of the federal government, and that the CIA had been asked to develop their own set of eyes and ears on major college and university campuses across the country to assist the government in developing a plan to respond to the increasing number of anti-war protests and the levels of violence associated with them. The CIA had been authorized to reach out to students and professors to identify students and others, both foreign and national, who might be involved at any level in anti-war activity. The CIA would be grateful for my help, he said. The agency would provide a small monthly stipend and an absolute guaranteed draft deferment while a selected student (me) successfully participated in the program as well as an offer of future employment with the government if both parties decided that would be the next step.

The agents went on to say, however, that if I accepted the offer, I could not share that fact with anybody, family included. If I did, I could face prosecution and fines. They said that even if I declined to work for them, I could face the same consequences as well as other unnamed evils and that my act of signing the confidentiality documents was proof that I had agreed to these conditions.

I sat there in stunned silence for several moments, trying to get a grasp on the situation they had presented to me. Unreal, I thought; had I entered a dreamland; a trap? I didn't know what to say. I finally managed to ask Harris if they had the right person. After all, I was a-political, destined to become an aerospace engineer with desires to become an astronaut. I knew nothing about intelligence operations and I certainly knew nothing about the techniques used to obtain the type of information they sought. Why had they even approached me of all people? I asked them the simple but obvious question, "Why me?"

After exchanging looks with his partner, Harris responded by delving into my past with a detail that astonished me. He recounted the fact that while a sophomore in high school I had been the cofounder of the Boone Rocket Society and had impressed many of my teachers. He knew I had taken the tough science and math courses in preparation for entering the engineering college at Iowa State, that I had begun taking flying lessons, and that my name had been passed on to them through independent but reliable resources they refused to identify. He went on to say that a thorough background investigation had already been done on me without my knowledge. Friends, teachers, family, and others had all been interviewed already by CIA personnel using various covers so as not to reveal their true identity. I could only assume that agents conducted these interviews pretending to be representatives of various aerospace firms I had contacted just wanting to know a little bit about my background. I knew that most positions I had applied for required a minimum security clearance just to start out and since most friends and my family knew what field I was studying, they would assume everything was on the up and up. Taking all of this into consideration, the CIA had made the decision to contact me with this surprising offer. It seemed to reflect my country's confidence and interest in me and it offered me a way to serve it without stopping a bullet in an Asian jungle 10,000 miles from home. They explained, however, that I would first need to complete a formal entry application process that would include more interviews, tests, and evaluations that, if passed successfully, would allow the government to begin my training and employment on campus during my senior year.

I contemplated my decision. Their offer seemed to present me with a win-win situation. After all, I could decline future involvement after graduation and I would have a guaranteed draft deferment, a monthly cash stipend, a secret life, and still feel proud about serving my country. In a patriotic moment filled with ego and pride, I signed the documents.

With handshakes all around I signed a few other procedural documents. They told me to expect a contact shortly with instructions on how and when I should come to Washington, D.C., for processing. I'd have to spend several days there so I would have to plan accordingly.

Then they asked if I had any other questions. I said yes and asked if university officials knew of this type of activity on the campus. Their response was affirmative but they admonished me to keep this to myself. Apparently some officials at Iowa State not only knew about the government recruiting on campus in this fashion but had actually submitted names of students as possible candidates for approach. They said nothing about the fact that my assignments would be illegal at worst or immoral at best. In fact, since this was a secret operation, I would be paid in cash with no other record keeping and the rest of the federal government wouldn't know that I was working for the same government. I never questioned the legality of all of this. How could I? Not being aware of the secrets and machinations at every level of the government, I just assumed that everything it did was somehow legal. Years later I learned that the then university president, William Robert Parks, and the dean of male students, Millard Kratovil, had known about the CIA and FBI recruiting on the ISU campus. Conducted on the hush-hush, only a handful of university officials knew about the program. I assume they, in turn, believed that the process was entirely legal and a serious national security secret as well. For years, the CIA used former officers and supporters who currently enjoyed comfortable positions in the academic community, law enforcement, financial institutions, and politics to identify potential recruits for the Agency. The CIA referred to these people as assets in the "Old Boys' Club." The president and dean of men at ISU must have been members of this elite and secret club.

Some years later that I became aware that a friend from both high school and the university might also have tossed my name in the CIA in-basket. Jerry C. had gone through the same college-prep courses in high school with me and driven in our car pool during my first three years of study at ISU. He enrolled in electrical engineering and succeeded at that field of study. But then he suddenly dropped out of school in our junior year and joined the Navy without really providing me or others an understandable reason for doing so. He ended up in Naval Intelligence and died while assigned to the U.S. naval spy ship the USS *Liberty* in 1967 when the Israeli Air force bombed and strafed the ship during the Seven Day War. The USS *Liberty*, a recycled Liberty ship left over from the Second World War and newly outfitted as an electronic listening ship, deployed to the Eastern Mediterranean to monitor all electronic communications coming from Israel and Egypt just before and during the War. The Israeli air force identified the ship as a U.S. navel vessel but attacked it anyway over a period of two days to stop their communications from being relayed to Washington. Several U.S. sailors and intelligence staff, including Jerry, died during the attacks. I recall a phone call I had received from him months before that incident when he told me that he was doing "interesting stuff" and that he had dropped my name to some people, supposedly as a reference. I had never been contacted by anyone about Jerry so today I can only assume they belonged to the Old Boys' Club at some level. I'll never know for sure.

As I left the Memorial Union that day, I found myself totally unprepared for this type of rude awakening to the demands and realities of the world beyond my campus. I had led a sheltered life in central Iowa, never been involved in politics, never traveled beyond the borders of the country, and always looked at events in Washington, D.C., and other world capitals as in another dimension and somehow not really connected to me. The world had just come knocking at my door demanding some heavy decisions from me at the tender age of 22. I felt bewildered and somewhat fearful of what I had just committed myself to.

To prepare for the trip to D.C., I looked at my class schedule and planned interview trips as well as holiday school breaks to determine when I could travel without raising any unwanted suspicions. Taking advantage of a previously arranged engineering related interview trip to add on the visit to D.C., I notified the CIA contact person assigned to me and gave them the dates I would be there. They instructed me to check into the downtown YMCA under the name of Gary Bryant. I would receive further instructions once I arrived. The flight to the capital was uneventful except for the uneasiness in my stomach. I kept going over all that had transpired since the interview and wrestled with the decision to accept the offer or reject it and let fate determine my draft status and future. It had been a few weeks since the interview and I still couldn't decide just what I should and/or would do.

I arrived at the YMCA the day before my appointments and used my real name to sign in, having forgotten the admonition to use the alias. The next morning I waited for the phone to ring but time passed and nothing happened. I went out to get something to eat, did a little sight-seeing, and returned to the YMCA about noon. As I started up the staircase, a man approached me quietly and asked if my name was Verne. I acknowledged affirmatively and he asked me to accompany him outside. He motioned me into one of the coffee stands that dotted downtown. He bought me a cup of coffee. He told me that I had caused some anxiety for the Agency because I had not used my alias at the Y but that would be understood as just having the jitters. I felt differently. I had just blown my first simple test. I thought my time in D.C. might not last very long with that type of blunder.

We walked to a bus stop and then boarded a small blue bus that pulled up. It carried no type of identification. It certainly didn't look like a public transportation vehicle. My guide flashed his identification and vouched for me. With that, the bus took off for a destination unknown to me.

We got off at a building in downtown D.C. after passing some well known monuments, including the White House. We went up several floors and entered an office with no number on the door. I sat in the waiting room as my guide spoke to the receptionist. He then told me I would spend the rest of the day there and that I would receive a schedule to follow for the next several days. The schedule given to me had the places and times listed for my future appointments. The little blue buses belonged to the agency and he told me to use them for transport. A small card with numbers on it represented my transportation pass. Showing it to the driver would get me to the indicated destination at the proper time. Additionally, I had to present the card at each building I entered during my stay to gain access and I would be required to return the card upon completion of the process. With that he wished me good luck and left me waiting. After a brief period of time, an escort ushered me into the adjoining room where three men sat at desks. They asked me to sit down and the process began. I don't recall if they offered their names or not but I do remember they mentioned something about the positions they held within the Agency and why they were there. I do remember that one of them specifically said that he represented the Office of Security. I believe that one of the others stated he represented the Directorate of Operation and the Domestic Contact Service. They said they wanted to briefly review my background and ask a few questions about my motives for accepting the offer. They told me that they knew I had worked my way through college, that I had no known debts, was not married and had no relatives who were subject to foreign governments. They had obtained copies of my driving record and any police reports that bore my name. They knew the names of most of the girls I had dated, my high school grades and my level of involvement with high school activities. In fact, they told me things that I had completely forgotten about my own life. Their list included the fact I received my first traffic ticket at the age of 14 while driving my home-built go-kart, the local police responses to numerous reports of my amateur rocket building efforts and launches and the types of firearms I possessed. I sat there on edge, nervous and in awe.

The men went on to discuss some of the overall goals of the program I intended to join. The agency wanted "resources" on selected campuses to provide reliable information regarding anti-war movements: their plans of action, membership, financial sources, etc.. They wanted their "resources" nondescript, disciplined, reliable, and able to build their anti-war credentials from scratch. No one said anything about maintaining these carefully crafted covers for anything beyond the life of the program.

As the interview concluded, they asked if I had any questions or comments but if I did, I don't recall them or their answers. The whole event seemed more like a history lesson or lecture rather than an interview. They photographed and fingerprinted me before I left the building and instructed me to obtain a temporary identification credential at my first stop the following day. Reminding me to catch the bus at the proper time and place the following morning, they also reassured me the driver knew exactly where to take me. Over the next several days I bused to several different locations and visited with psychiatrists and medical doctors, underwent a series of personality tests, and finally took a lie detector test. As the final step in the whole procedure, completing the lie detector would allow me to return home. After a thorough review of the week's events and results the agency would notify me if I had passed. At the lie detector test the examiner said very little. He explained the process and told me that I would not be informed of the results. He went on to say that the exam, called "vetting" in Agency terminology, never really ended and that if hired, I should expect to repeat this test on at least a yearly basis. Then he connected me to the machine, placing a flexible hose around my chest to measure my breathing and connecting electrodes to measure heart beat and skin response. The operator explained the exam. He told me that he would be out of sight but within voice range. I remember him saying that I shouldn't be surprised at any of the questions because they had to cover a lot of ground with very direct and pointed questions.

He instructed me to answer the questions with either a simple yes or no and not to offer any additional information. He asked several "test" questions designed to establish a baseline for my reactions. Then he moved on to the real questions: probing, personal, almost insulting questions at times. He asked about my sexuality, if I had even stolen anything, did I tell lies often, did I use drugs, did I know anybody from a foreign country, had I ever traveled outside the USA, had I told anybody about this trip to Washington, D.C., etc. The questioning continued for what seemed like hours but only lasted about 40 minutes. He asked some questions a second time. Then he disconnected me from the machine and escorted me back to a waiting room. An aide reimbursed me for my expenses while I signed a receipt. The aide admonished me once again about keeping the whole experience secret and added that I would be contacted within a few days. As I left D.C. for home I sure didn't feel like a spy. Not knowing the results of all the questions and probing done over the previous days left me feeling like a failure. Why couldn't they tell me if I had made the grade or not? If I passed, what would they expect of me? If I failed, would they cut my tongue out? I had felt out of place during my stay in D.C. and certainly felt the whole experience would end in naught except for a life-long obligation not to talk about what had happened. I felt violated by the entire process of being interrogated, probed, measured, and evaluated by complete strangers. I had gained nothing and had been stripped naked in front of people who now held my future in their hands. How stupid of me. Unlike a nightmare, I couldn't just wake up from this and continue a normal life. I cursed myself for having ever gotten involved in this morass and, as I returned to Iowa, I found myself secretly hoping I had failed. If that proved to be the case, I could deal with the fact as well as the never ending secrecy consequences that now seemed destined to follow me to the grave.

I returned to classes and, trying to forget about my brief stay in this nether world of clandestine service, threw myself into my studies, special projects, and thinking about plans after graduation. I had been interested in building model rockets since about the eighth grade and had designed and built dozens of small and mid size solid fuel rockets in my bedroom. In high school I co-founded the Boone Rocket Society and along with similarly minded friends and my brothers, we located and developed a launching site at an abandoned shale pile on the west edge of town. On weekends we would launch our latest designs. Some turned out spectacular failures sending observers and ourselves running for cover. We relentlessly built ever larger and more complicated devices and developed the fuel mixtures to match. We regularly gathered chemicals like zinc dust, sulphur, potassium per-chlorate, potassium chlorate, potassium permanganate, glycerin, black powder, as well as a host of other things, to make up our different witches' brews.

With this background, I obtained permission, as a special project, to design, build and launch the first liquid fuel rocket developed at Iowa State University. I designed it myself but needed the approval by my professors. We machined and fabricated the rocket's parts in the university's machine shops and then assembled the whole contraption in the back room of the Aero lab right next to the wind tunnel we used for experiments. Basic in design, the rocket featured a glass lined oxidizer tank filled with red fuming nitric acid (RFNA) and a fuel tank to hold aniline. The mixture would explode on contact when mixed in the combustion chamber. High pressure nitrogen gas contained in a third container pushed both liquids out of their respective storage tanks to the combustion chamber. As I assembled the rocket, my fellow students and professors would drop by, stare in amazement and wish me luck. We tested the final design with tanks full of water on a Saturday afternoon but when we hit the launch button, everyone in the immediate area received a shower, including me. It took hours to clean up the Aero lab. We fired the actual rocket later that spring but after rising only a few feet from the launching pad, a blockage developed in one of the feed lines and the launch failed. I recall Harris taking a great interest in this project and asking in-depth questions about my classes and my knowledge of rockets whenever we had the chance to talk.

Although I hadn't completely forgotten about the pending decision from the Agency, it had drifted to the back of my mind as I settled into my daily routine of classes, lectures, and other aspects of student life. I also tried to find time to spend with a girl I had developed a relationship with in my home town. We would try to spend time together and make plans for the future but I could tell that things weren't always going according to plan. We would talk about what we might do after I graduated but with this new commitment that I couldn't even tell her about, things just became more complicated and stressful. I hadn't even been accepted by the agency yet and it already affected my personal life and future plans. It was becoming an uncomfortable situation to say the least.

After what seemed an eternity, Harris called. He sounded upbeat and wanted to meet the next day so we agreed on a time and place. Once the meeting started, it didn't take him long to get to the point: I had been accepted into the program. He beamed as he offered his hand and welcomed me aboard. I didn't know quite what to say. I wasn't even sure the answer I had just received was what I really wanted. At any rate, over lunch he explained to me how the program would work, what I would be expected to do, how to prepare my reports, how I would be contacted each month or more frequently if necessary, how I would be paid and how to make contact if required. I recall him telling me that the phone number for the contact was in St. Louis and the answerer would always say something like. "This is the office." I would identify myself by my code name of Gary Bryant, then hang up and wait for a return call. Our meeting ended with me swearing to uphold and defend the Constitution of the United States of America against all enemies, be they foreign or domestic.

Harris gave me my first assignment to identify all student groups on campus that might have anything to do with political expressions opposed to stated government stands on domestic and international issues. Harris would contact me monthly with new assignments and expect me to turn in reports on past and current issues I was dealing with. He advised me to "blend" into the environment I was monitoring and avoid standing out if possible. I asked him if my draft board had been notified about the guaranteed draft deferment the agency had given me and his response was that they had not. He went on to explain that should I hear from the board, I should immediately notify the contact in St. Louis and things would be taken care of. I didn't pursue the subject any further.

Armed with my first mission, I began the long and tortuous path into the world of smoke and mirrors. As a secret agent, I felt important, exalted to a level of trust and confidence only those who had lived and worked in the *sanctum sanctorum* of the government could relate to. I served on the front lines, doing my part in the struggle against foreign infiltration of our society and our way of life. This feeling made me want to shout it out to the world but I could not tell a soul. The euphoria lasted for weeks.

As instructed, I first identified selected student groups that had activist agendas and then began to monitor them. The agency provided the identities of some selected students, assistant professors, full and tenured professors as well as foreign students who had voiced opinions over the involvement of the U.S. in the growing conflict in Vietnam. Additionally, as I got active politically and monitored the chosen groups and people, I became able to identify those who seemed to be the chief organizers and leaders as well. I had difficulty at first because I had never been politically active before and was not well informed about the issues or people being discussed. I had to quickly develop a basic knowledge of both and inform myself as to why these items were so important to the particular groups. I also had to deal with the fact that I might be at a meeting of campus Democrats one night and then attend a similar meeting with the campus Republicans the next. When asked about this, I offered a convincing answer: I needed to determine which groups offered ideas that matched mine before I committed myself. Without actually joining, I volunteered with many student organizations on campus including the Young Democrats, the Young Republicans, the fledgling Students for a Democratic Society (SDS), Ban the Bra, and several others. I would volunteer to staff their offices and booths at odd or late hours when I would be alone and then I would copy membership lists, donor lists, activities both planned and past, virtually everything I could get my hands on.

The CIA expressed particular interest in names and identities of the "travelers" list. This list contained the names of people who were not ISU students but who traveled from campus to campus organizing anti-war protests and demonstrations. These 'travelers' seemed well funded and the director of the FBI, J. Edgar Hoover, had determined that they were really duped agents of the Soviet Union financed to manipulate the anti-war activities nation wide. However, Hoover had not convinced President Johnson of this so Johnson authorized the CIA to undertake the largest covert and illegal operation ever run against the citizens of the U.S. The charter of the CIA mandated it to operate beyond the borders of our country. FBI turf lay within our national borders and the war between both agencies ran hot and fierce. The CIA didn't trust the FBI or vice-versa. The Agency and the Bureau did not routinely share intelligence or information. The CIA considered FBI agents to be nothing better than Keystone Kops; let them chase petty crooks, bank robbers and car thieves, the agency had bigger fish to fry.

Many of these groups on the watch list I received had very few members. The majority of their activities revolved around getting statements published in the university newspaper, the *Iowa State Daily*, known for its anti-establishment positions on most subjects. Many of these student groups had fewer than ten core members and perhaps an equal number of on-lookers when they held rallies on campus. Additionally, the groups seemed only semi-connected to larger national movements that bore the same names and ideas. A couple of the groups actually achieved charter status with the national affiliates but I don't recall which ones. I do remember that some of the information I secretly collected on these groups indicated they received some funding and literature from larger national groups but I don't recall the level of outside support achieving any real significance.

The campus cops always attended the public demonstrations but, to the best of my memory, they did not take photographs. However, I did notice a couple of individuals would usually show up, stand sort of on the fringe of the group and take pictures. At first I thought they worked with the campus newspaper but later learned that only one of them did. The other photographer I couldn't place and I determined to find out who he represented and why he regularly shot photos of the students. Sometime later the CIA gave the program they had recruited me into the official code name of MHCHAOS and I found out that the FBI had also developed its own sets of eyes and ears on most major university and college campuses to monitor the same student and faculty members and groups I was infiltrating at ISU. I believe that the person I almost always saw taking pictures at local events worked for the FBI even though I never really identified him. Did he know about me and my purpose? I doubt it but cannot be 100 percent sure.

A two story wood frame structure located only a couple of blocks from the campus, Memorial Union earned the name "International House." It housed some foreign students and provided office space for their activities. One of my fellow Aero E. students from the Middle East lived there so I commonly showed up and checked in on what they were doing and talking about. I learned from regularly monitoring the foreign students that they all planned on returning to their home countries to practice the skills they learned in the U.S. Few, if any, expressed feelings about staying in the states after graduation. Most came from wealthy and politically well connected families and seemed to have positions already secured in their home nations. They all expressed views about the involvement of the U.S. in Indochina but their points of view ranged all across the political spectrum. They worried more about grade point averages and graduation than anything else. I uncovered no dangerous foreign plots. At any rate, as foreigners I really had no concern how my reports would affect them down the line. I never expected to see any of them again, so what the hell.

I hand wrote all of my reports and I turned them over each month to the contact the CIA sent to campus to collect them. I would also receive my cash monthly stipend of $300 in a plain white envelope during this visit which usually took place on the first Monday morning of each month at the "Hub," a coffee and donut shack on the north side of Beardshere Hall. The exchange would be quick. The contact, always about my age, would stand just outside the door holding a red knapsack. I would approach him and ask if he wanted to see the campus newspaper. When he said yes, I would hand him a copy of a newspaper wrapped around an envelope containing my reports. In the same exchange he would slip me the envelope with the cash. We would exchange some meaningless small talk and he would ask if I needed anything. If so, I would relay it to him and he, in turn, relayed it to my case manager for action. The meetings never lasted more than a few minutes and looked quite normal for a campus setting. The money came in handy paying for gasoline in the commuter club I belonged to and it allowed me to enjoy a few beers and pizza with friends on the weekends.

My assignments varied and some seemed downright strange and time consuming. Usually if my superiors gave me the identity of a "target" they also supplied some basic information normally accompanied with a request for verification, follow up, or more in-depth investigation. Often the identity of the target amazed me because, at least on the surface, I could not identify any reasonable cause for the government's interest in that person. It seemed that people became targets for investigation by expressing nothing more than casual or innocent interest in the activities of a particular group. When I felt probable cause existed I might open a file on my own volition into some person or group without waiting for instructions from my superiors. However, when I found my studies adversely affected by the amount of time I needed to spend on gathering information on a particular person or group I began to fudge my reports in spots where I felt there could be no independent confirmation and no one could dispute my version especially if the target and I were the sole witnesses to events. After a few months of this routine, I felt certain that everything I did amounted to one big test and that the information I provided had no real relevance in the first place. Having scrutinized everyone at every event I monitored, I felt convinced that I was the only ISU student recruited into this program.

Since I had no real access to student academic records or files, I had to collect bits and pieces of information whenever and wherever I could. Sometimes it would be done through casual conversation with the target in the classroom or it might be at a rally or event of some sort. I would also use any mutual contacts that I and the target might have. I recorded personal history, like and dislikes, family size, where they were from, course of studies being pursued, plans after graduation, views on the university, staff members, and, of course, political views and feelings towards the War in Vietnam. I made my inquiries very carefully so as not to sound like I was interrogating them. For the most part, I found the subjects to be forthcoming and not paranoid about discussing these issues with another student. Up to that time nobody had presented any real history or evidence of the student movement being infiltrated at any level in our society so most students never imagined I was spying on them.

Altogether tougher was getting information about teaching assistants and professors. How does one go about gathering information about their affiliations, beliefs, and activities? You could always ask students who were enrolled in their classes but the information only dealt with class subject matter, its manner of presentation and if the teacher graded hard or easy. Did they grade on strict percentage or on the curve? Could you earn extra-credits? Did they frequent the local watering holes in town? Did they come off as party animals? You could also "monitor" one of their classes if you had the time. This allowed you to attend class without getting credit for a period of time and it did allow you to meet the instructor and sort of break the ice. I chose this route in several instances and found it allowed me to approach the instructor out of the classroom environment when I saw them in the book store, restaurant, or on the street. In fact, on several occasions while attending a campus political event or group rally in public, I could recognize some of the teachers and professors at the outer fringe of the group listening to the speakers. If they stayed around or lingered, you could assume interest on their part in the theme being discussed and go from there. Sometimes they would make a comment in class about their disgust or agreement with a military decision made by commanders in the field in Vietnam or by politicians in Washington, DC. I noted their statements and questions, both pro and con, regarding involvement in Vietnam and forwarded them to my handlers.

Sometimes the professors would ask their students what they thought about current issues and invite class discussion. Often the professor would then express an opinion or two, either personal or from an academic point of view, that students would remember. I worked painstakingly to piece all of this together into some sort of comprehensive report. I found it time consuming and my style of reporting veered from simple objective reporting. Subjectivity crept into the reports and I expressed my uneasiness about this to my case officer a few times. My superiors always responded that such misgivings and doubt were only normal reactions and I should continue without being concerned. I wondered who else was identifying these academics as targets because 90 percent of the time my case officer gave me the names of the people to collect intelligence on. The other 10 percent of the time I could initiate a file if a professor's actions or views came to me through independent sources. Rarely would I find one of my "targets" drinking alone in a campus bar and I don't recall gathering anything interesting or useful using that technique.

My doubts about the relevance of my spying efforts permeated my subsequent attitude towards the CIA. I felt uncomfortable sizing everyone up as to his "political correctness." After all, the Constitution I had sworn to defend guaranteed their freedom of expression and belief as Americans. In time I decided to pursue my engineering profession upon graduation and tell the CIA thanks but no thanks for their offer and move on with my life. If I accepted their offer after graduation, I knew I would go into their equivalent of the Office Candidate School (OCS) and become an employee in one of the several divisions of the CIA. Nothing would guarantee me a spot in the Deputy Directorate of Operations (DDO) where I would get an overseas assignment. I would need to take language classes and intern for awhile with the State Department under a special relationship between the two agencies. I wanted to be part of the moon race not a desk analyst.

I decided to continue with the program until just before graduation before telling the CIA that I was going to turn down their offer of full time employment. That would allow me additional time to collect the much needed monthly stipend and extend the guaranteed draft deferment. Several fellow students had gone to work for McDonnell Aircraft in St. Louis and had gotten their promised deferments. The various versions of the latest fighter aircraft, the Phantom F-4 were being designed and manufactured in St. Louis and I calculated that as long as the war in Indochina continued, I would have both a job and deferment. I also needed the time to plan exactly how I would announce my decision to the Agency. Several times during that senior year they had mentioned that I could continue my affiliation with them at less than full time. However, they had never offered any clear guidelines on just what form that would take.

I also had concerns about my pending application for the security clearance needed for my type of engineering work. I apparently had a clearance now through the CIA but I couldn't tell any prospective employers about it. If I chose to take a government position with NASA for example, I couldn't tell them I was already a federal employee or that I had been previously. The more I thought about the challenges that I would have to face, the more intimidated I felt. I didn't think I had made the correct choice. Sure, it filled my short term needs at the beginning of the year as it paid me some money, guaranteed me a deferment and made sure I had the time to finish my studies but looking at the long term, it didn't seem like such a wise choice. I didn't know how long those secret agreements I had signed would really be enforced. I always operated under the assumption they would follow me to the grave. This bothered me a great deal because I couldn't foresee the twists and turns my life would take 10, 20, even 30 years down the road.

I wrestled with these things on a daily basis as graduation approached. I also noticed that it affected my relationship with my girlfriend. I wasn't spending the time that I should have with her. We were growing apart and, even though we both may have been a fault, I felt I bore more of the responsibility than she.

As the end of the school year approached, I placed my activities with the agency on a back burner. I had accepted an offer from McDonnell Aircraft in St. Louis over a great offer from United Aircraft/Pratt and Whitney in Florida. Since St. Louis was closer to home I thought I might have a better chance of saving my relationship with my girlfriend if I remained nearby. When the day came to inform Harris, I felt nervous but managed to blurt out my decision and the reasons for it, including the fact I felt uncomfortable spying on people. He listened in polite silence and then asked a few questions. He thanked me for the time and energy I had given to the agency and told me they held me and my work in high esteem. He told me that he would always be available if I needed to contact him and that if I found myself in need of a recommendation one could be given through a special program in place for those who had done acceptable work. He did tell me that the agency would contact me from time to time just to check on how I was doing and ask if I had changed my mind. Hearing these offers, I made a counter-offer of my own. I told Harris that if the agency needed my help on a specific project, they could count on my and my patriotism. He seemed glad to hear that. We shook hands and went our separate ways. I felt as if a great weight had been lifted from my shoulders. The separation had gone smoothly with no apparent animosity on their part. I thought I had done the proper thing by offering to help if needed but I couldn't imagine them ever contacting me again. Why would they want someone who had walked away from them and their offers?

Just after graduation in the summer of 1966, I packed my belongings into my old 1956 Ford and drove to St. Louis and began working for McDonnell Aircraft. My assignments included working on the F-111 swing-wing fighter bomber being built by General Dynamics Corporation in conjunction with McDonnell and the Gemini two-man space capsule. I had found a small apartment near the airport and McDonnell Aircraft and began my life as an engineer. Several of my ISU classmates also had come there to work so it seemed like old times. It wasn't long, however, the agency and its aims impacted my life all over again. Before the year ended, I found myself involved in agency plans that embroiled me with the law, saw the end of my relationship with my girlfriend and took me to Mexico, Canada, and eventually Cuba as a full-time active duty covert agent. Over time, the work I subsequently did under CIA orders ate away at my naivety. I no longer saw my work as patriotic or moral. When I could take no more, I quit.

Today, I try to look back at my frame of mind as a 22-year-old college student and recall my perception of the world. I realize that I never truly thought or worried about what the consequences would be for the people I spied on. I can only assume that due to my efforts some of those poor souls paid high personal prices that I can't even begin to imagine. Foreign students may have been denied continued visas to study in the U.S. Professors may have applied for tenure and been turned down due to faulty conclusions drawn from one of my hastily written or fudged reports. Students may have been denied career opportunities because they couldn't obtain a security clearance or because of a negative foot note tucked away in some obscure government file. I also realize that my alma mater's active involvement in spying on its own students and faculty usurped their civil rights and convinces me that the almighty dollar reigns supreme. A system that allows an agency like the CIA, designed to lie, deceive, manipulate, coerce, and destroy, to operate on their campuses mocks the very premise of education as a search for truth and knowledge. It goes against everything the university proclaims to pursue. Academia and the secret government collection of intelligence within its hallowed halls stand diametrically opposed to each other.

In the years that have passed since I made the decision to be part of the U.S. government's secret intelligence community, I have not only paid a very heavy personal price with daily consequences but I have slowly come to the realization that the government increasingly distances itself from its very reason to exist: to serve the citizens of this country. The consequences of that choice I made back in 1965 have cost me my rights as a first class citizen; my right to bear arms; rights to a security clearance, access to employment in my field of engineering, loss of friends, and ever increasing levels of distrust of authority and confidence in our national government.

The CIA program that I had been part of gained the official code name of MHCHAOS in 1967. In conjunction with MHCHAOS, the CIA opened two other major domestic operations. One, called MHMERRIMAC, infiltrated peace groups and black activists for reasons not clearly defined at the time. However, as time went on, it included other groups and individuals as well. The U.S. Government wanted to expand its intelligence data base while it had the chance. The CIA also created project MHRESISTANCE to coordinate information related to actual or perceived plans aimed at creating disturbances or violence at CIA recruiting events, CIA facilities and those of its contractors as well. Originally targeted at the Washington, D.C. area where most CIA facilities are located, its scope expanded over the years to include the entire country and some overseas locations as well. Most of the information collected by projects MHMERRIMAC and MHRESISTANCE ended up at the doorstep of OPERATION CHAOS for attempted verification. MHCHAOS also involved spying on fellow U.S. Government employees.

The number of people recruited into the program topped 30 with several of them coming from the FBI where they previously worked. Many first got overseas assignments to strengthen their "radical credentials" and thus provide them with legitimacy within the anti-war movement. When the MHCHAOS operation was finally shut down in the mid 1970s, it had collected files on over 13,000 individuals, more than 7,000 of them U.S. citizens. It also had opened and maintained files on more than 1,000 legal organizations.

MHCHAOS caused dissension within the CIA almost from its inception because of its questionable legality. It also caused friction between the FBI and the CIA and between White House staffers. Everyone knew that those who had authorized the program and those who directed it skated on very thin ice. The CIA's Domestic Contact Service (DCS) had previously infiltrated and recruited agents from émigré groups located within the USA. The best known case involved the recruitment of displaced and disgruntled Cubans who had fled from Fidel Castro's revolution after 1959. It may have been a secret to American citizens but not to Fidel Castro and his intelligence agency, called G-2, and its agents. Other important cases involved groups of Europeans who had escaped from nations under Soviet control and domination. The DCS targeted these groups from Hungary, East Germany, Czechoslovakia, Lithuania, Poland, and other nations to glean information, recruit agents, and establish means of supplying material and money to underground political groups active in these captive countries. It seems almost impossible to ascertain the effectiveness of these operations due to the way the CIA is compartmentalized. The Deputy Directorate of Operations (DDO) is divided into country or regional specific groups and, because the whole Agency operates on a need-to-know basis, there is little cross-over of information. History shows us that even if the secret covert CIA operations implemented in Europe and Latin America were somewhat successful, nothing really changed until the collapse of the Soviet Union from internal pressures.

One thing is clear, however, and that is that those decades of secret operations that saw governments overthrown, economies ruined, a massive build-up of the military-industrial complex in the U.S. and the political paranoia here at home caused irreparable harm and change to our country. The federal government has closed off public buildings, public roads, access to its secret files and records, and has increased the size and scope of its intelligence activities not only against perceived foreign enemies but its own citizens as well. There are secret federal courts that have never refused the government's request to establish covert spying operations on citizens, dissident groups, or the rights of a citizen to be free of unreasonable searches and seizures as guaranteed by the Bill of Rights in our Constitution. As the level of paranoia grows within the government, the more it displays its distrust of its own citizens. Federal agencies don't respond to simple requests for information or action; people are more isolated from their elected representatives; crimes committed by high level government officials are not prosecuted or they are waived off with nothing more than a worthless apology. The federal government no longer represents the collective will of the governed; instead, it only represents its own self interests which are dictated by multi-national corporations, the military-industrial complex, and the ever increasing layers of security it places between those who govern and the governed.

My years with the agency provided me with a unique view into the *sanctum sanctorum* where U.S. foreign policy is implemented and sometimes created. Decisions and policies are made based at times on fact as well as fantasy but regardless of their source, the death and destruction caused by their adoption and implementation by the U.S. and its NATO partners is very real indeed. The decision and implementation process is politicized and often flawed to the point that we, as a nation and people, reap nothing but ill will from a suffering world.

Never Too Young:
The U.S. Intelligence Community's
Summer Spy Camp for Kids

Roberto González

Under the guise of generous "collaboration" between government and universities, a growing current of programs are drawing college, high school, and even junior high students into contact with the CIA and other U.S. spy agencies.

"Collaboration" is taking unusual forms. For example, during the summer of 2005, a select group of 15- to 19-year old high school students participated in a week-long program called Spy Camp in the Washington, D.C., area. It included a field trip to CIA headquarters in Langley, Virginia, an "intelligence simulation" exercise, and a trip to the $35 million International Spy Museum. According to the Spy Museum's web site, visiting groups have the option of choosing from three different Scavenger Hunts, in which teams are pitted against one another in activities ranging "from code-breaking to deceptive maneuvers. Each team will be armed with a top secret bag of tricks to help solve challenging questions" that can be found in the museum.[1]

On the surface, the program sounds like fun and games, and after reading about the program, one might guess that an imaginative social studies or history teacher organized it. But some saw Spy Camp as more than just fun and games — in fact, they saw it as very serious business. Trinity University of Washington, D.C. — a predominantly African-American university with an overwhelmingly female student population — carried out the high school program as part of a pilot grant from the U.S. Office of the Director of National Intelligence (ODNI) to create an "Intelligence Community Center of Academic Excellence" (or IC/CAE).[2]

At the University of Texas–Pan American (UTPA)—which has a predominantly Hispanic student population—a similar drama unfolded recently. Located on the north side of the Texas-Mexico border, UTPA sponsored a summer camp for high school students called Got Intelligence? from August 9 to 12, 2010. According to a university publication, teenage participants gained "first-hand knowledge" from FBI and Border Patrol agents in such topics as "criminal fingerprinting, where students learned to collect evidence and pick up fingerprints from glass surfaces; footprint casting, in which students learned the basics of casting footprints left behind in a crime scene; forensics; remote sensing; and an FBI mentoring program."[3]

According to the ODNI, IC/CAE programs that sponsor high school camps aim to increase the pool of future applicants for careers in the Central Intelligence Agency, the Federal Bureau of Investigation, the Defense Intelligence Agency, and the dozen or so other organizations that make up the U.S. "intelligence community"—in less euphemistic terms, America's spy agencies.

The idea for IC/CAEs developed in the wake of the September 11, 2001, attacks, when both the Senate and House of Representatives held hearings about how the country's spy agencies missed clues that might have foiled the World Trade Center and Pentagon attacks. As part of the response, Congress passed a sweeping law called the Intelligence Reform and Terrorism Prevention Act (S 2845). In the House Intelligence Committee hearings prior to the bill's passage, California representative Jane Harman (Democrat from California and chair of the House Intelligence Committee) put it bluntly: "We can no longer expect an Intelligence Community that is mostly male and mostly white to be able to monitor and infiltrate suspicious organizations or terrorist groups. *We need spies that look like their targets*, CIA officers who speak the dialects that terrorists use, and FBI agents who can speak to Muslim women that might be intimidated by men."[4]

For this reason, the IC/CAE program did not target students attending Harvard, Yale, Princeton, or other Ivy League schools, or internationally renowned universities like Stanford, Berkeley or the University of Chicago—longstanding centers of CIA recruitment dating back to the agency's founding in 1947. The program's architects consciously directed it at schools where so-called minority students are the majority—predominantly African-American and Hispanic universities and tribal institutions which are often even more chronically underfunded than other institutions of higher education. Perhaps this reflects the shape of "multiculturalism" in a militarized society: the government's spy agencies and armed forces recruit minority students from low-income regions in order to "monitor and infiltrate" people ("targets") that look and speak like them.

Spy Kids

Since 2005, the IC/CAEs at Trinity and UTPA have had their funding renewed each year, and Spy Camps have continued every summer since. In fact, beginning in 2006 the Director of National Intelligence dramatically expanded the IC/CAE program (of which the Spy Camp is only a part), and today there are a total of 22 such centers throughout the country. These are located at California State University–San Bernardino, Carnegie-Mellon University, Clemson University, Clark Atlanta University, Florida A&M University, Florida International University, Howard University, Miles College (Alabama), Norfolk State University (Virginia), North Carolina A&T University, Pennsylvania State University, Tennessee State University, Trinity University, University of Maryland–College Park, University of Nebraska, University of New Mexico, University of North Carolina–Wilmington, University of Texas–El Paso, University of Texas–Pan American, University of Washington, Virginia Tech, and Wayne State University (Michigan). Significantly, most of these universities have large numbers of minority students, which corresponds with the original objectives of the IC/CAE program's architects. Tens of millions of dollars have been appropriated for the programs, with some centers receiving individual grants of up to $750,000 annually. According to *The Washington Post*, the ODNI planned to expand the program to 20 universities by the year 2015, indicating that it has apparently met this goal far in advance.[5] (Since 2008, the ODNI has included universities with significantly higher percentages of "white" students. It may be that the ODNI quickly exhausted its supply of predominantly Hispanic and African-American universities.)

Though this is by no means the first time that U.S. military and intelligence agencies have funneled large sums of money into universities to advance their interests — the 1958 National Defense Education Act led to the creation of language and area studies programs focused upon Russia, Latin America, and Southeast Asia — those centers generally did not limit scholars' ability to pursue a wide range of research, including critical social science research building upon anti-imperial and leftist scholarship.[6] But there are clear indications that the IC/CAEs and other new recruitment programs have much more focused and narrow objectives.

The stated goals of the University of Texas–El Paso (UTEP) IC/CAE illustrate just how narrow these objectives can be:

Introduce students to the 16 agencies that make up the Intelligence Community
Interest students in careers within the Intelligence Community
Introduce students to a critical language
Provide students with the opportunity to begin developing the technical skills necessary to succeed in the Intelligence Community
Develop students' analytical and critical thinking skills.[7]

Not surprisingly, UTEP's curriculum is narrowly focused upon Arabic language instruction, political science, intercultural communication, GPS/GIS training, field trips to intelligence agencies, and meetings with "various guest speakers, including local and federal Intelligence Community representatives."[8]

Judging from some students' responses, it seems that the program is making an impact. News reports from college newspapers begin to tell the story. Najam Hassan, a 19-year old student at Trinity University, said: "It's a good opportunity. I have interest in the FBI." Reagan Thompson, who is 17, told a reporter, "I want to be a spy when I grow up. You learn different perspectives and it opens your mind." Meriam Fadli, also 17, said: "I was like 'Oh my God, I am so joining the FBI'.... She [the speaker] made it seem so interesting. It's not like a dull office job." Leah Martin, a 21-year old, decided that she wanted an intelligence career after getting involved in the program: "You get to travel, to do something different every day, you're challenged in your work and you get to serve your country. How cool is that?"[9] At UTPA, high school junior Robert Crumley said, "It was really cool to be able to meet and interact with several professionals from agencies around the country. I got more information through the week on different aspects of the Intelligence Community and how our nation uses intelligence to protect itself."[10] Another high school participant in UTPA's summer program noted: "I have learned a lot about the subject of law enforcement and laws. I am gad that I applied and was chosen to attend because this will look good on my resume and will show that I have experience and knowledge in these fields."[11]

The picture that emerges from these and other comments shows that students are drawn to the IC/CAEs because they offer exciting, challenging experiences that will serve the country — not unlike the reasons that draw many young people to the armed forces or JROTC programs. For students who belong to ethnic groups that have been historically disenfranchised due to segregationist or discriminatory policies, careers in the military — and now in intelligence agencies — seem to offer the prospect of an affordable education, upward social mobility, and first-class citizenship. For students from immigrant families, these careers appear to provide a straightforward way of "giving back" something valuable to the country — a means of reciprocating.

A powerful cultural apparatus supports these belief systems. For example, the immense popularity of TV series that glorify law enforcement agents (*CSI: Crime Scene Investigation*), intelligence operatives (*24*), and military personnel (*JAG*) romanticize these careers even further. Smart, sexy spies have been a Hollywood staple for nearly half a century (from the time that Sean Connery first played the role of James Bond in the 1962 movie *Dr. No*). In recent years, women (Angelina Jolie in *Salt*, Julia Roberts in *Undercovers*), African-Americans (Denzel Washington in the remake of *Manchurian Candidate* and the forthcoming

Safe House) and Hispanic actors and actresses (for example, Antonio Banderas in producer/director Robert Rodriguez's *Spy Kids* movies) have played roles that have greatly romanticized spy work.

University administrators and faculty like the IC/CAEs for other reasons, not just the issues of funding and job placement for graduating students. But some also emphasize the importance of building an ethnically and culturally diverse pool of intelligence agents who might blend in more easily abroad. Norfolk State University geology professor David Padgett told the journal *Diverse Online*, "When a lot of higher education funding shifted after September 11 into defense, a lot of Black colleges weren't in a position to take advantage of it. We saw an opening. In order to have a diverse work force in the intelligence arena, you have to get to minority-serving institutions. In intelligence, people have to go to areas populated by people of color."[12]

Economist Dennis Soden, executive director of the Institute for Policy and Economic Development, a University of Texas–El Paso unit that was awarded an IC/CAE grant, had this to say:

> In the intelligence community before, it was really a white male, Ivy League, Big-10 kind of place. All these guys who went to Harvard, Wisconsin, and Yale they looked like America and they got the jobs and ended up just slapping each other on the back telling each other how great they were. Of course, we found out they weren't very good because they couldn't find WMDs and they couldn't figure out what was going on. There is a real sense that the agencies were just recruiting from the same places all the time and getting the same people over and over again — it was like a type of inbreeding.... The U.S.-Mexico border is now a national security interest, but who really understands it? A guy at Yale who takes Spanish for a few years doesn't really understand it. The idea is to get people both for domestic and international intelligence purposes who reflect the country and understand all of its nuances.[13]

The Office of the Director of National Intelligence promoted the IC/CAE program heavily during its first few years of existence. The original IC/CAE program plan is a 25-page document that clearly lays out goals and procedures. Under the title "Pre-College/High School Outreach" is the subheading "Summer Camp (for elementary and junior high students)." The program plan notes: "Institutions may consider coordinating summer camps for junior high students. The camps should be at least one week in duration with high energy programs that excite the participants.... They should focus on developing the critical skill of 'thinking before you act.'"[14]

Spy agencies have supported the idea of youth outreach for years. The CIA, the FBI, the Department of Homeland Security, the National Security Agency, and the Defense Intelligence Agency all have "Kids' Page" websites that include games, puzzles, and occasionally, sanitized histories of the agencies. More shocking is the fact that some of the university-based IC/CAEs have recruited 11- and 12-year-old junior high students to participate in two-week summer camps. For example, Norfolk State University's IC July 2010 "summer academy" for middle schoolers included classes on "Arabic cu_ture," "Mexican culture," "Phillipino [*sic*] culture," "Use of DNA Fingerprinting," and "Ballooning as an Intelligence Weapon."[15]

Nearly all universities that have received funding for IC/CAEs have created high school outreach programs. For example, Norfolk State's program included a simulation exercise in which faculty asked Nashville-area high schoolers to locate ten simulated "weapons of mass destruction" hidden in the city using GPS locators.[16]

University officials used the name "Spy Camp" only once, at Trinity University. Now, the high-school outreach programs are known in many places as "Summer Intelligence Seminars," which is part of a larger effort to publicly distance IC/CAEs from spy work.

Intelligence Outreach: Infiltrating Schools.

What makes the new IC/CAEs across the country different from other institutes or research centers? Though there are numerous differences from one school to the next, all ten universities appear to be involved in three kinds of activities apart from high-school outreach programs like Spy Camp.

Curriculum development — especially the creation of new classes — is a common process for IC/CAE schools. Many if not most of the participating universities are creating new majors and minors in "intelligence studies," and developing new courses to meet the demands of spy agencies. For example, Trinity University developed a new course entitled "East vs. West: Just War, Jihad and Crusade, 1050–1450." While the title itself is benign (though it conjures up images of the "clash of civilizations" popularized by historian Samuel Huntington), the syllabus states that the course "seeks to develop the critical/analytical and writing skills that are particularly important to the intelligence community."[17] In some cases new masters' programs are also being developed, which might result in new faculty hiring. New classes in languages deemed important to U.S. security are being established as well (particularly in Arabic and Mandarin) and many campuses are purchasing books and films for these new courses.

Another group of activities includes organized events such as academic colloquia and guest lectures. Like all university special events, these can be intellectually stimulating, particularly when a thought-provoking or controversial speaker is invited to speak. But what might occur when a guest lecture or other campus event becomes a recruiting pitch for spy agencies?

Finally, nearly all of the IC/CAEs include scholarship and travel abroad programs. The same law that brought the IC/CAEs into existence also created the new Intelligence Community Scholarship Program (ICSP). Scholarship fellows take required intelligence-related courses and are typically eligible for study abroad experiences and internships with spy agencies. It is worth noting that according to the law, ICSP students who do not take jobs with U.S. intelligence agencies after graduating are required "to repay the costs of their education plus penalties assessed at three times the legally allowed interest rate."[18] Like PRISP (the Pat Roberts Intelligence Scholarship Program, a $25,000 one-year scholarship for undergraduate and graduate students which requires them to work for the CIA after graduation), the identities of students are not publicly announced. Congress established PRISP in 2004 as a kind of academic version of the ROTC (Reserve Officer Training Corps) program: it was designed to combine intelligence training skills with academic areas of expertise, such as anthropology or political science. Since its creation PRISP has placed hundreds of students in an unknown number of university classrooms. Although critics have referred to such programs as "debt bondage to constrain student career choices," President Barack Obama's former Director of National Intelligence, Dennis Blair, announced in 2009 plans to make PRISP permanent.[19]

In and of themselves, all of these activities might sound benign, even desirable. After all, who could argue against funding for new courses, films, guest speakers, conferences, and scholarships — particularly during this period of chronic underfunding of higher education? But there is a subtle danger posed by the deluge of funding now reaching universities through the IC/CAEs program — a danger very similar to that posed by military funding. Anthropologist Hugh Gusterson (who is based at George Mason University) has written eloquently about the ways in which this can bend the education process over time. A wide range of problems comes into focus:

> When research that could be funded by neutral civilian agencies is instead funded by the military, knowledge is subtly militarized and bent in the way a tree is bent by a prevailing wind. The public comes to accept that basic academic research on religion and violence "belongs" to the military; scholars who never saw themselves as doing military research now do; maybe they wonder if their access to future funding is best secured by not criticizing U.S. foreign policy; a discipline whose independence from military and corporate funding fueled the kind of critical thinking a democracy needs is now compromised; and the priorities of the military further define the basic terms of public and academic debate.[20]

In short, the IC/CAEs could potentially threaten the notion of the classroom as a free "marketplace of ideas." The fact that the "intelligence community" (headed by ODNI) includes heavy representation from Pentagon agencies (such as the Defense Intelligence Agency and Marine Corps Intelligence, to name but two) further underscores the significance of Gusterson's words.

Case Study: A South Texas IC/CAE

For me, learning about the creation of the IC/CAEs programs struck close to home — literally. I heard about IC/CAEs from an anthropology professor at one of the participating universities, the University of Texas–Pan American (UTPA), located along the U.S.-Mexico border deep in south Texas. The professor wanted to see an article I had written in which I criticized the "military-anthropology complex" — a web connecting U.S. social scientists to the Pentagon and military contract firms for counterinsurgency work. From him I learned that anthropologists constituted some of the key players at UTPA's IC/CAE, including the dean, and to their credit, they wanted to learn more about the history of such relationships and ethical dilemmas that might arise as a result. I sent my article to the anthropology professor, along with a request to interview the dean of the College of Social and Behavioral Sciences — a request which the department of anthropology quickly granted.

UTPA is located seven miles from my childhood home, and my parents both graduated from the university (though it was called Pan American College in those years). My first "academic" job was tutoring local high school students at UTPA more than 20 years ago as part of the Texas Pre-Freshman Engineering Program. I planned a trip to the university's anthropology department that would coincide with a summer visit to my hometown.

Arriving at the university brought back many memories. As I walked towards the social science building in the sweltering tropical heat of a south Texas summer afternoon, the sprawling campus, the long arched corridors connecting its buildings, and the beautiful palm trees lining its perimeter took me back to my youth.

Not a small university, UTPA has nearly 18,000 students, nearly 90 percent of whom are Hispanic. More than one out of three faculty are Latino, and it has more full-time Latino faculty members than any other Texas university. I learned that like many other universities around the country, UTPA has not grown quickly enough to meet local demand. Administrators (and corporate donors) have tended to give strong support to UTPA's engineering, health science, and business schools, while the social science and humanities departments have sometimes struggled.

For these reasons, the IC/CAE grant looked especially attractive to the College of Social and Behavioral Sciences. The applicants enlisted faculty from each of the colleges to support the grant proposal, as well as letters of support from the university president and a local school district superintendent. Their efforts paid off handsomely: in October 2006, the ODNI awarded UTPA a grant of $500,000 a year for five years, for a total of $2.5 million. The application process had moved forward quietly — so quietly that numerous UTPA professors felt completely blindsided by the introduction of the IC/CAE.

Within a year, UTPA's IC/CAE staff organized a high-school outreach program — a five-day "camp" involving 20 local students — which took place in August 2007. They called it Got Intelligence? (students wore black T-shirts with the phrase silk-screened across the chest), and according to the UTPA magazine *Los Arcos*, students "heard from speakers from intelligence community agencies, such as the CIA and FBI."[21] Other activities included workshops for geographic information systems training, resume preparation, and a solar-powered vehicle competition.

Just two months earlier, a smaller group of UTPA students had an even more dramatic experience: a one-month all expenses paid study abroad trip to Qingdao, China, reportedly the first trip ever taken by a UTPA group to China. Accounts of the trip in *The Monitor* (the local daily newspaper) did not mention the word "intelligence," nor the Office of the Director of National Intelligence. Instead, it described the Center for Academic Excellence as "promot[ing] international research and analytical thinking skills."[22] Later, the IC/CAE study abroad program expanded to Morocco as well.[23]

The dean, Van Reidhead — who has since moved on to become provost of East Stroudsburg University in Pennsylvania (another university with a strong IC/CAE program, though one run by the National Security Agency) — was very optimistic about the future of the IC/CAE. He described ongoing efforts to create a new minor in "intelligence" and eventually, a masters' degree program in "global security studies and leadership." He noted that courses in Mandarin Chinese would soon be offered for the first time at UTPA, and they were planning to introduce Arabic language courses in the near future. When I asked whether he worried about the possibility that students might be corralled into dangerous careers with agencies that have a record of human rights abuses, the dean emphasized the fact that this was primarily a program for better "global" understanding, not an intelligence gathering program. (In fact, the IC/CAE eventually changed its name to the Integrated Global Knowledge and Understanding Collaboration or IGkNU.) Even so, he acknowledged that the IC/CAE offered "many opportunities for dialogue" with "agency people" for internship opportunities and career placement for college graduates.

The UTPA IC/CAE staff treated me cordially in every way, but their benign view of the intelligence agencies, even naive given headlines in recent years, surprised me. For example, they expressed the idea that in future generations, a more ethnically diverse "intelligence community" would likely lead to better policies. Others seemed convinced that they could keep the program focused on sharpening students' "critical thinking" skills and other skills not limited to spy work. They repeatedly emphasized the idea that in a period of scarce resources, the IC/CAE grant benefited the entire campus because it made generous funds available to students and faculty.

However, a glance at the way in which the UTPA IC/CAE has used funding for library materials tells another story. According to the center's website, they have acquired eight new journals, nearly all published in the U.S. and with a heavy emphasis on national security and intelligence studies, including *Intelligence and National Security, International Journal of Intelligence and Counterintelligence, International Security,* and *Studies in Conflict and Terrorism.*[24] If the UTPA IC/CAE dedicates itself to international research and analytical thinking skills, one wonders why it does not provide funding for journals such as *Cultural Survival Quarterly, WorldWatch,* or the *Journal of Human Rights.* Could it be a case of UTPA's base of knowledge "bent in the way a tree is bent by a prevailing wind"?

Opposing Voices

Not everyone at UTPA approved of the IC/CAE. A group consisting of students from the university's chapter of MEChA (a nationwide Chicano student organization) and faculty members voiced opposition to UTPA's participation in the ODNI grant, and I contacted several of them.

These critics had an entirely different perspective on the IC/CAE. In particular, they feared the Center might lead to bias in the classroom, or a biased orientation of books and other materials purchased in the library — a concern borne out by the UTPA library website. In the words of a professor opposed to the IC/CAE (who requested anonymity), "I don't think they're going to be buying history books that examine the CIA's crimes in Central America, or the abuses of graduates of the School of the Americas." The professor noted that IC/CAE personnel appeared to suffer from a lack of awareness of the dark history of the CIA, the FBI, and other agencies making up the "intelligence community."

Another faculty member, UTPA political science professor Samuel Freeman, argued that "just as intelligence agencies are penetrating our universities today with phony 'Intelligence Community Centers of Academic Excellence'— like the center recently established at UTPA unfortunately — the CIA, in the 1950s and 1960s conspired with unethical university professors and administrators."[25] Freeman's concerns linked intelligence agencies' current recruiting efforts on college campuses to a broader history of co-optation on university campuses.

Some critics expressed concern about the way in which the intelligence agencies might manipulate "diversity" to meet their own interests, rather than the interests of students. A graduate student I spoke with particularly objected to the cloak of "multiculturalism" used by the ODNI and the IC/CAE to promote the program. The student requested anonymity, a pattern which suggested a climate of fear.

Another student, Nadezhda Garza, reportedly said of the UTPA program: "At this point, you have to decide if opportunity is really opportunity.... The [intelligence community] isn't pushing you academically, it's pushing you to recruitment. The [intelligence community] has its own agenda."[26] A report in the *San Antonio Express–News* appeared to confirm Garza's words, noting that "CIA recruiters were on [the UTPA] campus visiting mainly with students in the program who are earning an intelligence studies certificate."[27]

Still another concern I heard from critics of the program had to do with the safety of UTPA students participating in study abroad programs. "What kind of risk are students in China going to face if that country's government knows that they are connected to the Office of the Director of National Intelligence?" asked Samuel Freeman. He argued that Chinese officials might view them as spies.

Finally, both students and professors worried that academic freedom at UTPA might be threatened by the IC/CAE. What would happen to students or faculty who refused to "go along" with the current produced by waves of IC/CAE funding? How would university administrators (or campus police) deal with students or faculty who actively protested guest speakers from the CIA or FBI? According to the minutes of an April 2006 UTPA faculty senate meeting, a group of MEChA students expressed concerns over the proposed IC/CAE ranging from "possible restrictions to academic freedom" to "exploitation of UTPA students by intelligence communities"[28]. UTPA professor Philip Zwerling has noted that at a November 2008 conference underwritten by UTPA's IC/CAE, "FBI, CIA, DEA, ICE and U.S. Border Patrol Agents" presented while "twenty-five or so UTPA students and faculty [were] lining the entryway protesting the conference and leafletting attendees."[29]

Zwerling has also described how some of his colleagues have rejected the idea of IC/CAE on campus. For example, when asked about the CIA and other intelligence agencies funding courses, UTPA English professor Jose Skinner replied: "What kind of courses does the CIA have in mind? Advanced Waterboarding Techniques, Recruitment and Training of Unilaterally Controlled Latino Assets? Case Studies in the Destabilization of Democratically Elected Governments?" When Zwerling asked whether it mattered that the money came through the ODNI rather than directly from the CIA, Skinner responded:

If it doesn't matter where the money comes from. Why not ask the Gulf Cartel or the Mafia for funds? I hear they have lots. I assume such monies come with curricular strings attached, like the Intelligence funds do. That being the case, some course suggestions: Money Laundering Through the Ages, Polyploidy in Enhancement of THC in Cannabis Indica, Pablo Escobar: Hero of the People.[30]

When local media ran a handful of stories on the UTPA IC/CAE in 2007, reporters generally ignored the many criticisms that had been raised by concerned faculty and students. The CIA, FBI, and other spy agencies appeared to be scoring a "silent coup" at UTPA, a pattern that would be repeated at other universities as the IC/CAE program diffused throughout the country.[31]

Ignoring the Elephant in the Room

Once I began exploring the roots of the IC/CAEs by combing through dozens of documents, articles, government reports, websites, and interview transcripts, I saw that intelligence agents, congressional representatives, educators, and students had been ignoring the elephant in the room: outrageous and illegal actions that many U.S. spy agencies have been involved with over the last 60 years. I began to ask: What happened to teaching "critical thinking skills" at the IC/CAEs?

As Stephen Kinzer has noted in his book *Overthrow*, the CIA worked diligently in orchestrating coups, assassinations, and civil wars in such diverse places as Iran, Guatemala, Chile, Indonesia, and El Salvador, among many others over the past century.[32] We now know that the CIA supported social science research throughout the 1950s and 1960s to perfect psychological torture techniques later outsourced to Vietnam, Argentina, and other countries.[33] Phillip Agee, shocked by his discoveries of the CIA's covert operations in support of Latin American dictatorships, quit the agency in 1968 and spent the rest of his life criticizing it.[34]

In recent years many others have come forward to expose illegal acts carried out with impunity by the "intelligence community." Here are a few that illustrate the scope of operations:

December 2002: The *Washington Post* runs a front-page story describing CIA operatives sending suspected members of al Qaeda to third countries (at so-called secret "black sites") for brutal interrogations.[35] The report includes a chilling quote from a U.S. official involved in capturing and transferring accused terrorists: "If you don't violate someone's rights some of the time, you probably aren't doing your job."

November 2005: Investigative journalist Dana Priest reveals the presence of a secret CIA network of overseas prisons in Eastern Europe, southeast Asia, and other regions. The prisons are located in countries whose police and intelligence agencies are infamous for their egregious human rights violations, which have been extensively documented by human rights organizations.[36]

December 2005: The *New York Times* describes the NSA and Defense Intelligence Agency's use of illegal wiretapping at the request of the Bush administration. The report is based in part on leaks from NSA whistleblower Russell Tice. In a letter to Congress, Tice wrote, "It's with my oath as a U.S.

intelligence officer weighing heavy on my mind that I wish to report to Congress acts I believe are unlawful and unconstitutional."[37]

March 2006: Former CIA analyst Ray McGovern returns his Intelligence Commendation Award to protest the CIA's involvement in torture — a gross violation of the Geneva Conventions — and declares that the agency altered its reports on weapons of mass destruction in Iraq under pressure from the White House.[38]

April 2006: Former AT&T technician Mark Klein issues a public statement in which he describes AT&T's cooperation in a secret National Security Agency (NSA) operation that would allow it to conduct "vacuum-cleaner surveillance of all the data crossing the internet," a form of wiretapping prohibited by the U.S. Constitution.[39] (The NSA is among the agencies making up the "intelligence community.")

February 2007. An Italian court indicts 26 U.S. intelligence agents, most of them from the CIA, for the 2003 kidnapping of an Egyptian cleric, Usama Nasr. Agents took Nasr to Egypt where he was held for four years and reportedly tortured before being freed by an Egyptian court that ruled his detention to be "unfounded."[40]

January 2007. A German court issues arrest warrants for 13 U.S. intelligence agents (mostly CIA) involved in the 2003 kidnapping of a German citizen, Khaled el Masri. Masri was taken to Afghanistan, jailed for five months, and physically and psychologically tortured before being released without charges.[41]

June 2007. Following a Freedom of Information Act request filed in 1992, the CIA releases to the public a set of reports detailing illegal agency activities from the 1950s to the mid–1970s. The report includes revelations of illegal wiretapping, domestic surveillance, assassination plots, and experimentation on human subjects.[42]

Although these events (and many other similar violations) made headlines at the time the ODNI established the IC/CAEs on campuses across the country, few of the news articles about the centers mentioned any dilemmas that university collaboration with the agencies in question might pose either politically or ethically. Nor did they ask whether institutions of higher education ought to accept money linked to such sources. The 1975–1976 Church Committee reports of the U.S. Senate — which famously and publicly exposed the legal and political abuses carried out by U.S. intelligence agencies — seemed never to have existed.

Some scholars did make these connections, and raised questions that proved inconvenient for proponents of the program. For example, independent scholar, writer, and lecturer in the UTPA English department Dr. Kamala Platt noted that in overwhelmingly Hispanic south Texas, "decades of being among the poorest and most underserved regions of the country have laid the groundwork" for the program. In many ways, student participation in IC/CAEs resembles participation in JROTC programs. As Oberlin College anthropologist Dr. Gina Pérez argues, JROTC is "deeply rooted in notions of citizenship [and service to country] ... [a]nd informed by the realities of a local political economy with extremely limited employment opportunities for working-class youth."[43] Consquently both IC/CAEs and JROTC might be seen as programs in which "notions of exceptional citizenship [are] anchored in a distinctive and particularly valorized military culture."

But a militarized culture can lead to intellectual, moral, and ethical dilemmas. According to Dr. Platt, a range of contradictions inherently accompany such initiatives:

> Underlying ICC's interest in these [academic] fields is the identification, fear, and domination of "enemies" and the blowing up of bridges of communication.... The intelligence community's interest in these disciplines defiles them, and I could never in good conscience (i.e. with intellectual or moral integrity) participate in these junctures of university and IC-CAE. I could never teach a Chicana novel in a classroom where I knew some of the students were being trained to read the literature for knowledge that might endanger sister barrios.[44]

Once critics started to raise such points, some IC/CAEs began to drop the words "Intelligence Community" from their names. Now many style themselves as Centers for Academic Excellence. Similarly, the Spy Camp at Trinity became simply Summer Intelligence Seminar, while UTPA's version became the Got Intelligence? camp, implying that these were places where students would get smarter.

It may be that the ODNI's primary goal in creating the IC/CAEs is to increase the pool of minority youth seeking employment in spy agencies. But an important secondary goal appears one of public relations: to give an extreme makeover to the CIA, the FBI, the NSA, and other agencies for a generation too young to know about their past, and too overworked and distracted to study their current abuses. Only by whitewashing the past can the Office of the Director of National Intelligence hope to normalize spy work.

In Defense of the Public Trust

Is the IC/CAE program as benign and generous as its proponents claim? Is it really the "win-win relationship for everyone involved," to quote a sympathetic article?[45] Or somewhere down the line, does someone lose?

From one point of view, the program appears to be creating new opportunities for young people, especially African-American and Hispanic students who get excited by the possibility of challenging, adventurous work in service of country. On the other hand, we might ask: couldn't these young people play a more constructive role in our society if government agencies or private sector employers aggressively recruited them into careers in medicine, engineering, or education supported with generous grants like the ODNI millions?

We might also ask ourselves, what kind of a society do we live in where citizens define "serving your country" solely in terms of employment with the military or intelligence agencies, as if other institutions didn't matter? This propaganda strategy in the ODNI's effort to recruit "intelligence"— modeled after the military's techniques for recruiting soldiers — deserves much criticism, whether such methods target minorities and recent immigrants to our country or the general populace.

Clearly many of the IC/CAEs expose students to unrealistic scenarios if not outright deception. Like most recruitment processes — whether for cults, the military, or other authoritarian institutions — there exists an element of undue influence, what psychologists call "coercive persuasion."[46] If these centers soften children up through scavenger hunts and other exciting activities, we might ask whether they are being given the chance to freely explore other options. If a charismatic CIA analyst or military intelligence officer pumps up junior high or high school kids with stories about their global travels, they may easily convince them it "beats having an office job!" The official IC/CAE literature from the ODNI sanitizes the histories of its member agencies. Full disclosure is nonexistent. The ODNI literature does not mention CIA assassination plots, nor COINTELPRO (the FBI's illegal domestic surveillance program), nor any mention of secret prisons in the "war on terror." This reminds us of the military recruiter who promises high school students money for college and the chance to see the world without mentioning that they might be sent to the front lines of Afghanistan or Iraq for a year or two. Such techniques appear egregious, even more so when children are the victims.

In the words of professor Samuel Freeman:

> The [IC] Spy Center is part of nothing less than an attempt to legitimize the illegitimate, to manipulate us into condoning the unpardonable, and to accept the crimes of U.S. intelligence agencies as actions that are legitimate, acceptable, and even respectable.... Hopefully, protests raised by students and faculty will send a message to other UTPA organizations that consorting with IC-CAE/IGkNU is not worth the cost."[47]

On at least one campus, students and faculty are working against the IC penetration of their university. In 2009, University of Washington students protested the campus's IC/CAE, dubbed the Institute for National Security Research (or INSER). According to Adam James, a political science major who wrote a letter to the UW student newspaper, a campus coalition presented UW President Mark Emmert with a list of demands that included termination of INSER.[48] Over time, students and faculty may again organize themselves into a nationwide movement against CIA and FBI infiltration of university campuses as they did in the 1960s and again in the 1990s.

In the meantime (as mentioned above), some students are getting sucked into scholarship programs like PRISP that require mandatory service for intelligence agencies. For example, the Stokes Program (sponsored by the CIA, the FBI, and the NSA) targets high school seniors with the promise of paid tuition and a government salary in exchange for mandatory employment with these agencies. In the case of most of these programs, the cloak of secrecy surrounding the scholarships is extremely troubling. Typically, college students are secretly receiving money from the ODNI and no one — neither their peers, nor their professors, nor their administrators — know that they are receiving financial support. Under these circumstances, what is to keep the intelligence agencies from demanding that PRISP participants monitor political student groups, international students from the Middle East or central Asia, or professors for "subversive" activities such as participating in anti-war rallies or demonstrations opposing torture, as they did during the CIA's Operation CHAOS in the 1960s? The very possibility that these scenarios might play out has a chilling effect at a time when college campuses already face political pressure as the result of the PATRIOT Act and the proposed HR 1955 (the so-called Violent Radicalization and Homegrown Terrorism Prevention Act) currently being debated in Congress.

Perhaps it is not surprising that in a speech delivered to the Association of American Universities on April 14, 2008, Defense Secretary (former CIA Director and former President of Texas A&M University) Robert Gates announced the creation of the $60 million Minerva Consortium project which would provide Defense Department funding for new social science research projects related to national security. (The project is named after the Roman goddess of wisdom and war.) Gates outlined four areas of interest: Chinese military studies, religious studies, "Iraqi and Terrorist Perspectives," and the "New Disciplines Project." (The latter would help the Pentagon develop expertise in anthropology, history, and sociology.) But the architects of the Minerva Consortium have failed to understand how government funds might instead be used to address urgent priorities related to higher education in general. The $60 million that government officials will spend on Minerva could pay the annual tuition and fees of 15,000 students at my university, or hire more than 1000 new professors, or update the library collections of many colleges.

IC/CAEs, PRISP, the Minerva Consortium, and their ilk will likely erode academic freedom and distort the education of university students. Classes that support the needs of the "intelligence community" and the Pentagon will likely receive ample funding; those that expose the historical crimes of the CIA, FBI, and other spy agencies will not. Professors who accept the goals and perspectives of the ODNI will likely be supported in their efforts to secure tenure, internal grants, and facilities; those who don't accept them will not.

Similar situations in the past — in which universities or professional associations have succumbed to the pressures of commercialization — have tended to produce these results. Late 19th-century U.S. economists (such as Henry Carter Adams and Richard Ely) who proposed ideas for radical economic reform faced tremendous pressure to conform to the dictates of conservative administrators who sought to please industrial magnates. They and many others buckled under the pressure, until eventually, economic "studies and findings tended to be internal, recommendations hedged with qualifiers, analyses couched in jargon that was unintelligible to the average citizen."[49] The reform advocates became impotent professionals. In the early years of the 20th century, radical engineers such as C.E. Drayer, F.W. Ballard, and Morris Cooke called for public control of utilities, but professional associations (dominated by corporations) reprimanded them. Sometimes, these associations forced these professionals to give up engineering practice.[50] As a new wave of intelligence-based commercialization hits, we need to warn our colleagues of the dangers that it poses to academic freedom and the core principles of higher education. The university itself runs the risk of selling its soul for a quick financial fix that, in the end, does a disservice to the students and the entire society.

In many ways, today's problems began as early as the 1980s, when public universities shifted to a profit-driven corporate model. As state governments began cutting back public funding for higher education, universities came to rely more and more upon external funding, especially from corporations and other private sources. The private, profit-driven model has all but replaced our country's publicly funded university system. In the process it has inflicted widespread damage to a part of American culture that many people around the world still greatly admire.[51]

As noted earlier in this essay, military and intelligence agencies have aggressively infiltrated college and university campuses at other historical moments. However, the structures of the IC/CAE programs, PRISP, and other initiatives that now threaten to constrain free and open intellectual inquiry on our campuses should concern us all.

Universities in the United States have strayed far from their core values: academic freedom, open scientific inquiry not subject to secrecy, and commitment to high-quality education for the benefit of students, not for some ulterior motive.[52] But concerned citizens might still turn things around. In this context we should remember the words of Senator William Fulbright (who we honor today through the Fulbright Fellowship program). Just over 40 years ago, in the midst of the Vietnam War, he spoke on the floor of the Senate:

More and more our economy, our government, and our universities are adapting themselves to the requirements of continuing war.... The universities might have formed an effective counterweight to the military-industrial complex by strengthening their emphasis on the traditional values of our democracy, but many of our leading institutions have instead joined the monolith, adding greatly to its power and influence.... Among the most baneful effects of the government-university contract system, the most damaging and corrupting are the neglect of its students, and the taking into the government camp of scholars, especially those in the social sciences, who ought to be acting as responsible and independent critics of their government's policies.... When the university turns away from its central purpose and makes itself an appendage to the government, concerning itself with techniques rather than purposes, with expedients rather than ideals ... it is not only failing to meet its responsibilities to its students; it is betraying a public trust.[53]

Fulbright's words carry as much relevance today as when he first made them in 1967. Now students, faculty, and other citizens of conscience must ensure that wisdom and good judgment will prevail over a marriage of convenience between universities and spy agencies.

NOTES

1. "Special Events: Scavenger Hunts," International Spy Museum, http://www.spymuseum. org/special/hunts.php. Twenty-four high school students participating in Norfolk State University's two-week "National Security Scholars Leadership Development Conference" also traveled to the Spy Museum, where "they were able to learn about the history of spying, look at real life gadgets, learn about specific spies, etc." See "A Recap of the High School Program," Norfolk State University IC-CAE, http://www.nsu.edu/iccae/phprint.php (accessed October 10, 2010).

2. ODNI is an independent government agency subject to the authority of the president. The agency heads the "Intelligence Community" — 16 military and civilian government agencies comprised of the Central Intelligence Agency, the Defense Intelligence Agency, the Department of Energy (Office of Intelligence and Counterintelligence), the Department of Homeland Security (Office of Intelligence and Analysis), the Department of State (Bureau of Intelligence and Research), the Department of Treasury (Office of Intelligence and Analysis), the Drug Enforcement Administration (Office of National Security Intelligence), the Federal Bureau of Investigation (National Security Branch), the National Geospatial-Intelligence Agency, the National Reconnaissance Office, the National Security Agency/Central Security Service, the Air Force, the Army, the Marine Corps, the Navy and the Coast Guard. ODNI also directs and oversees the National Intelligence Program. When Congress passed the Intelligence Reform and Terrorism Prevention Act of 2004, it effectively created the ODNI as a means of coordinating the efforts of different intelligence agencies. In addition to the IC/CAE program — which the ODNI created — numerous other "Intelligence Community" agencies have created Centers of Academic Excellence. For example, the National Security Agency's CAE program (funded by the Department of Defense) consists of approximately 128 colleges and universities, most of which the NSA has designated CAE-IAs (Centers for Academic Excellence in Information Assurance). The NSA program focuses upon training computer-literate experts capable of defending the U.S. "information infrastructure," while the ODNI IC/CAE program is quite narrowly focused on drawing minority youth into intelligence careers. See "Centers of Academic Excellence — Institutions," National Security Agency/Central Security Service, http://www.nsa.gov/ia/academic_outreach/nat_cae/institutions.shtml (accessed December 26, 2010).

3. Amanda Perez, "IGKNU Collaboration Broadens Horizons through Intelligence Training," University of Texas-Pan American Division of University Advancement, August 16, 2010, http://ur.utpa.edu/publications/read/fl41de02b9d98a1c1063 (accessed October 12, 2010).

4. Jane Harman, quoted in U.S. House Intelligence Committee, "Building Capabilities: The Intelligence Community's National Security Requirements for Diversity of Language, Skills, and Ethnic and Cultural Understanding," November 5, 2003, http://www.fas.org/irp/congress/2003_hr/110503hpsci.pdf (accessed March 15, 2010).

5. U.S. Office of the Director of National Intelligence, "Intelligence Community Centers of Academic Excellence Program," *Intelligence Community Centers of Academic Excellence*, http://www.DNI.gov/cae/institutions.htm. See also Walter Pincus, "Howard, Virginia Tech Join U.S. Intelligence Program," *Washington Post*, September 7, 2009.

6. See, for example, Laura Nader, "The Phantom Factor: Impact of the Cold War on Anthropology," in Andre Schifflin, ed., *The Cold War and the University* (New York: New, 1997), 107–146; Bruce Cumings, "Boundary Displacement: Area Studies and International Studies during and after the Cold War," *Bulletin of Concerned Asia Scholars* 29, no. 1 (1999): 6–26. See also *Universities and Empire: Money and Politics in the Social Sciences during the Cold War*, ed. Christopher Simpson (New York: New, 1999).

7. University of Texas-El Paso, "IC-CAE High School Summer Program Application," http://academics.utep.edu/Portals/1729/pdf/ICCAE_Application.pdf (accessed October 15, 2010).

8. Ibid.

9. Joshua Garner, "University's 'Spy Camp' Lets Teens Learn about Intelligence Gathering," *Catholic News Service,* July 17, 2007, http://www.catholicnews.com/data/briefs/cns/2007 0717.htm; Richard Willing, "Intelligence Agencies Invest in College Education," *USA Today*, November 27, 2006.

10. Gail Fagan, "Students Gain Leadership Skills at 'Got Intelligence?' Summer Institute," *University of Texas-Pan American Online News*, August 10, 2009, http://www.utpa.edu/news/index.cfm?newsid=3798 (accessed October 14, 2010).

11. Amanda Perez, "IGKNU Collaboration."

12. Peter Galuszka, "Black Colleges Involved in Efforts to Boost Intelligence Community Talent Pool," *Diverse Online*, January 11, 2007, http://diverseeducation.com/article/6874/black-colleges-involved-in-efforts.html.

13. Ryan Poulous, "UTEP Camp Shows the World of Intelligence," *El Paso Inc.*, http://www.elpasoinc.com/showArticle.asp?articleId=1471.

14. U.S. Office of the Director of National Intelligence, *United States Intelligence Community Centers of Academic Excellence in National Security Studies: Program Plan for Fiscal Years 2005–2015* (Washington, D.C.: Office of the Director of National Intelligence, 2005), pp. 6–7.

15. Norfolk State University IC CAE, "Health and Science Summer Academy: Middle School," July 19–30, 2010, http://www.nsu.edu/iccae/pdf/MiddleSchoolSchedule.pdf (accessed October 20, 2010).

16. Galuzka, "Black Colleges Involved."

17. "Cloak and Gown," *Texas Observer*, April 21, 2006, http://www.texasobserver.org/archives/item/14790-2188-political-intelligence-marchers-mccain-y-mas.

18. Hugh Gusterson and David Price, "Spies in Our Midst," *Anthropology News* 46, no. 6 (September 2005): 39–40.

19. Ibid. See also David Price, "Obama's Classroom Spies," *CounterPunch,* June 23, 2009, http://www.counterpunch.org/price06232009.html.

20. Hugh Gusterson, "The U.S. Military's Quest to Weaponize Culture," *Bulletin of the Atomic Scientists*, June 20, 2008, http://www.thebulletin.org/web-edition/columnists/hugh-gusterson/the-us-militarys-quest-to-weaponize-culture.

21. "Center for Academic Excellence Creates New Opportunities for Valley Students," *Los Arcos: The University of Texas Pan-American*, Fall 2007: 18.

22. Daniel Perry, "The China Connection: UTPA Students Experience Chinese Culture, Academics," *The Monitor* (McAllen, Texas), July 24, 2007, http://www.themonitor.com/articles/china-4002-students-center.html.

23. Philip Zwerling, "The CIA on My Campus ... and Yours," *Nebula: A Journal of Multidisciplinary Scholarship* 6 (2009), no. 4, 255.

24. University of Texas Pan-American Library, "IGKNU Journals, http://lib.utpa.edu/research/subjectguides/igknu (accessed September 15, 2010).

25. Samuel Freeman, "Intelligence Agencies Are Penetrating Our Universities Today," *Rio Grande Guardian* (McAllen, Texas), April 10, 2007, http://www.riograndeguardian.com/index.asp.

26. Jesse Bogan, "Intelligence Grants in Valley Rile Some," *San Antonio Express-News,* December 2, 2006, http://www.mysanantonio.com/news/MYSA120306_04B_intelligencealert_2715c86_html8625.html.

27. Ibid.

28. "University of Texas-Pan American Faculty Senate Minutes," April 26, 2006, https://portal.utpa.edu/portal/page/portal/utpa_main/daa_home/senate_home/senate_imagesfiles/fs_0 60426_lm.pdf (accessed June 24, 2010). It is not clear whether the students' concerns materialized.

29. Philip Zwerling, "The CIA on My Campus," 256.

30. Ibid.

31. David Price, "Silent Coup: How the CIA Is Welcoming Itself Back onto American University Campuses," *CounterPunch,* January 16–31, 2010: 1–4; see also David Price, "The Spook School Program," *CounterPunch,* February 1–15, 2010: 7–8.

32. Stephen Kinzer, *Overthrow: America's Century of Regime Change from Hawaii to Iraq* (New York: Times, 2007).

33. Alfred McCoy, *A Question of Torture: CIA Interrogation from the Cold War to the War on Terror* (New York: Metropolitan, 2006).

34. Phillip Agee, *Inside the Company: CIA Diary* (New York: Bantam, 1984).

35. Dana Priest and Barton Gellman, "U.S. Decries Abuse but Defends Interrogations," *Washington Post,* December 26, 2002.

36. Dana Priest, "CIA Holds Terror Suspects in Secret Prisons," *Washington Post,* November 2, 2005.

37. James Risen and Eric Lichtblau, "Bush Lets U.S. Spy on Callers without Courts," *New York Times,* December 16, 2005.

38. Margot Patterson, "The Mission of Ray McGovern," *National Catholic Reporter,* October 27, 2006.

39. Shayana Kadidal, "NSA Surveillance: More Muck from the Bowels of AT&T," *Huffington Post,* April 14, 2006, http://www.huffingtonpost.com/shayana-kadidal/nsa-surveillance-more-muc_b_19128.html. See also Ellen Nakashima, "A Story of Surveillance," *Washington Post,* November 7, 2007, http://www.washingtonpost.com/wp-dyn/content/article/2007/11/07/AR2007110700006.html.

40. Tracy Wilkinson, Tracy and Maria De Cristofaro, "Italy Indicts CIA Agents in Kidnapping," *Los Angeles Times,* February 17, 2007.

41. Mathias Gebauer, "Germany Issues Arrest Warrants for 13 CIA Agents in El-Masri Case," *Spiegel Online,* January 31, 2007, http://www.spiegel.de/international/0,1518,463385,00.html.

42. Karen DeYoung and Walter Pincus, "CIA Releases Files on Past Misdeeds," *Washington Post,* June 27, 2007, http://www.washingtonpost.com/wp-dyn/content/article/2007/06/26/AR2007062600861.html.

43. Gina Pérez, "JROTC, Citizenship, and Puerto Rican Youth in Lorain, Ohio" (presentation, annual meetings of the American Anthropological Association, Philadelphia, PA, December 6, 2009). See also Pérez, Gina, "JROTC and Latina/o Youth in Neoliberal Cities," in *Rethinking America,* edited by Jeff Maskovsky and Ida Susser (New York: Paradigm, 2009), 31–48. For analysis of the legal and political implications of Latino non-citizens in the military (and their conversion to citizens), see Luis F.B. Plascencia, "The Military Gates of Non-Citizenship: Latino 'Aliens and Non-Citizen Nationals Performing Military Work in the U.S. Homeland," (presentation, annual meetings of the American Anthropological Association, Philadelphia, PA, December 6, 2009).

44. Kamala Platt, "How Can We Sleep? The Birthing of an Intelligence Center on University Grounds," *La Voz de Esperanza* (San Antonio, Texas), May 2007, 6–7. See also Kamala

Platt, "Latino/a Students and Covert "Securities": The Integration of Academic and Intelligence Communities," *Latino Studies* 6: 456–465.

45. "Intelligence Studies Initiative," *Trinity Magazine*, Fall 2005, http://www.trinitydc.edu/news_events/mags/fall05/intelligence_studies_initiative.php.

46. Edgar H. Schein, *Coercive Persuasion* (New York: W.W. Norton, 1971).

47. Samuel Freeman, "PACE and the 'Spy Center's' Shills," *Rio Grande Guardian* (McAllen, Texas), January 30, 2009, http://www.riograndeguardian.com/index.asp (accessed August 22, 2010).

48. David Price, "Silent Coup," 4.

49. Mary O. Furner, *Advocacy and Objectivity: A Crisis in the Professionalization of American Social Science, 1865–1905* (Lexington: University of Kentucky Press, 1975), pp. 128–142, 154–162, 324.

50. David Noble, *America by Design: Science, Technology, and the Rise of Corporate Capitalism* (New York: Oxford University Press, 1979), pp. 62–63.

51. Laura Nader, "Why Are We Destroying Public Education?" *Democracy Now!*, November 17, 2009, http://www.democracynow.org/2009/11/17/why_are_we_destroying_public_educationh; Christopher Newfield, *Unmaking the Public University: The Forty-Year Assault on the Middle Class* (Cambridge: Harvard University Press, 2008), p. 230, 265. See also Henry A. Giroux, *The University in Chains: Confronting the Military-Industrial-Academic Complex* (Boulder: Paradigm, 2007); Gaye Tuchman, *Wannabe U: Inside the Corporate University* (Chicago: University of Chicago Press, 2009).

52. Derek Bok, *Universities in the Marketplace: The Commercialization of Higher Education* (Princeton: Princeton University Press, 2004).

53. J. William Fulbright, "A Point of View," *Science,* December 22, 1967, 1555.

WORKS CITED

Agee, Phillip. *Inside the Company: CIA Diary.* New York: Bantam, 1984.

Bogan, Jesse. "Intelligence Grants in Valley Rile Some." *San Antonio Express-News,* December 2, 2006, http://www.mysanantonio.com/news/MYSA120306_04B_intelligencealert_2715 c86_html8625.html (accessed November 2, 2010).

Bok, Derek. *Universities in the Marketplace: The Commercialization of Higher Education.* Princeton: Princeton University Press, 2004.

"Center for Academic Excellence Creates New Opportunities for Valley Students." *Los Arcos: The University of Texas Pan-American*, Fall 2007: 18.

"Cloak and Gown." *Texas Observer,* April 21, 2006, http://www.texasobserver.org/archives/item/14790–2188-political-intelligence-marchers-mccain-y-mas (accessed February 20, 2010).

Cumings, Bruce. "Boundary Displacement: Area Studies and International Studies during and after the Cold War." *Bulletin of Concerned Asia Scholars* 29, no. 1 (1999): 6–26.

DeYoung, Karen and Walter Pincus. "CIA Releases Files on Past Misdeeds." *Washington Post,* June 27, 2007, http://www.washingtonpost.com/wp-dyn/content/article/2007/06/26/AR2007062600861.html.

Fagan, Gail. "Students Gain Leadership Skills at 'Got Intelligence?' Summer Institute." *University of Texas-Pan American Online News*, August 10, 2009, http://www.utpa.edu/news/index.cfm?newsid=3798 (accessed October 14, 2010).

Freeman, Samuel. "Intelligence Agencies Are Penetrating Our Universities Today." *Rio Grande Guardian* (McAllen, Texas), April 10, 2007, http://www.riograndeguardian.com/index.asp (accessed August 22, 2010).

_____. "PACE and the 'Spy Center's' Shills." *Rio Grande Guardian* (McAllen, Texas), January 30, 2009, http://www.riograndeguardian.com/index.asp (accessed August 22, 2010).

Fulbright, J. William. "A Point of View." *Science,* December 22, 1967, 1555.

Furner, Mary O. *Advocacy and Objectivity: A Crisis in the Professionalization of American Social Science, 1865–1905.* Lexington: University of Kentucky Press, 1975, pp. 128–142, 154–162, 324.

Galuszka, Peter. *"Black Colleges Involved in Efforts to Boost Intelligence Community Talent Pool."* *Diverse Online,* January 11, 2007, http://diverseeducation.com/article/6874/black-colleges-involved-in-efforts.html.

Garner, Joshua. "University's 'Spy Camp' Lets Teens Learn about Intelligence Gathering." *Catholic News Service,* July 17, 2007, http://www.catholicnews.com/data/briefs/cns/2007 0717.htm (accessed October 15, 2010).

Gebauer, Mathias. "Germany Issues Arrest Warrants for 13 CIA Agents in El-Masri Case." *Spiegel Online,* January 31, 2007, http://www.spiegel.de/international/0,1518,463385,00.html (accessed August 12, 2010).

Giroux, Henry A. *The University in Chains: Confronting the Military-Industrial-Academic Complex.* Boulder: Paradigm, 2007.

Gusterson, Hugh. "The U.S. Military's Quest to Weaponize Culture." *Bulletin of the Atomic Scientists,* June 20, 2008, http://www.thebulletin.org/web-edition/columnists/hugh-gusterson/the-us-militarys-quest-to-weaponize-culture.

_____ and David Price. "Spies in Our Midst." *Anthropology News* 46, no. 6 (September 2005): 39–40.

"Intelligence Studies Initiative." *Trinity Magazine,* Fall 2005. http://www.trinitydc.edu/news_events/mags/fall05/intelligence_studies_initiative.php (accessed February 12, 2010).

International Spy Museum. "Special Events: Scavenger Hunts." International Spy Museum, http://www.spymuseum.org/special/hunts.php (accessed October 15, 2010).

Kadidal, Shayana. "NSA Surveillance: More Muck from the Bowels of AT&T." *Huffington Post,* April 14, 2006, http://www.huffingtonpost.com/shayana-kadidal/nsa-surveillance-more-muc_b_19128.html

Kinzer, Stephen. *Overthrow: America's Century of Regime Change from Hawaii to Iraq.* New York: Times, 2007.

McCoy, Alfred. *A Question of Torture: CIA Interrogation from the Cold War to the War on Terror.* New York: Metropolitan, 2006.

Nader, Laura. "The Phantom Factor: Impact of the Cold War on Anthropology," in Andre Schifflin (ed.), *The Cold War and the University* (New York: New =, 1997), 107–146.

_____. "Why Are We Destroying Public Education?" *Democracy Now!* November 17, 2009. http://www.democracynow.org/2009/11/17/why_are_we_destroying_public_education.

Nakashima, Ellen. "A Story of Surveillance," *Washington Post,* November 7, 2007.

Newfield, Christopher. *Unmaking the Public University: The Forty-Year Assault on the Middle Class.* Cambridge: Harvard University Press, 2008, p. 230, 265.

Noble, David. *America by Design: Science, Technology, and the Rise of Corporate Capitalism.* New York: Oxford University Press, 1979, pp. 62–63.

Norfolk State University IC/CAE. "Health and Science Summer Academy: Middle School," July 19–30, 2010. http://www.nsu.edu/iccae/pdf/MiddleSchoolSchedule.pdf (accessed October 20, 2010).

_____. "A Recap of the High School Program." http://www.nsu.edu/iccae/phprint.php" (accessed October 10, 2010).

Patterson, Margot. "The Mission of Ray McGovern." *National Catholic Reporter,* October 27, 2006.

Pérez, Amanda, "IGKNU Collaboration Broadens Horizons through Intelligence Training." University of Texas-Pan American Division of University Advancement, August 16, 2010, http://ur.utpa.edu/publications/read/fl41de02b9d98a1c1063 (accessed October 12, 2010).

Pérez, Gina. "JROTC and Latina/o Youth in Neoliberal Cities," in *Rethinking America,* ed. Jeff Maskovsky and Ida Susser (New York: Paradigm, 2009), 31–48.

_____. "JROTC, Citizenship, and Puerto Rican Youth in Lorain, Ohio," (presentation, annual meetings of the American Anthropological Association, Philadelphia, PA, December 6, 2009).

Perry, Daniel. "The China Connection: UTPA Students Experience Chinese Culture, Academics," *The Monitor* (McAllen, Texas), July 24, 2007, http://www.themonitor.com/articles/china-4002-students-center.html.

Pincus, Walter. "Howard, Virginia Tech Join U.S. Intelligence Program." *Washington Post*, September 7, 2009.

Plascencia, Luis F.B. "The Military Gates of Non-Citizenship: Latino 'Aliens and Non-Citizen Nationals Performing Military Work in the U.S. Homeland." Presentation, annual meetings of the American Anthropological Association, Philadelphia, PA, December 6, 2009.

Platt, Kamala. "How Can We Sleep? The Birthing of an Intelligence Center on University Grounds," *La Voz de Esperanza* (San Antonio, Texas), May 2007, 6–7.

_____. "Latino/a Students and Covert "Securities": The Integration of Academic and Intelligence Communities." *Latino Studies* 6: 456–465.

Poulous, Ryan. "UTEP Camp Shows the World of Intelligence." *El Paso Inc.*, http://www.elpasoinc.com/showArticle.asp?articleId=1471 (accessed September 13, 2010).

Price, David. "Obama's Classroom Spies." *CounterPunch,* June 23, 2009, http://www.counterpunch.org/price06232009.html.

_____. "Silent Coup: How the CIA Is Welcoming Itself Back onto American University Campuses." *CounterPunch*, January 16–31, 2010: 1–4.

_____. "The Spook School Program." *CounterPunch*, February 1–15, 2010: 7–8.

Priest, Dana. "CIA Holds Terror Suspects in Secret Prisons." *Washington Post*, November 2, 2005.

_____ and Barton Gellman. "U.S. Decries Abuse but Defends Interrogations." *Washington Post*, December 26, 2002.

Risen, James, and Eric Lichtblau. "Bush Lets U.S. Spy on Callers without Courts." *New York Times*, December 16, 2005.

Schein, Edgar H. *Coercive Persuasion*. New York: W.W. Norton, 1971.

Simpson, Christopher. *Universities and Empire: Money and Politics in the Social Sciences during the Cold War*. New York: New, 1999.

Tuchman, Gaye. *Wannabe U: Inside the Corporate University*. Chicago: University of Chicago Press, 2009.

University of Texas-El Paso. "IC-CAE High School Summer Program Application." http://academics.utep.edu/Portals/1729/pdf/ICCAE_Application.pdf (accessed October 15, 2010).

University of Texas-Pan American Faculty Senate. "University of Texas-Pan American Faculty Senate Minutes," April 26, 2006. https://portal.utpa.edu/portal/page/portal/utpa_main/daa_home/senate_home/senate_imagesfiles/fs_060426_lm.pdf (accessed June 24, 2010).

University of Texas-Pan American Library. "IGKNU Journals." http://lib.utpa.edu/research/subjectguides/igknu (accessed September 15, 2010).

U.S. House Intelligence Committee. "Building Capabilities: The Intelligence Community's National Security Requirements for Diversity of Language, Skills, and Ethnic and Cultural Understanding." November 5, 2003. http://www.fas.org/irp/congress/2003_hr/110503hpsci.pdf (accessed March 15, 2010).

U.S. National Security Agency/Central Security Service. "Centers of Academic Excellence — Institutions." http://www.nsa.gov/ia/academic_outreach/nat_cae/institutions.shtml (accessed December 26, 2010).

U.S. Office of the Director of National Intelligence. "Intelligence Community Centers of Academic Excellence Program." *Intelligence Community Centers of Academic Excellence*, http://www.DNI.gov/cae/institutions.htm (accessed July 15, 2010).

_____ *United States Intelligence Community Centers of Academic Excellence in National Security Studies: Program Plan for Fiscal Years 2005–2015*. Washington, D.C.: Office of the Director of National Intelligence, 2005, pp. 6–7.

Willing, Richard "Intelligence Agencies Invest in College Education." *USA Today*, November 27, 2006.

Wilkinson, Tracy and Maria De Cristofaro. "Italy Indicts CIA Agents in Kidnapping." *Los Angeles Times*, February 17, 2007.

Zwerling, Philip. "The CIA on My Campus ... and Yours." *Nebula: A Journal of Multidisciplinary Scholarship* 6.4 (2009): 255.

8

Nine Steps to a Spy-Free Campus

Philip Zwerling

Step One: Research

Central Intelligence Agency analysts and operatives don't just hide out deep behind enemy lines dodging bullets and terrorist bombs. They scuttle in the shadows on college campuses as well sometimes evading snooping faculty and students. In each case, they don disguises. Overseas those disguises might include trench coats, wigs, and false beards. On campus, however, those disguises are usually front organizations, money passthroughs, and newly minted acronyms, like ODNI (Office of the Director of National Intelligence), IGkNU (the Integrated Global Knowledge and Understanding Collaboration), and IC/CAE (Intelligence Community Centers of Academic Excellence), that most people can't remember, pronounce, or identify but serve to obscure their connection with the CIA.

The CIA penetrates campuses to recruit students, seeking 10,000 applications to fill 1,000 vacancies at the agency each year. As part of that national effort they also "modify" curriculum, create academic courses and degree plans with an ideological bent, place agents in classrooms as professors, spy on faculty and students, and subvert the mission of the university. In 1986 CIA Director William Casey, speaking to the *New York Times* identified "the need to recruit, keep and reward high quality people — as his No. 1 priority"[1] and they want these high quality people from our schools. Most professors and students don't know the CIA is on campus, and that ignorance makes their work easier.

In the past, the CIA hid behind academic sounding programs like the Harvard/MIT Center for International Studies, the Asia Foundation at Michigan State University, Boston University's African Studies program, Harvard's Center for Middle Eastern Affairs, the International Police Academy and the

American Language Institute at Georgetown University, Cornell University's School of Industrial and Labor Relations, and the Institute for Social Research at the University of Michigan, all of which depended upon CIA collaborators and CIA covert funding.[2]

Today the CIA expends its secret budget through the ODNI and much of the money the CIA earmarks for campus activities flows through the CAE, so that on my campus and others collaborators can publicly proclaim that they do not receive CIA money. They can say, instead, that they receive ODNI money or CAE grants, and usually no one knows what that is.

After the U.S. intelligence agencies failed to detect or stop the 9/11 attacks against New York and Washington, D.C. Congress created the ODNI, the Office of the Director of National Intelligence. It is an umbrella group of the 16 U.S. intelligence agencies: the Defense Intelligence Agency, the Department of Energy (Office of Intelligence and Counterintelligence), the Department of Homeland Security (Office of Intelligence and Analysis), the Department of State (Bureau of Intelligence and Research), the Department of Treasury (Office of Intelligence and Analysis), the Drug Enforcement Administration (Office of National Security Intelligence), the Federal Bureau of Investigation (National Security Branch), the National Geospatial-Intelligence Agency, the National Reconnaissance Office, the National Security Agency/Central Security Service, the United States Air Force, the United States Army, the United States Coast Guard, the United States Marine Corps, the United States Navy, and, of course, the Central Intelligence Agency.

This collective roster goes by the acronym IC; the warm and fuzzy sounding Intelligence Community, but they don't gather around a campfire singing "Kumbaya." In their cozy "community" they're enticing young students into the biggest mistakes of their lives. Follow the money: the entire ODNI budget is $53 billion[3] but the CIA budget, an open secret, is $30 billion, or 57 percent of the total ODNI funds and leaves just billion dollar crumbs for the other 15 agencies to fight over. The CIA is the 700 pound gorilla in the ODNI.

The CIA is hiding on U.S. campuses. It takes some digging to find them and figure out what they're up to. The first thing to do is read. A literature search turns up lots of sources and I list 19 excellent books on the subject at the end of this essay. I suggest starting with two which are chock full of scary well researched facts. The first is the Pulitzer Prize winning *Legacy of Ashes: The History of the CIA* by journalist Tim Weiner. Weiner chronicles the long chain of U.S. intelligence disasters and political deceit from the comedically inept CIA precursor, the Office of Strategic Services, to the law breaking, coup planning, assassination plotting CIA of today with a tone of ironic disdain. A necessary complement is William Blum's *Killing Hope: U.S. Military and CIA*

Interventions Since World War II. (Monroe, Maine: Common Courage 2004), an angry polemic I quote from frequently in essay number 1.

Jonathan Feldman in his book *Universities in the Business of Repression* writes: "Universities are part of a complex web of intervention and militarism ... the university [is a] participant in both the U.S. war system and the transnational economy.[4] Weaving this web of deceit, the CIA wends its way across campus at 21 colleges and universities (see the complete list at the end of this essay), though the only people on your campus who may know where they are hiding are the faculty and students in the program and a handful of administrators and the law bars them from sharing this information. The program has expanded from just ten schools in 2004; so if your school is not on the list yet it may be soon. The less well known but equally secret NSA (National Security Agency) has its own IC/CAE program on 124 campuses. According to the excellent *Washington Post* series on "Top Secret America:" "30,000 [NSA] employees are reading, listening and analyzing an endless flood of intercepted conversations 24 hours a day, seven days a week." And the NSA will be recruiting 10,000 additional employees in the next fifteen years.[5] You can see a complete list of the NSA IC/CAEs on campuses at the end of this essay[6]. According to the *Washington Post* reports on our mushrooming secret government, the CIA and NSA (though among the largest such organizations) join some 1,271 other government organizations and 1,931 private companies working on "programs related to counterterrorism, homeland security and intelligences in about 10,000 locations across the United States. As estimated 854,000 ... hold top-secret security clearances."[7]

The CIA stakes out their corner of campus but they do not hang out a sign reading 'CIA At Work;' they are present themselves as CAE, IGKNU, Global Studies, Intelligence Analysis Campus, IC, and a dozen other covers so that collaborators cloak their work in "deniability" and can say they do not work for the CIA. A straight passthrough of funds would look like this:

CIA→UTPA

But to obscure and obfuscate, the passthrough goes like this:

CIA→IC/CAE→IGkNU→PACE→UTPA

Dr. Sandra Hansmann, an assistant professor of Rehabilitation Services at my campus, the University of Texas Pan American, who holds the title "Principal Investigator, UTPA Intelligence Community Center of Academic Excellence," has written publicly: "IGkNU is not and has never been a CIA program."[8] "IGkNU," she writes, "is funded by the Office of the Director of National Intelligence." But CIA money passes through the ODNI (57 percent of its budget) to IGkNU. IGkNU (The Integrated Global Knowledge and Understanding

Collaboration) is the UTPA campus entity created to disburse funds from the national CAE, the Centers for Academic Excellence program of the ODNI and CIA. IGkNU, like CAE, is a CIA program.

Earlier CIA recruiting at UTPA worked strictly on the level of marketing and recruitment as a for-credit business course. In 2005 a UTPA College of Business Administration's Advertising and Promotions class won a grant from the Central Intelligence Agency Collegiate Marketing Program through EdVenture Partners, which, according to a UTPA press release, develops private industry-education partnerships with universities across the country by "blending academic theory with practical, hands-on applications." The class developed a recruitment program aimed at their own campus, produced an advertising campaign, and hosted a job fair for the CIA. According to that same UTPA press release:

> The challenge for the class ... is to design and implement its own unique marketing campaign for the CIA, focusing on specific marketing objectives designed by the CIA. The goal is to increase awareness of the CIA and its career opportunities, market the CIA as an employer of choice to UTPA students and assist the CIA in positively marketing the agency and dispelling myths about the agency and careers within the agency.... [undergraduate student] Flores said UTPA was selected to participate in the project based on the institution's positive academic record, geographical location and diverse culture. "The CIA is interested in how to market to different ethnic groups and UTPA was the perfect candidate for this," Flores said.[9]

Note that this supposedly academic course doesn't have the merely pragmatic goal of selling the CIA as an employer of choice to fellow students but also the ideological goal of "dispelling myths about the agency." The entire history of CIA abuses is not subject to investigation, research, or critical discussion — the usual academic methods of education — but is instead dismissed as "myth," a common method of indoctrination and the antithesis of the educational mission of the University.

The press release continues:

> The marketing team had conducted a survey of UTPA students and determined that 57 percent had never been exposed to any CIA advertisement and 62 percent had never considered a career with the CIA. Flores said the survey also showed that most students thought the CIA was a very secretive organization and did not consider the CIA as a business organization with many job opportunities. "Our goal is to change those numbers significantly," Flores said. "Through diverse marketing strategies, we will increase CIA awareness and promote the CIA as an employer of choice."
> During the marketing event, representatives from the CIA visited the UTPA campus to inform students of job opportunities with the agency. In addition to a live band, free food and drinks and games, nearly 1,500 students were also able to register for door prizes such as concert tickets, cash prizes, T-shirts and a television. The marketing team will continue to track the level of awareness of the CIA among

UTPA students by conducting a follow-up survey of students in the coming weeks. Based on its research thus far, the team has made a few marketing strategy recommendations.

"To market to ethnically diverse populations, one must understand the culture. Furthermore, it is most effective to market to cultures individually rather than standardize the message," Flores said. "Our marketing agency chose a modern strategy—hosting an event — to create awareness, rather than the CIA's more traditional approach used in the past."

The project culminated ... when the marketing students presented their results and recommendations to the CIA and EdVenture Partners representatives in addition to many UTPA staff and faculty members. The students also proposed the CIA maintain frequent visits to the University to increase awareness of the agency. Marilyn Blatnikoff, diversity recruitment coordinator for the CIA, was impressed with the students' presentation and said their hard work and preparation was evident through their presentation and marketing suggestions. "Some of their recommendations are exactly in line with what we are trying to do," Blatnikoff said. "We are trying to narrow our range of schools and go more often to those schools, so their suggestions are great."[10]

After such a warm welcome mixing business and spycraft recruiting behind the EdVenture facade, the CIA returned to UTPA in 2006 with more money — 2,500,000 — a five year commitment, and a collaboration designed to change the academic curricula for decades, creating new courses and cobbling together old courses into a global studies minor and a master's certificate.

To further obscure its CIA connection, IGkNU partners with other campus groups in an interlocking daisy chain of organizations that on the surface seem to have nothing to do with the CIA. The $2.5 million CIA grant to IGkNU requires annual campus conferences but rather than sponsor its own conference IGkNU drew in two partners while retaining the purse strings. The UTPA Office of International Programs and PACE (the Pan American Collaboration for Ethics in the Professions) joined IGkNU in joint sponsorship of an ostensibly "academic" conference at UTPA in November 2008 entitled: "Ethics in Intelligence, Security and Immigration: The Moral and Social Significance of Gathering and Managing Information and Borders in the Global Community" and paid to print the proceedings, insuring that collaborating professors got a leg up on publications towards tenure. Although PACE Co-Director Dr. Cynthia Jones had a sign on her office door reading "Not funded by the CIA," the CIA has a very clear goal for such campus conferences where top speakers are cherry-picked for political reliability and a pro–CIA point of view, stating: "Colloquium ... should contain ... keynote addresses by senior IC officials and national level experts."[11]

Back in 1968, University of California Berkeley vice-president and covertly paid CIA consultant Dr. Earl Bolton wrote, in a secret memo widely circulated among U.S. universities, to advise the use of duplicity and deceit to hide the CIA connection to the campuses. He wrote:

> I suggest 'an affirmative action program' designed to improve the Agency's reputation in academic circles and thus decrease the risks (costs) of association with the Agency. However, until either the passage of time or an image bolstering plan changes the clichés of the moment an educational institution or individual electing to assist the Agency may be on the defensive.... It should also be stressed that when an apologia is necessary it can best be made ... with full use of the jargon of the academy.... There is sufficient vagueness in the total traditions of the profession to provide a skillful polemicist with formidable ammunition for defense.

Under the subhead "Contracts and Grants" he writes:

> Shouldn't the Agency have an insulator such as Rand or IDA? Such entities have quite good acceptance in academia ... and provide real protection against 'blow back.' Such an independent corporation should of course have a ringing name (e.g. Institute for a Free Society [or IGkNU or PACE?] should do work for the entire intelligence community and should really have a sufficiently independent existence so that it can take the heat on some projects if necessary....
>
> The real initiative might be with the Agency but the apparent or record launching of the research should whenever possible, emanate from the campus.... Follow a plan of emphasizing that CIA is a member of the national security community (rather than the intelligence community) and stress the great number of other agencies with which the Agency is allied.... Stress in recruiting, articles, and speeches that the Agency is really a university without students and not a training school for spies.... Do all recruiting off campus and try to time these visits so that the probability of reaction is decreased e.g. during the summer, between semesters, after the last issue of the student newspaper is printed for the semester, etc."[12]

IGkNU also founded a summer spy camp, a one week summer institute offered free to forty area high school students and advertised as "Got Intelligence?" The IGkNU website describes the outreach to teenagers in grades 9 through 11:

> The importance of intelligence gathering and analysis has become increasingly evident since September 2001, succeeding in a larger undertaking of U.S. engagement abroad. Numerous studies have indicated the need for U.S. intelligence analysts with diverse backgrounds and ethnicities, to become the new cadre of employees. As the challenges of the new century unfold, government agencies, private industry, consulting companies, and thinking tanks will increasingly rely on this new cadre of employees in formulating policies, and developing business strategies that are globally aware while at the same time protecting the interest of the U.S. Government and corporations. The "Got Intelligence?" Summer Institute is directed toward fostering Global Knowledge, Understanding, and Leadership skills to a new generation of students at the high school level. The Summer Institute will be multidisciplinary in nature, incorporating topics in History, Information Science, Engineering, Geology, Psychology, and Language studies, and designed to give the students critical tools which make them capable of analyzing events at the national and international level.[13]

At spy camp students play high tech games of hide and seek with GPS (global positioning) units and do water quality studies with GIS (Geographic Information Systems), but the emphasis remains on recruitment. UTPA's press release on the camp, posted 8/10/9 explained:

> [Said] Med High School senior Aleyda Cantu Munoz, from Donna [Texas] ... who along with medicine also has an interest in an intelligence career. "I have read about it but here it is more in depth and detailed. It was very helpful to hear from actual Intelligence Community representatives."[14] In the words of the ODNI, the high school outreach programs are designed to "increase the talent pool of students considering a career in the IC."[15]

In other words, it's never too young to join the CIA, for the ODNI also encourages summer spy camps for youth as young as "junior high school"[16] which will include: "several intelligence related exercises, scenarios, case studies."[17]

In our sit-down meeting on May 5, 2009, in newly refurbished offices in the Lamar building on the UTPA campus, program director Nick Weimer, hired out of a career in the hotel and tourist industry, told me IGkNU has "no affiliation with the CIA. We do not work with the CIA." As I've pointed out the ODNI funding comes mostly from the CIA budget and the IGkNU budget comes from the ODNI. "If a student wanted to work for the CIA," Weimer said, "we'd take them as we would a student who wanted to work for the State Department."[18]

Though the grant requires the university to hold an annual public conference, sponsor study abroad courses, institute some curricula in the intelligence field, and reach out to high school students, Weimer insisted "We build the program, not them. In no way is our program spy training."[19] However, the ODNI's own Guidance and Procedures bulletin for the IC/CAE states clearly that a major goal of the funding includes "curriculum modification activity," government-speak for not only for creating new IC courses but also increasing the number of courses "modified to include IC related topics"[20] as the CIA infiltrates an unlimited number of university classes.

At the same time, however, UTPA is not an independent partner since the ODNI requires that: "IC agencies and elements are actively involved in the development, implementation and operation of the IC/CAE Program."[21]

Certainly the ODNI gets its money's worth with a toe hold on campus. In the words of Dr. Van Reidhead, immediate past dean of UTPA's College of Social and Behavior Sciences, home to IGkNU, "The intelligence community needs people with a global knowledge foundation. They [the intelligence community] can teach the trade crafts."[22]

To this end, IGkNU sponsors two summer language immersion programs, one in China (presumably the U.S. rival for world preeminence in the

21st century), and Morocco (a representative of the Arab and Islamic worlds from which comes the contemporary terrorist threat). In addition they send students to career conferences in D.C. where undergraduates mingle with recruiters from the various intelligence services. IGkNU also sponsors a resource room in the UTPA library named for themselves, an annual speakers series, an annual National Conference on Global Security, and funding for faculty to develop new courses in the intelligence field.

Once again the Intelligence Community and the CIA reach out into issues of academic careers, promotion and tenure, linking the IC/CAE money to "support for sabbaticals, research, and related activities of faculty."[23] Scholars who play ball with the CIA gain access to the goodies that ensure successful academic careers.

IGkNU used the IC/CAE money to furnish and stock a conference room on the third floor of the UTPA library where many IGkNU speakers are presented. Though the conference room is open to all students, the ODNI is clear about its use requiring that collaborating colleges "ensure that books, magazines, and material about each of the IC agencies and components are readily available for students."[24] Again, imagine a "tobacco industry library room" stocked only with pro-smoking materials to propagandize students. Need I mention that no other program or department on campus has its own named and dedicated room in the library?

Where the CIA finds the university's own faculty insufficiently reliable to promote the CIA, the ODNI will "Provide curriculum development assistance. Assistance may include officers-in-residence, contractors, local and national level experts and retired IC cadre to assist in IC/CAE Program Development."[25] One group eager to aid the effort is the Association of Former Intelligence Officers whose editor wrote in their monthly bulletin of May 2007:

> I recently visited the campus and found the students very engaging and eager to learn. I believe it would serve the nation well if AFIO members in the vicinity of UTPA made themselves available to visit the university and interact with the students. Of course there are the self proclaimed experts that are critical of the program, and anything we can do to support this DNI effort will serve our community well.[26]

The involvement of the Office of International Programs with IGkNU and PACE is particularly disheartening as the recruitment of tens of thousands of foreign students studying in the U.S. has long been a CIA priority with a history of blackmail, threats and intimidation aimed at coercing students to spy against their native countries.[27] Often such students return to their home countries both compromised and terrified. According to author Ami Chen Mills over forty such foreign student agents recruited from U.S. campuses by the CIA committed suicide between 1948 and 1991.[28]

CIA recruiters put the rosiest picture possible on their future vocation, even assuring recruits they will get desk jobs far from the field and distanced from covert actions like assassinations and torture. For example, according to UTPA political science associate professor Dr. Samuel Freeman, who raised the issue of CIA recruitment of Mexican-American students to become field agents and possibly involve themselves in torture and assassinations:

> The College of Social and Behavioral Sciences Dean [Dr. Van Reidhead] repeatedly stated publicly that students recruited into the program who join intelligence agencies upon graduation would become analysts, and denied they would become operatives. When asked why he believed IC-CAE students at UTPA would not become operatives, he responded CIA officers told him the students would not become operatives; and the Dean said he believed them. He believed the CIA.
>
> This raises an interesting question. If they will be analysts, why is there any particular need to recruit minority students? One does not need to be African-American or Mexican-American or Oriental-American or Arab-American to be an analyst. One's ethnicity does not necessarily mean a person has any cultural ties with or understanding of Latin America or Africa or Asia or the Middle East that would enhance their ability to analyze intelligence from those regions. Furthermore, analysts generally are not considered to be "spies." Operatives who travel to these regions are "spies."[29]

Although the number of CIA employees and their job descriptions, like the CIA budget, is secret, conservative estimates put the number of field agents engaged in covert operations at 20 percent of the workforce[30] and no CIA employee can be assured of keeping his/her hands clean.

College students in CIA undergraduate programs can go to work as spies even before they join the CIA as Trinity College in Washington, D.C., learned in January 2010 when the FBI accused the Assistant Director of the Intelligence Community Center of Academic Excellence at Trinity, Stan Dai, also a speaker at Georgetown University's CIA summer program, with "aiding and abetting" the installation of an electronic eavesdropping operation at the New Orleans office of U.S. Senator Mary Landrieu. Trinity's President Patricia McGuire, though admitting her campus received $250,000 from the IC/CAE annually for four years, denied Trinity trains spies.[31]

Step 2: Teach

According to former CIA agent Ralph McGehee, "The CIA wants active, charming, obedient people who can get things done in the social world but have limited perspective and understanding and who see things in black and white and don't like to think too much."[32] Our job on campus is to teach: to get our students to see all sides of issues, to think, and to understand.

A CIA recruitment flier for a campus meeting.

I am not a fan of proselytizing in the classroom, and teaching creative writing does not give me much occasion to talk about the CIA. But I do talk about the book and articles I'm writing on the subject and that often leads to further discussion. History, political science, government, psychology, anthropology, journalism, and philosophy professors can certainly assign readings and lead class discussions about the spy agency.

Teaching doesn't just take place in the classroom, however. Some of the most effective means of building the intellectual underpinnings of the anti–Vietnam War movement were the 'Teach-ins,' organized debates, often on campuses, between supporters and opponents of that War. At UTPA we've taken advantage of venues like Pan-American Days, the annual Social Justice and Peace Conference, and International Days to offer panel discussions on the CIA and IGkNU. At first I wanted to balance the speakers' points of view but after every colleague associated with IGkNU whom I invited declined to speak I realized that, like the CIA itself, they avoided public scrutiny. I settled for a series of anti–CIA speakers, making sure to recruit new faces from the faculty each time and to publicize the refusal of collaborators to face the public.

It's also possible to bring special speakers to campus, especially former CIA agents like Verne Lyon, Bill Blum, Ralph McGehee, and others whose personal stories and first hand experiences provide a rare look behind the cloak of this secret agency. Many such ex-agents, including the late Philip Agee, are also available in film documentaries for a small rental fee or from Netflix, or free internet download. Look for *On Company Business, Secrets of the CIA,* and *An Unholy Alliance.* Or, plan a series of showings of classic movies on the misdeeds of the CIA. *Missing, Lumumba, Three Days of the Condor, The Good Shepherd, The Quiet American, Syriana, Latino, The Battle of Chile,* and *Under Fire* are all available and lend themselves to after-viewing discussions of CIA morality, efficacy, and secrecy and its place on campus.

Set up a table in the student union to sell this book and the other books cited here. Make sure this book and others like it are ordered by your campus library. Invite one of our authors to speak at your campus.

Use the movie screenings, teach-ins, and book tables to build faculty-student alliances. Faculty can best organize faculty and only a student led movement can organize students. There are many groups to partner with on campus and off: LGBT groups might join to protest the CIA's treatment of gays; Black, Latino, and Asian civil rights groups might join to protest the CIA's targeting of vulnerable minorities, feminists may join to oppose the organization's role in world-wide male dominance.

Gather email lists at public events and keep people informed of anti–CIA activities on campus. All kinds of people will attend events and sign up including those who are opposed to the cause, but while the CIA operates in secret, we cannot and our actions must be transparent and overt.

Spokespeople need to make use of every media outlet, including stories for the campus newspaper and radio station and off-campus television news shows, talk shows and daily and weekly newspapers. Remember that every panel held, every movie showing, and every speaker is a news event worthy of a press release and calls to the local media for additional coverage.

When the movement is large enough to look substantial it's time for public rallies, leafletting, and the picketing of CIA recruiters. Make use of organs of campus governance: student can pass motions in student government, faculty have recourse to college councils and the faculty senate. See a copy of the resolution we submitted and passed unanimously at our College Council at the end of this essay.

It's also necessary to talk to people: faculty colleagues, department chairs, deans, and the college president. Newly appointed UTPA President Robert Nelsen gave three of our professors a full hour in his office to present our opposition to the CIA on campus. He didn't share his own thinking on the subject but we did, at least, begin a dialogue on the issue at a high level of campus decision making. While it may be true, in the words of former CIA agent Philip Agee, that "University administrators and presidents are not known in this country as people with great backbone in standing up to the government,"[33] they are thoughtful people who may listen to well-reasoned arguments presented in a rational manner. After all, while all administrators want to increase cash flow to their institutions, many want to avoid paying the price of a divided campus and a media spotlight.

Fight the notion, which you will hear, that stopping CIA recruiters on campus deprives them of free speech. We champion free speech; public speech, dialogue, debate, and intellectual discovery are our goals. The CIA, as a secret organization, with a history of dissembling, lies, and fraud, is opposed to each of these. Invite the CIA to public events to debate the issues and see if they come. But keep in mind that recruitment is not speech. The speech that goes on in a CIA job interview is not for education; it is private, individual, and based on lies. As ex–CIA Verne Lyon said twenty years ago, and as it remains true to this day: "They don't tell [interviewees] that the CIA is geared for subverting treaties and circumventing international law, that it is a criminal organization, that it has participated in drug dealing."[34]

Your colleagues may also tell you that campus recruitment is necessary to reform the Agency and that enlisting "good," educated, humane people, (i.e., college students, professors and administrators) into the CIA might ameliorate their activities. But this only begs the question of how much worse they would have been if left solely in the hands of "bad guys." Over time individuals' scruples have had less impact than the culture, mission, history, and the very *raison d'etre* for this secret organization. A bad system does not allow much room for good people to do good; it only makes them "bad."

You're not alone; national help for this effort comes from organizations like the American Civil Liberties Union, the Center for Constitutional Rights, and the National Lawyers' Guild. The American Friends Service Committee and magazines like CounterPunch and the Nation and National Public Radio, as well as the blog Boiling Frogs Post (http://www.boilingfrogspos.com/tag-/podcast-episode/) and The Independent (http://www.indypendent.org/) regularly cover these issues and can keep you updated of the anti–CIA struggle on other campuses.

Step 3: Oppose

Just say "no" to the CIA. Say "no" to colleagues, administrators and students: it is not o.k. to collaborate with the CIA on campus. Sometimes one loud voice saying "no" is what it takes to give others the courage to also oppose the CIA. Movements start with a single expression of commitment. Commitment often begins with a single example of courage, as Rosa Parks' simple refusal to surrender her bus seat to a white person sparked the 1955–56 Montgomery Bus Boycott and ultimately integrated that Alabama city. Refuse to collaborate with the CIA. Dispute with those who do collaborate. Take a further step and circulate a faculty and/or student petition not to collaborate with the CIA.

Collaboration confers many benefits, however, for the academic careerist. The Intelligence Community (CIA) reaches out to manipulate academic careers, promotion and tenure, linking the IC/CAE money to "support for sabbaticals, research, and related activities of faculty."[35] Scholars who play ball with the CIA gain access to the goodies that ensure successful careers. UTPA Political Science Professor Samuel Freeman, who opposed the ODNI funding on his campus, was told by his College of Social and Behavioral Sciences Dean, Van Reidhead, that if he dropped his opposition to the CIA funding "faculty participating in the program could get spy center funding for research abroad."[36] In an academic atmosphere where success and the relative security of tenure are based on research and publications, such CIA money for travel is pure gold. In the past, CIA funded scholars on editorial boards have helped other CIA collaborating scholars gain acceptance of their articles at journals subsidized in part or whole by the CIA. Putting together a list of faculty on your campus who refuse CIA inducements helps "out" collaborators when they refuse to sign the petition and identify allies when they do sign.

Action that begins with a no advances to a yes as steps lead to building an anti–CIA movement and personal protest turns into public action. Speakers and teach-ins lead to identifying more allies who are then enlisted in further actions. Educational outreach leads to the direct action of picketing and leafletting. At schools like the University of Colorado at Boulder in 1984 that led to civil disobedience outside the campus building where the CIA recruiter set up shop, arrests by campus police, more public demonstrations, more arrests, and more demonstrations. The CIA stopped visiting the University of Colorado for the next ten years.[37] In April 2005 the CIA pulled out of recruiting events at New York University when they learned of planned student protests.

Step 4: Persevere

This is not a campaign won in a semester or a year; it is a slow process of building awareness of and opposition to the CIA. After discovering the CIA programs on your campus and beginning the process of public education you may well run into an air of aloof disdain from colleagues who, perfectly comfortable in the insulation and detachment of the ivory tower, are suspicious of both politics and social engagement. They may mock colleagues for their commitment and concern and marginalize them as single-issue ideologues who have lost their scholarly perspective. None of us want to stand out as the oddball in the conformist society of academics but, as we learned in grade school, we cannot worry about what others think of us. It's amazing how, when you take a stand, you encourage others to step forth and stand with you.

We will persevere. In the words of one Nicaraguan peasant: "When you say, 'What can I do? Nothing!' I agree with you. But, when you ask another: 'What can *we* do?' I would say: 'Everything.'"[38]

We will wear them down. I subscribe to the notion that right eventually makes might and that the truth eventually will out. I don't know how long that will take but I do know that in the end truth trumps money, connections, and ambition, the main values the other side has going for it.

Step 5: Caution

Do not, however, underestimate the power of the CIA and its collaborators on campus. Even with the truth on your side, you must act cautiously. The academic world is steeply hierarchical and power comes from the top down. The people who bring in the money in the form of CIA/ODNI grants — sometimes in the millions of dollars — rise to the top, recruit and reward other collaborators, and together bring in more money and recruit more collaborators in a daisy chain of shared interests and mutual support.

Tenure, like money, is power. Collaborators are rewarded with lighter teaching loads, research and travel money, and choice committee assignments. For them tenure is assured. Those who oppose the CIA on campus, however, can be bullied, intimidated, and even denied tenure. The official reasons for denying tenure can be lack of publications, below average teaching skills, or less than stellar service, all of which often come down to subjective decisions by committees rather than a clear qualitative judgment. Unofficially, people are denied tenure in confidential votes just because their colleagues don't like them and their colleagues don't like them because they are seen as troublemakers who ask too many questions or disturb too many consciences.

We might wish that tenured professors would use their secure status to lead this effort. Sometimes they do, but the sad fact of academic life is that the seven years spent worrying abut earning tenure and trying to keep your head down and not alienate the powers that be often condition you to live the rest of your life that way. It is likely that this is the very intention of the tenure process: by the time you've earned the security to speak and act boldly you no longer remember how to do so.

When I first got involved in this issue, a colleague — one of contributors to this book, in fact — warned me of the dangers and advised me to leave the work to tenured colleagues. I thought long and hard about his words and decided that while I was willing to avoid controversy on most issues, this one was simply too important as simultaneously a professional, a political, and a moral issue to not take a stand. That decision will always be an individual and personal one but I do believe lives, the lives of our students and others beyond our borders, are at stake.

Opponents will use the university governance structure and the tenure process against us. Intimidation is one of their weapons. For example, on April 7, 2010, several colleagues and I sponsored a panel on the CIA/IGkNU connection at UTPA as part of the annual Pan American Days on campus. Following that event I received a phone call in my office from another colleague threatening he would "come over and beat the shit out of me." Not exactly the words you expect to hear on campus. He was angry about remarks attributed to me but which I had not made. He had not been present at the teach-in. (Happily, he called back ten minutes later to apologize.) Better yet, I had several witnesses in my office at the time of the call and we all wrote the incident up and sent copies to our department chairs. At least they'd know where to find our bodies.

The following day another colleague collaborating in the IGkNU grant sent out an email copied to each participant speaker at the teach-in but addressed to the Provost, our department chairs, and, most tellingly, to the Equal Opportunity Affirmative Action Officer in the Office of the UTPA President alleging that our speakers had made racist comments, badgered a student with a disability, and made "sexual insinuations veer[ing] dangerously close to sexual harassment." She wrote: "In sum, I have serious concerns about the possible racist and harassing behaviors of Drs. Zwerling, Carlson, and Anshen at their Pan American Days presentation. I thank you for your consideration of my concerns."[39]

Few more serious charges could be leveled at anyone, but especially at three untenured professors. Luckily for us, the events she described (she also was not present at the event) never occurred and we had plenty of witnesses to these inaccuracies. We responded to all the folks she had emailed denying every incident she had described.

A week later she responded disingenuously in another mass email: "I did not and do not intend to raise any charges against anyone, and I do not make any formal complaints. Had I intended to make a charge or complaint, I would have stated so clearly in my letter. Also, I didn't request any response from anyone, and need none. My intent was simply to raise these concerns in an attempt to continue academic debate and further intellectual inquiry into issues critical to all of us."[40] Allegations of "racist and harassing behaviors" are rarely considered part of an academic debate and are more clearly understood as intimidation. Thankfully, the Provost, chairs, and EEOAA officer made no comment and took no action.

Our teach-ins often attracted students enrolled in various IGkNU classes, some of whom had come to defend their program, as well as students and faculty opposed to IGkNU or those simply undecided on its merits. One student attended two such events wearing a T-shirt with the provocative motto "I'd rather be waterboarding." It was difficult at times to keep emotionally charged opinions in check and we required a moderator at each event to set guidelines and keep time limits. With these in place, we facilitated civil discussions and reached hundreds of students.

Step 6: Diversify

Speakers, films, and panel discussions all work well to bring this issue to the campus community but there are more arrows in our quiver of opposition, including but not limited to guerrilla theater, public demonstrations, counter recruitment, anti–CIA conferences, underground newspapers, and artistic expression (posters, murals, chalk drawings, gallery shows, T-shirt designs, etc.). Our faculty and students in the theatre, art, english, psychology, and political science departments have diverse talents vital to the anti–CIA movement.

I earned my Ph.D. in theatre and I studied agitation/propaganda and political plays from Aristophanes' *Lysistrata* to Jane Martin's *Flags*. The Lysistrata project, founded by two actresses in the months leading up to the U.S. invasion of Iraq in 2003, sponsored 1,000 public readings of the 2,500 year old anti-war play *Lysistrata* in a single night in 59 countries and all 50 states before a combined audience of 200,000 people while raising $100,000 for peace oriented charities.[41] The rights to *Lysistrata* lie in the public domain and anyone can stage a reading. Other powerful anti-war plays include Euripides' *The Trojan Women*, Kenneth Brown's *The Brig*, Bertolt Brecht's *Mother Courage and Her Children*, Irwin Shaw's *Bury the Dead*, James Duff's *Home Front*, John DiFusco's *Tracers*, and Emily Mann's *Still Life*.

Or, you can always write your own. It doesn't have to be a full length play. Try a short play, a skit, or borrow some tricks from the Living Newspaper. The 1930s Living Newspaper (and its later adaptation by playwrights like Augusto Boal) mixed drama and the latest headlines. Try dramatizing a waterboarding torture session while reading aloud the CIA Charter, or read the script of a possible CIA job interview while projecting images of Abu Ghraib on a screen behind it. You get the idea.

Puppets work (Punch and Judy reenact the CIA overthrow of Allende, perhaps, or torture a suspected terrorist?). The Vermont based Bread and Puppet Theatre long performed at anti-war demonstrations and has left a legacy of effective skits. Announcing the waterboarding of a student on the Quad at a certain date and time will draw a crowd ripe for a discussion of CIA tortures. Just don't actually waterboard anyone.

Non-violent and legal public demonstrations come in all shapes and sizes from a circular picket line, to an immobile line of students and faculty with their mouths gagged each holding a name tag of someone tortured or killed by the CIA.

Meet each CIA recruiting appearance on campus with a counter-recruitment protest in which students sign a pledge not to join a secret terrorist organization. Have students sign up for CIA interviews to engage the interviewers in political discussions and express student opposition to their presence on campus.

Organize an art show dedicated to peace. Art speaks more powerfully to some people than argument or debate. Campus artists can produce original work on the themes of peace, war and the CIA that will grab campus and media attention. T-shirt sales fund the movement and spread the message. Shirts with peace signs, lists of CIA assassinated heads of state or coup attempts, no torture graphics, etc. can be worn daily and in class to spark discussions. Cover available campus spaces with posters, murals, and chalk drawings. Back in the day we covered the Quad with a hundred white crosses to memorialize

Vietnam War victims. Make sure the campus newspaper and yearbook get photos before they are removed.

Step 7: Publish

Academics write and the CIA on campus is a subject worth writing about. It is a subject fit for academic conferences and academic publications. This book began as a conference presentation. The discovery of the CIA on my own campus led me to consider asking more questions, interviewing collaborating and opposing faculty and writing a paper. Delivering the paper for the first time at an international conference led to further discussion. Scholars then received electronic transcripts of the conference proceedings and further discussions ensued. I determined to publish my work and turned a twenty minute conference paper into an 8,000 word article. Twenty-seven paper and on-line journals rejected that article for a variety of stated reasons: too long, not long enough, of interest to only a narrow audience, no space, no time, no interest, etc. I never considered giving up and methodically pursued new venues. Finally the article was accepted by *Nebula*, an online academic journal published from Australia, of all places.

Colleagues and I circulated that article to more colleagues on campus and received both thanks and threats. I linked the journal site to my Facebook page and included the link as a tag at the end of all my email correspondence. Then I went looking for a publisher and tracking down scholars across the country to contribute to this volume and shepherded their work into this final form. An informal network of anti–CIA scholars and activists is growing. Next step would be an electronic clearinghouse with news of anti–CIA activity from correspondents at campuses across the country.

Academics research and write and we need to apply those special skills to getting the CIA off campus. Our venues range from academic conferences and journals to popular media, local newspapers, and throwaway leaflets. We do have the skills and means to reach and teach and win this battle.

Step 8: Celebrate

I understand the righteous wrath that underlies the anti–CIA work and the likely frustrations and dangers of taking on a multi-billion-dollar-a-year secret entity but I think we need to the keep the work positive and affirm small successes along the way of a seemingly unending struggle. We don't need negativity, self-righteousness, cynicism, or misplaced anger. Not everyone who disagrees with us is an enemy. An opponent today can be an ally tomorrow if we don't make the struggle personally vituperative.

One way to stay positive is to celebrate real campus values and be clear about what we are for as well as what we oppose. Academic freedom, freedom of speech, collegial cooperation, unbiased and shared research, freedom of association, international solidarity, helping our students succeed, and strengthening our communities are the things we are working for and the things we believe collaboration with the CIA subverts.

The past inspires us, from the anti-apartheid/South Africa divestment campaigns of the 1980s to the anti-sweatshop movement of the 1990s. Campus activism exemplifies campus idealism and energy since the anti-war movements of the '60s and '70s and anchors learning and teaching in real world activism. Yes, campus anti–CIA work is educational and actually part of our job as educators.

Step 9: Win

We are in this struggle to win. That anti-apartheid movement of the 1980s pressured 155 universities to divest from racist South Africa investments.[42] Between 1987 and 1991 in the last great campus movement against the CIA, anti–CIA activities actions blossomed at 75 colleges and universities[43] and in the late 1980s CIA recruiters met demonstrations at one-third of the campuses they visited.[44]

Universities in Mexico, France, and elsewhere are autonomous centers of academic endeavor and government forces (police, army, security agencies) may not enter. In the U.S. we too can stop the militarization of higher education. At UTPA the College Council resolution against IGkNU funding passed unanimously. The university-wide Faculty Senate then received the resolution and scheduled their own open debate on the issue for next semester. The IC/CAE grant to IGkNU ended in May 2011 and will not be renewed. In December 2010, UTPA President Nelsen told me he knew of no further ODNI funding to the university. It appears plans to establish an Intelligence Analysis Campus are, for the present at least, stillborn.

The future of our democracy hangs in the balance. In the words of Professor Henry Giroux, the Global Television Network Chair in English and Cultural Studies at McMaster University in Canada:

> While higher education is only one site, it is one of the most crucial institutional and political spaces where democratic subjects can be shaped, democratic relations can be experienced, and anti-democratic forms of power can be identified and critically engaged. It is also one of the few spaces left where young people can think critically about the knowledge they gain, learn values that refuse to reduce the obligations of citizenship to either consumerism or the dictates of the national security state and develop the language and skills necessary to defend those institutions and social relations that are vital to a substantive democracy.[45]

Books relevant to the CIA/Campus Connection

Blum, William. *Killing Hope: U.S. Military and C.I.A. Interventions Since World War II.* Monroe, ME: Common Courage, 2004.

_____.*Rogue State: A Guide to the World's Only Superpower.* Monroe, ME: Common Courage, 2000.

Caute, David. *The Dancer Defects.* Oxford: Oxford University Press, 2003.

Corson, William. *The Armies of Ignorance: The Rise of the American Intelligence Empire.* New York: Dial, 1977.

Feldman, Jonathan. *Universities in the Business of Repression: The Academic-Military-Industrial Complex in Central America.* Boston: South End, 1989.

Giroux, Henry A. *The University in Chains: Confronting the Military-Industrial-Academic Complex.* Boulder, CO: Paradigm, 2007.

Grandin, Greg. *Empire's Workshop: Latin America, the United States, and the Rise of the New Imperialism.* New York: Henry Holt, 2006.

Halperin, Morton, Jerry Berman, Robert Borosage, and Christine Marwick. *The Lawless State: The Crimes of the U.S. Intelligence Agencies.* New York: Penguin, 1976

Jagan, Cheddi. *The West On Trial: The Fight for Guyana's Freedom.* Berlin: Seven Seas, 1971.

Kwitny, Jonathan. *Endless Enemies: The Making of An Unfriendly World.* New York: Penguin, 1984.

McGehee, Ralph W. *Deadly Deceits: My 25 Years in the CIA.* New York: Sheridan Square, 1983.

Mills, Ami Chen. *CIA Off Campus: Building the Movement Against Agency Recruitment and Research.* Boston: South End, 1991.

Prados, John. *Safe for Democracy: The Secret Wars of the CIA.* Chicago: Ivan R. Dee, 2006.

Saunders, Frances Stonor. *The Cultural Cold War: The CIA and The World of Arts and Letters.* New York: New, 1999.

Schlesinger, Stephen, and Stephen Kinzer. *Bitter Fruit: The Untold Story of the American Coup in Guatemala.* New York: Doubleday, 1982.

Trento, Joseph. *Prelude to Terror: The Rogue CIA and the Legacy of America's Private Intelligence Network.* New York: Carroll and Graf, 2005.

Weiner, Tim. *Legacy of Ashes: The History of the CIA.* New York: Doubleday, 2007.

White, Geoffrey D., with Flannery Hauck, eds. *Campus, Inc.: Corporate Power in the Ivory Tower.* Amherst, NY: Prometheus, 2000.

Wilford, Hugh. *The Mighty Wurlitzer: How the CIA Played America.* Cambridge: Harvard University Press, 2008.

Resolution

Resolution passed unanimously October 14, 2010 by the College Council of the College of Arts and Humanities of UTPA and forwarded to the UTPA Faculty Senate and university president.

Whereas the U.S. Intelligence Agencies grouped in the Office of the Directorate of National Intelligence [ODNI] that sponsor IGkNU and the program in Global Security Studies include the Central Intelligence Agency [CIA], an agency that has repeatedly violated all manner of international and national laws and conventions, up to and including grave human rights violations, e.g., overseeing and funding torture, illegal detention, assassination, infringements of national sovereignty, and other illegal and immoral actions;

Whereas the CIA and other intelligence agencies have often promoted deliberate misinformation to mislead citizens of the U.S. and other nations to the detriment of universal principles of sovereignty, mutual respect, self-determination, and/or human rights; Whereas despite numerous efforts and declarations of reform, a demonstrable consistent pattern of behavior and abuses by the CIA has remained the norm, as seen in the past two presidential administrations, and therefore any present or future claims to reform must be taken with the greatest skepticism;

Whereas public universities should maintain the highest standards of autonomy and self-governance, as well as a necessarily critical distance from any kind of official state authority, particularly in areas that involve government agencies that have repeatedly manipulated information or used universities to perpetuate crimes and unconscionable and unethical acts incompatible with the mission of universities;

And whereas the very nature of such intelligence organizations requires secrecy and prevents public scrutiny and open access of ideas, which leads to functioning that is necessarily undemocratic, secretive, and antithetical to the highest ideals of academic freedom and public accountability, which form part of our University mission and values; for these reasons,

Be it resolved: The College of Arts and Humanities College Council opposes accepting further ODNI funding for academic programs at UTPA and rejects establishing an "Intelligence Analysis Campus," inasmuch as these appear incompatible with the independence of the University, the traditional mission of liberal education, the stated Value of the UTPA Mission Statement, which reads "We value ethical conduct based on honesty, integrity, and mutual respect in all interactions and relationships" and the Mission Statement's Goal of "infus[ing] Inter-American and global perspectives throughout the University community." We in the CoAH College Council ask the Faculty Senate to initiate an inquiry into the appropriateness of the cooperation between the University and this consortium of intelligence agencies and ask that the Faculty Senate, should it reach similar conclusions as the College Council of the Arts and Humanities regarding this incompatibility, to oppose further funding from the ODNI.

The National Security Agency on Campus

ALABAMA

Auburn University
Jacksonville State University
University of Alabama Huntsville

ALASKA

University of Alaska Fairbanks

ARIZONA

Arizona State University
University of Advancing Technology
University of Arizona Tucson

ARKANSAS

University of Arkansas Little Rock

CALIFORNIA

California State Polytechnic University Pomona
California State University Sacramento
California State University San Bernardino
Naval Postgraduate School
University of California Davis
University of California Irvine

COLORADO

Colorado Technical University
Regis University
U.S. Air Force Academy
University of Denver

CONNECTICUT

University of Connecticut

FLORIDA

Florida State University
Nova Southeastern University

GEORGIA

Clark Atlanta University
Georgia Institute of Technology
Kennesaw Sate University
Southern Polytechnic State University

IDAHO

Idaho State University
University of Idaho

ILLINOIS

De Paul University
Illinois Institute of Technology
Illinois State University
Moraine Valley Community College
University of Illinois at Chicago
University of Illinois at Springfield
University of Illinois at Urbana-Champain

INDIANA

Indiana University
Purdue University

IOWA

Iowa State University

KANSAS

Fort Hays State University
Kansas State University
University of Kansas

LOUISIANA

University of New Orleans

MARYLAND

Anne Arundel Community College
Capitol College
Johns Hopkins University

Hagerstown Community College
Prince George's Community College
Towson University
U.S. Naval Academy
University of Maryland Baltimore County
University of Maryland College Park
University of Maryland University College

MASSACHUSETTS

Boston University
Northeastern University
University of Massachusetts Amherst

MICHIGAN

Eastern Michigan University
University of Detroit Mercy
Walsh College

MINNESOTA

Capela University
Metropolitan State University
St. Cloud State University
University of Minnesota

MISSISSIPPI

Mississippi State University

MISSOURI

Missouri University of Science and Technology
University of Missouri Columbia

NEBRASKA

University of Nebraska Omaha

NEVADA

University of Nevada Las Vegas

NEW HAMPSHIRE

Dartmouth College

NEW JERSEY

New Jersey City University
New Jersey Institute of Technology
Princeton University
Rutgers, the State University of New Jersey
Stevens Institute of Technology

NEW MEXICO

New Mexico Tech
University of New Mexico

NEW YORK

Pace University
Polytechnic University
Rochester Institute of Technology
State University of New York Buffalo
Syracuse University
U.S. Military Academy West Point

NORTH CAROLINA

East Carolina University
North Carolina A&T State University
North Carolina State University
University of North Carolina Charlotte

OHIO

Air Force Institute of Technology
Ohio State University

OKLAHOMA

Oklahoma City Community College
Oklahoma State University
Rose State College
University of Tulsa

PENNSYLVANIA

Carnegie Mellon University
Drexel University
East Stroudsburg University of Pennsylvania
Indiana University of Pennsylvania
The Pennsylvania State University
University of Pittsburgh
West Chester University of Pennsylvania

PUERTO RICO

Polytechnic University of Puerto Rico

SOUTH CAROLINA

University of South Carolina

SOUTH DAKOTA

University of South Dakota

TENNESSEE

Fountainhead College of Technology
University of Memphis
University of Tennessee Chattanooga

TEXAS

Our Lady of the Lake University
Southern Methodist University
Texas A&M University
University of Dallas
University of Houston
University of North Texas
The University of Texas Dallas
University of Texas El Paso
University of Texas San Antonio

VERMONT

Champlain College
Norwich University

VIRGINIA

George Mason University
James Madison University
Norfolk State University
Virginia Polytechnic Institute and State University

WASHINGTON

University of Washington

WASHINGTON, D.C.

The George Washington University
Georgetown University
Information Resources Management College

WEST VIRGINIA

West Virginia University

NOTES

1. Qtd. in Ami Chen Mills, *CIA Off Campus: Building the Movement Against Recruitment and Research* (Boston: South End, 1991), 20.
2. Ibid., pp. 31, 35.
3. *The Monitor,* October 29, 2010, p. 5A.
4. Qtd. in Mills, p. 19.
5. http://projects.washingtonpost.com/top-secret-america/articles/secrets-next-door/, accessed December 29, 2010.

6. Website of the National Security Agency, http://www.nsa.gov/ia/academic_outreach/nat_cae/institutions.shtml#tx, accessed October 11, 2010.

7. http://projects.washingtonpost.com/top-secret-america/articles/secrets-next-door/, accessed December 29, 2010.

8. Qtd. in *La Nueva Raza News,* http://nuevaraza.wordpress.com/2010/06/03/rio-grande-valley-statement-concerning-national-security-center at-utpa-by-professors/, accessed October 9, 2010.

9. Mellisa C. Rodriguez, "UTPA Business Students Participate In National Marketing Project" in UTPA News, June 27, 2005, http://www.utpa.edu/news/index.cfm?newsid=2954 accessed April 22, 2009.

10. Ibid.

11. Guidance and Procedures of the Intelligence Community Centers of Academic Excellence Program published by the Office of the Director of National Intelligence, Spring 2008.

12. http://www.namebase.org/foia/ac01.html, accessed October 14, 2010.

13. posted August 10, 2009, at http://www.utpa.edu/igknu, accessed June 23, 2010.

14. Ibid.

15. IC Gidelines and Procedures, p. 5

16. Ibid.

17. Ibid.

18. Interview with author.

19. Ibid.

20. IC Guidance and Procedures, p. 11.

21. Ibid., p. 4

22. Daniel Perry, "Intel Center Kicks Off with Lecture Tonight" in *The Monitor,* March 1, 2007, http://www.themonitor.com/common/printer/view.php?db=monitortx&id=418, accessed April 22, 2009.

23. Guidelines and Procedures, p. 7.

24. Ibid., p. 8.

25. Ibid., p. 9.

26. *AFIO Weekly Intelligence Notes* #05–07 at http://www.afio.org/section/wins/2007/2007-05.html#Texas_Panamerican, accessed July 23, 2009.

27. Mills, pp. 24–35.

28. Mills, p. 26.

29. Dr. Samuel Freeman, "Ethics in Intelligence Agencies: An Oxymoron," unpublished manuscript submitted to *Global Virtue Ethics Review.*

30. Mills, p. 79.

31. http://www.newser.com/story/79434/phone-bust-cohort-worked-for-us-intelligence.html, accessed October 28, 2010.

32. Qtd. in Mills, p. 30.

33. Ibid., p. 31.

34. Ibid., p. 81.

35. IC Guidance and Procedures, p. 7.

36. email to the author, October 16, 2010.

37. Mills, p. 108.

38. Qtd. in Mills, p. 52.

39. Email to the author, April 8, 2010.

40. Ibid.

41. http://www.kathrynblume.com/LysProj.htm, accessed October 23, 2010.

42. Mills, p. 45.

43. Ibid., p. 139.

44. Ibid., p. 138.

45. Henry Giroux, *The University in Chains: Confronting the Military-Industrial-Academic Complex* (Boulder, CO: Paradigm, 2007), p. 210.

WORKS CITED

Academic Freedom. http://www.criticalthink.info/webindex/academia.htm, accessed April 22, 2009.

AFIO Weekly Intelligence Notes #05–07. http://www.afio.org/section/wins/2007/2007–05.html# Texas_Panamerican, accessed July 23, 2009.

Bogan, J. http://www.mysanantonio.com/news/12/1MYSA120306_04B_intelligencealert_2715 c86_html8625.html, accessed December 11, 2009.

Cockburn, Alexander. "CIA on Campus: Cloak and Gown Connection." *CounterPunch*, January 26, 2005. www.counterpunch.org/cockburn01262005.html, accessed March 15, 2009.

Freeman, Dr. Samuel. "Ethics in Intelligence Agencies: An Oxymoron," unpublished manuscript submitted to *Global Virtue Ethics Review.*

Giroux, Henry A. *The University in Chains: Confronting the Military-Industrial-Academic Complex.* Boulder, CO: Paradigm, 2007.

_____ "Spying, Secrecy, and the University." *CounterPunch*, April 7, 2003.

Guidance and Procedures of the Intelligence Community Centers of Academic Excellence Program published by the Office of the Director of National Intelligence, Spring 2008.

La Nueva Raza News, http://nuevaraza.wordpress.com/2010/06/03/rio-grande-valley-statement-concerning-national-security-center at- utpa-by-professors/, accessed October 9, 2010.

National Security Agency. http://www.nsa.gov/ia/academic_outreach/nat_cae/institutions.s html#tx, accessed October 11, 2010.

Perry, Daniel. "Intel Center Kicks Off with Lecture Tonight." *The Monitor*, March 1, 2007. http://www.themonitor.com/common/printer/view.php?db=monitortx&id=418, accessed April 22, 2009.

Rodriguez, Mellisa C. "UTPA Business Students Participate In National Marketing Project." UTPA News, June 27, 2005 http://www.utpa.edu/news/index.cfm?newsid=2954, accessed April 22, 2009.

The Texas Observer, April 21, 2006 http://www.texasobserver.org/article.php?aid=2188, accessed April 22, 2009.

UTPA Fall 2008 Stats at a Glance. Office of Institutional Research and Effectiveness, University of Texas Pan American.

Weimer, Nick. Interview with the author. May 5, 2009.

Willing, Richard. "Intelligence Agencies Invest In College Education." *USA Today*, November 28, 2006. http://usatoday.com/news/education/.

9

Which Side Are You On?
Intelligence Agencies on Campus
and the Class Struggle

DAVID ANSHEN

Introduction to a Problem: How to Avoid Being
Blackmailed by What Everybody Knows
Thinks They Know

Class divisions in society become more visible all the time. Since the financial crisis of 2008 led to a wave of government bailouts which temporarily stabilized profits for the richest, the working class increasingly hears we must "tighten our belts" and accept austerity measures that show no sign of letting up. Out of these conditions we can expect greater social conflict and class struggle to eventually sharpen. Those who prosper off the existing order seem to sense this since we no longer hear talk about the "end of history"[1] or the "new world order" that accompanied the end of the Cold War. Talk of a "peace dividend" evaporated. Instead, the media pundits and politicians tell us we need guns but not butter. All sectors of mainstream public opinion accept, with varying degrees of hesitation, the need for a growing militarization of society. This includes constant war preparations, interventions abroad and a growing apparatus for spying, surveillance and other covert operations. Truly George Orwell's *1984* describes our condition of perpetual war and constantly dwindling civil liberties. This disturbing state of affairs signifies the ruling class[2] increasingly fears that long-term economic and political stability remains elusive. Discontent, here and abroad, haunts those in power. Both history and common sense show that declining standards of living combined with protracted military adventures form an explosive combination.

However, public discourse presented by the media, universities, and so-called experts strives to manufacture assent for the unfolding situation. Mainstream American political discussions construct an elaborate portrayal of an imaginary world composed of a noble and unified United States that responds to irrational terrorist threats and various evil forces, here and abroad. Those who shape discussions in the public arena hope to conceal or distract us from the real conditions that grow increasingly unbearable for millions worldwide. Yet, even a superficial glance at the daily headlines makes it increasingly difficult to ignore the growing horrors that lie beneath the veneer of American interests and ignore what is coming, the class struggle.

This larger context shapes a series of small but important debates and protests taking place on several universities and colleges. The various intelligence agencies struggle to gain an official institutional foothold at more centers of higher education, as well as throughout society at large. They want to use the universities to promote their interests and to legitimize a growing police state. They use the guise of national defense and the claim that we must trust them as the guardians of our common interests. Concerned faculty and students who remain skeptical oppose this. We believe in the ideal that higher education should serve the goal of critical thought and disinterested inquiry and are trying to oppose the direct linkage of the organs of state repression, spying, and militarism with education.

However when the demand for "CIA off Campus" gets raised, objections from various quarters, some sincere, others not, get presented. They argue: "American society needs to acquire intelligence for the security of the nation. We must reform the Intelligence Community since surely it is impossible and even irresponsible to call for them to be abolished? It might be best to join such organizations and change them from the inside, perhaps by the influence of new blood, especially by incorporating people of traditionally disadvantaged groups or people with a liberal humanist education? Do you really think, in this world, it is anything other than the most utopian daydream to expect that the United States will ever function without some degree of surveillance, intelligence gathering and even covert operations designed to protect 'American interests?'"

They continue: "We have real enemies; the terrorists want to hurt us Americans and therefore even if torture, Guantanamo Bay, incarcerations, renditions, etc. remain unfortunate aspects of realpolitik and probably should be stopped — perhaps for pragmatic reasons since they hurt the image of the U.S. — we need protection." Often they will concede the point that such agencies don't belong on campuses, traditionally thought of as bastions of free thought and disinterested inquiry and research, still and all....

Finally, they pose the question in its most bare and naked form: "Since the CIA and various repressive agencies of the state remain necessary and unavoidable, isn't the ultimate logic that either we reform them or put ourselves into the untenable position of leaving the nation defenseless and the people who reside in America[3] at the mercy of their enemies?"

These questions usually go unanswered and disarm support for struggles against the activities of intelligence agencies at universities and society in general. In this essay, I will argue simply that all of these arguments ignore the different class positions and interests that compose American society. The common "we" assumed to represent American society is a fiction that breaks apart. This may appear exaggerated since it flies in the face of so many common sense assumptions about the U.S. However, the reality of the conditions of our lives and the unfolding logic of capitalist society bring to the fore new needs and new ways of thinking. The necessity and possibility of fundamental alterations in American society will become clearer to all. What types of changes society undergoes remain open.

Independent working class politics does not, yet, exist in a form that can be seen and discerned on a mass level. Indeed, there are not voices that can be easily heard over the roar of political unity — held together by common values when issues of war, so-called "national security" and the need to bail out those financial institutions deemed "too big to fail" bring together virtually all wings of mainstream politics. This unity alternates with political polarization lead by the rightward drift of mainstream politics. The alternative to mainstream politics seems limited to the various rightist forces that dominate aspects of the media such as Fox News or the Tea Party groupings that claim to speak for the disenchanted majority while receiving funding and backing from a wing of the very wealthy.

And yet, the mainstream press has more and more begun employing terms like "main street" and "Wall Street"; terms used by media pundits to describe contrasting interests between working people and big business. The cover of *Newsweek* presented the surprising headline "We are all Socialists now" in the midst of the crisis.[4] These new types of discussion reflect, in the most minimal and obfuscating way, the reality of the class structure of U.S. society, and the implicit recognition of class rifts that may develop into conflict. The world situation dictates what the long-term objectives for the CIA off campus movement should be.

Slavoj Zizek, the Lacanian/Neo-Marxist philosopher and cultural critic, has usefully coined the term "double blackmail" for situations where the very structure of questions posed forces you to answer in ways that foreclose getting to the root of the problem.[5] In this case, those concerned with ending the growing role of intelligence agencies either (1) get positioned as naïve and foolish in the face of real terroristic threats or (2) take the morally bankrupt position exemplified by Ward Churchill and Amiri Baraka (not to mention

Al Queda itself) of equating the people who live in America with the policies and politics of the governing regime. However, this way of formulating these questions contains an implicitly false dichotomy. The choice seems to offer complete rejection of all concern for the people who live in the United States by leaving them defenseless or, on the other hand, unqualified support for "national security." In the final analysis, "national security" means siding with the policies of war and domestic repression, not to mention growing class inequalities in society. As Zizek points out, such dichotomies obscure "the hidden TRUTH of the New World Order."[6] Here I side with Zizek: let us reject two bad choices and critique the assumptions behind the assertion that "we" need the CIA and various assorted intelligence agencies for "our" security. Instead we should reject ways of thinking about the U.S. government and its agencies within the framework of this "double blackmail." A real third choice is needed.

The logic of our times presents two interrelated facts that should call into question the existence of a unified "American society": first that the capitalist economy is revealing itself to be deeply crisis-ridden, unable to avoid the built in possibility of greater and greater commercial and financial crises alongside high rates of unemployment and cutbacks in social service for working people. We have reached the absurd state where Medicaid recipients in Arizona who need organ transplants will be denied them, amounting to a death sentence, justified by the logic of so-called fiscal responsibility.[7] Meanwhile the government gifts trillions of dollars to the richest financial institutions. Such stark and desperate conditions will lead to class struggle and to the situation Karl Marx and Fredrick Engels described in the Communist Manifesto in words that read as if they were written today:

> The modern bourgeois society [...] has not done away with class antagonisms. [...] it has simplified the class antagonisms. Society as a whole is more and more splitting up into two great hostile camps, into two classes directly facing each other: Bourgeoisie and Proletariat.[8]

The second feature of our times that we must place in the context of the reality of class polarization concerns the seemingly unrelated expansion of the Intelligence Community and its activity throughout society, including our college campuses. The only way to make sense of these phenomena lies in recognizing their interconnections and drawing the necessary conclusions. This leads to the conclusion that rather than one society, one nation, or one world, there exist two, class-divided and with separate and even opposing interests. If valid this should guide how we approach the question of the function of intelligence agencies on campuses and society in general. Interestingly, those in the ruling class or the bourgeoisie often understand the class nature of society very well. A *New York Times* reporter quoted Warren Buffet in

2006: "There's class warfare, all right," Mr. Buffett said, "but it's my class, the rich class, that's making war, and we're winning."[9] This liberal capitalist humanitarian deserves to be taken at his word: class struggle marks our time. When we work to find political and social solutions that challenge the prerogatives of capital and articulate a different set of interests, we have good reasons to believe that the rapidly expanding national security apparatus, will target the real "us," the vast millions who suffer including the majority of people who reside in America. That includes those of us who attend or work at universities and colleges. Intelligence agencies and related institutions do not function as reliable instruments against "our" enemies, meaning enemies of the entire United States, both the majority and the economic elite; history and the logic of events suggest intelligence agencies will act against the vast majority of the population.

As the Elite loses Confidence, Intelligence Services Increase

Opposition to intelligence agencies on campus develops as part of the broader objective of ending U.S. imperialism and developing a radical transformation of U.S. society, while rallying together all who recognize these developments as a threat to the traditional freedoms allowed on colleges and in society. If we can succeed in creating an inhospitable climate for the ODNI (the Office of the Director of National Intelligence, which oversees the blanket of intelligence agencies), by debate, information, protests, and working within forms of faculty and student representation (and we know that anything other than completely peaceful means would prove disastrous and counterproductive), this advances the fight for a better society and prepares for a future that may seem unimaginable but for which we must prepare now.

The expansion of the intelligence agencies takes place at a rate that shocks and startles even those who might not expect anything different. The multipart *Washington Post* series "Top Secret America: A Hidden World Growing Beyond Control" presents fascinating and terrifying details about the increasing scope and pace of intelligence operations.[10] The title describes these developments as an out-of-control world that is "growing" and "hidden." The information provided by this respected mainstream newspaper forms a surprisingly damning vision of the expanding "hidden world." The picture that emerges from these accounts concerning the size, scale, inefficiency, and possibility of abuse by these agencies makes shocking reading. However the information provided on the scope and scale of the intelligence community remains at best an approximation because as the reporters note:

The top-secret world [...] has become so large, so unwieldy and so secretive that no one knows how much money it costs, how many people it employs, how many programs exist within it or exactly how many agencies exist within it or exactly how many agencies do the same work [...] the system put in place to keep the United States safe is so massive that its effectiveness is impossible to determine.[11]

Difficulties in gauging the actual size of intelligence agencies results, in the first instance, because these agencies are a merger of private and public agencies and contractors, organized in fragmented, isolated, bureaucratic fashion. The agencies are decentralized, geographically into "clusters" of hidden yet large-scale, top-security zones; like espionage industrial parks or sets of office buildings but larger and on a greater scale. The article sounds like something out of the most fantastic James Bond type spy novels. For example, it describes a secret "manhole cover" near these "clusters" which functions as an "access point to government cables" transmitting "sensitive-compartmented information." This is the technological mechanism for monitoring and conveying information about individuals and developments to whatever government unit wants this data. We indeed live in a strange new world where one has to be careful where stepping.

The reporters for *The Post* based their information on "government documents and contacts, descriptions, property records [...] and hundreds of interviews" despite the obstacle that "most" interviewed remain "prohibited from speaking publicly [...] because, they said, they feared retaliation at work for describing their concerns."[12] The inherent lack of transparency surrounding information on the growing leviathan that intelligence agencies are becoming prohibits any reasonable notion of democratic control or accountability over the government. This should remain in mind when activists opposed to making universities into havens for such elements face the accusation that they stand in opposition to free speech or academic freedom. The irony of such a charge lies in the fact that the public gets excluded from the information necessary to judge the actions of the agencies acting on behalf of a supposedly democratic society. The Intelligence Community itself opposes free speech and academic freedom by clinging to secrecy.

The facts reported in *The Post* article, which likely understate the problem but give a piece of the truth available for public knowledge, include the following:

1,271 government organizations and 1,931 private companies work on programs related to some form of intelligence "in about 10,000 locations across the United States."

An estimated 854,000 people hold top-secret security clearances which the Post article notes forms a population "nearly 1.5 times as many people as live in Washington D.C."

In just the area around Washington D.C., the "building complexes for top-secret intelligence work" built or in the process of construction since September 11th "occupy the equivalent of almost three Pentagons or 22 Capitol buildings — about 17 million square feet of space."
Many of these agencies overlap responsibilities for the same type of information or work, which reveals redundancy, inefficiency, and the highly compartmentalized nature of this so-called information gathering.
The information obtained from various agencies result in "50,000 intelligence reports each year — a volume so large that many are routinely ignored."[13]

Lest one conclude that all of this information leads to security the article quotes various officials including retired Army Lt. General John R. Vines, who reviewed the tracking information for the Defense Department's "most sensitive programs," and concluded the impossibility of "assess[ing] whether it is making us more safe."[14] On the other hand, this "hidden world" creates massive potential for invasion of personal liberties and privacy. We cannot know whether this enormous amount of scrutiny over all forms of communications, whether phones, email, Facebook,[15] other online sites, computers or even people in their homes can effectively deter threats of "terrorism." To quote *The Post* again:

> Lack of focus, not lack of resources, was at the heart of the Fort Hood shooting that left 13 dead, as well as the Christmas Day bomb attempt thwarted not by thousands of analysts employed to find lone terrorists but by an alert airline passenger who saw smoke coming from his seatmate.[16]

Even a CIA inquiry into the December 2009 suicide bombing of a CIA headquarters in Afghanistan, by a double agent employed by the CIA, which killed several CIA operatives, concluded the incident resulted from "systematic errors where all of us have some responsibility" according to Leon Panetta, director of the CIA. These errors resulted in no firings or punitive actions for mistakes leading to lapses in security.[17] The obvious point to recognize is how little evidence anyone has that any of the heightened security measures protect anyone.

But perhaps security for the average American is not the real issue. The merger of traditional methods of political repression with new technology paints a scary picture. For example, Forbes magazine reported that portable vans that can see through walls, using a variant of the body scanning technology currently implemented at many airports, is now being deployed in Iraq, Afghanistan and the United States.[18] According to *Forbes*, American Science and Engineering, the company that designs these scanners, sells these vans to foreign governments, the U.S. government, border patrol centers and law enforcement agencies.

The Z Backscatter Vans, or ZBVs, as the company calls them, send a narrow stream of X-rays off and through nearby objects and read which ones bounce back.
Absorbed rays indicate dense material such as steel. Scattered rays show less-dense objects that can include explosives, drugs or human bodies. That capability has made AS&E's scan vans powerful tools for security, law enforcement and border control.[19]

The article also reports that these "X-Ray Vans" have been sold to law enforcement agencies such as the New York Police Department which has, according to *Forbes,* refused to discuss their use. Beyond the potential for abuses of privacy in general in relation to the right to association, privacy in one's home, or place of association, the "X-Ray Vans" also see through clothing, leaving targets both physically and politically naked and violating personal dignity. Apparently anything goes, however, when the stakes include so-called "National Security," fears of immigration, and crime.

Class Divisions Stretch Around the World

We must consider whether it is possible for any security system to really protect the people who live in the U.S., if terrorists remain determined to strike. As Noam Chomsky states, "The only way we can put a permanent end to terrorism is to stop participating in it."[20] As long as U.S. foreign policy continues to generate massive suffering and treats the people and resources of the world as a little toy,[21] terrorism remains a deadly threat. That the victims of U.S. terrorism lack sufficient mass movements with the moral and political capacities to seriously challenge the root problems in their own societies (which, of course is no easy task) and to distinguish between the American people and the U.S. government and its policies compounds the tragedy. This makes indiscriminate attacks against the people who live in the United States, or elsewhere, quite likely.

Logically the only way for the majority of people who reside in the U.S. to protect ourselves from remaining potential targets, over the long run, involves serious analysis of the root causes of discontent in the Middle East and elsewhere combined with effectively opposing the U.S. government's policies. The economic crisis we live through reveals that U.S. policies serve a narrow few, which we see through the juxtaposition of corporate profits with high levels of unemployment. It seems likely that the already existing skepticism about whose interests foreign policies serve will grow. As U.S. troops remain bogged down oversee in multiple conflicts with no end in sight, and as the gap between the "haves" and "have-nots" deepens, the connection between domestic and foreign policies will clarify. An awareness of this interconnection can lead to what Marxists term class consciousness and class struggle. Without building real international solidarity of the working class, we will increasingly become the targets of misguided and immoral attempts to strike back at what may get perceived, for good reasons, as imperial aggression and national and religious indignities.[21]

This situation contrasts with the memories many political activists have of their experiences in the 1980s and early 1990s in Central America where we were told by common people, who suffered the brutality of real terrorist operations organized by the CIA, that they distinguished the people of the U.S. from the U.S. government. Speaking personally, my most formative experience politically was in my early twenties when I visited a remote peasant village in Nicaragua, during the U.S.-organized Contra War, and met women who had lost all of their sons, husbands, and brothers to mercenary forces paid, trained, and organized by the CIA. They told me not to feel guilty; they could not hold me responsible since the government in Washington did not represent the people. They humbly asked our group of peace activists to send a message to then President Reagan informing him that they had no intention of invading the U.S., not even through Texas. I do not believe he ever got the message.

The majority of people within U.S. borders (and in the occupied countries) who have gained little from the wars for oil and who face growing economic deprivation need to think about whether we, the majority, want to identify with U.S. foreign policy. Before there is a resolution to these economic and military crises, the fate of humanity may rest in the balance. The alternative way to fight terrorism, making clear which side we stand on and struggling for a new international social and economic order in the interests of the majority of the human race, will eliminate terrorism.

Security Agencies Repress Social Change

Already labor activists and critics of U.S. foreign policy find themselves on the receiving end of government repression and investigation by the political police. Reports in the media[22] reveal that anti-war activists, unionists, and defenders of the rights of Arab Americans became the targets of raids by FBI agents sweeping through the homes and offices of various individuals in Chicago, Minneapolis, and other cities on September 24, 2010. As reported in the Socialist newspaper *The Militant*, "The FBI seized computers, cell phones, passports, and other documents and issued subpoenas to 11 people in Minnesota, Illinois, and Michigan to appear before a federal grand jury in Chicago."[23] The article quotes FBI spokesman Steve Warfield explaining that the raids occurred as part of an "ongoing Joint Terrorism Task Force investigation into activities concerning material support to terrorism."[24] The raids targeted individuals such as long-time antiwar and union activists, Joe Iosbaker and Stephanie Weiner as well as Hatem Abudayyeh, executive director of the Arab American Action Network. Iosbaker has been a "staff member at the University of Illinois at Chicago and chief steward for Service Employees International Union Local" and Weiner "a professor at Wilbur Wright College."[25] Tom Burke, a member of the Columbia Action Network, "was also subpoenaed."[26] The article points out that Iosbaker "reported that 25 FBI agents searched his house from top to bottom for 12 hours."[27] According to *the Chicago Tribune* Warfield, the FBI agent said the individuals represented "no imminent danger." Further according to the attorney for the couple 30 boxes of personal information was taken and the agents said "they would determine what was evidence later."[28] Another activist under investigation, Mike Kelly, works as "a union cafeteria worker at the University of Minnesota" and serves as the "editor of *FightBack!*, a Minneapolis-based newspaper and website and a leader of the Anti-War Committee, also based in Minneapolis."[29] FBI agents did not charge these activists with any direct participation in terrorist activities but rather "according to *the Chicago Tribune* the subpoenas are for records detailing their travel to the Middle East and South America as well as for donations to Abudayyeh's group [the Arab American Action Network] and two groups on the State Department's list of terrorist organizations."[30] The warrant for Mike Kelly listed "providing ,attempting and conspiring to provide material support" to Hezebollah, the Popular Front for the Liberation of Palestine, and the Revolutionary Armed Forces of Colombia (FARC)" as well as the "Freedom Road Socialist Organization."[31] The foreign organizations mentioned do not represent anything progressive or positive for working people in the Middle East or Colombia, in my view, but we must note that these raids make inroads upon democratic rights. Travel becomes suspect and even attending meetings where speakers that belong to organizations the U.S. government deems terrorist present their views served as part of the justification and basis for the investigations.[32] Membership in a socialist group, never accused of any crime, gets slipped into the investigation for good measure.

Given the documented history of past and present slanders, misrepresentations, and deliberate lies that the FBI and other intelligence agencies have perpetrated upon anti-war activists, socialists, radicals, advocates of black rights, Chicano rights fighters, the American Indian Movement, and other dissidents, including liberals and the moderate left, we have no reason to believe these allegations truthful or in good faith. This type of governmental activity featuring accusations and arrests of political activists based on undisclosed evidence, shows precisely the dangers coming. We must maintain a healthy distrust of this type of activity by the forces of law and order which develop into attacks on democratic rights. This may become more important if the future involves greater economic, political, and militarist adventures that increasingly require greater resistance.

One positive result of these recent raids and seizures has been the response of people who are protesting and opposing such actions. The same article in *The Militant* reports that over 350 people protested in front of the FBI headquarters in Chicago, denouncing the raids, while around 150 others protested in Minneapolis.[33] Some demonstrators participated who knew the individuals arrested while others took part because they defend free speech, freedom of association, or have gained a healthy distrust of the U.S. government.

At almost the same time, another article in the same issue of *The Militant* reports on a city hall meeting held in San Francisco on September 23, called by the San Francisco Human Rights Commission and the Arab Resource Center to oppose FBI probes and "visits" on "campuses or at [...] places of work" according to "Veena Dubal, an attorney for the Asian Law Caucus." Dubal explained to listeners, "The agents do not need any basis to do this other than a person's race or religion."[34] Another part of the meeting involved speakers challenging plans by San Francisco's police chief to reactivate a "police intelligence" unit that had been shut down due to a successful ACLU lawsuit in the 1990s.[35] Perhaps the most interesting part of the meeting reported on was the comments by Michel Shehadeh, "a defendant in the frame up case of seven Palestinians and a Kenyan known as the Los Angeles Eight"[36] accused of aiding terrorism but after 20 years established their complete innocence and had charges dropped (so much for the reliability of police intelligence operations) who pointed out to the crowd:

> Police actions to suppress opposition to government policies is not a new thing [...]. This has a history going back to the Palmer Raids, when immigrant workers, including thousands of Jews, were deported in the 'Red Scare' after World War I.[37]

His description points to the historical context of intelligence agencies in the U.S. which must be part of understanding the nature and role of the changes we are now living through. Equally important for the future, these raids did not go unanswered. This represents the beginning of movements to defend democratic rights against the political police which the CIA off campus movement must link to and learn from.

A Long Sordid Record of Trying to Prevent Class Struggle and Liberation Movements

The persistence of the belief that we can somehow trust the CIA or FBI or any of the intelligence agencies to defend the U.S. people or to promote democracy abroad seems amazing given the long history of repression of legal political dissent in this country[38] and crimes against humanity abroad which reach horrific numbers.[39] Part of the problem lies in the commonsense perception that nations comprise a homogeneous group with common interests. Even a brief glance at the kinds of activities that drive institutions of the U.S. government can reveal the unpleasant reality of a class-divided society that does not operate in a neutral, reliable fashion for all. In discussions of the role of intelligence agencies in society and on campus we need to remember Shehadeh's historically accurate point made above and that repression does not operate in a vacuum; economic and social struggles precipitate and develop alongside responses by those in charge of maintaining order.

The Palmer Raids rank among the first cases of large scale centralized political police style repression of dissidents in the U.S.[40] The Attorney General and Justice Department presented these raids to a credulous public as a response to anarchist bombings they loudly claimed threatened our national security; an interesting parallel to the use of 9/11 to justify all manner of government malfeasance that has no link to the tragic events of that day. Another obvious comparison concerns the bombing of Pearl Harbor that was cited as justification for the forced internment of Japanese Americans.

The Palmer Raids commenced on January 2, 1920, and involved midnight raids on "4,000 alleged radicals, socialists, anarchists, communists and immigrants who were rounded up in over thirty three cities, in over twenty three states (over 200 aliens were subsequently deported)."[41] Ideologically, these raids had the advantage for the government of combining charges of terrorism, communism, and anti-immigrant sentiments as their justification. However, their importance lies in the broader context in which the Palmer Raids took place. They occurred after a massive strike wave swept the United States. In ten states workers went on simultaneous strike. This process initially involved textile workers, copper miners, shipyard workers, and others. Eventually developments led to a walkout of 365,000 steelworkers and around 500,000 coal miners. The steel companies worked hand-in-hand with local state government and hired thugs until the federal government feared these forces of repression would prove inadequate. President Woodrow Wilson unleashed the larger forces of the U.S. state. As a supposedly "progressive" Democrat he showed his class loyalties when drawing America into World War I after campaigning on promises of non-involvement and then serving the bosses against the workers after the war. To break the strike, early on, local state forces and private contractors used force and violence on behalf of the private companies, murdering eighteen workers.

We must situate these domestic events as part of the international class struggle; they transpired in the context of a deep worldwide radicalization inspired by the Russian Revolution. A short-lived revolutionary government formed in Hungary in 1918, and the workers rose up in Germany and formed workers, soldiers, and farmers councils, as newly formed communist parties and radical formations spread throughout Europe and the world. This led to extreme repression and bitter class struggle, and ended with great working class leaders murdered in Germany and counterrevolution triumphant in Hungary. By the 1920s the state forces had largely contained the revolutionary upswing and counterattacked with brutal repression. Nascent communist organizations in the United States found themselves forced underground for a time. The repression resulted from real fear on the part of the rulers and business interests haunted by images of the spread of worldwide revolution and the strong appeal of the early Russian Revolution.

By the mid-twenties, after the Palmer Raids ended, the FBI continued functioning as a national security force for a short time. However, general indignation against these FBI abuses combined with the decline in labor militancy and strikes led the government to decentralize repression. Instead of the national centralized agency working to contain class struggle, responsibility for monitoring and stopping dissent fell to the local wings of the police known as "bomb squads," "radical divisions," and "Red Squads" which worked with private detective agencies and Pinkerton outfits.[42] These private agencies received tacit approval and freedom to use violence and other means by the government in the interests of business. They bring to mind Blackwater USA, renamed XE Service LLC after committing horrific killings of unarmed civilians in Iraq, a private company contracted out by the U.S. government, and other mercenary forces that serve similar functions today.

The next major expansion of large-scale centralized repression and surveillance which focused on unionists, socialists, black rights fighters and Chicano militants took place in the late 1930s. Franklin Roosevelt met with J. Edgar Hoover — who eagerly participated in political repression during the Palmer Raids and went on to a glorious career trying to destroy any social progress whatsoever, whether targeting working people, blacks or any oppressed group — and the two planned the transformation of the FBI into the major centralized force of disruption, surveillance, monitoring and violence it grew into. The growing labor radicalization in the early thirties that led to the rise of the Congress of Industrial Organizations (CIO) particularly concerned them. The CIO represented industrial unionization that replaced traditional craft unionizing, and impelled the growing working class militancy that spread throughout the decade. Another concern, for the rulers, remained the possibility that blacks, Chicanos and other oppressed groups in the United States might not subordinate their struggles to unconditional support for the impending U.S. entry into the Second World War.[43] In his essay "Workers Rights Against the Secret Police" Larry Seigle writes,

But with the rise of the CIO and the deep-going labor radicalizat.on, the rulers knew [...] this whole operation [needed] to be centralized, upgraded, and brought directly under federal government control. In September 1936, J. Edgar Hoover, head of the FBI, acting under instructions from President Roosevelt, informed all FBI offices that 'the Bureau desires to obtain from all possible sources information concerning subversive activities being conducted in the United States.[44]

Roosevelt and Hoover made this decision after the strike wave of 1934 in which Teamsters, Longshoreman, and the Toledo Auto-Lite Workers carried out such broad and militant struggles that the CIO formed and spread like wildfire, transforming the history of the labor movement. The actions by the government in 1936 anticipated by two years the big sit-down strikes in Flint Michigan which made the United Auto Workers (UAW) a force in American politics — although presently one that has withered away to such a degree that the gift of the bailout to General Motors included the negotiated sell off of large part of contracted UAW pension benefits. What a wonderful example we inherit when workers, bosses, and the government all pull together and we all tighten our belts in the face of a national economic crisis.

After the Second World War ended, the "anti-labor, anticommunist witch-hunt, began with the establishment by the Truman administration of the Attorney General's list of 'subversive' organizations, an official government blacklist."[45] This expanded into the establishment of McCarthyism and other forms of repression of freedom of speech, association, and assembly. The damage done in this period inflicted on so many individuals in Hollywood, at universities and throughout society remains a black stain in American history.

The Intelligence Community next explicitly targeted political dissent in the Cointelpro Programs. We learned of these programs only after they had damaged many law abiding citizens who participated in the social movements of the Sixties. Hoover outlined the aim of these efforts, which targeted an unknown number of black rights fighters, student activists, socialists and others, in a memo from 1968 which targeted the "New Left," a broad term for many different types of activists:

> The purpose of this program is to expose, disrupt, and otherwise neutralize the activities of the various New Left organizations, their leadership and adherents [...]. We must frustrate every effort of these groups and individuals to consolidate their forces or to recruit new or faithful adherents.[46]

In addition to targeting the "New Left," the FBI also sought to discredit and destroy black rights fighters including Martin Luther King and Malcolm X, the Chicano movement, the Committee in Solidarity with the People of El Salvador (CISPES) and many others. However, FBI targeting of free speech and thought at universities, colleges, high schools, and even down to pre-schools remains less well known. This history connects directly to the movement against intelligence agencies on campus today. Both students and teachers had their rights trampled on. Famous cases involve the CIA funding and overseeing of the National Student Association to manipulate its politics and the targeting of other student groups; we should note the significance of documented abuses aimed directly at teachers.

A lawsuit initiated by the Socialist Workers Party against the FBI, CIA, and other assorted agencies revealed, among other things, multiple attacks against the rights of teachers to teach. Evelyn Sell, a preschool teacher, described by her FBI persecutors as "an intelligent, excellent teacher who was well qualified in her field,"[47] lost her job as the victim of a combined effort of the Austin Texas police department and the FBI to get her fired as a Head Start teacher. The FBI in Detroit, where she had publicly run for office as a Socialist, contacted their San Antonio office about her political affiliations (which she had not hidden). They further contacted the Austin Police Department which encouraged the Austin School Board not to renew her contract, which they did. Previous to this her high school-aged son, an active participant in the anti-war movement, met with his school principal who told him that the FBI had come to his school to investigate him and that they knew his mothers' political views.[48] Not coincidentally the year before her firing, 1969, 11,000 opponents of the war in Vietnam marched to the state capitol as part of the burgeoning anti-war movement which Sell was involved in organizing.

Two other prominent cases where academic freedom faced threats from the political police involve university professors. The same year that Sell lost her job, Arizona State University dismissed professor of philosophy Morris Starsky after the Phoenix office of the FBI sent "an anonymous letter slandering him to a faculty committee reviewing his case."[49] Although 3,000 students and over 250 professors signed petitions to get him reinstated and protect his academic and personal freedom, the dismissal stood. Another round of "poison pen" letters secretly authored by the FBI's office in Detroit, listing 17 years of political activity by Professor David Herreshoff, a professor at Wayne State University, but signed "A fed up Taxpayer!" and addressed to a Michigan State Senator, agitated for firing the professor.[50] In his case, Professor Herreshoff retained his job despite government efforts to ruin him.

These cases document just a few known incidents where intelligence agencies targeted professors or teachers and used deception and defamation to interfere with the normal academic review process. They provide historical examples of the types of government actions that pose grave threats to academic freedom and the interchange of ideas. This bears directly on the potentially dangerous role of these organizations in setting up spy centers at universities. If colleges and universities play the role, in the future as they have in the past, as centers of discussion and political organizing, such attacks seem likely. The point of this very brief survey of the history of centralized U.S. intelligence agencies and their role in domestic repression lies in recognizing their nature as a response to social movements. Each time political activity develops momentum on a growing scale these agencies move into action. This means that if radical social change or big political struggles begin to percolate in the future, we can expect that these agencies will once again act as they have traditionally, at home and internationally. They will attack and subvert movements for change.

A Capitalist Crisis Means Working Class Cuts

Reading the economic news on a daily or weekly basis produces a surreal feeling. Ever since the recent economic crisis that started with the escalating wave of home foreclosures in 2006, followed by a series of bank failures which eventually led to numerous government bailouts of large financial institutions, the news features alternating reports about the return to a stable economy and those that highlight greater anxiety about the future. The so-called "Great Recession," the worst economic downturn since the Great Depression, ended in the early summer of 2009 according to the National Bureau of Economic Research, the group that officially declares when recessions begin and end. For working people who continue to suffer high rates of unemployment, greater financial instability, and waves of budget cuts that target desperately needed social services, such pronouncements of economic health seem a cruel joke. Despite the supposed recovery, however, in early November 2010, AP news headlines, posted by Yahoo Finance, seem oddly ambivalent: "Job crisis eases, but economy has long way to go,"[51] "Economy recovering but recession casts a long shadow,"[52] and "Small banks failing as larger firms regain health."[53] These articles arrived in a single week, a year and a half or so since the official recovery. These strange headlines recur, on and off, both claiming the economy is improving and nevertheless sounding strangely ominous. The specter haunting the news seems to be the continuing possibility of the virtually never spoken "D" word. Yet a strange optimism lingers in these reports; perhaps, as the old Depression-era song put it, "Happy Days are Here Again!"

When reading these articles carefully, one finds disturbing facts hidden among the positive sounding descriptions. For example in the AP report "Economy recovering but recession casts a long shadow," we learn that U.S. households lost 17 percent of their wealth over the past three years and that household debt rose to about 140 percent of disposable income. Consumer spending represents 70 percent of economic activity but the average debt burdened American buys less and more on credit.

Retail sales are off by 2.6 percent since the recession began in December 2007. That's a stark contrast to the last 60 years. At this stage in an economic recovery, retail sales on average were up 25 percent, according to Gluskin Sheff.[54]

On the other hand, Bank of America has assets worth over 2.3 trillion dollars.

The article on banks reports that though big banks are doing well, thanks in part to the bailout, the rate of bank closings is the highest in two decades. About 160 to 200 banks are expected to fail this year and approximately the same next year. But the article quickly reassures, "No the financial crisis hasn't returned. Wall Street doesn't need another bailout [...] Still the wave of plant closings points to the persistent struggles of many communities and states."[55] This sentence points to the class nature of the bailouts; Wall Street is making sufficient profits but smaller communities continue to suffer. The bailouts of 2008 reveal, in the starkest manner imaginable, that both political parties unify around the needs of capital while showing little care or compassion for the vast majority of working people who face a continuing unemployment rate that hovers just below 10 percent officially, and also continue to face escalating foreclosures and debts.

We should not forget that the Clinton Administration altered how unemployment rates get tabulated. Since Clinton any worker, unemployed for over a year, no longer counts as part of the labor force at all. This sleight of hand trick minimizes how many job age workers, who need jobs, get counted as unemployed.[56]

In addition, the expansion of personal debt means more and more people, competing for fewer and fewer jobs, turn over a larger share of their income to banks and financial companies. This serves as redistribution of wealth from the poor to the rich. Calling for budget cuts, whether on the federal, state, or local level serves as another trend that politicians unify around. These "cuts" mean fewer resources for everything from health care and jobless benefits, to education, yet never affect the military or the expansion of intelligence agencies. Diminishing revenues and the need to pay back the wealthy bondholders (read "capitalists") make these "cuts" sound like an inevitable law of nature or economics. The big capitalists and bondholders count on governments to back up their interest bearing loans to governments and use the force or persuasion necessary to slash the living standards of everyone else.

However, the waves of struggle that have swept Europe (Spain, Greece, Ireland, France and Iceland) show that the working class can and will resist the dominant economic logic which would balance "budget deficits" on their backs. But if the finance capitalists get in too much trouble they get support from government because they are "too big to fail" and threaten to bring down the rest of us with them. Either way, workers get squeezed or find their only hope lies in resistance. The situation is well described in one of the AP articles from the same week in November 2010:

> Mark Zandi, chief economist at Moody's Analytics, holds out hope that "the preconditions are coming into place for much better job growth. Big companies, midsize companies are very profitable." [...] Job creation used to bounce back faster after recessions. When manufacturing occupied a bigger part of the economy, factories would quickly revive the labor market by recalling laid-off workers once conditions improved.[57]

This description depicts reality; we have growing profits for those on top of the economic structure and continuing unemployment combined with so-called shrinking budgets that economists can only hope will change.

Why has manufacturing dropped in the United States? Capitalists currently find greater rates of return when they invest in what Marx termed "fictitious capital" which means speculation, lending, banking, currency trading, the host of financial derivatives and various ways of accruing profits that bypass production of goods and services. The noted scholar David Harvey argues that the capitalists face a crisis of "sustained capital accumulation" going back to the sixties due to the relative strength of labor then.[58] "Labour was well organized, reasonably well paid and had political clout"[59] leading, says Harvey, to various strategies of trying to break labor which have included encouraging immigration, labor-saving technologies, the use of state power to crush unions, the movement of capital globally and eventually:

> Strange new markets arose, pioneered within what became known as the 'shadow banking' system, permitting investment in [...] everything from trading in pollution rights to betting on the weather [...]. This was the environment in which hedge funds flourished, with enormous profits for those who invested in them.[60]

When all this came crashing down, the government acted quickly for the only class it really serves, the capitalist class. The rulers make clear that they plan to continue to act on behalf of a small minority. But to do so they also plan to build the largest system of repression and force ever known to humanity.

What We Can Accomplish Opposing Intelligence Agencies on Campus

Another vexing objection that presents itself to the approach offered in this essay, accepted by many sincere activists who want to improve society, comes as a belief in a strict dichotomy between the objectives of gradual change in contrast to radical struggle against the system and its institutions- traditionally labeled "reform or revolution." Often activists argue that some-day, in the far-off future, there might be a revolution or deep changes in which we can fundamentally restructure society from the ground up. Humanity will deal, at that point, with the pressing needs of mass starvation, economic and military instability, and even environmental issues that concern the future of the planet, but not now. Therefore, logic dictates incremental reforms and working within the system as the best hope for progress at the present time.

However, history shows that virtually all world-historic, earth-shaking revolutions, whether the French, American, Russian, or Cuban, either completely or almost completely surprised the majority of people of the time, including the revolutionaries who carried them out. Those opposed to the injustices of their time discovered in the process of striving for real improvements that these could not be achieved within the current systems. On the surface a pragmatic approach suggests that truly systemic change is off the agenda, and therefore long-term objectives wait upon so-called "realistic" objectives. The working class and liberation movements have much experience with the focus on day-to-day politics at the expense of grander objectives. The stark presentation of the alternatives of accepting capitalism or consigning one's politics to remaining beyond the pale does not exhaust political options.

Looking back to the last wave of capitalist crises and their repercussions also remains useful. Leon Trotsky argued in his work "The Transitional Program for Socialist Revolution" that the traditional socialist parties mistakenly divided their activity and ideas into a "minimum program, which limited itself to reforms" and a "maximum program, which promised the substitution of socialism for capitalism in the indefinite future."[61] Trotsky contrasted this idea with a "bridge" or "transitional program" which recognizes the need for "democratic" and "transitional" demands as part of relating short term and long-term objectives. The goal of education, protests, and organizing is to overcome this separation of long-term and short-term objectives through common struggle that can transform consciousness. But this is an unfolding process that develops possibilities previously deemed inconceivable. Trotsky derived his approach from an observation of how revolutions and radical change have actually happened historically, particularly drawing conclusions from the unexpected pace and radicalism of the French Revolution and what he knew best, the 1917 October Revolution, when the Bolsheviks came to power. The short term objectives of political education, agitation, and organizing against intelligence agencies on campus should serve the broader objectives of educating youth and working people about the nature of imperialism and the class basis of the U.S. government. This remains the only way to solve the grave problems facing humanity.

Interestingly we begin to hear a few voices today — in popular academic discourse among contemporary cultural critics — which openly challenge the capitalist consensus. Several prominent intellectuals including the previously mentioned Slavoj Zizek, but also Alain Badiou and, even Jacques Derrida all make a turn to explicit political and social concerns and to deconstructing the ideology of capitalist permanence itself.[62] Whatever limitations the new critics may or may not have as political thinkers, they have the courage to call the incredibly oppressive conditions by their name: capitalism. They also show the courage to oppose the tendency to make peace with this system under the guise that it is (1) ever-present or inescapable or (2) can only be reformed and improved upon from within. Zizek notes:

> It thus seems that Fukiyama's utopia of the 1990's had to die twice, since the collapse of the liberal-democratic political utopia on 9/11 did not affect the economic utopia of global market capitalism; if the 2008 financial meltdown has a historical meaning then, it is a sign of the end of the economic face of Fukiyama's dream.[63]

Francis Fukiyama wrote a supposedly Hegelian account of the end of the Cold War, which posited that humanity had reached the "end of history" because capitalism had showed itself superior to its "Communist" rivals and therefore would face no major, world historic challenges ever again, certainly not from Marxism. Zizek turns the discussion on its head by referring to the idea, noted earlier, that media rhetoric proclaimed that the end of the Cold War meant a "peace dividend" was at hand and that peace and prosperity would blossom. Things did not turn out this way. Similar claims were made about "the new economy" that was supposedly being ushered in by revolutions in information technology; claims that in hindsight merit Zizek's description of the "new economy" as utopian thinking.[64] Zizek counterintuitively, but persuasively, argues that September 11th, while horrible on a moral level and certain to be manipulated for greater foreign policy objectives and to justify greater domestic and foreign repression (which undeniably describes our present conditions) actually revealed the weakness and failure of U.S. imperial power after the end of the Cold War. The "second utopia" where capitalism would become friction free also sustains fewer adherents. However, despite more anxiety about the economy this does not mean that socialism waits around the corner, even if things get much worse. The short term results of capitalist crisis often strengthen the far right and move society towards greater authoritarianism. Events clearly are proceeding in this manner. Indeed, we can interpret the growing national security apparatus as a sign of the rulers' lack of confidence in the long-term viability of the liberal democracy that only a few years ago they proclaimed beyond threat. However, the possibility of bridging the gap between day-to-day political struggles and the search for getting to the root of the problem, seem more possible now and will, hopefully, become more so in the future. To quote Zizek again, "The moral of the story: the time for liberal-democratic moralistic blackmail is over. Our side no longer has to go on apologizing; while the other side had better start soon."[65]

In the spirit of Zizek's comments, we should boldly stand our ground when detractors challenge our position of opposition to intelligence agencies on campus. When confronted with the challenge to explain how "we" should respond to threats internal and external, we should proudly follow the logic exemplified in the old joke about the Lone Ranger and Tonto. When surrounded by Indians, the Lone Ranger asks, "What are we going to do?" to which Tonto responds, "Who'se 'we,' paleface?"

NOTES

1. The most famous example was Francis Fukiyama's well received book, *The End of History and the Last Man* (New York: Free, 1992).

2. By the term ruling class, and the term bourgeoisie, I mean the class of people who own the means of production and the commanding heights of the economy. My goal is not to use terms that seem old-fashioned but to use the terms I find most precise.

3. The issue of immigrants or workers without papers is relevant here. To talk about national defense or national interests without recognizing the fact that a growing sector of the population within the boundaries of the United States are not citizens, even though as the general strike of 2006 proved, they are indispensable to the economy, means to ignore reality.

4. Jon Meachum, "We Are All Socialists Now," *Newsweek,* January 14, 2011. http://www.newsweek.com/2009/02/06/we-are-all-socialists-now.html.

5. Zizek uses this term first in an article for *New Left Review* titled "Against the Double Blackmail" to criticize the way leftists often felt obligated to support the bombing of Serbia because of the horrors of ethnic cleansing or alternatively to support the Milosovekic regime. He writes: "However, what if one should reject this double blackmail (if you are against NATO strikes, you are for Milosevic's proto-Fascist regime of ethnic cleansing, and if you are against Milosevic, you support the global capitalist New World Order)?" Slavoj Zizek, "Against The Double Blackmail," *New Left Review* 234 (March-April 1999). http://www.egs.edu/faculty-/slavoj-zizek/articles/against-the-double-blackmail/ .

6. Although Zizek uses the term New World Order he is not using it as the far-right has taken to doing as a form of fascist conspiracy theory. For a time, the official post cold war rhetoric among politicians used this term. This has been almost immediately scrapped by the political spin doctors because the idea that we are living through any "order" old or new, sustains less traction. As this essay notes, the whole focus of Zizek's recent books, such as *First as Tragedy, Then as Farce* is to demonstrate how the concept of a "new world order" along with the so-called "end of history" and other claims have been discredited in the face of events; the crime that is September 11 and the financial crisis that began in 2008, are the tragedy and farce that sweep away previous ideological claims. Slavoj Zizek, *First as Tragedy, Then as Farce* (London: Verso, 2009).

7. The news reports two patients dying of lack of transplants since the new measures went into effect. Jane E. Allen, "Medicaid Cuts Make Organ Transplants Unaffordable for Some," ABCNews.com, January 10, 2011. January 14, 2011, http://abcnews.go.com/Health/Health_Care/medicaid-cuts- make-organ-transplants-unaffordable/story?id=12177059.

8. Karl Marx, Friedrich Engels, and Leon Trotsky, *The Communist Manifesto* (New York: Pathfinder, 2008).

9. Ben Stein, "In Class Warfare, Guess Which Side is Winning," *The New York Times*, November 26, 2006. http://www.nytimes.com/2006/11/26/business/yourmoney/26every.html.

10. Dana Priest and William M. Arkin, "Top Secret America: A Hidden World Growing Beyond Control," *The Washington Post*, December 15, 2010. projects.washingtonpost.com/top-secret-america/.../a-hidden-world-growing-beyond-control.

11. Ibid.

12. Ibid.

13. Ibid.

14. Ibid.

15. It recently hit the worldwide press that Facebook has been sharing information that is supposed to be private. However, prior to that, less media attention was focused on accounts that information on Facebook was being used for political surveillance. See Cindy Jacquith, "Police Use Facebook and Twitter to Spy and Entrap," *The Militant* (New York), January 4, 2010. Print.

16. Ibid.

17. Kimberly Dozier and Adam Goldman, "Ignored Warnings, Lax Security Lead to 7 CIA Deaths," *Denver Post*, October 20, 2010. http://www.denverpost.com/breakingnews/ci_16 384453?source=rss.

18. Andy Greenberg, "Scanner Vans Allow Drive-By Snooping," Forbes.com, September 27, 2010. http://www.forbes.com/forbes/2010/0927/technology-x-rays-homeland-security-aclu-drive/.

19. Ibid.

20. Quoted in Maral Shamloo, "Chomsky Discusses Terrorism," *The Tech*, October 19, 2001. http://tech.mit.edu/V121/N52/52chomsky.52n.html.

21. Recent anti–Islamic prejudice clearly concerns, to some degree, leading figures in the U.S. government who fear that it will backfire on U.S. efforts in the Middle East. General Petraeus publicly called upon a religious nut who planned to burn the Koran not to, since he recognized it would have deleterious effects upon efforts in the Arab world, particular Afghanistan and Pakistan and the president of the United States weighed in, for an evening, on the controversy around whether a mosque could be built in the vicinity of where the World Trade Center previously stood. The next day, Obama waffled and offered a position that few could make any sense of: that he recognized the right of mosques to be built but had no opinion on whether one should be built in the location announced. The cynicism of such gestures where respect for religious rights relates to foreign policy objectives or political expediency reveals the unprincipled but pragmatic nature of the rulers of the United States.

22. See Andy Grimm and Cynthia Dizikes, "FBI Raids Anti-War Activists' Homes," *Chicago Tribune*, September 24, 2010. http://articles.chicagotribune.com/2010–09–24/news-/ct-met-fbi-terrorism-investigation-20100924_1_fbi-agents-anti–war-activists-federal-agents. Also see Alyson Kennedy, "Protests Denounce FBI Raids in Chicago and Minneapolis," *The Militant* (New York), October 11, 2010, http://www.themilitant.com/2010/7438/743803.html.

23. Ibid.

24. Ibid.

25. Ibid.

26. Ibid.

27. Ibid.

28. See Grimm and Dizikes.

29. See Jacquith.

30. Ibid.

31. Ibid.

32. See Grimm.

33. See Kennedy.

34. Betsy Stone, "Hearing Protests FBI Targeting Arabs, Asians," *The Militant* (New York), October 11, 2010. http://www.themilitant.com/2010/7438/743854.html.

35. Ibid.

36. Ibid.

37. Ibid.

38. See Nelson Blackstock, *Cointelpro: The FBI's Secret War on Political Freedom* (New York: Pathfinder, 2000); Ward Churchill and Jim Vander Wall, *Agents of Repression: The FBI's Secret Wars Against the Black Panther Party and the American Indian Movement* (Cambridge, MA: South End, 2002).

39. CIA operations in Indonesia, Guatemala, Iran, Iraq, Vietnam, Central America, etc.,

are undoubtedly responsible for, directly or indirectly, by a conservative estimate hundreds of thousands of deaths and almost certainly the number reaches into the millions. See Noam Chomsky and Edward S. Herman, *The Political Economy of Human Rights* (Boston: South End, 1979).

40. Although, we should be clear, the Palmer Raids were not the first cases of political repression of ideas or individuals in American society. Even if we leave aside the horrors of the destruction of the Indians, the brutal enslavement and lynching of blacks and Mexicans on the grounds that these weren't political ideas being repressed but racism and national expansion (and, obviously, morally we should never forget these atrocities) we still have the Alien and Sedition Acts, the repression of Shay's rebellion and other farmers movements, the Jim Crow Laws established after the defeat of Radical Reconstruction, not to mention the legal execution of the Haymarket Martyrs in 1886.

41. Noam Chomsky, Introduction, *Cointelpro: The FBI's Secret War on Political Freedom*, ed. Nelson Blackstock (New York: Vintage, 1976).

42. Larry Seigle, "Appendix A: Workers Rights Versus the Secret Police," *FBI on Trial: The Victory in the Socialist Workers Party Suit Against Government Spying*, ed. Margaret Jayco (New York: Pathfinder, 1988), 214–48.

43. Which indeed they didn't as documented, among other places in the book by C. L. R. James, George Breitman, Ed Keemer, and Fred Stanton, *Fighting Racism in World War II: A Week-by-Week Account of the Struggle Against Racism and Discrimination in the United States during 1939–45* (New York: Pathfinder, 2009).

44. See Seigle.

45. Ibid.

46. See Blackstock, p. 8.

47. Ibid., p. 163.

48. Ibid., p. 162.

49. Ibid., p. 164.

50. Ibid., p. 165.

51. Paul Wiseman, "Jobs Crisis Eases, but Economy Has Long Way to Go," Yahoo! News, November 10, 2010. January 25, 2011, http://news.yahoo.com/s/ap/20101105/ap_on_bi_ge/us_economy_job_creation_4.

52. Rachel Beck and Anne D'Innocenzio, "Economy Recovering, but Recession's Shadow Is Long," Yahoo! Finance, November 10, 2010. Web. January 25, 2011, http://finance.yahoo.com/news/Economy-recovering-but-apf-2800294185.html?x=0.

53. Marcy Gordon and Daniel Wagner, "Small Banks Failing as Larger Firms Regain Health," Yahoo! Finance, November 10, 2010. Web. January 25, 2011, http://finance.yahoo.com/news/Small-banks-failing-as-larger-apf-162632968.html?x=0.

54. Beck and D'Innocenzio.

55. Gordon and Wagner.

56. Jack Barnes, "The Clinton's Anti-Labor Legacy: Roots of 2008 World Financial Crisis," *New International* 14: 26. Print.

57. Wiseman.

58. David Harvey, *The Enigma of Capital and the Crises of Capitalism* (Oxford: Oxford University Press, 2010), p. 12. Print.

59. Ibid., pp. 13–4.

60. Ibid., p. 21.

61. Joseph Hansen, George Novack, and L. Trotsky, *The Transitional Program for Socialist Revolution* (New York: Pathfinder, 1974), p. 75. Print.

62. It should be noted that these are not marginal figures in contemporary academic life. Slavoj Zizek gets described in an article in the *New Yorker* as "the Elvis of Cultural theory," Alain Badiou is arguably justifiably considered the major contemporary, living French philosopher in many popular and intellectual or academic circles and the works he writes or has written are being translated at quick rate, Jacques Derrida clearly will go down in intellectual history for inventing deconstruction and remains at the center in debates in many disciplines including literary theory, philosophy, and even political, social, linguistic, and legal analysis.

63. "First as Tragedy," p. 5.
64. One of the best critics of such claims who is not an orthodox Marxist but a radical critic of capitalism and a powerful popular writer on economics is Doug Henwood. See his important and useful demystification of the prevailing mystifications and utopian ideological hopes of the '90s and early years of the twenty-first century, *After the New Economy* (New York: New, 2005). Print. Even this title, written in 2003 with an afterword added in 2005, shows how much more sober and accurate his analysis remains in contrast to the wisdom of the time.
65. See "First Time Tragedy," p.8.

Works Cited

Allen, Jane E. "Medicaid Cuts Make Organ Transplants Unaffordable for Some." ABCNews. com, January 10, 2011. January 14, 2011, http://abcnews.go.com/Health/Health_Care-/medicaid-cuts-make-organ-transplants-unaffordable/story?id=12177059.

Barnes, Jack. "The Clinton's Anti-Labor Legacy: Roots of 2008 World Financial Crisis." *New International* 14: 26. Print.

Beck, Rachel, and Anne D'Innocenzio. "Economy Recovering, but Recession's Shadow Is Long." Yahoo! Finance, November 10, 2010. Web. January 25, 2011, http://finance.yahoo.com/news/Economy-recovering-but-apf-2800294185.html?x=0.

Blackstock, Nelson. *Cointelpro: The FBI's Secret War on Political Freedom*. New York: Pathfinder, 2000.

Chomsky, Noam. Introduction. *Cointelpro: The FBI's Secret War on Political Freedom*. Ed. Nelson Blackstock. New York: Vintage, 1976. Print.

_____, and Edward S. Herman. *The Political Economy of Human Rights*. Boston: South End, 1979. Print.

Churchill, Ward, and Jim Vander Wall. *Agents of Repression: The FBI's Secret Wars Against the Black Panther Party and the American Indian Movement*. Cambridge, MA: South End, 2002. Print.

Dozier, Kimberly, and Adam Goldman. "Ignored Warnings, Lax Security Lead to 7 CIA Deaths." *Denver Post*. October 20, 2010. http://www.denverpost.com/breakingnews/ci_16 384453?source=rss.

Fukiyama, Francis. *The End of History and the Last Man*. New York: Free, 1992. Print.

Gordon, Marcy, and Daniel Wagner. "Small Banks Failing as Larger Firms Regain Health." Yahoo! Finance, November 10, 2010. Web. January 25, 2011, http://finance.yahoo.com/news/Small-banks-failing-as-larger-apf-162632968.html?x=0

Greenberg, Andy. "Scanner Vans Allow Drive-By Snooping." Forbes.com, September 27, 2010. http://www.forbes.com/forbes/2010/0927/technology-x-rays-homeland-security-aclu-drive/.

Grimm, Andy, and Cynthia Dizikes. "FBI Raids Anti-War Activists' Homes." *Chicago Tribune*, September 24, 2010. http://articles.chicagotribune.com/2010-09-24/news/ct-met-fbi-terrorism-investigation-20100924_1_fbi-agents-anti-war-activists-federal-agents.

Hansen, Joseph, George Novack, and L. Trotsky. *The Transitional Program for Socialist Revolution*. New York: Pathfinder, 1974. Print.

Harvey, David. *The Enigma of Capital and the Crises of Capitalism*. Oxford: Oxford University Press, 2010. Print.

Henwood, Doug. *After the New Economy*. New York: New, 2005. Print.

Jacquith, Cindy. "Police Use Facebook and Twitter to Spy and Entrap." *The Militant* (New York), January 4, 2010. Print.

James, C.L.R., George Breitman, Ed Keemer, and Fred Stanton. *Fighting Racism in World War II: A Week-By-Week Account of the Struggle Against Racism and Discrimination in the United States During 1939–45*. New York: Pathfinder, 2009.

Kennedy, Alyson. "Protests Denounce FBI Raids in Chicago and Minneapolis." *The Militant* (New York), October 11, 2010. http://www.themilitant.com/2010/7438/743803.html.

Marx, Karl, Friedrich Engels, and Leon Trotsky. *The Communist Manifesto*. New York: Pathfinder, 2008. Print.

Meachum, Jon. "We Are All Socialists Now." Newsweek. 14 January 14, 2011. http://www.news week.com/2009/02/06/we-are-all-socialists-now.html.

Priest, Dana, and William M. Arkin. "Top Secret America: A Hidden World Growing Beyond Control." *The Washington Post*, December 15, 2010. projects.washingtonpost.com/top-secret-america/.../a-hidden-world-growing-beyond-control.

Seigle, Larry. "Appendix A: Workers Rights Versus the Secret Police." *FBI on Trial: The Victory in the Socialist Workers Party Suit Against Government Spying*. Ed. Margaret Jayco. New York: Pathfinder, 1988. Print.

Shamloo, Maral. "Chomsky Discusses Terrorism." *The Tech*, October 19, 2001. http://tech.mit.edu/V121/N52/52chomsky.52n.html.

Stein, Ben. "In Class Warfare, Guess Which Side is Winning." *The New York Times*, November 26, 2006. http://www.nytimes.com/2006/11/26/business/yourmoney/26every.html.

Stone, Betsy. "Hearing Protests FBI Targeting Arabs, Asians." *The Militant* (New York), October 11, 2010. http://www.themilitant.com/2010/7438/743854.html.

Wiseman, Paul. "Jobs Crisis Eases, but Economy Has Long Way to Go." Yahoo! News, November 10, 2010. Web. January 25, 2011. http://news.yahoo.com/s/ap/20101105/ap_on_bi_ge/us_economy_job_creation_4.

Zizek, Slavoj. "Against The Double Blackmail." *New Left Review* 234 (March-April 1999). http://www.egs.edu/faculty/slavoj-zizek/articles/against-the-double-blackmail/ .

_____. *First as Tragedy, Then as Farce*. London: Verso, 2009. Print.

About the Contributors

David **Anshen**, an associate professor of English at University of Texas–Pan American, works to oppose the connections between UTPA and the intelligence agencies. He has written on William Faulkner, Norman Mailer and the films of Jean-Luc Godard. His next project will be a book on culture and commodity fetishism.

David **Carlson** is an assistant professor of history at the University of Texas–Pan American, where he teaches courses on colonial and modern Latin America. A specialist in nineteenth-century Cuba, he is also a member of Historians Against the War.

Roberto **González** is an associate professor of anthropology at San José State University. His books include *Zapotec Science: Farming and Food in the Northern Sierra of Oaxaca* (2001), *American Counterinsurgency: Human Science and the Human Terrain* (2009), and *Militarizing Culture: Essays on the Warfare State* (2010). He is a founding member of the Network of Concerned Anthropologists.

Verne **Lyon** is a native Iowan, aerospace engineer, former CIA deep cover intelligence officer and former political prisoner. Resigning after CIA domestic and Latin American postings, he co-founded the Association of National Security Alumni, an activist group of former CIA, FBI, and State Department officers. He lectures on CIA covert operations excesses.

Deirdre **McDonald** is a doctoral student in library science at Texas Woman's University. She received her MLS from North Carolina Central University in 2003. Her research interests include national security states' archives and the politics of access, academic labor, and literacy education.

David **Price** is a professor of anthropology at St. Martin's University. He is the author of *Threatening Anthropology: McCarthyism and the FBI's Per-*

secution of Activist Anthropologists (2004) and *Anthropological Intelligence: The Deployment and Neglect of American Anthropology during the Second World War* (2008).

Stephen **Soldz**, a professor at the Boston Graduate School of Psychoanalysis, is a psychologist, public health researcher, and psychoanalyst in Boston. He is president of Psychologists for Social Responsibility. Soldz is a leader in efforts to remove psychologists from coercive interrogations. He served as consultant on several Guantánamo trials.

Philip **Zwerling**, an assistant professor of English at the University of Texas–Pan American, is the author of *Nicaragua: A New Kind of Revolution* (1985) and *After School Theatre Programs for At-Risk Teenagers* (2008) as well as numerous journal, magazine, and newspaper articles.

Index

*After School Theater Programs for At Risk
Teenagers* 15
Agee, Philip 40, 202
Algeria 68
Allende, Salvador 13, 62
American Anthropological Association 38
American Friends of the Middle East 25
American Institute for Free Labor Develop-
ment 18
American Library Association 90, 91, 92, 94,
95, 96; Code of Ethics for Librarians 91,
92; Library Bill of Rights 91, 92
American Psychological Association (APA)
114, 116, 120–125, 127–129, 132–133
Americans for Intellectual Freedom 37
Ames, Aldrich 29
Angleton, James Jesus 36
Arbenz, Jacobo 14, 27, 65, 73, 77
Argentina 68–69
Armas, Castillo 14, 73
Armies of Ignorance 47
Asia Foundation 25
Association of Former Intelligence Officers
198

Bacevich, Andrew 72
Batista, Fulgencio 75, 76
Battle of Algiers 70
Bay of Pigs 15, 43, 76, 79
Bessac, Frank 39
Bishop, Maurice 8, 11
Blasier, Cole 80–81
*Blowback: The Costs and Consequences of
American Empire* 71
Blowing My Cover: My Life as a CIA Spy 54
Blum, William 16, 20, 192–193
Boland Amendment 19, 22
Bolton, Earl 195
Brandon, Susan 123, 126
Braverman, Kate 8

Brazil 13, 27
Buchanan, Patrick 16
Buckley, William 24
Burnham, Forbes 25
Burnham, James 37
Bush, George H. 21
Bush, George W. 63, 71

Cameron, Ewan 24
Cardenal, Ernesto 20
Cardenal, Fernando 20
Carter, Amy 51
Carter, Jimmy 16, 18
Casey, William 16, 18, 19, 191
Castro, Fidel 13, 79
Castro, Raul 13, 79
Chamorro, Violeta 18
Chile 13, 35, 62
China 14, 43
Chomsky, Noam 61, 65
Church, Frank 48
*CIA Off Campus: Building the Movement
Against Agency Recruitment and Research*
51
Clarridge, Duane 11, 18, 19
Clinton, William J. 66
Cloak and Gown: Scholars in the Secret War
36
Coe, Michael 41
COINTELPRO 46, 229
Colby, William 29
Columbia University 39
Contras 19, 20, 21, 22, 23, 69
Cornell University 25, 192
Corson, William 47
Costa Rica 17, 22
Counter Spy 51
Cuba 9, 10, 13, 14, 15, 28–29, 37, 68, 69,
72, 74, 75, 76
Cuban Missile Crisis 79

Cultural and Scientific Conference for
    World Peace 37
The Cultural Cold War 41
Cumings, Bruce 43

Davis, Martha 125
Deception detection 119, 121, 125, 127–128
Defense Department Counterintelligence
    and HUMINT Center (DCHC) 125–126
Defense Department Counterintelligence
    Field Activity (CIFA) 125, 128
D'Escoto, Miguel 13, 20
Diamond, Sigmund 34
Diem, Ngo Dinh 13, 41
Dominican Republic 13
Donovan, William, "Wild" Bill 34
Doolittle, James 40
Dulles, Allen 73, 75, 77, 78
Dulles, John Foster 73

Eagleton Institute for Research 25
Eisenhower, Dwight David 3, 28, 72, 76, 93
Ellsberg, Daniel 46
El Salvador 13, 14, 16, 26
Empire's Workshop 63
enhanced interrogation (torture) 66, 113, 114,
    115, 122
extreme (or extraordinary) rendition 54, 66,
    69
Exxon 18

The Family Jewels (CIA) 46
Federal Bureau of Investigation 46, 97–98
Federal Training Programs Center 26
Feldman, Jonathan 193
Figueres, Jose 13
First Unitarian Church of Los Angeles 14
Foster, Sharon 26
Foundation for Youth and Student Affairs 25
Freedom to Read 92–93
Freeman, Samuel 177, 178, 182, 199, 203
Fulbright, William 184–185

Gairy, Eric 9
Gates, Robert 55, 183
Georgetown University 192
Giroux, Hnery 209
Goffman, Erwin 42
Goss, Porter 27
Grand Anse 8
Graves, Theodore 47
Grenada 7, 8, 9, 12, 13, 14, 18, 23, 27
Guardiola-Rivera, Oscar 63
Guatemala 13, 14, 27, 35, 37, 38, 65, 72,
    73, 74
Gusterson, Hugh 174
Guyana 25

Haig, Alexander 17
Haiti 14
Harbury, Jennifer 67, 69
Harman, Jane 169
Harvard University 39, 50; Center for Inter-
    national Studies 191; Center for Middle
    Eastern Affairs 52, 191; International
    Summer School 39; Russian Research
    Center 38
Helms, Richard 24, 44
Heritage Foundation 9
Hersh, Seymour 46
Hidden Terrors 67
Honduras 14, 17, 22, 70
Hook, Sidney 37
House Select Intelligence Committee (Pike
    Committee) 49, 50
Huntington, Samuel 26, 52

Indonesia 13, 25, 27
Integrated Global Knowledge and Under-
    standing Collaboration (IGkNU) 176,
    191, 194–196, 198, 205
Intelligence Community/Centers for Aca-
    demic Excellence 4, 52–53, 56, 102, 105,
    168–170, 172, 174–185, 192, 197–199, 203
Intelligence Community Scholarship Pro-
    gram (ICSP) 174
The International Catholic Youth federation
    26
The International Student Conference 25
Iowa State University 148, 157
Iran 13, 17, 22, 27, 35, 37, 38, 66, 72
Italy 35

Jacobowitz, Daniel 17
Jagan, Cheddi 25
Janey, F.W.M. 3, 23
Jeffreys-Jones, Rhodri 45
Jessen, Bruce 116, 117, 121, 122
Johnson, Chalmers 71
Johnson, Lyndon 24, 44
Jones, Cynthia 195
Jones, Jim 25

Katzenbach, Nicholas (and Katzenbach
    Commission) 44–45
Kennedy, John F. 28
Kent, Sherwood 36
Killing Hope 16
Kirkpatrick, Jeanne 22
Kissinger, Henry 24, 39
Kluckhohn, Clyde 41
Kozol, Jonathan 14
Kruckewitt, Joan 21
*KUBARK Counterintelligence Interrogation
    Manual* 42, 70

Laguna, Noel 23
Langguth, A.A. 67
Legacy of Ashes 28
Library Awareness Program 94, 95, 96–97, 104
Linder, Benjamin 20, 21, 22
Literacy Crusade 15
Lumumba, Patrice 13, 27

Manley, Michael 13
Mansbach, Richard 26, 51
Massachusetts Institute of Technology 25, Center for International Studies (CENIS) 38, 39
Matarazzo, Joseph D. 116–117
McCoy, Alfred W. 69
McGehee, Ralph 51, 199
McSherry, J. Patrice 69
Meyer, Cord 35
Michigan State University 25, 41; Asia Foundation 191
The Militant 224, 226
Millikan, Max 38
Mills, Ami Chen 51, 198
Minerva Consortium 183
Mitchell, James 116, 117, 120, 121, 122
Mitchell, Jessen and Associates 116
Moran, Lindsay 54
Mossadegh, Mohammed 13, 27, 66, 72

Nasser, Gamal 13, 28
National Endowment for Democracy 18
The National Review 39
National Student Association 25, 44, 230
Nehru, Jawaharlal 13
Nelsen, Robert 202, 209
New Jewel Movement 8, 9
Nicaragua 13, 14, 15, 16, 18, 19, 20, 21, 22, 23, 27, 75, 224
Nicaragua: A New Kind of Revolution 19
Nixon, Richard 13, 18
Norfolk State University 173
Noriega, Manuel 17
North, Oliver 17
Northwestern University Traffic Institute 26

Obama, Barack 33, 54, 71
Office of Medical Services (OMS) 118–119
Office of Public Diplomacy 1
Office of Strategic Services (OSS) 34
Office of the Director of National Intelligence 4, 102–103, 105–106, 168–170, 172, 192, 197, 198
Officers in Residence Program (CIA) 26, 51
Operation CHAOS (MHCHAOS) 24, 25, 46, 47, 160, 165, 183
Operation Condor 69

Operation Mongoose 76, 78
Operation PBSUCCESS 6, 71, 77
Operation TPAJAX 72
ORDEN (El Salvador) 69

Pan American Collaboration for Ethics in the Professions 195, 198
Parrales, Edgard 20
Pat Roberts Intelligence Scholars Program (PRISP) 52, 55, 174, 183
Pearson, Norman Holmes 36
People's Temple 25
The Philippines 38
Phillips, John 2
Pike, Otis 49
Platt, Kamala 180–181
Point Salines 7, 9, 10, 12
Posada, Luis 80
Praeger Press 45
La Prensa 18
Project Artichoke 24
Project MKULTRA 24, 25, 41–42, 115–115
Psychological Operations in Guerrilla Warfare 22

Rahman, Omar Abdel 29
Ramparts Magazine 25, 44
Rather, Dan 20
Reagan, Ronald 8, 9, 11, 16, 17, 18, 20
Reidhead, Van 176, 197, 199, 203
Rochester Institute of Technology 26
Rockefeller Commission 47
Rogers, Karl 42, 115
Roosevelt, Franklin Delano 14, 74
Roosevelt, Kermit 72
Rostow, Walt 38
Rutgers University 25

Safran, Nadav 26, 51
Sanchez, Nestor 9
Sandinistas 13, 15, 16, 17, 21
Sandino, Augusto 16
Saunders, Frances Stonor 41
Schneider, Rene 13
School of the Americas (SOA) 67
Schulman, Jay 42
Seligman, Martin 117, 118
Skinner, B.F. 42, 115
Skinner, Jose 178
Socialist Workers Party 230
Society for the Investigation of Human Ecology 42
Somocistas 19
Somoza, Anastasio, Jr. 14, 17, 18
Somoza, Anastasio, Sr. 13, 14, 16
Somoza, Luis 14
South of the Border 63

Soviet Union 9, 14
Special Access Program 119
Spock, Benjamin 14
Spy Camp 168
Standard Fruit Company 18
Steinem, Gloria 4
Stephenson, Richard 42
Stern, Sol 44
Stockwell, John 51
Stone, Oliver 63
Studies in Intelligence 35
Suez Canal 28
Suharto 27
Sukarno, Ahmed 13, 25, 27
Survival, Evasion, Resistance, and Escape
    (SERE) 70, 115–116, 119

Texas A&M University 55
Torrijos, Omar 1
Trinity University 168, 173, 199
Truman, Harry 40
Turner, Stansfield 28

United Fruit Company 73
United States Senate Select Committee to
    Study Governmental Operations with
    Respect to Intelligence Activities (The
    Church Committee) 48, 49, 64
United States Youth Council 26
University Associates Program 38
University of Colorado 204

University of Iowa 147
University of Pennsylvania 117
University of Texas El Paso 4, 53, 170–172
University of Texas Pan American 53, 103–
    104, 169, 171, 175–179, 193–195, 205–
    206, 209, 210
University of Washington 53, 105, 182–183
USA PATRIOT Act 33, 50, 98–100, 102,
    107

Venezuela 13
Vietnam 29, 68
Vijil, Felix 15, 16

Walz, Skip 23
Warsaw Pact 16, 17
Weimer, Nick 197
Weiner, Tim 12, 24, 28, 192
Western Hemisphere Institute for Security
    Cooperation (WHISC) 67
Wikileaks 88
Winks, Robin 36
Wisner, Frank 13
World Court 21

The Yale Report 36
Yale University 36

Zhou Enlai 13
Zinn, Howard 51
Zizek, Slavoj 218–219, 235

www.ingramcontent.com/pod-product-compliance
Lightning Source LLC
Chambersburg PA
CBHW031126270326
41929CB00011B/1517